The Routledge Guidebook to Hobbes' *Leviathan*

Hobbes is widely regarded as one of the most important figures in the history of ideas and political thought, and his seminal text *Leviathan* is widely recognised as one of the greatest works of political philosophy ever written.

The Routledge Guidebook to Hobbes' Leviathan introduces the major themes in Hobbes' great book and acts as a companion for reading this key work, examining:

- The context of Hobbes' work and the background to his writing
- Each separate part of the text in relation to its goals, meanings and impact
- The reception the book had when first seen by the world
- The relevance of Hobbes' work to modern philosophy, its legacy and influence.

With further reading included throughout, this text follows Hobbes' original work closely, making it essential reading for all students of philosophy and politics, and all those wishing to get to grips with this classic work.

Glen Newey is Professor of Political Theory at the Université libre de Bruxelles.

THE ROUTLEDGE GUIDES TO THE GREAT BOOKS

Series editor Anthony Gottlieb

Available:

Forthcoming:

Routledge Guides to the Great Books

The Routledge Guidebook to Hobbes' *Leviathan*

Glen
Newey

Routledge
Taylor & Francis Group

LONDON AND NEW YORK

First published in the Routledge Philosophy Guidebook series in 2008
First published in The Routledge Guides to the Great Books series in 2014
by Routledge
2 Park Square, Milton Park, Abingdon, Oxon OX14 4RN

and published by Routledge
711 Third Avenue, New York, NY 10017

Routledge is an imprint of the Taylor & Francis Group, an informa business

© 2008, 2014 Glen Newey

British Library Cataloguing in Publication Data
A catalogue record for this book is available from the British Library

Library of Congress Cataloging in Publication Data
Newey, Glen.
The Routledge guidebook to Hobbes' Leviathan /
Glen Newey. -- 1 [edition].
pages cm. -- (Routledge guides to the great books)
Includes bibliographical references and index.
1. Hobbes, Thomas, 1588-1679. Leviathan. 2. Political science--Early works to 1800. 3. Political science--Philosophy. I. Title.
JC153.H659N49 2014
320.1--dc23
2013040156

ISBN: 978-0-415-67131-6 (hbk)
ISBN: 978-0-415-67132-3 (pbk)
ISBN: 978-1-315-78115-0 (ebk)

Typeset in Garamond
by Taylor & Francis Books

CONTENTS

SERIES EDITOR'S PREFACE

'The past is a foreign country', wrote a British novelist, L. P. Hartley: 'they do things differently there.' The greatest books in the canon of the humanities and sciences can be foreign territory, too. This series is a set of excursions written by expert guides who know how to make such places become more familiar.

All the books covered in this series, however long ago they were written, have much to say to us now, or help to explain the ways in which we have come to think about the world. Each volume is designed not only to describe a set of ideas, and how they developed, but also to evaluate them. This requires what one might call a bifocal approach. To engage fully with an author, one has to pretend that he or she is speaking to us; but to understand a text's meaning, it is often necessary to remember its original audience, too. It is all too easy to mistake the intentions of an old argument by treating it as a contemporary one.

The *Routledge Guides to the Great Books* are aimed at students in the broadest sense, not only those engaged in formal study. The intended audience of the series is all those who want to understand the books that have had the largest effects.

Anthony Gottlieb

*Series editor **Anthony Gottlieb** is the author of*
The Dream of Reason: A History of Philosophy
from the Greeks to the Renaissance.

PREFACE TO THE SECOND EDITION

This new edition of *Hobbes and Leviathan* differs from the first edition of 2008 mainly in the addition of a new chapter, which deals principally with the early reception of *Leviathan* (Chapter 11). In addition, I have gone through the whole text and amended passages, generally in the name of improving lucidity or readability. I have augmented the bibliography, and the further-reading suggestions appended to each chapter, to take account of new scholarly work published in the interim. In one or two places I have also modified substantive claims made in the first edition where my views have evolved since the first edition came out. This is particularly so in Chapter 7, on sovereignty. I have also corrected some errors. I am grateful to Taylor & Francis for giving me the time to prepare a new edition, and particularly for the editorial advice and forbearance of Iram Satti.

September 2013

ACKNOWLEDGEMENTS

The writing of this book has taken an unconscionable amount of time – far longer, embarrassingly enough, than the composition of *Leviathan* itself – and I have incurred a number of debts.

My overriding debt is to Linda Holt. She read the entire manuscript several times, an act far above and beyond the call of marital duty. Her sharp critical eye spotted mistakes that had escaped me, and her constant prodding to be clearer, while not always welcomed at the time, has invariably proven justified on closer reading. There can be very few academic writers who have the daily benefit of advice from someone with such acute critical intelligence and so strong an ability to empathise with the intellectual content of an academic book such as this. More importantly, her companionship and engagement have provided constant support in the process of writing it. Her influence is present on every page.

Several other people also read the book in draft and made valuable suggestions. My former doctoral supervisor and now colleague, John Horton, corrected a number of infelicities and encouraged me to clarify a number of passages that were unclear in the manuscript. I would also like to take this opportunity to thank him for many professional and personal acts of kindness over a period now of over twenty years.

A beneficial consequence of my arrival at Keele has been access to the vast erudition of John Rogers, whose landmark scholarly edition of *Leviathan* appeared while this book was being written. His blend of philosophical acumen and expert knowledge of Hobbes has been an extremely valuable resource during the latter stages of writing this book.

My series editor for the first edition, Jonathan Wolff, also read the whole manuscript more than once. He has been a model editor, dispensing encouragement and advice in equal measure. His interventions have helped to make this a far better book than it would otherwise have been.

I am also indebted to the lengthy list of editors at Routledge who have been involved with the project. All have shown forbearance in the face of my near-pathological inability to complete the book. I am particularly grateful to Priyanka Pathak for balancing the scholarly and commercial constraints with which any project of this kind has to contend. I am also indebted to suggestions made by an anonymous reader for Routledge.

I am also very grateful to the Human Values Center at Princeton University. The Center provided unmatched research facilities during a very enjoyable year I spent as a Laurance S. Rockefeller fellow there, where the first draft was written. I would particularly like to record my gratitude to George Kateb, now retired from the Center, and to Stephen Macedo.

The arrival of Attila Newey during the writing of the book, and his increasingly animated interactions with his sister Laura, have provided a vivid domestic illustration of the state of nature. As time has worn on, he has learned how to switch off my computer with a single well-aimed jab of his forefinger, thereby saving me from numerous errors. Like everybody else mentioned above, he is not to be held responsible for any errors that remain.

FIGURES

INTRODUCTION

THE POLITICS OF CHAOS

A spectre haunts *Leviathan*, one of the foremost works of political philosophy. The spectre takes the form of political breakdown, and the chaos that follows from it. And the emotion pervading the pages of *Leviathan*, which this vision of chaos evokes, is terror. As its author, Thomas Hobbes, wrote in his autobiography, 'fear and I were born twins together'.

His mother gave birth to him on 5 April 1588, his delivery hastened – or so Hobbes liked to say in later life – by the reported approach of the Spanish Armada, the fleet sent by King Philip II of Spain to invade England. During his adult years, much of Europe was convulsed by war. Hobbes was forced into political exile in 1640 by the political strife between King Charles I and Parliament. From exile in France, Hobbes observed the collapse of Charles' rule in England, and the King's eventual overthrow and execution at the hands of republican revolutionaries.

In the most famous passage in *Leviathan*, Hobbes graphically expressed this dread of violent turmoil. The passage is known to many people, who have never read the rest of the book. Hobbes is discussing what life is like in the state of nature, when human beings lack effective government.

> Whatsoever is consequent to a time of war, when every man is enemy to every man, the same is consequent to the time, wherein men live without other security, than what their own strength and their own invention shall furnish them withal. In such condition, there is no industry, because the fruit thereof is uncertain, and consequently no culture of the earth [i.e. agriculture]; no navigation, nor use of the commodities that may be imported by sea; no commodious building; no instruments of moving, and removing such things as require much force; no knowledge of the face of the earth; no account of time; no arts; no letters; no society; and which is worst of all, continual fear and danger of violent death; and the life of man solitary, poor, nasty, brutish and short.
>
> (L 89)[1]

In short, Hobbes is saying, a life without the security provided by government is not worth living.

Leviathan was first published in 1651, over 370 years ago. Why should we still bother to read it now? After all, in many respects our world is quite unlike the one in which Hobbes lived and wrote. Mid-seventeenth-century Europe was shaken by religious, political and military conflict. The tolerant liberal democracies familiar to us today, with their freedom of religious worship and political expression, lay far in the future. Many countries were still subject to the rule of an absolute monarch, as in the France of King Louis XIV. There were few international institutions or organisations of the kind we know, such as the United Nations, or the European Union. Similarly absent was the worldwide mobility of labour and capital that marks our world, as were the international corporations whose power rivals – indeed, exceeds – that of some sovereign states. In these respects, Hobbes' world looks quite alien.

However, some of its major features remain recognisable to us today. The violence born of political breakdown, for example, is all too familiar. In the late twentieth and early twenty-first century the collapse of empires has led to enduring political instability, with dire results for those caught up in the ensuing struggles for power. Sometimes the weakness of newly independent governments has left them prey to foreign invasion, while elsewhere failed states have fought civil wars or massacred their own citizens. Violent seizures of power through revolution or invasion, the waging of war against foreign citizens or one's own, massacre and genocide – these are all real-life horrors from our own time. Since the end of the Cold War, too, religious conflict has become or continued to be a prominent feature of international and, in many cases, national politics.

As a result, many of the political problems with which Hobbes was grappling remain with us. Some of these arise from differences of opinion – in belief, doctrine and their associated cultural or religious practices. Citizens of modern states are troubled, as was Hobbes, by fears about security. In some cases these fears are well founded, as when the state is unable or unwilling to muster the executive force needed to protect its citizens. In other cases, as with the post-9/11 panic over the 'terrorist threat', the fears are exaggerated, but for all that have political impact. What is more significant, however, is that the rhetoric of 'security', mobilised against the supposed threat, remains extremely potent even in secure and stable liberal democracies. The dread of political collapse lurks in every page of *Leviathan*, and as Hobbes was keenly aware, it is seldom far below the surface in the real world too.

Religion has come to the fore again politically, despite having been dismissed as outmoded by so many modern secular and progressive political and moral creeds. This is not just because of the confrontation between the secular 'West' and the Islamic world, which looms so large in modern international politics. Even the 'West' itself remains deeply imbued with religiosity, particularly in the United States. Again, this is not exclusively because Western countries have absorbed significant numbers of Muslim immigrants. In many occidental societies such as Italy and the USA, religion remains politically potent among the population, and this is unlikely to change soon.

Sometimes a work of political theory captivates its readers less by the power of its arguments than through a compelling vision of what politics is, or what it can be. It may do this by holding out the prospect of a different and better world, as in utopian writings. On most readings of him, Hobbes does the opposite,[2] offering a nightmare vision of political breakdown. *Leviathan*'s state of nature is in fact a world without politics, since the conditions needed for political life are not met: there is nothing for politics to be about, since there are no public goods, and no way of doing politics, because there are no ways of concerting joint action. The social and economic disintegration described in the extract above is both a cause and a consequence of the absence of politics. By contrast with anarchists, Hobbes detects in the absence of politics the seeds not of opportunity, but disaster.

Leviathan stresses the role of sheer force in human affairs, and force can be used for good or ill. Again, this is an aspect of the book which modern readers can readily grasp. Force is, of course, no less present for being, as it often is, invisible. Like the gravitational force acting between bodies distant from one another, the presence of political force can be detected via its effects. These effects include citizens' compliance with the law – notice the effect on car drivers, for instance, when they come within range of what they think is an operating speed camera. In fact, it is precisely when force is not directly visible that the power of the sovereign is working as Hobbes intended. It works when the sovereign is powerful enough to instil in citizens a well-founded fear of the consequences if they break the law.

'The passion to be reckoned upon', Hobbes says, 'is fear' (*L* 99). At the same time, of course, the state of nature – the alternative to politics – is so awful precisely because it is also a state of constant fear. Hobbes, then, has to navigate between two opposite fears, of life without political authority, and life with it. *Leviathan* would not have survived as long as it has if Hobbes had merely tried to scare his readers. The fearfulness of the state of nature carries its own political message. If we have good reason to be afraid of the state of nature, we have at least that reason to prefer anything which prevents it, or helps us to get out of it – assuming, which some readers of Hobbes have always disputed, that his alternative is less terrible than the state of nature.

This brings us to the double-edged core of Hobbes' theory. For his solution, in effect, is to create something that is fearful – the *Leviathan* of the book's title. This is an absolute ruler, in the form either of a single all-powerful individual or (as Hobbes also allowed) a 'sovereign assembly' such as a ruling council. The point of creating an all-powerful sovereign is precisely that it will be more terrible than the purely private force that any individual can muster in the state of nature. The sovereign's overwhelming power is what gives everybody reason to agree to obey; anyone who fails to do so, having already agreed to do so, is a 'Fool' (L 101). That is, those who are subject to the power of the sovereign are cowed into obedience. But of course the other side of this coin is the danger, well known to us now, of tyranny by the sovereign. In his efforts to ensure that the sovereign is strong enough to enforce order, Hobbes risks making the sovereign a despot. Like Hobbes, our fate is to be caught between two opposed fears: of life without effective government, and life with a government which (at least in its tyrannical form) is all too effective.

LEVIATHAN AND POLITICAL PHILOSOPHY

Hobbes' fork of fear is familiar enough to us. For instance, the dread of tyrannical government, and the dread of lawlessness, have been felt by turns by the citizens of Iraq first under Saddam Hussein's dictatorship, and then since the 2003 invasion in murderous internecine conflict, followed by lower-level but still chronic violence and insecurity. However, I have also pointed out some basic differences between our world and the mid-seventeenth-century environment in which Hobbes was writing. Much of *Leviathan*, particularly Part 3 and Part 4, is devoted to matters that many people would now regard as being politically marginal at best: for example, the authorship of books of the Bible (chapter 33), the significance of miracles (chapter 37), the legitimate extent of the political power of the church (chapter 42). This has meant that over the last 100 years Parts 3 and 4 have received much less attention than Part 1 and especially Part 2, which contains the kernel of Hobbes' political theory.

Nonetheless, even when Hobbes addresses matters that may seem politically marginal to us, he never forgets their political significance. For him the key political question is 'Who rules?', particularly in the face of deep disagreements about religion, morality and politics. Hobbes' detailed discussion of miracles in Part 3 seems at first to be devoid of political relevance. He notes that what is regarded as miraculous depends on the education and experience of the observer, and also, more importantly, of those who receive reports of miracles. Moreover, because they are taken as signs of God's will, and those who witness them are regarded as divinely inspired, miracles are potent political weapons. Then Hobbes argues (L 305–6) that because different people will have different opinions both on what counts as a miracle, and whether a given report of a miracle should be believed, we need an authority to decide these questions. Since reports of miracles always make claims to power, to allow a public free-for-all is a recipe for anarchy. Judgement on miracles has to be handed over to the ruler: 'private reason must submit to the public' (L 306). In his insistence that public reason must trump private opinion, Hobbes in fact anticipates a central claim of modern philosophical liberalism.

Modern theories have sometimes lost sight of Hobbes' insights. Modern academic political philosophy, at least in the English-speaking world, often tries to base political arrangements on moral considerations, such as the idea that everyone is owed equal respect, or that nobody should try to enforce a political regime which others could reasonably reject. Most often, it assumes that we are all subject to certain moral norms, and tries to work out what these norms require of us politically. However, as modern liberals are well aware, societies are beset by internal disagreement over morality. The problem then is to try to withstand the forces of moral conflict; for example, modern political theorists sometimes try to devise a set of principles that are morally acceptable because they can command universal agreement.

But such arguments tend to undermine themselves. They start with the political problems posed by disputes over morality or 'values', and then try to resolve these disputes by coming up with a moral solution. The risk is that the solution is open to disputes similar to those that had caused the political problem in the first place.[3] If so, the agreement is no longer 'universal', and theorists find themselves reduced to saying, in effect, that people who do not agree with the suggested principles, at any rate ought to do so. This is a journey up the hill and then back down again.

Hobbes would have had little time for this approach to political philosophy. His starting point is admittedly the same as many modern liberal thinkers: the fact of persistent disagreement, which nowadays is often ascribed to the pluralism or multiculturalism of modern societies. But from there, Hobbes' approach diverges radically. Modern liberal theories typically seek to find a common moral grounding for political principles. By contrast, Hobbes tries to identify a basis for action that can have overriding force for people, and then asks what set of political arrangements will result if people act on the motive in question. He finds it in the natural impulse towards self-preservation: 'the final end', Hobbes says, which people have in setting up political authority over themselves, 'is the foresight of their own preservation' (L 117).

Precisely because Hobbes gives such weight to the motive of self-preservation, he thinks that people will be prepared to relinquish a great deal in exchange for a secure state (or 'commonwealth', as he calls it). Thus he believes that they will readily hand over responsibility for law-making to the sovereign – who may be an individual, a monarch, or an assembly like Parliament or Congress – and with it full discretion over the content of the law. This makes Hobbes' state a good deal more authoritarian than those of modern liberal democracies profess to be. Hobbes' sovereign has the power, for instance, to impose religious uniformity on the population, in the name of civil peace. To allow private belief, dogma or superstition to run riot in the public sphere is to risk chaos.

Despite Hobbes' authoritarian conclusions, this makes the concerns of *Leviathan* very similar to those of modern liberal philosophers. Their overriding aim is to arrive at principles for governing political life which can command reasonable agreement despite the fact that people disagree so strongly about morality, politics and religion. The important point for political theorists who intend, as Hobbes did, to lay a basis for stable government, is not whether it is possible to gain knowledge of these matters, but the fact that people disagree strongly. This problem would still exist even if one side in an ideological conflict had knowledge of the relevant truths, since this leaves the question of what to do about the other side. They still have their beliefs, and they may indeed form the majority.

There would still be a political problem to solve even if some specific religious or moral doctrine was true, and could be known to be true. The problem arises as long as people disagree deeply about the truth of the doctrine. Early in *Leviathan* Hobbes makes it clear how this can lead to political turmoil:

> when there is a controversy in an account, the parties must by their own accord set up for right reason, the reason of some arbitrator or judge, to whose sentence [i.e. judgement] they will both stand, or their controversy must come to blows or be undecided for want of a right reason constituted by nature ... when men that think themselves wiser than all others clamour and demand right reason for judge, yet seek no more but that things should be determined by no other men's reason but their own, it is as intolerable in the society of men, as it is in play after trump is turned, to use for trump on every occasion that suit whereof they have most in their hand. For they do nothing else that will have every of their passions, as it comes to bear sway in them, taken for right reason.
>
> (L 32–33)

Here Hobbes is saying that, in the face of bitter disputes, we need an agreed procedure to resolve them, just as nowadays irreconcilable parties (such as employers and workers, or landlords and tenants) may refer their dispute to an independent arbiter in order to resolve it. This is a pragmatic solution to the brute fact of disagreement. It is a response to the need for a method of resolution, given that it is worse for everyone if the dispute remains unsettled.

But, of course, someone who advocates a certain set of political arrangements as best, as Hobbes does in *Leviathan*, makes a claim that seems to aim at truth. It is, however, consistent with this to say that we can aim at the truth without knowing whether we have hit it. Moreover, as I shall suggest, Hobbes' goal is to reach political conclusions that we find we have to agree to. This is one way of getting round doubts about morality or politics, since if we can't help agreeing to a conclusion, then the question of its truth, at least for political purposes, lapses. We have to live with the conclusion because we can do nothing else.

As Hobbes notes, the problem is to find a conclusion that impresses itself on reason with just this force. If we do,

> we are not to renounce ... our natural reason ... By the captivity of our understanding is not meant a submission of the intellectual faculty to the will of any man, but of the will to obedience where obedience is due. For sense, memory, understanding, reason and opinion are not in our power to change ... [and] are not effects of our will, but our will of them. We then captivate our understanding and reason, when we forbear contradiction.
>
> (L 255–56)

Reason is both strong and weak, and has to be in order to serve Hobbes' purposes. It is weak insofar as its power to discover the truth about certain aspects of the world (such as the nature of God) is very limited. But it is strong to the extent that, just because of this, it imposes a stringent standard on belief: if this power is indeed weak, then reasonable belief and action need to take account of this. While reason cannot stop people from holding beliefs which are irrational, reason can devise means to counter the ill effects of their doing so. Or so Hobbes hoped.

He thought not that reason should withdraw from the public sphere, but that the sovereign – the supreme ruler – should decide which religious and political doctrines should be publicly endorsed. He knew that it would be impossible to force all individuals to believe these doctrines, as private citizens (e.g. L 323). Again this offers a strong contrast with most modern political philosophy, and in particular the doctrine of neutrality – the idea that the state should remain neutral or impartial between different ideas of the good life, or of the meaning of life, including such matters as religion. The most widely held justification for neutrality runs as follows: since reasonable people hold widely differing views on the nature of the good, any such view is reasonably rejectable; if a view is reasonably rejectable, it cannot be justified to enforce that view politically (e.g. by force of law); but all views are reasonably rejectable; so the state, to be justified, must endorse no such view. It must remain neutral between different ideas of the good life.

Thus, liberals who support neutrality rule out theocratic states of the kind that exist in today's Iran, or indeed an established religion such as the Church of England. They argue that beliefs about the good life or the meaning of life are inevitably controversial, so that it is unjustifiable for the state to impose specific beliefs about these matters on everybody. On this view, the state should be like a referee, rather than one of the competing teams, impartially enforcing rules which apply equally to all sides.

Hobbes knew well that questions about the meaning of life were controversial. But he thought that these views had to take second place behind the maintenance of the state. Suppose we grant the claim of neutrality that the state cannot justifiably impose its idea of the good on everybody, in the face of reasonable disagreement about what the good is. It is clear that this approach assumes that certain goods, and in particular that of security, are already in place. But what if the only way to maintain the state were to impose some such idea, however controversial? It is clear that the neutrality argument assumes that security is already guaranteed – without it, there is no state to act as a referee. Worries about justification are, to this extent, a luxury, which can be indulged in only when the fundamental political good of security is already in place.

It may be said that an unduly repressive political authority may itself undermine security. That was what made the creation of an all-powerful sovereign double-edged. But, first, this view is itself controversial, and relies on assumptions about individuals' motivations within a repressive regime.[4] And, second, even if it is the case that security is best served by a regime of toleration rather than repression, the argument is no longer about justification in the abstract, as it is with neutrality, but about the best way to promote security.

Hobbes' alternative view, then, puts to one side questions of justification in favour of a more pragmatic approach. The sovereign – whether it is an individual or assembly – can and should decide controversial matters of doctrine. The fact that, in the abstract, it may be impossible to justify these doctrines – in the sense of providing adequate warrant for believing them – is not the point. It is not the point, for Hobbes, because there are political goods that take precedence over truth.

This is why Hobbes is a deeply troubling figure for philosophers, who usually see themselves as engaged in a project of inquiry – and if the notion of inquiry is to make sense, it is hard put to do without the notion of truth, at which inquiry aims. Hobbes says, not that we cannot get hold of the truth, but that other things matter more. As he says about law, it 'depends not on the books of moral philosophy. The authority of writers, without the authority of the commonwealth, makes not their opinions law, be they never so true ... yet it is by the sovereign power that it is law' (L 191). The nature and limits of the 'sovereign power' lie at the heart of *Leviathan*.

NOTES

1 *L* 89 = *Leviathan*, p. 89. All citations of *Leviathan* are to Tucker ed., Hobbes 1991.
2 It should be said that one school of interpretation – that of Richard Tuck – argues that *Leviathan* itself is a utopian work. See Tuck's 'The Utopianism of *Leviathan*', in Sorell and Foisneau 2004.
3 It is obviously unfair to select a single example to illustrate what I see as a widespread tendency within modern political philosophy. But the work of John Rawls exemplifies the short circuit, both in his early work (*A Theory of Justice*) and his later theory (*Political Liberalism*). In both cases Rawls tries to construct in theory what he takes to be a moral foundation that s implicit in the beliefs of citizens – although in the case of *Political Liberalism* the construction is deemed to have extra authority because it is held not to be rooted in controversial sectarian moral doctrine. I cite Rawls not only because his work is very well known, but because it embodies this method of argument in a particularly clear but also sophisticated form.
4 It is far from clear that Hobbes' personal preference was for repression: at the end of *Leviathan* he describes the early Christian churches, which operated in freedom from central control, as 'perhaps the best' system of church government (*L* 480); for more on this, see Chapter 9 below.

1

HOBBES' LIFE

HOBBES' LIFE AND TIMES

The life of Thomas Hobbes was sociable, rich, pleasant, cultured and long. Hobbes was deeply enmeshed in the society of his time, both in his long involvement with the aristocratic Cavendish family, and in his contact (see the correspondence collected in Hobbes 1994a) with many of the leading European intellectuals of the day. At his death, Hobbes left over £1,000, a substantial sum for the time. In his English verse *Autobiography* (see Hobbes 1994b, lxiii) he notes that 'My sums are small, and yet live happy so'. He was a highly cultivated intellectual figure, producing translation from (and into) Latin and Greek, and engaging in speculation about philosophy, physics, theology, biblical interpretation, natural science and mathematics, among other subjects. Hobbes died at the age of ninety-one.

He was born on Good Friday, 5 April 1588, in Westport, north Wiltshire, not far from Malmesbury (he was known, indeed, known as 'Thomas Hobbes of Malmesbury'). Another biographer, Anthony Wood, wrote that Hobbes' followers were apt to say that 'as our Saviour Christ went out of the world on that day to save the men of the world, so another savior came into the world on that day to save them' (Wood 1817, vol. III, 1206). Many of Hobbes' contemporaries took a less flattering view of him, as we shall see.

Hobbes' father, also named Thomas Hobbes, was a rural clergyman, curate of the neighbouring parish of Brokenborough. Little is known about Hobbes' mother, but she may have been Alice Courtnell, who married a Thomas Hobbes in St Martin, Salisbury, not far from Malmesbury, on 3 May 1578. Hobbes had an older brother, Edmund, and a younger sister, Anne. Despite his clerical vocation, Thomas Hobbes senior was a notorious wastrel, though not untypical of the rural clergy of the day. He was illiterate, and apparently often drunk. According to John Aubrey, Hobbes' friend and biographer, Hobbes' father was given to falling asleep in church, once stirring from his slumbers to exclaim, 'trafells [i.e. clubs] are trump[s]'. He was excommunicated – in effect, expelled from the church – for beating up a fellow vicar, Richard Jeane, in Malmesbury churchyard. Hobbes senior had previously been tried in a church court for slandering Jeane, and after the churchyard incident reportedly left the county for good. Afterwards Hobbes' uncle Francis, a prosperous glove merchant, seems to have acted as the young Thomas' guardian.

Hobbes attended elementary school in Westport, near Malmesbury, and later went to school in Malmesbury itself. By the age of fourteen he had translated the ancient Greek playwright Euripides' *Medea* from Greek into Latin verse. Between about 1602–3[1] and 1608, Hobbes attended Magdalen Hall (now Hertford College) at Oxford University. At Oxford he received the usual training in classical languages and literature, particularly in the works of the ancient Greek philosopher Aristotle, which Hobbes would later dismiss in *Leviathan* as 'Aristotelity' (*L* 462). According to Aubrey he amused himself when not at his studies by perusing maps in shops, and by catching birds. An antipathy to the 'Schools', the medieval philosophy derived from Aristotle, remained with him for the rest of his life (e.g. *L* 59, 227, 418, 472–73).

On the recommendation of Magdalen Hall's Principal John Wilkinson in 1608, Hobbes was recruited to act as a tutor to the future second Earl of Devonshire, William Cavendish. In fact Hobbes' duties extended beyond those of a tutor (Hobbes was only about two years older than his master), to acting as a general factotum in the Cavendish household. This passage into the service of the aristocracy was one made by many intellectually able young men of humble origins. Hobbes spent most of the seventy-one further years of his life as a member of the household either of the Earls of Devonshire, or of their cousins, the Earls of Newcastle.

Not much is known about Hobbes' activities between 1610 and 1614. It was once thought that he was in Europe with his protégé William Cavendish during this period, but there are strong grounds for thinking that they did not leave England until 1614 (Martinich 1999, 29–30). In that year he and Cavendish undertook a tour of France and Italy, where Hobbes learned Italian. They returned in 1615. He seems to have made the acquaintance of Francis Bacon, the Lord Chancellor (1561–1626), soon after his return to England in 1615, perhaps helping Bacon to translate the latter's *Essays* from English to Italian before their publication in 1618. Hobbes was the source for John Aubrey's claim, in his biography of Bacon, that the Lord Chancellor died from a chill caught during a disastrous refrigeration experiment, which involved stuffing a (dead) chicken with snow. In 1620 an anonymous volume was published, entitled *Horae subsecivae* ('Leisure Hours'), comprising a number of essays, some of which, it has been argued, were written by Hobbes himself. It is possible to see the foundations of Hobbes' mature philosophy in two of them, 'A Discourse upon the Beginning of Tacitus' and 'A Discourse of Laws' (see Hobbes 1995).

Hobbes continued in the Cavendish family service, and was a board member and nominal shareholder on the Virginia Company, in which the Cavendish family maintained substantial interests (Malcolm 2002, ch. 3). William Cavendish died in 1628, having succeeded as second Earl of Devonshire only two years earlier. This temporarily left Hobbes without employment in the Cavendish family. Through the good offices of the Earl of Newcastle, however, he soon secured employment with Sir Gervase Clifton, a friend of the Cavendish family. After a second European tour to France and

Switzerland as the tutor of Sir Gervase's son in 1629–30, he returned to the service of the Cavendish family in the household of William's widow, the Dowager Countess of Devonshire, at Hardwick Hall. In 1629 he published a translation of the ancient Greek historian Thucydides' *History of the Peloponnesian War*, 'to the end that the follies of the democratic Athenians might be laid open', as Anthony Wood said (Wood 1817, vol. III, 1206). In his *Autobiography* Hobbes wrote that Thucydides was a favourite of his among historians because he showed 'how stupid democracy is' (Hobbes 1841, vol. I, lxxxviii).

Thereafter Hobbes extended his intellectual contacts and reputation both in England and abroad. During the 1630s Hobbes associated with members of the so-called 'Tew circle', which met at the home of Lucius Cary, Viscount Falkland (1610–43), in the village of Great Tew in north Oxfordshire, and was involved in the intellectual coterie which met at the Earl of Newcastle's home in Welbeck, Nottinghamshire. The Tew Circle included such friends (and sometimes future ex-friends) of Hobbes as Edward Hyde (1609–74), who later became Earl of Clarendon. Hyde wrote a history of what is usually referred to as the 'English Civil War',[2] the religious and political conflicts that raged across the British Isles between 1642 and 1651. Other acquaintances included the lawyer and political theorist John Selden (1585–1654), the poet Edmund Waller (1606–87), theologian William Chillingworth (1602–44) and the Oxford cleric Gilbert Sheldon (1598–1677). The Circle was familiar with the work of Hobbes' great contemporary, the Dutch legal and political theorist Hugo Grotius (1583–1645), and with continental philosophical doctrines to which Hobbes had already been exposed.

This exposure arose from a third tour of mainland Europe which Hobbes undertook from 1634 to 1636, accompanying the third Earl of Devonshire (who, though still a minor, had succeeded to the title when his father died in 1628). They visited France and Italy, including two prolonged stays in Paris. There he met Marin Mersenne (1588–1648), a friar from the order of Minims, who kept in contact with a wide range of European philosophers and intellectuals, and helped to spread their ideas. Hobbes also met the great astronomer Galileo in Florence. Of his acquaintance with Mersenne, he proudly writes in his verse *Autobiography* that after showing the friar his writings on motion, 'I was reputed a philosopher' (l. 136). His translation of Aristotle's *Rhetoric*, with the English title *A Briefe of the Art of Rhetorique*, was published in 1637. The translation incorporated radical revisions to Aristotle's text (it was in fact a translation of a Latin summary of the work which Hobbes had previously used for tuition purposes). During the later 1630s Hobbes also wrote a tract in Latin on optics.

The 1630s were also years of political unrest in England. King Charles I failed to summon Parliament during the eleven years between the dissolution of 1629 and the Short Parliament of April 1640. In the election for this parliament, Hobbes stood as a candidate for Derby, but the influence of Devonshire was not enough to secure Hobbes' election. The King's eleven years of personal rule (i.e. rule by Charles I and his advisers without summoning Parliament) were marked by growing dissent, including the famous Ship Money case of 1637, which raised the question whether there were any limitations on royal prerogative. Charles also launched a disastrous invasion of Scotland to enforce the Anglican prayer book in 1639. As political ferment grew, Hobbes published the pro-royalist *Elements of Law* in May 1640.

Moves against Charles' supporters by the Long Parliament, which opened later in 1640, caused Hobbes to leave for Paris in November of that year – 'the first of all that fled', as Hobbes himself said later. He would remain in exile for eleven years. In France he renewed his acquaintance with Mersenne and the other French intellectuals he had met on his visit to Paris in 1634–36. His second major work of political theory, the Latin work *De cive*, was circulated in a limited edition in 1642 and published in 1647 (an English version was published in 1650, a French translation by Hobbes' friend Samuel Sorbière having appeared in 1649), though it may have been substantially complete by 1640. *De cive* was part of a projected trilogy whose other two parts did not appear until the 1650s. Hobbes also wrote a lengthy refutation of the Catholic philosopher Thomas White's book *De Mundo*, which was not published during Hobbes' lifetime (now usually referred to as the *Anti-White*) (Hobbes 1976).[3] He wrote a tract on optics in English, later incorporated into *De homine* (Hobbes 1841, vol. II).

Hobbes remained in France until after the publication of *Leviathan* in mid-1651, by which time Charles had been defeated in the civil wars, executed and replaced by a republican regime. Hobbes seems to have begun writing the book in 1649, and must have composed it very rapidly: he had written thirty-seven of the chapters (which became forty-seven in all, together with the 'Review, and Conclusion', though Hobbes had originally projected fifty) by May 1650 (Malcolm, in Hobbes 2012, vol. I, 2). The rest of the book was more or less finished by the end of that year. It was published in London in April or May 1651.[4]

When he was asked by his old friend Edward Hyde why he had published it, Hobbes famously replied – in a mood, Hyde recorded, 'between jest and earnest' – that '[t]he truth is, I have a mind to go home' (as Hyde recounted in his 'A Survey of Mr Hobbs His Leviathan', in Rogers 1995, 184). This presumably indicates that Hobbes thought *Leviathan* would help him to find favour with the new republican regime in England, despite his association with royalism during the civil wars. If this was indeed Hobbes' calculation, it was correct (see Collins 2005). He returned to England in 1651–52 and remained unmolested by the republican regime.

However, the book's vehement hostility to Roman Catholicism – chapter 47 of the book compares the Papacy with 'the Kingdom of Fairies' – incurred the displeasure both of the French clergy and the English court in exile (Charles I's widow Henrietta Maria was a Catholic). The book's views on church government, sovereignty and controversial points of theology were also unwelcome in orthodox royalist circles and indeed Anthony Ascham, one of the so-called 'de facto' apologists for the new English republican regime, whose views bore a passing similarity to Hobbes', had recently been murdered in Spain by royalist agents. Just as the *Elements of Law* had prompted Hobbes' departure from England to France in 1640, the publication of *Leviathan* sped him back from France to England eleven years later.

Back in England Hobbes continued to publish prolifically, though he was now well into his sixties and in poor health. He engaged in a lengthy dispute with Bishop John Bramhall (1594–1663) on free will, and published the first and second parts of the *Elements of Philosophy*, the *De corpore* (1655) and *De homine* (1658). The latter adds some important material to the political theory set out in *Leviathan*. The publication of *Leviathan* made Hobbes famous. A number of attacks on the book soon appeared in print, such as Alexander Ross' (1591–1654) *Leviathan Drawn Out With a Hook* of 1653, George Lawson's (1598–1678) *An Examination ... of Mr Hobbs His Leviathan*, which appeared in 1657, and Bramhall's *The Catching of Leviathan*, published in the following year.

In 1660 Charles II returned from exile as the restored Stuart monarch. As a supporter of the King during the civil wars, Hobbes was not initially threatened by the persecution of former republicans and regicides that followed the Restoration. But with the Restoration of the monarchy came that of the Church of England too, and a series of statutes reasserted religious orthodoxy after the free-for-all of the late 1640s and 1650s. Hobbes duly found himself under threat of investigation by the House of Lords as part of the proceedings on a bill against 'Atheism and Profanity' in 1666–68. This episode is discussed in greater detail in Chapter 11.

During this decade, as he approached the age of eighty, Hobbes remained very active: the Latin version of *Leviathan* dates from this decade (for the dating of the Latin text, see Chapter 2), as probably does his *Dialogue between a Philosopher and a Student of the Common Laws of England*.[5] Hobbes' sight was failing by this time, and because he was no longer capable of writing in person he had to dictate to an assistant. *Behemoth*, his narrative of the background to the civil wars in Britain in the 1640s, was written in 1670, though it was not published until 1679, the year of his death.

In the final decade of his life Hobbes lost little of his intellectual vigour. He continued to engage in polemics. One of these involved John Fell (1625–86), the Hobbes-hating Dean of Christ Church, Oxford. Fell demanded changes to a (largely favourable) biography of Hobbes which was included by Anthony Wood in the latter's *History and Antiquities of the University of Oxford*. In the 1670s Hobbes also wrote and published a history of the church, the *Historia Ecclesiastica*, and two works on mathematics, as well as a translation of Homer, *The Travels of Ulysses*, which went through several editions before Hobbes died. According to Bishop White Kennett, at this stage of his life Hobbes would have 'dinner' at about noon, and would then retire to his study 'with 10 or 12 pipes of tobacco laid by him'; he would then start 'smoking, and thinking, and writing for several hours'.

Hobbes was a man of idiosyncratic likes and dislikes. He engaged, for example, in a long and vituperative dispute with the mathematician John Wallis (1616–1703). This resulted in part from Hobbes' project of 'squaring the circle', in which he persevered for decades. Squaring the circle was an ancient puzzle for mathematicians. It was the task of constructing, from a given circle, a square equal in area to it, using only an unmarked ruler and a compass; it is in fact impossible (see Hardy Grant, 'Hobbes and Mathematics', in Sorell 1996a). Wallis, an accomplished mathematician, was reduced to exasperation and eventually silence. In fact, Hobbes' last publication, the *Decameron Physiologicum* of 1678, included yet another attempt to refute Wallis' geometrical claims.

He antagonised the Dutch mathematician and natural scientist Christiaan Huygens (1629–95) for similar reasons, and made prolonged and bizarre attempts to show that Robert Boyle's (1627–91) claim to evacuate a glass jar by means of an air-pump must be misguided or fraudulent (Shapin and Schaffer 1985; see also Douglas Jesseph, 'Hobbes and the Method of Natural Science', in Sorell 1996a). Hobbes developed a morbid fear of mountains, which he seems to have regarded as abominable excrescences. This was unfortunate for Hobbes, who spent much of his adult life in Derbyshire's Peak District, in the Cavendish family seat at Hardwick Hall. In 1636 he published a long Latin poem on the subject, *De mirabilibus pecci* ('Concerning the Wonders of the Peak'), which dealt with a peak in the neighbourhood of Hardwick known locally as the 'Devil's Arse' – no doubt an attempt to 'work through' this phobia.

Hobbes had other oddities. He was a hypochondriac. He believed that death was caused by the reabsorption in old age of one's own perspiration, causing the victim to drown. This belief caused him to engage in much pointless exercise, and to wear thick garments even in warm weather, in an attempt to sweat out the supposedly lethal fluid. He sang a lot, apparently in the belief that doing so would counteract the tendency of the lungs to shrivel in old age; this seems to have caused him respiratory problems. He played tennis, and indeed *Leviathan* employs an extended and rather strange tennis metaphor at the end of chapter 25 (*L* 182). He never married, though Aubrey remarked, with perhaps intended ambiguity that 'he was not a woman-hater'. Indeed, White Kennett's memoir of Hobbes, as well as Anthony Wood's, alleged that he had fathered an illegitimate daughter, though no hard evidence has been found to support this claim; according to Wood, Hobbes referred to her as his *delictum juventutis* (the sin of his youth).

Anthony Wood summarised Hobbes' personality as follows:

> Tho' he hath an ill name from some, and good from others, yet he was a person endowed with an excellent philosophical soul, was a contemner of riches, money, envy, the world &c. He was charitable and beneficial to his relations and others. He was a severe lover of justice, and endowed with great morals. Among those that he lived with and was conversant, he was cheerful, open, and free of his discourse, yet without offence to any, which he endeavoured always to avoid.
>
> (Wood 1817, vol. III, 1208)

Aubrey's pen-portrait of Hobbes the man is also vivid enough to be worth quoting at some length.

> From forty or better, he grew healthier, and then had a fresh ruddy complexion [Hobbes had apparently looked rather pallid in his younger days] ... In his old age he used to sing prick-song [written music for voices] every night, for his health ... He had a good eye, and that of a hazel colour, which was full of life and spirit, even to the last. When he was earnest in discourse, there shone, as it were, a bright

live-coal within it. He had two kind[s] of looks: when he laughed, was witty, and in a merry humour, one could scarce see his eyes; by and by [later], when he was serious and positive, he opened his eyes round ... He was six foot high, and something better, and went indifferently erect, or rather, considering his great age, very erect ... He was, even in his youth, generally temperate, both as to wine and women ... For his last 30 + years, his diet etc. was very moderate and regular. After 60 he drank no wine, his stomach grew weak, and he did eat most fish, especially whiting, for he said he digested fish better than flesh. He rose about seven, had his breakfast of bread and butter, and took his walk, meditating till ten; then he did put down the minutes of his thoughts, which he penned in the afternoon ... he did twice or thrice a year play tennis (at 75 he did it); then went to bed there and was well rubbed. This he did believe would make him live two or three years the longer.

Hobbes lived until he was ninety-one, a great age for a seventeenth-century man. In October 1679 he fell ill with strangury, a bladder complaint (Wood 1817, vol. III, 1216). About a week before he died he had what Anthony Wood described as a 'dead palsy', which seems to have been what would now be called a stroke. Shortly before his death he was moved from Chatsworth to Hardwick, about 10 miles away, swaddled in a feather blanket. He died on 4 December 1679. His body, wrapped in a woollen shroud, was buried at the Parish Church of Hault Hucknall, a mile or so from Hardwick. The Latin inscription on the headstone records Hobbes' years of service to the Cavendish family, though according to a sermon preached by Bishop Kennett at the funeral of William Duke of Devonshire in 1708, Hobbes had previously requested that the headstone inscription should read: 'this is the true philosopher's stone'.

HOBBES' THOUGHT AND *LEVIATHAN*

Hobbes' intellectual background was eclectic. It has often been observed that his early intellectual development owed much to his 'humanist' training – that is, to his education in the classical languages of ancient Greek and Latin, and their literature and philosophy. Apart from the early translation of Euripides that he produced while still a schoolboy, his first substantial publication was, as we have seen, a translation from the Greek of Thucydides' *History of the Peloponnesian War*. Similarly, much of his own training and early pedagogic career – the European tour, the teaching of Latin and learning of Italian, instruction in rhetoric – formed a standard part of humanist education at the time.

Hobbes never entirely outgrew this early humanist training. It is certainly true that his intellectual interests diversified as he grew older (his comparatively late engagement with geometry being a case in point). His interest in contemporary science, particularly astronomy, seems to date from his time at Oxford. To think of Hobbes' life as segmented into distinct 'phases', in any case, risks misrepresenting it. Hobbes' humanistic pursuits continued throughout his life, including his late translation of Homer into English, as well as his own Latin verse compositions. He also published a lengthy Preface to Sir William Davenant's epic poem *Gondibert* in 1650, and in old age he produced English translations of the Homeric epics the *Iliad* and the *Odyssey*.[6] The diverse range of intellectual interests that Hobbes pursued is as well represented in *Leviathan* as in any of his works.

It is more useful, as well as more realistic, to think of Hobbes' intellectual interests as an amalgam of distinct but coexisting elements – humanist, scientific, theological and so on – in creative tension with one another, rather than as marking out a succession of distinct phases of his life. Part of his aim in *Leviathan* is to make a case against some of the central tenets of humanist political theory, such as those upheld by republican writers such as Marchamont Nedham (1620–78) in his *The Excellencie of a Free State*, and others influenced by the Florentine Niccolò Machiavelli. Important among these ideas is the claim that individual citizens can only enjoy liberty under a republican constitution, where each citizen has the right to engage actively in political affairs. Hobbes' scornful remarks in *Leviathan* (L 149) about the city of Lucca, often upheld as a model of republican freedom, seem clearly designed to repudiate the notion that citizens are freer in a republic than in a monarchy; but in *Leviathan* Hobbes also draws freely on humanist rhetorical devices in making his argument, perhaps because he came to see that persuasion required more than reason to be effective, as indeed Aristotle had argued in the *Rhetoric*, which Hobbes translated (Skinner 1996). His background in humanism was not something he simply outgrew.

Hobbes was also immersed in the natural scientific discoveries of his day, and indeed regarded himself as a man of science. It was a long-standing cause of grievance to him that he was not admitted to the Royal Society (Skinner 1969b; Malcolm 2002, ch. 10). His travels on the continent brought him into contact with scientific advances in fields such as optics, mechanics, chemistry and astronomy, while he knew or had met many of the most eminent scientists in England, including William Harvey (1578–1657), William Petty (1623–87) and Robert Hooke (1635–1703), as well as Francis Bacon. Hobbes seems to have regarded his scientific writings, which include such voluminous works as the *Anti-White* of 1643 and the *De corpore*, published in 1655, as at least equal in importance to his political writings – certainly to *Leviathan*. At the very end of the book he returns, with what sounds like relief, to 'my interrupted speculation of bodies natural' (*L* 491).

Three major features of Hobbes' scientific work, and particularly of his views on metaphysics and scientific method, are significant for our understanding of *Leviathan*. Hobbes was an out-and-out materialist, system-builder and sceptic.

MATERIALISM

Hobbes believed that physical matter alone was real. Hobbes proclaims towards the end of *Leviathan*: 'the world (I mean not the Earth only ... but the Universe, that is, the whole mass of things that are) is corporeal, that is to say, body' (*L* 463). His position is also clearly set out in the objections he made in the early 1640s to the *Meditations on First Philosophy* of the French philosopher and mathematician René Descartes (1596–1650). While Descartes argued that humans are essentially mental rather than physical beings, Hobbes maintained that in order for mental phenomena – such as thoughts – to exist, there must be some *body* that experiences them.

Moreover, Hobbes believed that there was a single type of cause that operated to bring about natural phenomena. This cause was matter – material bodies – in motion. For example, in *De corpore* (ch. 26, §7),[7] Hobbes conjectures that magnetism will prove to consist in the movement of matter: 'it is not known what magnetic force is, but when it is known, it will be found to be the motion of matter'. This makes it sound as though Hobbes was a kind of determinist – that is, someone who believes that every event in the universe results by causal necessity from a previous state of the universe. Though Hobbes was a kind of determinist, as we shall see, it should be noted that determinism does not follow from materialism itself: it is possible that the world could be nothing but matter, but that it combines randomly. At any rate, Hobbes applies the idea that the world can be comprehensively understood as matter in motion not only to areas such as ballistics or astronomy, but to optics and human psychology. Indeed, the opening of *Leviathan* asks 'what is the heart but a spring; and the nerves, but so many strings; and the joints, but so many wheels, giving motion to the whole body … ?' (*L* 9). For Hobbes, if we wish to know the cause of some natural phenomenon, we need to know how it has been produced by material motion.

SYSTEM-BUILDING

In both his political writings and his other philosophical and scientific pursuits, Hobbes aimed to bring order to phenomena via a cohesive intellectual system. His pattern for this was the deductive certainty provided by mathematical proofs, and especially geometry. His friend John Aubrey told the famous story of how, around 1630, Hobbes

> was in a gentleman's house in which a copy of Euclid's *Elements* lay open on a desk. When he read proposition 47, he said, 'By G –, this is impossible.' So he read the demonstration of it, which referred him back to such a proposition; which proposition he read. *Et sic deinceps* [and so on back to the start, i.e. the initial proposition], that at last he

was demonstratively convinced of that truth. Th s made him in love
with geometry.

(Aubrey 1898, vol. I, 301)

Whether or not Aubrey's tale is true, it illustrates a key aspect
of Hobbes' intellectual endeavours. He hoped to extend the
demonstrative certainty of geometry to all areas of human
knowledge. The idea was to start off with axioms – in other
words, propositions that are treated as true by definition. From
the axioms one proceeds via rules of inference, which enable us
to move from known truths to further truths which may be
previously unknown.

Hobbes sets out this idea of gaining knowledge through a
process of deduction in *Leviathan*, chapter 5:

> Reason [is] attained by industry, first in apt impos ng of names [i.e. by
> appropriate definitions], and secondly by getting a good and orderly
> method [i.e. a rule of inference] in proceeding from the elements,
> which are names, to assertions made by connection of one of them
> to another ... till we come to a knowledge of all the consequences of
> names appertaining to the subject in hand; and that is it, [which] men
> call 'science'.

(*L* 35)

He expresses a similar idea in the earlier *Elements of Law*, where he
says that we should proceed 'from the imposition of names' to 'the
truth of their first propositions; and from two of the first, a third;
and from any two of the three a fourth, and so on, according to
the steps of science' (Hobbes 1969, 66).

This is relatively uncontroversial as an account of geometry, or
mathematical reasoning in general. It becomes much more controversial when it is extended, as Hobbes sought to do, to what
we would now call natural science – including not only physics,
but human physiology and psychology – let alone to what is
hopefully known as 'political science', the study of political
institutions and behaviour. In particular, we need to know how
the geometric mode of reasoning purely from abstract definitions
can deliver truths about matters of fact, as natural science aims to

do. Deduction requires, as Hobbes realised, great care in framing the initial definitions: 'in reasoning, a man must take heed of words' (*L* 31). Some words, such as the names of virtues and vices, are particularly treacherous, because there is no agreement about what they apply to: 'one man calls "wisdom", what another calls "fear"' and so on (*L* 31). But, however important this may be, it is unclear how we can proceed purely on the basis of definitions and rules of inference to knowledge of empirical fact.

Hobbes' claim that his political theory was scientific is one that other political philosophers, notably Karl Marx, have made about their own theories. It is a further question whether Hobbes intended the whole of knowledge, including politics, to be brought within a single intellectual system. Some writers (Sorell 1986; Malcolm 2002, ch. 5) argue that Hobbes' political theory can be detached from his wider scientific views while other (often less recent) writers disagree (Goldsmith 1966; Watkins 1973); I discuss this question further in Chapter 3.

Hobbes was also a form of nominalist, that is, someone who denies that there are real properties in the world which correspond in a systematic way to our use of general terms such as 'dog', 'tree' and so on. Of course we use these words in a mutually intelligible way, and no doubt most people assume that these words apply to dogs and trees because of certain properties that dogs really have in common and that trees really have in common. But this, according to Hobbes, is an illusion. '[T]here [is] nothing in the world universal but names; for the things named are every one of them individual and singular' (*L* 26). However Hobbes immediately qualifies this by distinguishing between proper names, such as 'Thomas Hobbes', which refer to just one object, and universals, such as 'dog' and 'tree', which refer to many, and says that the latter can be so applied because of the 'similitude' between different things (*L* 26).

One reason why Hobbes held this position was that he wished to avoid committing himself to accepting, or risking having to accept, the existence of objects that he thought obscure. This is quite an important part of *Leviathan*'s argument, stated both in Part I and in chapter 46, 'Of Darkness from Vain Philosophy'. There he traces the 'absurdities' of medieval scholasticism that arose because of its tendency to create abstract nouns based on reified properties and this, rather than the radical denial that there are any such 'similitudes' at all, is the position that Hobbes wants to defend. In chapter 8, for instance, in attacking scholasticism, he argues that philosophers who use scholastic terms and styles of argument are in fact

> mad, or intend to make others so. And particularly, in the question of transubstantiation [the doctrine that said that the 'accidents' of bread and wine are miraculously transformed into the body and blood of Christ at communion]; where, after certain words spoken, they that say, the white*ness*, round*ness*, magni*tude*, quality, corruptibility, all which are incorporeal, and go out of the [communion] wafer into the body of our blessed Saviour, do they not make those *nesses, tudes* and *ties* to be so many spirits possessing his body?
>
> (*L* 59)

Hobbes' answer to this rhetorical question is basically 'Yes', and this is held to be 'absurd' in itself since being incorporeal is *defined* as 'not having the attributes or properties of a physical object', or something similar, and yet the incorporeal properties are also said to be capable of physical relocation. Hobbes certainly has an animus against abstraction. But his political aim is to reform thought in such a way that philosophical and theological conflicts of the sort that marked the prelude to the civil wars would be shown up as pointless. By achieving what Confucius called 'the rectification of names' the misunderstandings that engender conflict can be defused. Without regimentation of this sort, chaos is liable to ensue, as when one person calls 'good' the satisfaction of her own desires by something than another person also wants (who, if deprived of it, will call this situation 'bad'): 'when we conceive the same things differently, we can hardly avoid different naming of them' (*L* 31). One and the same thing can be described as stemming from a sense of fear, or wisdom; from cruelty, or justice; from prodigality, or magnanimity – and so on. 'And therefore such names can never be true grounds of any ratiocination [rigorous reasoning]' (*L* 31).

SCEPTICISM

Philosophical scepticism also influenced Hobbes' thought. The ancient form of this scepticism, professed by writers such as Carneades, Pyrrho and Sextus Empiricus, sought to undermine the claims to knowledge made by the ancient Greek philosopher Plato and others. Ancient sceptics held that, since equally strong arguments could be made on either side of a question, the only sensible response was to suspend one's judgement. The sceptical position extended to claims about both knowledge of the physical world and moral knowledge. Scepticism had enjoyed a revival during the last few decades of the sixteenth century among humanist writers such as Michel de Montaigne (1533–92).

This sceptical strain of European humanism rejected the common-sense understanding of the world based on sensory perception. Ancient sceptics were fond of showing that our 'knowledge' of quantities such as temperature through direct physical experience must be ill-founded: if I submerge one foot in a bucket of crushed ice, and the other in a bucket of hot water, then transfer both to a bucket of lukewarm water, it will feel hot to one foot and cold to the other; so to think that immediate sensory experience is identical with the world itself is to say that the lukewarm water is both hot and cold at once, which is absurd. Examples like these were used to cast doubt on the very possibility that sensory experience could provide knowledge of the world.

The revived concern with scepticism of late sixteenth- and seventeenth-century humanism sought a foundation for knowledge that could avoid the treacherousness of sensory experience. During his sojourns in Paris (during 1629–31, 1634, 1637 and 1640–51, which of course covered the period of *Leviathan*'s composition), and by correspondence when he was in England, Hobbes was in close contact with intellectuals strongly influenced by scepticism, including such friends as Pierre Gassendi (1592–1655), and particularly Samuel Sorbière (1615–70).

Some commentators have questioned the importance of scepticism for Hobbes' thought (Sorell 1993; Malcolm 1996, 26; Zagorin 2000; Skinner 2002, 88). There is certainly little direct discussion in *Leviathan*, or indeed elsewhere in Hobbes' writings, of scepticism in the radical form associated with Pyrrho. But *Leviathan* is certainly strongly marked by what might be called *practical* scepticism. This asserts that, whether or not we can actually attain knowledge, disagreement in fact rages about questions of politics, religion, morality, and so on, and that this state of affairs will go on for as long as there is no authority to impose uniformity. Practical scepticism makes no controversial claims about whether we can know the truth about these questions, or indeed whether there is any truth to be known about them. Knowing the truth about morality, religion and so on, would not suffice to deal with political conflict. So it is not the unavailability of the truth itself that poses the political problem, so much as the fact that it is not something on which people will converge of their own accord.

Hobbes thought that this was a political disaster. Seen from this angle, the political project is to find a basis for practical convergence, irrespective of people's personal convictions. If this is what Hobbes is trying to achieve, his project seems much closer to the concerns of modern politics and theory than is often thought. It is then a recognisable forerunner of Rawls' concerns in his later book *Political Liberalism*, which sets out to answer this question: how can we provide a just basis for political society, given the wide divergence in people's beliefs? Except that the circumstances in which Rawls imagines that the theory applies are ones where the Hobbesian problem seems already to be solved, as some commentators have pointed out (e.g. Williams 2005, ch. 1): people *already* converge in accepting each other's status as defined by Rawls' 'two moral powers' and can deliberate about how to assign the social surplus in conditions far more secure than Hobbes' 'war of all against all'. In this sense Hobbes is pursuing a similar project to Rawls, but at a more fundamental level.

READING *LEVIATHAN*

Leviathan is a book both in and out of its time. When it was first published in 1651, Hobbes was already sixty-three. He was, by seventeenth-century standards, an old man, who might not expect to live much longer – he had suffered a serious illness during the late 1640s – though in fact he lived for a further twenty-eight years. Moreover, most of his distinctive political ideas had already been developed and published, and helped to make Hobbes' name both in England and on the continent. Why then did he set out to restate his views, and at much greater length than before?

One suggestion can be largely discounted: the idea that the turmoil of the civil wars explains Hobbes' political theory, together with the interpretation of the state of nature in *Leviathan* as a lightly fictionalised version of 1640s England, is still occasionally encountered, though seldom in the scholarly literature. The most obvious fact which refutes this view is that most of his mature political theory is already presented in *The Elements of Law*, which, though not published until 1650, was written a decade earlier, and in the Latin *De cive*, which was published in a limited edition in 1642, the year the civil wars began, when Hobbes was a mature man of fifty-four. Although relations between King Charles I and Parliament were already under severe strain in 1640–42, nobody foresaw in this period the civil tumult which would convulse the country in the decade to come, still less the triumph of Parliament, the execution of the King, and his replacement by a republic.

Hobbes does say in the 'Review, and Conclusion' at the end of *Leviathan* that the book was 'occasioned by the disorders of the present time' (*L* 491). But in fact, given the length of *Leviathan*, and when it was written (i.e. in 1649–50; see Chapter 2), it is more noticeable how few references there are to the civil wars and their consequences. Furthermore, Hobbes in this passage characteristically chooses his words carefully: he says that the book was *occasioned* by the disorders of the time, but this does not show that the leading ideas in *Leviathan* were produced by those disorders, in the sense that the ideas would have been radically different or not have come into being at all without them.

A better guess, due to the eminent Hobbes scholar Quentin Skinner, suggests that Hobbes was nudged into writing the book, while exiled in France, by the press of events at home in England. On 11 October 1649 Parliament called on the adult male population to swear its allegiance by an 'Oath of Engagement' to the new republican regime (Skinner 2002, vol. III, 19; ch. 10). Skinner argues that Hobbes wrote *Leviathan* to convince former supporters of King Charles I (like Hobbes himself) that they could in good conscience accept the rule of Parliament and the Council of State (the executive body which ruled the country after Charles' defeat in the civil wars), despite the abolition of the monarchy. As an incidental benefit, Hobbes could hope to win credit with the new regime, by encouraging Charles' supporters to accept the new order.

The key passages for this reading appear in the 'Review, and Conclusion' at the end of *Leviathan*, where Hobbes says that he wrote the book 'with no other design, than to set before men's eyes the mutual relation between protection and obedience' (*L* 491). And Hobbes says that he aims to set out the truth in order to correct 'diverse English books lately printed', which misstate 'in what point of time it is that a subject becomes obliged to the conqueror' (*L* 484). The answer to this question is that a subject vanquished by a stronger opponent becomes obliged, not when he is defeated, but when he consents to the authority of the vanquisher (cf. *L* 141). Here Hobbes seems to have in his sights 'de facto' theorists such as Anthony Ascham or Marchamont Nedham, who had argued that the mere fact of conquest confers political authority. I consider further the claim that *Leviathan* addressed the 'Engagement' controversy, in Chapter 11.

***

In general, attempts to read off Hobbes' political theory from the historical circumstances in which it was written can be pressed too far. The 'Review, and Conclusion' of *Leviathan*, and Hobbes' attempts at self-justification in the *Considerations*, amount to marginal tinkering with the theory. The local circumstances in which *Leviathan* were written are of great interest, but do not provide 'the' key to interpreting the book. Hobbes produced a new version of *Leviathan* in Latin in the late 1660s, in a radically changed political climate. He did not think that these new circumstances demanded any major change to the political theory of *Leviathan*. It is true that the more repressive political atmosphere at the time forced him to delete passages which he had felt free to let stand in the English edition – the diarist Samuel Pepys noted on 3 September 1668 that the English *Leviathan* was 'a book the bishops will not let be printed again', and Hobbes had recently been investigated for blasphemy, as I explain in further detail in Chapter 11. But Hobbes saw no reason to abandon the main arguments, despite the fact that the Stuart monarchy had been restored to power in England. Nor did he modify the argument significantly to take account of the fact that the Latin translation was aimed at a quite different audience of European intellectuals, rather than the English political class.

Sometimes it is said that the meaning of a historical text like *Leviathan* is fixed by the author's intentions, which can only address the historical circumstances or 'context' in which the text was written. So, it is said, we can only 'recover' the meaning of the text by understanding that context. Such an approach is associated particularly with the 'Cambridge School' of intellectual history. But attending to historical context fails to fix the meaning of the text. One problem is that the context in which a book like *Leviathan* was written has itself to be interpreted, causing problems of 'hermeneutic circularity'. We are supposed to fix the meaning of the text by looking at its historical context, but interpreting the context will demand, in turn, that we understand the meaning of statements made within it, including in texts such as *Leviathan*.

Furthermore, there is no obvious reason to think that there is any fixed thing that is the intention of the author in writing a text. The story is told that during a rehearsal of one of his own plays, the British playwright Harold Pinter was asked by an actor what he had intended by a certain line. Pinter said: 'I have no idea what the author's intentions were at this point.' It is tempting to appeal, in making judgements about whether an interpretation is right or not, to claims about what Hobbes would or would not have said about it. The question to ask in response to such claims is, 'Would have if what?'; there is no definitive way to fill out the 'if what'. Everything depends on what contrary-to-fact suppositions are made, and even then there may be no obvious answer to the question.

This is not to argue that we can say whatever we like, and claim for example that *Leviathan* is really about space travel. It is not even to dispute the claim that we can appeal, in reading *Leviathan*, to claims about Hobbes' intentions. But, when we ask of some specific passage what his intentions were, there may either be no relevant intention, or an indefinite number of possibilities, none of which is demonstrably better than all the others. We can only try to make the best sense of the book we can, and this is a constructive process, not one which is simply given to us by historical facts.

In any case, to read *Leviathan* as if it were written entirely with a view to local historical conditions itself risks misunderstanding Hobbes' own intentions in writing it, at least if we go on an obvious reading of what he says about them. At the end of Part 2, he despairs that, 'this [i.e. *Leviathan*'s] doctrine' is so different 'from the practice of the greatest part of the world' that 'it is impossible for the disorders of state and ... civil war, ever to be taken away'; but he consoles himself that 'at one time or other' it will fall into the hands of a sovereign who will 'convert this truth of speculation' into practice (*L* 254). In other words, Hobbes aspired to produce a theory whose validity did not depend on current conditions. His ambitions were grander than that.

To focus exclusively on context also narrows unduly our approach to *Leviathan* today. It is not just that the book loses much of its interest if it is viewed simply as a tract for its own time. Indeed, the 'Review, and Conclusion' which Hobbes appended to *Leviathan* aimed to explain how the general and abstract theory presented in the main text should apply in these conditions (Burgess 1990, 676). The 'Review, and Conclusion' was duly dropped in the Latin version of the late 1660s, when political conditions had changed radically.

In contrast to the Cambridge School, the approach I favour could be described as rational reconstruction. Rational reconstructors sit down, open the book, and make the best sense of it they can, where 'best' means 'most coherent' or just 'most interesting, given what sense we can make of the text'. Rational reconstructors are happy to state, for example, that 'the best statement of Hobbes' theory is one he never explicitly gave' (Skinner 2002, vol. III, 190). We bring to bear modern political concerns, both theoretical and practical; other information that may be of interest, such as what Hobbes seems to be saying in his other writings; and such competence as we can muster in the English language. We then use these materials to paint a picture of what may be going on, while remaining aware that the text does not always speak with one voice.

Since those who practise this approach are often interested in modern political theory, they are inclined to ask what significance historical texts such as *Leviathan* have for today's debates. This obviously influences the interpretation that I offer in this book. Whether this reflects the 'real' intentions of the historical figure Hobbes is not an obviously answerable question. I shall, however continue to refer unselfconsciously to 'Hobbes' in what follows.

A political theory of the kind set out in *Leviathan* abstracts from local conditions by appealing to general norms that guide action, derived, for example, from human nature. It is then a necessarily ambiguous matter how exactly theory bears upon political practice. A question that *Leviathan* poses in an unusually sharp form, as we shall see, is how, and how far, political theory can guide political practice at all.

FURTHER READING

SOURCES BY HOBBES

Hobbes wrote an autobiography in Latin verse towards the end of his life, reprinted in the edition of Hobbes' Latin works by William Molesworth (Hobbes 1841, vol. I, lxxxv–xcix, which is however not the definitive version: this is Hobbes' *Thomae Hobbesii malmesburiensis vita* (London, 1679)). An English version of the verse autobiography, which appeared in 1680 and may be Hobbes' own translation, is in Edwin Curley's edition of *Leviathan* (Indianapolis, IN: Hackett, 1994), liv–lxiv. There is also a partial translation of Hobbes' Latin prose autobiography in the same edition at lxiv–lxv. Important biographical materials can also be found in Noel Malcolm's two-volume edition of *The Correspondence of Thomas Hobbes* (Oxford: Oxford University Press, 1994).

OTHER CONTEMPORARY SOURCES

The sources for Hobbes' life are numerous. Contemporary sources include the invaluable biography by his friend and younger contemporary John Aubrey in *Brief Lives, chiefly of contemporaries*, set down by John Aubrey, between the Years 1669 and 1696, ed. A. Clark (Oxford: Clarendon Press, 1898), on which this chapter has drawn. It remains the best single original source for details of Hobbes' life. This is available in hard copy in many modern editions, and also on various online sites, for example at the McMaster University website, socserv.mcmaster.ca/~econ/ugcm/3ll3/hobbes/life. The edition of *Leviathan* edited by Edwin Curley contains extracts from Aubrey's biography.

Apart from Aubrey, the fullest contemporary source on Hobbes' life is Anthony Wood's entry on Hobbes in Wood's *Athenae Oxonienses*, vol. III, 1206–18 (London, 1817). Some details about Hobbes' final years, and in particular his involvement in the dispute between Anthony Wood and John Fell, can be found in Allan Pritchard, 'The Last Days of Hobbes: Evidence of the Wood manuscripts', *Bodleian Library Record* 10 (1980), 178–87. Further interesting biographical material, from which I have quoted in the text of this chapter, is contained in White Kennett's *Memoirs of the Family of Cavendish* (London: H. Hills, 1708).

MODERN BIOGRAPHIES OF HOBBES

Full-length

For a long time the standard full-length biography of Hobbes was George Croom Robertson's *Hobbes* (London: William Blackwood & Sons, 1886). The most recent life of Hobbes is A.P. Martinich, *Thomas Hobbes: A biography* (Cambridge: Cambridge University Press, 1999). This includes some updated material (e.g. on the chronology of Hobbes' first tour of Europe), but is prone to digression, and contains some mistakes. It is also written with Martinich's own theistic interpretation of Hobbes' political writings firmly in view. See also Miriam Reik, *The Golden Lands of Thomas Hobbes* (Detroit, MI: Wayne State University Press, 1977), chs 3 to 5, for further details about Hobbes' humanist intellectual background and his encounter with geometry. Arnold Rogow's biography *Thomas Hobbes: Radical in the service of reaction* (New York: Norton, 1986) is also full of detail but not always reliable. There is also a good deal of biographical material in Jeffrey Collins, *The Allegiance of Thomas Hobbes* (Oxford: Oxford University Press, 2005). Collins argues on fairly thin evidence (mainly the remarks Hobbes makes at the end of the English *Leviathan*) that Hobbes' enduring allegiance was to the Independent faction that gained the upper hand on the Parliamentary side after the defeat of Charles I.

Shorter

The best available short biography of Hobbes by a modern writer is chapter 1 of Malcolm's *Aspects of Hobbes* (Oxford: Clarendon Press, 2002). Quentin Skinner also provides a short life of Hobbes that lays particular stress on Hobbes' rejection of humanist approaches to politics, in Skinner, *Visions of Politics*, vol. III: *Hobbes and civil science* (Cambridge: Cambridge University Press, 2002), ch. 1. Otherwise see Malcolm's 'A Summary Biography of Hobbes', in Tom Sorell (ed.), *The Cambridge Companion to Hobbes* (Cambridge: Cambridge University Press, 1996), or A.P. Martinich, *Hobbes* (London: Routledge, 2005), ch. 1, which presents a similar view of Hobbes to that contained in Martinich's full-length biography.

INTELLECTUAL BIOGRAPHIES OF HOBBES

Quentin Skinner gives an outline intellectual biography of Hobbes in his *Visions of Politics*, vol. III: *Hobbes and civil science*, ch. 1. See also Richard Tuck, *Hobbes* (Oxford: Oxford University Press, 1989), and the same author's 'Hobbes and Descartes', in G.A.J. Rogers and Alan Ryan (eds), *Perspectives on Thomas Hobbes* (Oxford: Oxford University Press, 1988). See also chapter 7 on Hobbes in Tuck's *Philosophy and Government 1572–1651* (Cambridge: Cambridge University Press, 1993). It should be borne in mind when reading these texts, especially *Philosophy and Government*, that Tuck is concerned to advance his sceptical interpretation of Hobbes. See also Reik, *The Golden Lands of Thomas Hobbes*. Interesting information on Hobbes' involvement in the Cavendish family's affairs can be found in Noel Malcolm, 'Hobbes, Sandys, and the Virginia Company', *Historical Journal* 24 (1981), 297–321. This and several other highly informative essays on Hobbes' intellectual milieu can be found in Malcolm's *Aspects of Hobbes*.

NOTES

1 The uncertainty over dating arises from the fact that no matriculation record for Hobbes survives.
2 This term is a misnomer: theatres of war extended to Scotland, Wales, Ireland and the Channel Islands as well as England, and in the view of some historians involved a number of separate but intermeshing conflicts rather than only one.
3 It was finally published in an edition by Harold Whitmore Jones in 1976.
4 Information about the early publishing history can be found in Chapter 2.
5 The dating of the *Dialogue* is disputed, but the main evidence for this date is a letter from Aubrey to John Locke of 1673, which states that Aubrey had 'importuned' Hobbes to write 'a treatise concerning the law ... about eight years since' (Tuck 1990, 154–55).
6 For a useful corrective to the 'segmentation' view of Hobbes' intellectual development, see, for example, Johnston 1986; Condren 1990. See also Skinner 1996.
7 I translate from the 1655 (first) edition of *De corpore*, 247, i.e. '& vis magnetica quae sit ignoratur, & quando erit cognita, invenietur esse motus corporis'.

2

LEVIATHAN
THE BOOK

INTRODUCTION: THE TITLE OF *LEVIATHAN*

Hobbes took the name 'Leviathan' from the Bible. It occurs in a number of places in the Old Testament, particularly in the books of Isaiah and Job. 'Leviathan' denotes a mighty and terrifying beast, usually thought of as a monstrous sea-dweller, such as a sea-dragon or serpent (though sometimes it seems merely to refer to crocodiles). In fact, 'Leviathan' is one of three monster-names used in Job. Hobbes borrowed one of the others – 'Behemoth' – for the title of another of his books, on the causes and political issues underlying the civil wars of the 1640s. Leviathan's main appearance is in Job, chapter 41, from which Hobbes incorporated a verse into the title-page of *Leviathan*: 'upon earth there is not his like, who is made without fear'. In the King James Version, the passage runs as follows:

> Canst thou draw out leviathan with an hook? or his tongue with a cord which thou lettest down? ...

Will he make a covenant with thee? wilt thou take him for a servant for ever? ... Behold, the hope of him is in vain: shall not one be cast down even at the sight of him? None is so fierce that dare stir him up: who then is able to stand before me? ...

He esteemeth iron as straw, and brass as rotten wood. The arrow cannot make him flee: slingstones are turned with him into stubble. Darts are counted as stubble: he laugheth at the shaking of a spear ...

Upon earth there is not his like, who is made without fear.

He beholdeth all high things: he is a king over all the children of pride.

(Job 41:34)

The impression conveyed by this passage is one of sheer power. God's argument to Job is based not on His justice or righteousness, but on the fact of brute strength: He is powerful enough to crush Job if he wishes. The overpowering of justice, or its dependence upon, brute force is central to *Leviathan*.

The biblical origins of the name 'Leviathan' evoke ironies that were not lost on Hobbes' contemporary readers. While the Leviathan in the Bible threatens chaos, Hobbes' Leviathan is intended to bring order. Whereas the biblical story tells of the vanquishing by God of Leviathan, Hobbes sets up Leviathan as a 'mortal God' to quash human rebelliousness. Perhaps he acknowledges here that the very creation of a civil authority whose claims to subjects' allegiance might conflict with those of God (or at least the claims made on His behalf by clerics) is an act of rebellion. In these respects, the name already carries with it a tension that pervades the book: between rebelliousness and order, between the need to curb the 'children of pride', and the hubris of setting up a 'mortal God' over them (*L* 120).

The subtitle of *Leviathan* is *The Matter, Form, and Power of a Commonwealth Ecclesiastical and Civil*. Only Part 2, 'Of Commonwealth' (today, by far the most intensively studied and commented upon of *Leviathan*'s four parts), deals directly with political questions, while about half of the whole work is devoted to questions of biblical interpretation and the church's relation to the state. The subtitle's ordering of 'Ecclesiastical and Civil', and the fact that Part 3, 'Of a Christian Commonwealth', is the longest of *Leviathan*'s four parts, suggest that the issue of church government is meant to be at least as important in the book as that of civil government. But this is not, of course, to say that the ecclesiastical discussion is as important or as interesting for us now.

Nonetheless, the very fact that Hobbes talks of a single 'commonwealth, ecclesiastical and civil' is fundamental to the book. The phrase announces Hobbes' pivotal contention: secular and religious matters must fall under the jurisdiction of one authority.

THE TEXTS OF *LEVIATHAN*

There is no single definitive text of *Leviathan*, for reasons to be explained. However, since the first edition of this book appeared, Noel Malcolm's edition of *Leviathan* has been published by Oxford University Press in the Clarendon edition of Hobbes' works (Malcolm ed., Hobbes 2012). This sets a new standard of scholarship in the publishing history of *Leviathan*. It not only brings together the Latin and English texts on facing pages, but also exhaustively compares textual variants between seventeenth-century printed variants of the text, as well as checking the manuscript presentation copy referred to below.

As already noted, the first edition appeared in English in 1651. When taken together, the various early editions of the book are more like a word-processed document that exists in a number of different versions, corresponding to different edits, but with a good number of typographical errors thrown in. The historical circumstances of *Leviathan*'s composition and publication are the main reason why this is so. As already mentioned, there is a Latin version of *Leviathan*, also composed by Hobbes, but in numerous minor respects and some quite major ones the Latin text is not a straightforward translation of the English. In addition, there survives a handwritten presentation copy that Hobbes commissioned as a gift to the exiled Prince Charles, the future King Charles II, which is now held by the British Library.[1] I shall deal with the English, Latin and handwritten versions of the text in turn.

THE ENGLISH TEXT

The true first edition of the English *Leviathan* is the so-called 'Head' edition (the name of this and the other early editions is taken from the printer's devices which appear on the title-page), published in April or May 1651, which appeared with the legend 'London, Printed for Andrew Crooke, at the Green Dragon in St. Pauls Churchyard, 1651'.[2]

Although three editions bear the date 1651, it seems that only one edition was actually published in that year. There was an attempt to print an edition of *Leviathan* in London in 1670: in that year some unbound sheets of 'a book printing entitled 'Hobbs' Leviathan' were seized by the authorities (Macdonald and Hargreaves 1952, 29). Noel Malcolm (Malcolm 2002, ch. 11; also Malcolm ed., Hobbes 2012, vol. I, 226ff.) argues that a substantial proportion of the sheets from this printing were in fact retained or recovered by the printer, and these sheets were included in what became the 'Bear' edition, ostensibly dated 1651, whose completion sheets were printed in the Netherlands. However, Rogers and Schuhmann (ed., Hobbes 2003) argue that these sheets may have found their way into the 'Ornaments' (i.e. the third) edition of *Leviathan*, which is also dated 1651 but, it is generally agreed, was published some time after that date. This thesis is disputed by Malcolm, who argues that the 'Ornaments' dates from 1695–1702 on the basis of publishing data (Malcolm ed., Hobbes 2012, vol. I, 258ff.).

Given the complex publishing history of *Leviathan*, it would be naive to claim that there is or could be anything amounting to a single definitive version of the text; indeed, there is a live question in textual philology as to what it *means* for a text to be definitive. If the author's intentions are what determine a work's content, how do editors decide what to do when faced with errors? In some cases, it will be obvious what the correct version should be; for instance, a famous and glaring misspelling of the publisher's name as 'Andrew Ckooke' appears on the title-page (for a reproduction of a 'Bear' edition, see Malcolm ed., Hobbes 2012, vol. I, 227). In other cases, however, mistakes may be more prominent, or there are simply different versions of a given passage and decisions have to be made about inclusion and exclusion – even if the variants are given in a footnote.

How much does all this matter? In many respects, not much. Most of the variations between different copies of the same edition of *Leviathan*, catalogued in the Rogers and Schuhmann edition of 2003 and in Malcolm's 2012 edition, are of a quite trivial kind. Only rarely does a variant reading alter the sense of the sentence in which it occurs, and then seldom in a substantial way. In some cases readings derived from the handwritten presentation copy differ materially from those in the contemporary printed editions, though not always for the better. In a couple of places the differences seem to be explicable by the fact that the handwritten copy was prepared for Prince Charles and includes some derogatory references to Charles' political opponents, which are eliminated from the published versions of the text.

The overall conclusion, then, is that most of the variations between and within different editions of the English text are not very significant. However, there is one significant exception for us: the Latin version of *Leviathan*.

THE LATIN TEXT

There now exists a full translation into English of the Latin text for the first time, made by Noel Malcolm (Malcolm ed., Hobbes 2012, vols II and III). The Latin text was important in the contemporary reception of Hobbes' political thought on the continent of Europe. Latin was the common language of European intellectual life. Many continental scholars, such as the philosophers Spinoza and Leibniz, made their acquaintance with *Leviathan* via the Latin rather than the English text, as earlier many continental thinkers had read the Latin *De cive*. Later on, translators into European languages such as German used the Latin rather than the English text of *Leviathan*.

Nowadays proportionately fewer educated people read Latin than when Hobbes was alive. But it would be mistaken to adopt the dismissive stance of one recent editor of *Leviathan*, that '[t]he Latin version is a relatively obscure work for scholars' (Hobbes 1996, xlix). The main reason for paying some attention to it, apart from its reception in Europe (see Chapter 11), is twofold. First, as already mentioned, the Latin version is not a straight-forward translation of the English text. So we can compare possible changes in Hobbes' thinking between the composition of the two versions, or passages that were transformed under the pressure of political circumstances. Second, the Latin version can also shed light on obscure or contentious passages in the English *Leviathan*.

The major textual differences between the two versions of the book are that at the end of the English version there is the 'Review, and Conclusion' which is absent from the Latin, while the Latin version has a three-part Appendix on theological questions that is absent from the English text. In addition, some of the Latin chapters are severely abridged versions of the English original, and in particular Hobbes toned down some of his discussions of religious politics and theology, which are often polemical or scurrilous in English. *Leviathan* Part 4, 'Of the Kingdom of Darkness', is a drastically pruned remnant of the English text. The most obvious explanation for this is that the political and religious climate was much more relaxed during the period 1649–50, when the English *Leviathan* was written, than when Hobbes came to translate the work into Latin in the mid-1660s. It is also possible that he was frightened into softening the caustic treatment of church organization and theology by the threatened proceedings against the English text as part of the bill before Parliament against blasphemy and atheism, introduced in 1666 (see Chapter 11).

In his introduction to the French edition of *Leviathan*, François Tricaud argued that the Latin text in fact served as a first draft for the English *Leviathan*, a claim endorsed by Edwin Curley (Hobbes 1994b, lxxiii). However, there is no manuscript record of a full or near-full Latin text dating from before the 1660s. More decisively, however, the Tricaud hypothesis is circumstantially implausible. As Tricaud himself noted, Hobbes engaged in correspondence with Henry Stubbe, a young Oxford academic, who began (but never finished) translating the English text into Latin several years after the English *Leviathan* appeared. Hobbes corrected early drafts of Stubbe's translation. It is hard to see why

Hobbes would have gone to the effort of correcting Stubbe's drafts if he had already a complete Latin version to hand. The conclusion must be that there was still no Latin translation in existence some years after the appearance of the English *Leviathan*.[3]

THE SCRIBAL COPY

The other original source text for *Leviathan* is a scribal copy of the work that Hobbes caused to be made for presentation to Prince Charles, the future King Charles II; this seems to have been written by a francophone scribe in Paris with little or no knowledge of English (Malcolm ed., Hobbes 2012, vol. I, 199–200). This copy has survived, and is now in the British Library. The manuscript is written in a minute hand on vellum (sheepskin parchment). There are some crossings-out, which may sometimes be scribal mistakes, though on at least one page Hobbes seems to have had second thoughts, where some one hundred words have been entered and subsequently struck through, rendering them illegible. Rogers and Schuhmann's 2003 edition of *Leviathan* provides a full account of variations between the scribal copy and the large-paper edition of the book, as does Malcolm's edition of 2012.

THE TITLE-PAGE OF *LEVIATHAN*

The first edition of *Leviathan*, as well as subsequent editions produced in the seventeenth century, contain the famous engraved title-page (Figure 2.1) which has also been reproduced on or inside many of the book's modern editions.[4] While it may seem that the details of the title-page are minor or peripheral, it can be argued that the illustration is integral to the whole work and was fully intended to be seen as such. The most arresting feature of the title-page – the visual incorporation of the subjects into the body of the sovereign – is a literal image of *Leviathan*'s theory of the commonwealth as an artificial man (Prokhovnik 1991, 146). This image is central to the argument of the book.

The engraver's identity is not known. Keith Brown (Brown 1978) conjectures the title-page to be the work of the Bohemian artist

Figure 2.1 The frontispiece of *Leviathan* (1st edn, 1641)

Wenceslaus Hollar, who is also thought to be responsible for the ink drawing which appears on the scribal copy and which was an initial sketch for the engraving (Tricaud 1979, 297).[5] The imagery of the title-page itself is richly suggestive. It has been suggested that the figure of *Leviathan* resembles Oliver Cromwell, or the future Charles II, or possibly even an amalgam of the two of them. Commentators have proposed that the figure is meant to be William Cavendish, who became third Earl of Devonshire in 1628 (Rogow 1986, 115), or even Jesus Christ (Martinich 1992, 363). Martinich claims that the crozier or bishop's crook held by Leviathan in his left hand 'is strong evidence that a major feature of *Leviathan* is the significance of religion as practised by the Church of England' (Martinich 1992, 364).

A more plausible view, however, would be that it reaffirms a central claim of Part 3 of *Leviathan*, that the Church should be completely subordinated to the political authority. The crozier is probably simply a generic symbol of ecclesiastical authority, rather than a specifically episcopal symbol: bishops no longer existed in the England of 1651. Similar remarks apply to the bishop's mitre depicted in one of the lower right-hand panels, and to the sector containing an illustration of a thunderbolt, the traditional visual symbol of excommunication (i.e. expulsion from the Christian church).

The lower panels carefully incorporate elements of both spiritual and secular power in rhetorical opposition (Condren 1990, 717). Included here are depictions of battle, of cannons, a fortress, muskets and drums; in balance with these images, on the right there are panels showing a church, thunderbolts, bishop's mitre, and a scene of disputation – perhaps a civil tribunal, church court, or some other forensic business. Again, however, this need not be taken to mean, as has been suggested (Martinich 1992, 366), that 'secular power cannot be divorced from spiritual power'. It may show that the pretensions of the church to political power should be rebuffed.

The central image of a political authority composed of a multitude of people was not a novel one. Above the engraving is the quotation from the Book of Job in the Latin Bible, chapter 41, verse 33: 'Non est potestas super terram quae comparetur ei', that is (in the King James Version, which Hobbes cites), 'upon earth there is not his like'. It is said of the 'Leviathan', that he rules as 'king over all the children of pride' (L 221). The figure dominates a part-rural, part-urban landscape in the upper half of the engraving; a notable feature of the townscape shown in the foreground of this part of the engraving is the dominating presence of a cathedral or large church. This need not mean that Hobbes saw the church's role in civic life as being dominant. Rather it symbolises, if anything, the importance of a single public religion, for which Hobbes argues at length in *Leviathan* (e.g. *L* 253).

The British Library scribal copy also contains a version of the title-page, which is however not the original edition's engraving but a graphically similar ink drawing. This is reproduced in the Cambridge edition edited by Richard Tuck (1991) on p. 2; it can usefully be compared with the famous printed version of the title-page, which is reproduced a few pages earlier in Tuck's edition, at xciii. The major variation on the engraved version of the title-page is that the people who go to make up the body of Leviathan are now depicted, not with their backs to the reader, but as faces gazing out at us from the page.

Noel Malcolm (Malcolm 2002, ch. 8, esp. 222–28) argues that the ink drawing is intended as an anamorphic picture, in which the apparent image can be transformed by viewing it from a certain angle,[6] or with an optical device such as a mirror or lens. One such device was a tube with a multifaceted lens at one end: the effect of this was to resolve discrete lines into a unified image. Malcolm conjectures that such a tube was intended to be used with the ink drawing, its effect being to fuse all the faces which make up Leviathan's body into a single visage, providing a graphic illustration of a key feature of Hobbes' theory – the binding together of each citizen through being represented by the sovereign, as Hobbes describes in *Leviathan*, chapters 16 to 18 (see below, Chapter 7).[7]

While the layout of the scribal copy title-page remains the same as the engraving for the printed edition, this variation suggests that the engraver was advised to make the faces look up at the Leviathan – a graphic representation of their 'obedience' to the sovereign, who in turn wields the sword of 'protection'. The sovereign holds a bishop's crozier in his left hand, but in such a way as to make it look like another offensive weapon. As Maurice Goldsmith argues (1981), the depiction of the Leviathan's subjects in the printed title-page is not a rogue departure from the original ink drawing, but was probably made at Hobbes' own instigation. The graphic layout of the title-page would require a familiarity with the text of *Leviathan* which few people if anybody apart from Hobbes would have had at the time; it is also hard to believe that such a radical change to the design would have been made without Hobbes' express authorisation.

GETTING TO GRIPS WITH THE TEXT

The English *Leviathan* is divided into four parts, comprising forty-seven chapters in all. Hobbes describes the contents of each of the four parts briefly in the Introduction to *Leviathan*. He says that the work will be concerned with the making of a 'Leviathan', or 'artificial man' – the person of the political community, or commonwealth – and continues:

To describe the nature of this artificial man, I will consider

- First, the matter thereof, and the artificer, both of which is man.
- Secondly, how and by what covenants it is made; what are the rights and just power of a sovereign; and what it is that preserves and dissolves it.
- Thirdly, what is a Christian Commonwealth.
- Lastly, what is the Kingdom of Darkness.

(L 10)

This pared-down synopsis of *Leviathan* does indeed give the title and main subject matter of each of the four parts, though it hardly makes clear Hobbes' strategy in writing it. Modern readers opening the book and expecting a work of political theory or philosophy may be surprised to find that much of Part 1 is devoted to human physiology and psychology, the nature and interrelationship of the sciences, the definitions of words, and the nature of religion. Meanwhile, the longest is Part 3, 'Of a Christian Commonwealth'. A considerable amount of space, at least in the English version, is devoted to Part 4, 'The Kingdom of Darkness', which ridicules the claims of the Church, especially the Roman Catholic Church, to exercise political power.

I shall focus on the part of the book that has received the overwhelming bulk of critical attention, at least in modern times, namely chapters 13 to 31 (along with the 'Review, and Conclusion' at the end). So this book is not a chapter-by-chapter commentary on *Leviathan*, and does not give equal weight to each part of the book. These nineteen chapters form the core of *Leviathan*'s political theory, and I concentrate on them because it is as political theory that the book is most often read and studied. My exposition of this theory will very roughly follow Hobbes' ordering of the theory in *Leviathan*. But just as a map may exaggerate certain features of the terrain for a certain purpose, and relegate others to the background, I shall devote more attention to some chapters of *Leviathan* at others' expense. For example, I deal with chapters 1 to 12 of *Leviathan* in a single chapter (Chapter 3), while *Leviathan*, chapter 13, gets a whole chapter of this book to itself (Chapter 4).

Hobbes' short summary above does convey a central concern in *Leviathan*: how to make an 'artificial man' who will bear the person of the commonwealth, or in other words act as the political representative of the people as a whole. The individual subjects incorporate themselves into the political body, as a way of creating a unitary political authority with the power to compel obedience. At the same time, Hobbes aimed to be a systematic thinker, and claimed to have created a 'civil science'. I examine this claim in the next chapter.

Unfortunately, in the early pages of *Leviathan*, Hobbes does not help his readers much. He gives few signals about his intentions in the book as a whole. Instead, after the Introduction, Hobbes simply launches into the early chapters of Part 1, 'Of Man', with a series of discussions of topics concerning human perception, imagination, language use, reasoning, knowledge, motivational states and so on – in other words, topics in what we would now call human psychology or physiology.

It is important not to be thrown by this. Of course there is absolutely nothing wrong with reading these chapters as making independently interesting claims about human knowledge and motivation. But if the reader's main reason for studying *Leviathan* is to find out about Hobbes' political theory, it is not necessary to wrestle with the arguments of these opening chapters in great detail. The claims about human motivations in the state of nature, which Hobbes makes in chapter 13, certainly are important for the rest of the book, and we will consider these in Chapter 4 of this book. But there Hobbes is making specific claims about how people are motivated to act in certain conditions, rather than general contentions about the nature of motivation itself, as in some of the earlier chapters of *Leviathan*.

Why, then, does Hobbes start the book in this way? For the time being, it is useful to bear in mind the following. First, as we saw in Chapter 1, Hobbes was a system-builder and all-round intellectual. He did not think of himself as being a political theorist rather than a mathematician or a general philosopher. Moreover, he saw the political theory of *Leviathan* as being continuous with his other philosophical and intellectual concerns.

Second, as a materialist, Hobbes is at pains to show how human behaviour in general, and specifically in the state of nature, can arise intelligibly from an understanding of how material bodies act. Whatever else they may be, human beings in fact belong to the class of material bodies. So, from Hobbes' viewpoint, human beings should be subject to the same laws to which material bodies are subject. This includes laws of thinking: since thinking is a natural phenomenon, it must be explicable by the same material processes as other natural phenomena. In this Hobbes' views contrast sharply with those of his contemporary, the French philosopher Descartes, for whom thought, and beings that are capable of thought, are quite different in kind from material bodies and their modifications.

Third, Hobbes takes a close interest in the use and misuse of language. In part, no doubt, his aims here are simply explanatory – to explain the psychological mechanisms that lead human beings to use language as they do. But at the same time his aims are also diagnostic. He wants to trace the wrong thinking back to its source, in the words through which it is expressed. The point of this is not so much to correct error for its own sake. It is rather that mistaken beliefs – and mistakes about belief itself – form one of the prime causes of the 'disorders of the present time' (L 491), to which the political theory of *Leviathan* offers itself as a remedy.

MODERN EDITIONS OF *LEVIATHAN*

TUCK

The most useful edition for the student or other beginning reader of *Leviathan* is Richard Tuck's (1991) edition in the *Cambridge Texts in the History of Political Thought* series. In this book I cite Richard Tuck's Cambridge University Press edition because of its ready availability and affordability; it is also a genuine edition, in comparison with some others currently available. Valuable features of Tuck's edition include a useful analytical and separate name index, and a concordance of the pagination with that of other widely used modern editions, such as those of Oakeshott and Macpherson. However, it should be noted that this edition, though valuable in highlighting the previously neglected handwritten copy of *Leviathan* and Hobbes' corrections to it, suffers from a number of scholarly flaws. For example, Tuck introduces into the text certain errors not in his source text (a 'large-paper' copy of the Head edition in Cambridge University Library, printed in large format as a deluxe edition). More generally, the premise on which Tuck's edition is based, namely that the large-format edition of *Leviathan* contains the most accurate guide to Hobbes' final intentions regarding the text, has been questioned (Hobbes 2003, 111ff.).

MALCOLM

Since the first edition of this book appeared, the long-awaited edition of *Leviathan* edited by Noel Malcolm has been published (3 vols; Oxford: Clarendon Press, 2012). Of the three volumes comprising the edition, the first is devoted to the editor's introduction, and the last two to the two main textual sources of

Leviathan, namely the English and the Latin versions, which are printed on facing pages. It should be added that this edition offers the first full continuous-text translation of the Latin version, which relies on Hobbes' English text where it was the basis for the Latin, but adds Malcolm's translation of those parts of the text, notably in some of Part 4 and the Appendix, which have no equivalent in the English text. At around £200, this is a work for scholars and others with a special interest in Hobbes rather than general readers and students. Malcolm's editorial judgement is extremely acute and his knowledge of the field exhaustive. The edition is a work of meticulous textual scholarship.

In his introductory volume, however, Malcolm does not attempt much in the way of interpretation of the text of *Leviathan*, where this means (roughly) trying to explain what Hobbes was saying there, rather than getting clear, with regard to particular redactions of the text, what words may credibly be attributed to him. Inevitably these two tasks are not perfectly separable, but there is a difference between identifying a series of words as having been produced by an author and, more expansively, attempting to understand what the author meant by producing them. Malcolm may reasonably have decided that as there is hardly a shortage of different interpretations of the book available, little was to be gained by adding another; or simply have judged that any adequate interpretative exercise would have demanded yet a further volume to itself. There is a useful overview of early critical responses to *Leviathan* (Malcolm ed., Hobbes 2012, vol. I, 146ff.).

Though there are many online versions of *Leviathan*, there is not yet to my knowledge a scholarly hypertext edition of the work of the kind that for example Perseus (www.perseu.tufts.edu) have produced with classical texts. *Leviathan* is clearly ripe for this treatment, and Malcolm's edition is the ideal basis for it.

ROGERS AND SCHUHMANN

G.A.J. Rogers and Karl Schuhmann (eds), *Thomas Hobbes Leviathan*, 2 vols (London: Continuum, 2003), offers a full introduction to the publishing history of *Leviathan*. For a two-volume work it is also reasonably priced, though the Introduction is aimed mainly at specialist readers and offers little guidance as to the content of Hobbes' political theory. A briefer account of the early publishing history, to which the present chapter is indebted, is contained in the 'Note on the Text' in the Tuck edition.

CURLEY

Edwin Curley's edition of *Leviathan*, published by Hackett, readily available in paperback (Indianapolis, IN: Hackett, 1994), is a useful alternative edition to Tuck's. As well as the full English text, Curley incorporates some other material, such as excerpts from John Aubrey's biography of Hobbes and Hobbes' prose and verse autobiographies, a glossary, and most valuably, an extended account of variations between the English and Latin editions. Curley also includes a full translation of the three Appendices to the Latin text, which have no counterpart in Hobbes' original English *Leviathan*. George Wright has also published a full translation of the Latin appendices: see his 'Thomas Hobbes: 1668 Appendix to *Leviathan*', *Interpretation* 18 (1991): 323–413.

MARTINICH

In his edition of *Leviathan* published by Broadview, A.P. Martinich also includes as appendices some useful extracts from contemporary responses to *Leviathan* by writers such as George Lawson, John Bramhall and Edward Hyde (Peterborough, ON: Broadview, 2002).

OTHER

Other modern editions currently available include those edited by C.B. MacPherson (Harmondsworth: Penguin, 1968); and by J.G.A. Gaskin (Oxford: Oxford University Press, 1996). Michael Oakeshott, a distinguished political theorist in his own right, published an edition of *Leviathan* in 1946 which is still quite widely used. Abridged versions, for example those published in the Norton Critical Editions series and the one-volume version of Martinich's Broadview edition, are best avoided.

ONLINE

Full text versions of *Leviathan* are now also widely available on the Internet, for example on the Project Gutenberg website (www.gutenberg.org), and on many libraries' local networks. These are useful when carrying out text searches, but in general a hard-copy edition such as Tuck's is to be preferred.

THE LATIN TEXT

Early copies of the Latin edition published at Amsterdam in 1670 (the first edition published in 1668 is rarer) are deposited in certain United Kingdom libraries (e.g. the British Library in St Pancras, London; the Bodleian; the University Library at Cambridge), but the volume in Molesworth's nineteenth-century edition of Hobbes' Latin works is more readily available. Unfortunately this contains some editorial errors and no scholastic apparatus. As noted above, Curley's English addition usefully contains (with translations) variant passages from the Latin text.

FURTHER READING

SCHOLARLY PUBLICATIONS ABOUT THE TEXT OF *LEVIATHAN*

Variant editions

By far the best source on the publishing history of *Leviathan*, which compares in scrupulous detail the variants between the different '1651' editions of *Leviathan* as well as the handwritten and Latin versions, as already stated, is Noel Malcolm's edition of *Leviathan*, which gives a full account of the book's publishing history and points out some difficulties with the textual criticism in other editions, such as Rogers and Schuhmann 2003.

A single-volume facsimile copy of the full text of a 1651 Head edition was published by the Scolar Press in 1969. William Molesworth also published the English *Leviathan* as volume III of his *The English Works of Hobbes*, which appeared between 1839 and 1845.

Was there a Latin first draft of *Leviathan*?

Hobbes' modern-day French translator, François Tricaud, gives indications of the differences between the English and Latin texts in his French-language edition of *Leviathan* (Tricaud's introduction to his French edition of *Léviathan* (Paris: Sirey, 1971)). For the earliest claim that the Latin predated the English text, see Zbigniew Lubiénski, *Die Grundlagen des ethisch-politischen Systems von Hobbes* (Munich: Ernst Reinhardt, 1932), 254–70. An early systematic comparison of the two texts is also contained in chapter 7 of Julius Lips, *Die Stellung des Thomas Hobbes zu den politischen Parteien der großen englischen Revolution* (Leipzig, 1927; repr. Heinrich Scheffler, Frankfurt am Main, 1970), 75–82.

Tricaud provides a bibliographical essay in his 'Quelques éléments sur la question de l'accès aux textes dans les études hobbesiennes', *Revue Internationale de Philosophie* 129 (1979), 393–414.

Interesting comparative material is also contained in Karl Schuhmann's '*Leviathan* and *De cive*', in Tom Sorell and Luc Foisneau (eds), *Leviathan after 350 Years* (Oxford: Oxford University Press, 2004). Schuhmann argues that many passages in *Leviathan* are taken directly from the Latin version of *De cive*, so to this extent there was a Latin original for the English *Leviathan*. See also the Rogers and Schuhmann edition of *Leviathan*, vol. I, 236–40.

The correspondence between Hobbes and Henry Stubbe relating to the latter's plans for a Latin translation of the English text is published in Noel Malcolm's edition of *The Correspondence of Thomas Hobbes* (Oxford: Oxford University Press, 1994), vol. I; see especially Letters 80, 87, 91, 98, 113, 119, 123. For further details of *Leviathan*'s early publishing history, see also H. Macdonald and M. Hargreaves, *Thomas Hobbes: A bibliography* (London: Bibliographical Society, 1952).

THE TITLE-PAGE

For an interesting discussion of the title-page, see K.C. Brown, 'The Artist of the *Leviathan* Title-Page', *British Library Journal* 4 (1978), 24–36, and Noel Macolm, 'The Title-Page of *Leviathan*, Seen in a Curious Perspective', in *Aspects of Hobbes* (Oxford: Clarendon Press, 2002). Maurice Goldsmith, 'Picturing Hobbes' Politics', *Journal of the Warburg and Courtauld Institutes* 44 (1981), 232–37, provides some interesting comparative material on the title-pages to and other works, as does Raia Prokhovnik, *Rhetoric and De cive: Philosophy in Hobbes' Leviathan* (New York: Garland, 1991), 130–48. See also Arnold Rogow's biography, *Thomas Hobbes: Radical in the service of reaction* (New York: Norton, 1986), 156–60, and Conal Condren, 'On the Rhetorical Foundations of *Leviathan*', *History of Political Thought* 9 (1990), 703–20, especially 717–18. Further details, including information on the identity of the title-page engraver, may be found in M. Corbett and R. Lightbown, *The Comely Frontespiece* (London: Routledge & Kegan Paul, 1979). See also Martinich 1992, appendix C for an interpretation of the title-page.

NOTES

1 Shelf mark Egerton 1910.
2 Though Crooke was the publisher, material differences between copies of the Head may indicate that he farmed out the printing of some copies to other printers.
3 The more sophisticated version of the hypothesis is that an early Latin draft of *Leviathan* (not a complete Latin text) already existed in the late 1640s, and that this was in turn reworked in the light of the English text and to take account of subsequent political developments. This answers the objection about Hobbes' correspondence with Stubbe, but at the cost of largely dissolving the main point of the original hypothesis, which was to show that the Latin text that we now have was already extant in the late 1640s. However, it is undeniable that much of *Leviathan* derives from a known Latin text, namely Hobbes' *De cive* of 1642; in addition, it has been suggested (Rogers and Schuhmann ed., Hobbes 2003, 236–40) that some additional Latin material that Hobbes wrote independently in the second half of the 1640s about the Roman Catholic theologian Robert Bellarmine may underlie some of the later chapters of the English *Leviathan*, especially chapter 42.
4 Strictly speaking illustrated matter which appears at the start of a book but does not include the book's title is a frontispiece, though the title-page of Leviathan is sometimes referred to as its 'frontispiece'.

5 Others have suggested that the engraver was the Frenchman Abraham Bosse (Corbett and Lightbown 1979, 221–22).

6 A well-known example is Holbein's painting *The Ambassadors*, in the National Gallery in London, which includes an image that is hard to interpret when viewed from directly in front of the picture, but that turns out to be a skull if the viewer stands at a sharply acute angle to it.

7 Hobbes describes such a device in his 'Answer' to Sir William Davenant's 'Preface' to *Gondibert*, that was written in January 1650 when Hobbes was well into writing *Leviathan* (Malcolm 2002, 202).

3

HUMAN KNOWLEDGE, REASON
AND IGNORANCE

INTRODUCTION

Leviathan was written at great speed. Hobbes churned out its
250,000-odd words in under a year. As a result, he sometimes
expresses himself less scrupulously, and in less rigorously
argued ways, than is the norm not just in modern analytical
philosophy, but in many of Hobbes' other works. This is particularly true of the early chapters of *Leviathan*, as Hobbes never
says very clearly how they are meant to fit together into a unified
argument.

I shall suggest that, although his detailed philosophical claims
are controversial, Hobbes' aims in chapters 1 to 9, taken as a
whole, are fairly plain. But he also lays a number of false trails,
which can lead the unwary reader astray. The aim in this chapter
is both to lay bare these false trails, and to show how the early
chapters of *Leviathan* contribute to the argument of the book as a
whole.

LEVIATHAN: A FALSE START?

One of the false trails that Hobbes lays is the diagram of the relation between the branches of human knowledge in chapter 9. This picks up a theme from Hobbes' other writings. For example, in *De corpore*, which he wrote shortly before *Leviathan*, Hobbes set out systematically his views about human knowledge, the nature of reasoning and – an important theme given his wider aims – the roots of ignorance and misunderstanding. The chapter 9 diagram, together with other passages in Part 1, has led some commentators to think that *Leviathan* presents a unified theory of knowledge.

On this reading, Hobbes thought either that

(i) politics can be reduced to or subsumed by other more fundamental natural sciences (such as physics);

or, at any rate, that

(ii) natural scientific methods can be applied, without much modification, to politics.

Of course, if (i) is true, then (ii) follows as well, since if politics is subsumed by natural science, the latter's methods will simply comprise those of political science. On the other hand, (i) does not follow from (ii): it might be that politics is an autonomous discipline, in the sense that its subject matter is not reducible to that of physics, but that nonetheless it shares the methods of natural science. After all, sharing a method does not entail sharing a subject matter. For example, the methods of statistical analysis can be applied to the study of many different subjects, such as genetics, crime, microeconomics and even politics.

Many commentaries on *Leviathan*'s scientific theorising have little to do with what Hobbes actually says there. As regards (i), it has often been claimed that Hobbes, as a materialist, thought that the universe consisted of matter in motion – that is, part of the subject studied by physics – and therefore thought that political behaviour must be analysable as matter in motion. As we saw in Chapter 1, Hobbes was a materialist, and readily talks in *Leviathan* of 'politic bodies' in a calculated analogy with material bodies. Indeed, the second part of his first book of political theory, *Elements of Law*, is entitled *De corpore politico* ('about the body politic'). He also, of course, imagines the Leviathan as a giant body, composed of smaller bodies, though it is unclear, to say the least, how this image can be taken literally. In a famous passage in Hobbes' earlier work *De cive*, he compares the way in which states work to the operation of a watch, which some interpreters use as a basis for attributing (i) to him.

But some things that Hobbes says in *Leviathan* cast doubt on this reading. Indeed, the diagram of the branches of knowledge in chapter 9 conflicts with it, since its principal division is between 'natural philosophy' and 'civil philosophy' (*L* 61). Although he was a keen system-builder – his *De cive* ('about the citizen') forms the final part of a philosophical trilogy also comprising *De corpore* ('about body') and *De homine* ('about man') – Hobbes says in *De cive* that his political theory is detachable from his other philosophical theories. He regards the subject matter of physics as being the nature and modifications of material bodies, whereas politics or 'civil philosophy' studies the rights and duties of sovereigns and subjects (*L* 61).

It is sometimes suggested that Hobbes endorsed (i) because of his determinism, that is, his belief that every event in the world follows, as a matter of necessity, from a prior cause. Hobbes concluded that determinism must also apply to the actions of human beings: 'because every act of man's will and every desire and inclination proceeds from some cause, and that from another cause, in a continual chain ... they proceed from necessity' (*L* 146–47). So, as a closed physical system, such as gas particles in motion in a sealed jar, human actions could be thought of as determined, that is, as 'proceeding from necessity'.

But the fact that Hobbes was a determinist about human action does not show that he thought the study of human action, including politics, could be subsumed within some other deterministic science. More to the point, though, he did not believe that the study of politics requires conversance with some other area of knowledge, such as physics, even if politics is in some sense determined by physics. Hobbes may indeed have believed that true statements about politics were ultimately reducible to physical truths, such as the laws governing the motions of bodies, and that these laws operated deterministically. But he did not think that it was necessary to grasp the truths of physics in order to understand his political theory. He concludes Part 2 by saying that 'the science of natural justice is the only science necessary for sovereigns ... they need not be charged with the sciences mathematical' (L 254).

What about claim (ii)? Here there is more room for debate. Part of the reason for this is that 'science' as Hobbes uses it is not reducible to what we would now understand by 'natural science'. He does say at various points that there is one thing, science, which provides knowledge (e.g. L 32, 36–37, 73), and that the methods of science are common to what we would now regard as very different intellectual disciplines (e.g. L 32, 34). He contrasts 'science' with mere opinion, 'belief' or 'faith' (L 48, 406), each of which depends on trusting someone else's word, or one's own, however unreliable.

Thus 'science' sets the standard for intellectual endeavour. It discredits the claims not only of people talking politics in the saloon bar, but of political theorists too. Both 'pretend to know [their opinions] are true, when they know at most, but that they think so' (L 48). A contrast between knowledge and opinion is fundamental to the book. But knowledge or 'science', as contrasted with mere opinion, can encompass a wide range of different methods of discovering the truth. I shall return to this point later in the chapter.

* * *

Leviathan is first and foremost about politics. It presents a theory of how human beings can create and maintain a government that will last. But Hobbes' way of presenting his theory in the book is rather oblique. The first-time student of *Leviathan* who starts reading from chapter 1, expecting a work of political theory, is in for a surprise. The first nine or ten chapters of Part 1, which Hobbes entitles 'Of Man', contain very little direct discussion of political matters. Instead Hobbes launches into lengthy examinations of such topics as human psychology, perception, language, right and wrong reasoning, motivation, the nature of knowledge, power and social esteem. Few of these topics bear much obvious relation to what he calls 'civil philosophy' (e.g. *L* 61), that is, political and moral theory.

It is not merely that this list of subjects seems not to have much to do with politics. The elements of the list do not seem to bear any very obvious relation to one another, except that they could all be seen as branches of the humanities or human sciences – studies of human nature, or of human beings as parts of nature. As a result, the following questions arise:

- Why does Hobbes embark on this ambitious survey of the human sciences at all?
- How, if at all, are the subjects of early chapters of Part 1 interrelated?
- How, in Hobbes' view, does 'civil philosophy' relate to other branches of knowledge, and how do these chapters help to provide a theory of political authority?

HOBBES' INTRODUCTION TO *LEVIATHAN*

I have said that Hobbes' way of approaching politics in Part 1 of *Leviathan* is oblique. But before he reaches Part 1, the Introduction to the book does convey his main theme, and gives clues to his wider argumentative strategy. Hobbes begins thus:

> Nature (the art whereby God has made and governs the world) is by the art of man, as in many other things, so in this also imitated, that it can make an artificial animal. For seeing life is but a motion of limbs, why may we not say, that all automata (engines that move themselves by springs and wheels, as does a watch) have an artificial life? For what is the heart, but a spring; and the nerves, but so many strings; and the joints, but so many wheels, giving motion to the whole body, such as was intended by the artificer? Art goes yet further, imitating that rational and most excellent work of nature, man. For by art is created that great Leviathan called a 'commonwealth' or 'state'

(in Latin *civitas*) which is but an artificial man, though of greater sta-
ture and strength than the natural, for whose protection and defence
it was intended.

(*L* 9)

Hobbes then draws a long and slightly laboured analogy between
the parts of a state and the parts of the body.

On the face of it the passage above likens a natural man, created by
God, to the artificial man, the Leviathan, whose creation by humans
will be described later in the book. However, the bracketed aside
in Hobbes' opening sentence slyly undermines the very idea of
distinguishing the natural from the artificial. For nature, according to Hobbes, is itself artificial, since the natural world is God's
creation, just as a watch or a robot (an artificial animal) is created by
human beings. In this sense, everything is artificial – it is just that
some things are made by God, and others by humans. In creating
an artificial man, the Leviathan, humans imitate God as creator.

Hobbes adds that in Part 1 of *Leviathan* he will, in understanding
the 'nature of this artificial man', consider 'the matter thereof, and
the artificer, both [of] which is man' (*L* 10). This provides a first
clue to the subject matter of Part 1, 'Of Man'. Hobbes needs to
discuss 'man' because human beings bear a triple relation to the
Leviathan: they both compose it, that is, they are its constitutive
parts, as illustrated on the book's title-page; and they are its
creator, just as God makes man. They are also the model in whose
likeness the artificial man is made. Hobbes later describes the
Leviathan as a 'mortal God' (*L* 120). It is created in man's image.
We might then be led to think that the reason why we need to
know about human nature is because we need to refer to it if we
really are to create an artificial man.

Hobbes' presentation of his argument, then, looks roughly
like this:

- I am going to describe the creation of an artificial person, the
  Leviathan.
- The Leviathan is composed of human beings.
- The Leviathan is created by human beings.
- Therefore, I am going to begin by discussing human beings.

But of course talk of a 'Leviathan' is figurative. Doesn't Hobbes risk being taken in by his own metaphor (something he repeatedly warns against in stern tones (e.g. *L* 26, 31, 35, 52))?

We do eventually learn how Hobbes thinks that the Leviathan is constructed out of its components (chapters 14 to 17), but he gives few clues about this construction earlier in the book. In fact, the project of creating an artificial man is put on hold for most of Part 1.

Nevertheless, Hobbes does fulfil his pledge to discuss human beings in Part 1. As quickly becomes clear, his initial concern in discussing reason and knowledge is remedial. He aims to lay bare the infirmities of human reasoning, diagnosing why people fail to achieve knowledge, before setting them on the right path. He thinks that society will break down if people persist in inept reasoning, as occurred in the civil wars (e.g. *L* 127). If human reasoning causes the problem of political disorder, Hobbes will eventually have to show how an appeal to reason can also contribute to its solution.

HOBBES ON METHOD

The theme of human reasoning, and how it can go well or badly, runs through chapters 1 to 9 of *Leviathan*. Hobbes wants to set out a basis for distinguishing 'right reason' or 'ratiocination' from mere 'superstition'. In this connection one of his prime aims is to debunk the pretensions of medieval scholastic philosophy, based mainly on the writings of the ancient Greek philosopher Aristotle. Hobbes' main objections to this philosophy, which he denounces as 'vain' and 'false' (*L* 465), are fourfold.

First, it generates pseudo-names for things that do not really exist, such as 'essence' (*L* 464). Second, because of this, it generates bogus philosophical questions, which when understood correctly, are so much hot air (Hobbes speaks derisively of scholastic debates over the supposed transubstantiation of the communion wafer into the body of Christ (*L* 59)). Third, as he argues at length in chapter 46, false names not only spread misunderstanding, but also weave a mystical veil by which those in power – here Hobbes has in mind particularly the Roman Catholic Church – can hoodwink the faithful into obedience (e.g. *L* 477). Finally, Hobbes regards as seditious Aristotle's alleged belief that there is no measure of good and evil beyond what each individual happens to desire, because this leaves no room for any notion of a public good (*L* 469).

Hobbes saw the philosophy of Aristotle and his followers – for which Hobbes uses the derogatory term 'Aristotelity' – as an abdication of reason. If politics can indeed be brought within the scope of 'science', or in other words knowledge, he needs to show how political science can, like other branches of knowledge, be subjected to reason. But, on the face of it, even once this has been achieved, it still leaves us some way from showing how political authority is justified. It seems that the most that Hobbes will be able to show, if politics can be construed as an authentic form of knowledge, is that it should follow a certain method. But how can this tell us how we should be governed?

The short answer is that by itself the method will not tell us this. But it may be able to lay down conditions that a valid justification of political authority must meet. At some points, Hobbes seems to advocate an introspective method. In the Introduction to *Leviathan* he says that people 'might learn truly to read each other' if they followed the Latin maxim *nosce teipsum*, or 'read thyself' (*L* 10). Here he seems to suggest that an inquirer can find out truths about human beings simply by looking into the contents of his or her own mind and then generalising them to humanity as a whole. There are some points, such as the discussion of the state of nature in chapter 13, where Hobbes appeals to something like this method (*L* 89). However, as I shall suggest later in this chapter, its main use is as a double-check, which validates conclusions which can also be reached more long-windedly via the use of reasoning.

The principal methodological contrast Hobbes draws is between 'science' (which includes political theory, if it is done properly), and arbitrary supposition. This contrast relies in turn on a distinction between reasoning and hearsay. Reasoning is a step-by-step process in which each stage logically depends on the previous one. As Hobbes says, 'there can be no certainty of the last conclusion without a certainty of all those affirmations and negations on which it was grounded and inferred' (*L* 33). By contrast, hearsay is conveyed either orally or in books. Relying on hearsay to form one's beliefs is a bad idea: 'to forsake [one's] own natural judgement and be guided by general sentences read in authors ... is a sign of folly' (*L* 37). At the same time, Hobbes' attitude towards reason is not wholly enthusiastic. The problem is that if everybody relies on his own reason to decide about politics or religion, a jumble of competing opinions will ensue, with each person claiming that reason is on his side (e.g. *L* 48). So Hobbes has to show how his account of reason can avoid this.

In the first nine chapters of *Leviathan*, his purpose is largely negative. His remarks about human reasoning in Part 1 are critical and diagnostic: he aims to show how conventional moral and political thinking goes wrong. He rails at the manifold failings of human cognition, particularly people's tendency to be taken in by superstition or absurdity (e.g. *L* 59, 74, 147). Hobbes has two different kinds of explanation for human credulity, and both prove to be politically significant. One is a thesis in the sociology of belief – that is, a social explanation of why people end up with the beliefs that they do. The other is a thesis in the psychology of belief – an explanation based on individual humans' cognitive dispositions.

Hobbes' sociological claim is that people are far too willing to set up others as authorities on matters of religion, morality and politics. People take the claims of these supposed authorities on trust (*L* 49, 73). He pours scorn on scholars who think they can gain wisdom from books (*L* 10, 37). Similar derision is heaped on philosophers and 'Schoolmen' (i.e. followers of the ancient Greek philosopher Aristotle: *L* 24, 30, 35, 59), and on those who make false claims to divine inspiration (*L* 49, 58), particularly oracles and priests (*L* 85–86). As Hobbes says,

> there can be nothing so absurd, but [it] may be found in the books of philosophers. And the reason is manifest. For there is not one of them that begins his ratiocination from the definitions, or explications of the names they are to use; which is a method that has only been used in geometry, whose conclusions have thereby been made indisputable.
>
> (*L* 34)

Relying on the authority of others, rather than reasoning things out for oneself, sows ignorance and provokes blind clashes of dogma. When many supposed authorities vie for credence, Hobbes thinks that chaos will result. By contrast, as we saw in Chapter 1, he upholds the demonstrative methods of geometry which he describes in *Leviathan* as 'the only science that it has pleased God hitherto to bestow on mankind' (*L* 28). It is 'the mother of all natural science' (*L* 461).

As for the psychological thesis, Hobbes thinks that differences of belief result from the fact that 'men give different names to one and the same thing' (*L* 73). For example, he notes, if someone approves of a doctrine, they may call it 'opinion', whereas if they disapprove of it, they brand it 'heresy'. The main problem is not that people ultimately want different things; Hobbes says that 'all men' seek a 'contented life' (*L* 70). It is rather that people have different views on the best way to secure contentment, and nobody treats anybody's view as authoritative for all.

He sums up the source of the problem as '[i]gnorance' – ignorance both of 'causes', and of 'the signification of words' (*L* 73). It is important to see that, given Hobbes' views about the problem, two different solutions suggest themselves. One solution, which we may call 'realism', seeks to dispel ignorance by finding out the truth and then getting everyone to believe it, whether by force or persuasion. The second, which we may call 'conventionalism', dispenses with finding out the truth. Instead, it sets up an authority to decide and then enforce orthodoxy, so that everyone believes – or more accurately, acts as if he or she believes – the same thing. Hobbes draws on each of these solutions at different stages of his argument, as we shall see in later chapters. For now the salient point is that the key task of civil philosophy is to remedy ignorance by 'exact definitions' (*L* 36). Why does Hobbes think that words matter so much?

Geometry involves the manipulation of mathematical symbols. In explaining how its methods can be applied to politics, Hobbes draws an analogy between the initial axioms or postulates of geometry and names. He asserts that there is 'nothing in the world universal but names; for the things named are every one of them individual and singular' (*L* 26). Hobbes is denying here that there are real objects, often called 'universals', which underlie our uses of language. Take bananas. We routinely apply the term 'banana' to certain specimens of curvaceous yellowish soft fruit. Someone who believes that the world really contains universals will hold that there is a universal property of bananahood, which all bananas possess. But, for a nominalist like Hobbes, the only property which all bananas possess is that of being called 'bananas'. His scepticism towards universalism in part reflects his wider hostility to the obfuscations of medieval scholasticism, mentioned earlier. But it also carries a political and moral point in itself.

People bandy claims about what is good, just, right and so on. For Hobbes there is nothing 'out there' which answers to these claims. This philosophical position, which denies that there can be an objective basis for moral judgements, may seem innocuous. But if there is nothing that answers to ideas of right and wrong, justice and injustice, then people cannot claim external warrant for their views about what is right, wrong and so on. There is no 'common rule of good or evil to be taken from the nature of the objects themselves' (L 39). In particular, dissidents who assert that the government is acting unjustly or wrongly cannot appeal to God's revealed will, or abstract notions of morality, in making their case. But appeals to moral right, grounded for example in conscience, were and are very often made in order to challenge political authority. If no such appeals can be made, an important ground for dissent is cut away.

Beyond this, nominalism makes the category of 'nature' unstable. Our concepts cannot correspond to how the world is anyway, and in particular how it is if we set aside human intervention. For nominalists, there is nothing that answers to the description 'how the world is anyway'. In formulating our definitions, we create our own world, rather than being lumbered with what is given to us by nature.

Hobbes also thinks that words matter because political conflict – which is both symptom and cause of the failure of political authority – arises directly from conflicts of beliefs. The prime source, in turn, of conflicting beliefs is failure to agree, in the absence of an established authority, on the definitions of words.

The ills caused by varying definitions are not confined to the academic disputations of philosophers or theologians. They have a direct political impact. 'Ignorance of the signification of words', Hobbes says, 'disposes men to take on trust, not only the truth they know not, but also the errors, and which is more, the nonsense of them they trust' (L 73). Without an adequate grasp of the meanings of words, it is impossible to detect error, or nonsense. As a result, people appeal 'from custom to reason, and from reason to custom' (L 73) as it suits them.

Moral vocabulary is particularly potent in this respect. 'For one may call "wisdom" what another calls "fear"; and one [calls] "cruelty" what another [calls] "justice"', and so on (L 31). Hobbes has an explanation for this. Individuals' desires distort moral vocabulary:

> whatsoever is the object of any man's appetite or desire, that is it, which he for his part calls 'good'; and the object of his hate and aversion, 'evil'. And of his contempt, 'vile' and 'inconsiderable'. For these words of 'good', 'evil' and 'contemptible' are ever used with relation to the person that uses them, there being nothing simply and absolutely so.
>
> (L 39)

Hobbes here endorses a form of subjectivism, which says that moral terms like 'good' and 'evil' are not really true of the objects to which people apply them, but are simply used in order to express the speakers' personal attitudes towards the objects. If people fail to realise this, they will be drawn into dispute. A powerful cause of strife is thus the fact that 'men give different names to one and the same thing, from the difference of their own passions' (L 73). Indeed 'the same man, in diverse [i.e. different] times, differs from himself; and one time praises, that is, calls "good", what another time he dispraises, and calls "evil". From whence arise disputes, controversies, and at last war' (L 110–11).

In Hobbes' view, then, the geometric mode of reasoning is the only way to dodge the pitfalls into which political thinkers have blundered. What does this involve? It might seem that the subject matter of geometry is so different from that of political thought that no single method could fruitfully apply to each of them. Hobbes thinks, however, that the geometric method of deriving consequences via rules of inference from settled initial definitions can both expose what he calls the 'intellectual defects' of philosophers, and show how these defects may be avoided. The geometric method promises to lay falsehood and absurdity bare, and thereby point the way to consensus about morality.

In politics, similarly, 'ignorance of the causes and original constitution of right, equity, law and justice' (L 73) leads people to appeal to custom or precedent, which Hobbes regards as superstition. As a result, 'the doctrine of right and wrong is perpetually disputed both by the pen and the sword; whereas the doctrine of lines and figures [i.e. geometry] is not so' (L 74). 'The light of human minds is perspicuous words, but by exact definitions first snuffed and purged from ambiguity'; those who rely on 'false rules' are worse off than those who have no rules at all (L 36).

So the geometric method promises to rectify error by exposing the inadequate definitions on which political and moral disagreements rest. This is not to say that Hobbes thinks that all such disagreements are empty. On the contrary, people are drawn into dispute not merely because they are working with different verbal definitions (of, say, the word 'good'), but because the judgements they make with these words express their desires or 'passions'. The passions are often really in conflict, as Hobbes makes very clear in his account of the state of nature in chapter 13. When two or more people desire the same thing in conditions of scarcity, they will become enemies (L 87). Thus correct definitions will not, by themselves, put paid to all conflict. Indeed, Hobbes admits that even geometric propositions such as that the internal angles of a triangle equal two right angles could give rise to conflict if it were 'a thing contrary to any man's right of dominion' (L 74). But correct definitions do allow us to see the conflicts for what they are, and thereby perhaps help us to resolve them.

CAUSES AND CONSEQUENCES

Hobbes' appropriation of 'geometric' reasoning extends from definitions to their 'consequences' (L 34). By this he means theorems, that is, propositions logically derived from others whose truth has already been established, or which are taken as true for the purposes of argument. Hobbes describes the laws of nature, which tell people in the state of nature how to achieve peace, as 'theorems' about how to preserve oneself (*L* 111). In starting from adequate definitions, we in effect begin with names and their consequences (*L* 35). Words, Hobbes adds, 'are wise men's counters, they do but reckon by them; but they are the money of fools' (*L* 29).

We can now see more clearly the truth in claim (ii), which said that for Hobbes, political and natural science share a common method. However, modern readers may well think that Hobbes is confusing two senses of 'consequence' (Malcolm 2002, 155). One is logical consequence, as it is a consequence of the proposition that Eric is a fat man, that Eric is a man. Hobbes gives as an example the inference 'if he be a man, he is a living creature' (*L* 27). The geometric model is clearly to the fore when Hobbes uses 'consequence' in this sense. He argues that 'in the right definition of names lies the first use of speech; which is the acquisition of science' (*L* 28). This makes it sound as though gaining knowledge is in general a matter of providing correct definitions, and then drawing correct inferences from them.

On the other hand, Hobbes also uses the term 'consequence' to refer to the effect of some prior natural cause. Thus he says that 'in sum, the discourse of the mind, when it is governed by design, is nothing but seeking ... a hunting out of the causes of some effect, present or past; or of the effects of some present or past cause' (*L* 21). Hobbes also identifies 'science' with the knowledge of consequences in this causal sense. For example, he identifies '[w]ant [i.e. lack] of science' with 'ignorance of causes' (*L* 72). Hobbes sums up: 'knowledge of all the consequences appertaining to the subject in hand is [what] men call science' (*L* 35).

So Hobbes understands 'cause' and 'consequence' in senses that nowadays we would regard as distinct. Accordingly, the term 'science', which he readily applies to the study of cause and consequence in either sense, seems to lump together quite different kinds of intellectual enterprise, corresponding to different senses in which we now use the term 'consequence'. In its logical sense, a 'consequence' is (roughly) what can be deduced from a statement or set of statements. So in this sense, it is a consequence (i.e. it logically follows) from the statements that 'Kevin is a man' and 'All men are mortal', that 'Kevin is mortal'. By contrast, causal consequences are a matter for empirical investigation, in the sense that conjunctions of cause and effect yoke together phenomena that might not have turned out to be so related, such as that the moon's gravity causes tidal movement on earth.

It is a real question, then, whether Hobbes can achieve the demonstrative certainty of geometry, while also devising a civil philosophy with empirical content, which succeeds in describing the world as it is. He certainly seems to believe that he can. In chapter 5 he describes mathematicians who 'add and subtract' to calculate sums, and then says that 'writers of [i.e. about] politics add together pactions [i.e. agreements made between individuals] to find men's duties'. The idea here seems to be that, since duties are determined by individuals' agreements with one another, we can only list all the duties to which they are subject by adding together the agreements they have made. He goes on to affirm that in general 'reason ... is nothing but reckoning (that is, adding and subtracting) of the consequences of general names' (L 32).

This still leaves the question of how tracing 'the consequences of names' can yield an account of politics with empirical content. Part 1 of *Leviathan*, like the rest of the book, contains a good deal of empirical matter regarding, for instance, human beliefs and motivation. However, it is clear that Hobbes does think he is producing a civil philosophy that describes aspects of the world, rather than merely producing definitions and drawing inferences from them. He gives a clue to what he is trying to do in chapter 5:

[s]cience is the knowledge of consequences, and dependence of one fact upon another, by which, out of that we can presently do, we know how to do something else when we will, or the like, another time. Because when we see how anything comes about, upon what causes, and by what manner, when the like causes come into our power, we see how to make it produce the like effects.

(L 35–36)

Hobbes' thought here seems to be roughly this. In order to get what I want, I need knowledge of how causes produce effects. For instance, suppose I want an omelette. Suppose further that I already know that if I crack an egg into a bowl, beat it with some milk, and pour the resulting mixture into a hot pan, I stand a good chance of concocting this dish. This is a kind of knowledge: as a would-be omelette-eater, I am better placed than someone who also wants an omelette but has no idea how to make one. It is also causal knowledge, since performing the series of actions described is a way of bringing it about that an omelette exists. More generally, to achieve one's purposes, one needs causal knowledge or, in other words, what Hobbes calls 'science'.

Moreover, this causal knowledge can be expressed as a conjunction of names – at least if 'names' can include descriptions as well as pure referring terms, as Hobbes allows ('by a name is not always understood ... one only word' (L 26)). Thus the affirmation 'omelette is egg-and-milk mixture, solidified by cooking' or something similar, conjoins two names (one being a description). It also supports an inferential structure, as follows:

(1) This stuff was created by cracking an egg, beating it, and mixing it with milk.

So,

(2) This stuff is a mixture of egg and milk.
(3) The mixture referred to in (2) has been solidified by cooking.
(4) Omelette is solidified egg-and-milk mixture.

So,

(5) This stuff is omelette.[1]

Clearly, this chain of reasoning still relies on a causal claim, namely that cooking solidifies the mixture (i.e. causes it to become solid). So there is still empirical content in the reasoning, which is introduced in (3); a different (and false) empirical claim would have been made if (3) had read 'the mixture has been solidified by passing it through a sieve', or something similar.

Hobbes does not in fact discuss omelettes in *Leviathan*. But he does talk about malformed beliefs, and their political consequences. For example, in chapter 11 he notes that people fail to distinguish between 'one action of many men, and many actions of one multitude'. This may seem a rarefied distinction, but the confusion means that they 'take for the action of the people, that which is a multitude of actions done by a multitude of men, led perhaps by the persuasion of one' (*L* 73; cf. 128).

This is, as it turns out, a crucial distinction for Hobbes' theory of sovereignty. The failure to define 'the people' either as a corporate entity or as a collection of individuals sows misunderstanding. Nobody 'is so dull as to say, for example, "the people of Rome made a covenant [agreement] with the Romans, to hold the sovereignty on such or such conditions"' (*L* 123). But Hobbes thinks that those who believe that political authority rests on an agreement between the people and the sovereign (and therefore that any sovereign who fails to keep to the agreement may be deposed), are committed to saying exactly this. To base authority on an agreement is to ignore the fact that 'the people' becomes a single entity only by being represented, and to imagine falsely that the interests of the people can be opposed by a monarch who represents them (*L* 114). These are controversial claims; they will be discussed further in Chapter 7. My purpose at this stage is only to show how Hobbes thinks that his rules of thought have political implications.

The definitional model leaves some questions. For example, it would be troubling if Hobbes' theory of human knowledge deprived his political theory of empirical content. This danger looms, given his account of names. A proposition of the form '*N* is *M*', where *N* and *M* are names, seems to be necessarily true, if taken as what philosophers call a *de re* claim: if 'Spiderman' and 'Peter Benjamin Parker' name the same individual, then it seems that 'Spiderman is Peter Benjamin Parker' must be necessarily true, since every individual is necessarily self-identical. But, it might be said, necessary truths are given prior to experience; for example, it is necessarily true that it is either raining or it isn't, but to know this truth, I do not need any empirical data (e.g. about the weather). And since, it may be said, true propositions conjoining names are necessarily true, and necessary truths are given prior to experience, propositions of the form 'N is M' cannot have any empirical content.

In response Hobbes could deny that necessarily true propositions always lack such content. He could do this by allowing (as he in fact does: L 26) that 'names' include not just singular terms such as 'Brenda', but also individuating descriptions.[2] For example, the description 'the first man on the moon'[3] names the US astronaut Neil Armstrong in this world. But had things turned out differently, somebody else might have satisfied this description: if the Soviet Union had been first to get to the moon, a Russian might have satisfied this description. Surely, though, the identity of the first man on the moon is clearly something we learn empirically – it's not something we could know in advance of all experience. So, if descriptions are allowable as names, the scope for empirical inquiry clearly remains open, its role being to determine what satisfies a given description.

More obviously, perhaps, Hobbes could say simply that the necessity bears not upon the initial definitions, but on the derivation of their consequences. Hobbes does say that 'when we reason in words of general signification, and fall upon a general inference which is false; though it be commonly called "error", it is indeed an absurdity' (L 33). Mistaken inferences give rise to absurdity rather than mere error, presumably, because they state something that is necessarily false. Again this leaves room for empirical inquiry, since it allows empirical investigation to provide the premises on which the relevant inferences are based. Some conclusions can be reached only with the aid of empirical premises (as in (3) above).

IS CIVIL PHILOSOPHY DETACHABLE?

Did Hobbes see his civil philosophy as self-contained? Or did he believe that it formed a strict deductive system along with natural science? Hobbes certainly planned his writings as a comprehensive system, whose major expression is the three-part *Elements of*

Philosophy. But the parts were composed separately (indeed *De cive*, the final part, was published first, in 1642,[4] not to be followed by the others until the 1650s). And, of course, *Leviathan* itself was conceived and written as an entirely free-standing work: he says that '[t]o know the natural cause of sense, is not very necessary to the business now in hand' (*L* 13).

Hobbes provides further remarks about the relation between the different branches of his philosophy in *De corpore*, the first part of the *Elements*. He notes that 'civil and moral philosophy ... may be severed' from one another, since

> the causes of the motions of the mind are known, not only by ratiocination, but also by the experience of every man that takes the pains to observe these motions within himself. And, therefore, not only they that have attained the knowledge of the passions and perturbations of the mind ... from the very first principles of philosophy, may by proceeding in the same way, come to the causes and necessity of constituting commonwealths, and to get knowledge of what is natural right, and what are civil duties ... they also that have not learned the first part of philosophy, namely geometry and physics, may notwithstanding attain the principles of civil philosophy.
>
> (Hobbes 1839–45, vol. I, 73–74)

This sets out some of the positions already identified: the primacy of geometry and the role of introspection in examining 'the passions and perturbations of the mind'. Hobbes' argument here has two aspects. First, as we saw earlier, we do not need to work out the nature of the passions from first principles, since we have direct acquaintance with them. There is nothing wrong with seeking to proceed from first principles. But this is not necessary, since the information required can be gathered as raw data. Second, the dual aspect of scientific method itself shows how we can legitimately pursue 'civil philosophy' as an apparently free-standing inquiry, even though it also can be seen as deriving ultimately from 'the very first principles of philosophy'. There is no incompatibility between these two conceptions of inquiry. So we can check whether these principles are correctly formed by asking whether they successfully predict the observed data – in this case, the 'passions' and 'perturbations' of the mind. In other words, the principles must at least yield predictions consistent with what we know to be true.

In addition, we can also work forward from the passions to establish the conclusions which go to make up civil philosophy, and then we will again be proceeding analytically; this is why people who have not learned the 'first part of philosophy' may 'attain the principles of civil philosophy', as Hobbes says. The passions, the contents of the mind, thus mediate, in the chain of inquiry, between the ultimate first principles, at one end, and civil philosophy, at the other. We may start at the beginning, but we may also start in the middle, and this is where the real argument of *Leviathan* does start. What underwrites this starting point is the fact that the data themselves lie beyond doubt.

This explains the otherwise puzzling fact that while Hobbes makes geometry queen of the sciences, he makes no real attempt in the book to derive civil philosophy from ultimate first principles. In describing how the scientific method is applied to understanding 'the causes and nature of commonwealths' in chapter 20, Hobbes does indeed say that '[t]he skill of making and maintaining commonwealths consists in certain rules, as does arithmetic and geometry' (L 145). But in *Leviathan*'s main treatment of the subject in Part 1, he confines himself to relatively brief and schematic remarks about knowledge. Presumably this is because he thought a lengthier discussion unnecessary to his aims in the book.

On this evidence, then, it seems that Hobbes did have a scientific conception of his own political theory, albeit one which relied on his own understanding of 'science'. Hobbes understands 'science' to cover both the mathematical and the natural sciences. At the start of the *Six Lessons to the Professors of the Mathematics*, Hobbes declares that 'civil philosophy is demonstrable, because we make the commonwealth ourselves' (Hobbes 1839–45, vol. VII, 184).

There is nonetheless an underlying tension, since Hobbes cannot take a purely predictive view of civil philosophy. As he observes at a number of points (e.g. L 3, 254, 484, 491) his aim in writing *Leviathan* is to persuade, and this suggests that he hopes it will induce people to behave differently from how they would behave otherwise. It is apparent throughout the book that Hobbes sees a prime seed of disorder as lying in human error, and that errors based on individuals' unwarranted confidence in their own private judgements (e.g. *L* 33, 48, 127, 223, 400) are very widespread. Moreover, these errors, and the behaviour that results from them, can be corrected. So what becomes of the claim that his civil philosophy is predictive, rather than (if people heed it) a self-fulfilling prophecy?

The answer must be that Hobbes thought that his civil philosophy was not straightforwardly a prediction of what would happen in any case, but that it laid down guidelines for what could and should happen if individuals acted so as to pursue what was in their own best interests. It can still be seen as conditionally predictive in the following way: what people unconditionally want is security; they will gain security if and only if they form a commonwealth in accordance with the law of nature; so any commonwealth which provides them with security must conform to the law of nature. This of course is not the same as predicting that they will form such a commonwealth. The passions themselves are discovered by introspection, and the way to satisfy the passions is by the law of 'natural reason' (*L* 248), which shows us the 'theorems' (*L* 111) that demonstrate what is most conducive to our own preservation.

CONCLUSION

At the start of this chapter I set out to explain, first, why Hobbes addresses the human sciences in the opening chapters of *Leviathan*. His main aim is the negative one of showing how human psychology and cognition make people blunder in their thinking about questions of science, or politics and morality. They take refuge in 'opinion' rather than seeking knowledge. In Hobbes' view, the true path to knowledge goes via the geometric method, which sets the pattern for other areas of human science, including politics and morality. Gross error in moral and political thinking can only be avoided by using this method.

I asked, second, how the different topics addressed in *Leviathan* chapters 1 to 9 relate to one another. Despite Hobbes' various false cues these chapters share a fairly clear theme: the fallibility of human cognition, and how to remedy it. He ascribes error to the vividness of human imagination, wrong definitions, and the malign influence of those, such as priests, who have an interest in propagating superstition (*Leviathan*, chapters 1 to 3, 6 and 8). Hobbes sets out the corrective to these errors – the method of reasoning by the consequences of definitions – in chapters 4 and 5, and underlies the diagram depicting the branches of knowledge in chapter 9. On the basis of his own corrected definitions, Hobbes gives a list of the human 'passions' in chapter 6, and distinguishes knowledge from mere opinion in chapter 7. He then shows how the passions distort people's thinking (chapter 8).

Finally, I asked how civil philosophy relates to other branches of knowledge and how Hobbes' discussion of the latter contributes to his theory of political authority. He analyses the causes of cognitive failure because he thinks that they make humans unfit for 'civil obedience' (L 19). It is worth noting in this connection that Hobbes has a good deal to say about madness (e.g. L 28, 51, 54–59, 271, 442–43). Error is particularly likely when 'passions' lead people astray: 'passions unguided are for the most part mere madness' (L 55), and the 'abuse of words' is also a form of madness (L 58). 'Right reason' will make people fitter for 'obedience' and therefore also for 'protection'.

In the end, Hobbes thinks that the method of definition and consequence simply offers a longer route to conclusions which can be reached by common sense. In *Leviathan* he often appeals to 'reason', and not infrequently sounds a note of exasperation that truths which he regards as obvious are so little heeded by others (e.g. L 48, 130, 484). So reason is double-edged for Hobbes. On the one hand, he regards the truths of *Leviathan* as derived from 'natural reason' (L 254). But on the other hand, he thinks that people's reliance on their reasoning powers to reach conclusions about the best form of government, or religious truths, is disastrous for public order (L 33, 233). *Leviathan*, accordingly, aims to tame reason's power to trigger war, and to make it fit for peace.

FURTHER READING

Leviathan, chapters 1 to 9, especially 3 to 6; chapter 46

HOBBES' VIEWS ON 'SCIENCE'

The best writer on Hobbes' views on knowledge and its relation to his political philosophy is Tom Sorell. See his *Hobbes* (London: Routledge, 1986). A more compressed statement of Sorell's views can be found in his 'The Science in Hobbes' Politics', in G.A.J. Rogers and Alan Ryan (eds), *Perspectives on Thomas Hobbes* (Oxford: Clarendon Press, 1988). Sorell's article 'Hobbes' Scheme of the Sciences', in Sorell (ed.), *The Cambridge Companion to Hobbes* (Cambridge: Cambridge University Press, 1996), argues that Hobbes' scientific writings were less an expression of his own views than an attempt to present and systematise recent scientific developments. For criticism of Sorell's views, see the chapter on Hobbes in Roger Woolhouse, *The Empiricists* (Oxford: Oxford University Press, 1988).

HOBBES AND 'SCIENTIFIC' METHOD

For Hobbes' relation to European philosophy and natural science, see Richard Tuck, 'Hobbes and Descartes', in Rogers and Ryan (eds), *Perspectives on Thomas Hobbes* and, for Hobbes' relationship with the contemporary scientific establishment, Noel Malcolm's 'Hobbes and the Royal Society', in the same volume, reprinted as chapter 10 of Malcolm's *Aspects of Hobbes* (Oxford: Clarendon Press, 2002); on this see also Quentin Skinner, 'Thomas Hobbes and the Nature of the Early Royal Society', *Historical Journal* (1969), 217–39, reprinted in updated form as 'Hobbes and the Politics of the Early Royal Society', in *Visions of Politics*, vol. III: *Hobbes and civil science* (Cambridge: Cambridge University Press, 2002), ch. 12. More on Hobbes' relationship with contemporary natural scientists can be found in Miriam Reik, *The Golden Lands of Thomas Hobbes* (Detroit, MI: Wayne State Press, 1977), ch. 7.

Steven Shapin and Simon Schaffer's *Leviathan and the Air-Pump: Hobbes, Boyle, and the experimental life* (Princeton, NJ: Princeton

University Press, 1985) gives a full account of Hobbes' engagement with experimental science, particularly his contemporary Robert Boyle's attempt to create a vacuum mechanically. Shapin and Schaffer argue that Hobbes' hostility to the idea of a vacuum, rooted in his own materialism, has significant parallels with the political theory of *Leviathan*. On the vacuum dispute, see also Noel Malcolm, 'Hobbes and Roberval', in Malcolm, *Aspects of Hobbes*. Douglas Jesseph, *Squaring the Circle: The war between Hobbes and Wallis* (Chicago, IL: The University of Chicago Press, 1999), argues that the bitterness of his wrangle with Wallis can be put down to the centrality of mathematics to Hobbes' assault on traditional metaphysics.

THE 'SCIENTIFIC' METHOD AND POLITICS

For a classic statement of the view that Hobbes' political philosophy is largely disconnected from his understanding of natural science, see Leo Strauss, *The Political Philosophy of Hobbes* (Chicago: University of Chicago Press, 1952). For a contrasting view, see Noel Malcolm, 'Hobbes' Science of Politics and His Theory of Science', reprinted as chapter 5 of his *Aspects of Hobbes*. Malcolm argues that political and natural science really were distinct enterprises, but that Hobbes himself, abetted by his interpreters, makes a determined but doomed attempt to reconcile them. However, Malcolm's argument relies on a distinction between different 'levels' of knowledge (2002, 147) which is held to involve the introduction of concepts at one level (e.g. that of politics) which are absent from and therefore allegedly irreducible to those present at another level (e.g. that of physics). It is not clear that Hobbes believed in any such distinction of levels, let alone that he held that the relevant concepts at one level were irreducible to those at another.

For the view that Hobbes applied the methods of natural science directly to his political philosophy, see Thomas Spragens, *The Politics of Motion* (London: Croom Helm, 1973). Maurice Goldsmith, *Hobbes' Science of Politics* (New York: Columbia University Press, 1966), argues that Hobbes' conception of scientific method is modelled directly on Galilean science and applies a uniform explanation to the motion of bodies and to politics, mediated by a similarly structured account of human behaviour. A similar view is expressed in Richard Peters, *Hobbes* (Harmondsworth: Penguin, 1956). J.N.W. Watkins, *Hobbes' System of Ideas*, 2nd edn (London: Hutchinson, 1973), argues that Hobbes' conception of scientific method owed more to William Harvey than to Galileo.

For further information on Hobbes' views on natural science and the geometric method, see the following three articles from Sorell (ed.), *The Cambridge Companion to Hobbes*: Yves Charles Zarka, 'First philosophy and the Foundations of Knowledge'; Hardy Grant, 'Hobbes and Mathematics'; and Douglas Jesseph, 'Hobbes and the Method of Natural Science'. D.W. Hanson enters some qualifications to the idea that Hobbes was aiming at a strictly deductive method in 'The Meaning of "Demonstration" in Hobbes' Science', *History of Political Thought* 11, no. 4 (1990), 587–626.

SCEPTICISM

Hobbes as a sceptic

For the influence of contemporary philosophical scepticism on Hobbes' thinking, see a number of important articles by Richard Tuck, perhaps most notably 'Optics and Sceptics: The philosophical foundations of Hobbes' political thought', in E. Leites (ed.), *Conscience and Casuistry in Early Modern Europe* (Cambridge: Cambridge University Press, 1988). See also Tuck's *Philosophy and Government 1572–1651* (Cambridge: Cambridge University Press, 1993), ch. 7; and 'Flathman's Hobbes', in Bonnie Honig and D.R. Mapel (eds), *Skepticism, Individuality and Freedom: The reluctant liberalism of Richard Flathman* (Minneapolis, MN: University of Minnesota Press, 2002), ch. 9. For a similar view, see Ross Harrison, *Hobbes, Locke, and Confusion's Masterpiece: An examination of seventeenth-century philosophy* (Cambridge: Cambridge University Press, 2003). See also Richard Flathman, *Thomas Hobbes: Skepticism, individuality, and chastened politics* (Newbury Park, CA: Sage, 1993), ch. 3.

Hobbes as a non-sceptic

For a rejection of the idea that Hobbes' political philosophy was heavily influenced by scepticism, see Perez Zagorin, 'Hobbes' Early Philosophical Development', *Journal of the History of Ideas* 54 (1993), 505–18, and 'Hobbes without Grotius', *History of Political Thought* 21 (2000), 16–40. See also Richard Popkin, 'Hobbes and Scepticism', in L. Thro (ed.), *History of Philosophy in the Making* (Washington, DC: University Press of America, 1982). For a balanced assessment of the pros and cons of seeing Hobbes as a sceptic, see Marshall Missner, 'Skepticism and Hobbes' Political Philosophy', *Journal of the History of Ideas* 44 (1983), 407–27. For further critical discussion of Tuck, see Andrew Lister, 'Scepticism and Pluralism in Thomas Hobbes' Political Thought', *History of Political Thought* 19 (1998), 35–60.

NOTES

1 Of course, the transition to (5) would not go through if other things also satisfied 'is solidified egg-and-milk mixture', for example, scrambled egg. I am indebted to Linda Holt for this observation.

2 The opposite possibility would be to distinguish between proper names and individuating descriptions and argue that true statements conjoining names with other names, but not those conjoining names with descriptions, are necessarily true. In this case, of course, it would be possible to retain the claim that necessarily true statements lack experiential content.

3 I set aside here the complication that the description could be taken (*de re*) to refer to the same object in all possible worlds.

4 Strictly this would now be called 'quasi-publication' as it was intended for limited distribution among Hobbes' personal circle, and no copies of this edition were sold commercially (Tuck 1998, xiii); full publication of *De cive* followed in 1647.

4

THE STATE OF NATURE
LAW AND RIGHT

INTRODUCTION: THE STATE OF NATURE
IN *LEVIATHAN*

Like many other works of political philosophy written in the
seventeenth century, *Leviathan* contains a description of the state of
nature. This is a situation in which human beings have no government, no political institutions, and no executive forces such as a
police force or army – in other words, it is a condition of anarchy.

Other seventeenth-century writers who included an account
of the state of nature in their theories, such as Hugo Grotius
(1583–1645), Samuel Pufendorf (1632–94) and John Locke
(1632–1704), depicted life without a political authority as less
turbulent than Hobbes did. But in each case, despite the differences between them, the idea of a state of nature serves a broadly
similar purpose in all these theories. This purpose is to show that
political authority is justified.

In some theories the state of nature is treated as real, while
others only call for it as a possibility. Is the state of nature in

Leviathan meant to be an actual – that is, historical – stage of human development, superseded by political authority, or is it merely a thought experiment or hypothesis, introduced to help make Hobbes' case for political authority? My final answer to this question will be: 'A bit of both; and a bit of neither.' But it will take this chapter, and the next two after it, to reach this conclusion and explain it.

Rather confusingly, the authority that emerges from the state of nature, or forms the alternative to it, is often also called the 'state' in modern political philosophy. But, as we will see in a later chapter, Hobbes uses the term 'state' in a different and more specialised sense in *Leviathan*. Hobbes himself frequently uses the term 'commonwealth' to refer to what we would normally call the state, but this too has potentially misleading connotations. So I shall generally use the term political authority instead.

Hobbes' state of nature includes what modern philosophers might call *descriptive* and *normative* elements. The descriptive aspect tells us what life in the state of nature is or would be like. The normative aspect tells us what rights, obligations, laws and so on exist in the state of nature. I deal with these aspects in turn.

THE NASTINESS OF *LEVIATHAN'S* STATE OF NATURE

It has seemed obvious to many readers of *Leviathan* that what is crucial to the state of nature's justificatory role is the fact that life there is, to put it mildly, not much fun. Hobbes certainly goes to some effort, when describing the state of nature in chapter 13, to depict it as grim: indeed its grimness prompts the most famous passage in the book, which was quoted in the Introduction. It is worth citing the passage that leads up to it.

> Whatsoever therefore is consequent to a time of war, where every man is enemy to every man; the same is consequent to the time, wherein men live without other security, than what their own strength, and their own invention shall furnish them withal [i.e. with]. In such a condition, there is no place for industry; because the fruit thereof is uncertain: and consequently no culture of the earth; no navigation,

nor use of the commodities that may be imported by sea; no commodious building; no instruments of moving, and removing such things as require much force; no knowledge of the face of the earth; no account of time; no arts; no letters; no society; and which is worst of all, continual fear, and danger of violent death; and the life of man, solitary, poor, nasty, brutish, and short.

(L 89)

In this passage, Hobbes claims only that the state of nature is as bad as a state of war. Elsewhere in chapter 13, though, he identifies the state of nature *as* a state of war. There Hobbes uses 'war' in an extended sense, to include not just armed hostilities but any situation where there is no reasonable expectation that hostilities will not erupt. Hobbes compares the situation to unsettled weather: in such conditions, although it may not actually be raining at any given time, there is no reasonable expectation that a sudden downpour will not follow soon. He argues that the known readiness to engage in acts of aggression amounts in itself to a state of war: 'war consists not in battle only, or the act of fighting, but in a tract of time wherein the will to contend by battle is sufficiently known' (L 88).

Why is the state of nature so nasty? In chapter 13, Hobbes cites 'three principal causes of quarrel' which throw people into hostilities. Together they ensure that the state of nature is a state of 'war' in his extended sense. Hobbes calls these causes of quarrel 'competition', 'diffidence' and 'glory' (L 88).

REASONS TO BE FEARFUL

Competition

By 'competition' Hobbes means that goods – things that people need to live at all, or to make life bearable or pleasant – are in relatively short supply in the state of nature. There are not enough good things to go round. Some goods, like food, merely happen to be scarce some of the time. Other goods, like excellence at music or sport, are necessarily scarce because it is part of what it is to excel in these pursuits that one is better at them than most other people. Whether the goods are necessarily or contingently scarce, the fact that people are competing for them is enough to make them enemies.

Nor does Hobbes think that there comes a point at which someone has enough of a good, so that there is no need to compete for more of it. People want goods not merely for their own sake, but in order to be secure with respect to them. As Hobbes says, this is a desire for power – the power to control goods or resources into the future. 'I put for a general inclination of all mankind, a perpetual and restless desire of power after power, that ceases only in death' (L p70). The reason is that nobody can 'assure the power and means to live well, which he has present [i.e. which he already has] without the acquisition of more' (L 70). The motivation for this is not greed, but insecurity.

Diffidence

Chief among scarce goods, in the state of nature, is security itself. Security is not a necessarily scarce or 'zero sum' good: if I have security, it need not follow that others lack it. Indeed Hobbes' whole case in *Leviathan* is that everyone can have it. But security is necessarily scarce in the state of nature. By 'diffidence' Hobbes refers to the fact that, where nobody feels secure, each person will have a reason to attack any other person, for fear of being attacked first. The thinking that dominates in the state of nature can be summed up in the old adage that attack is the best form of defence. And, because each person has roughly equal killing power, everybody is both a potential killer and a potential victim.

The launching of pre-emptive attacks is a matter of simple prudence: 'there is no way for any man to secure himself [which is] so reasonable as anticipation' (L 87). Where no political authority is placed over people, the fact that each of them is liable to aggression from others means that each person has to treat every other person as an enemy, that is, as a prospective assailant. Each rational person will assume that where everybody has to regard everyone else as if they were an enemy, everyone else is an enemy. Hence diffidence makes people 'invade' one another for 'safety' (L 88). Thus the reason each person has for pre-emptive aggression – 'diffidence' – makes the state of nature a state of 'war' in Hobbes' sense.

Glory

Hobbes also thinks that 'glory' is of great importance to most people. Glory is 'joy arising from imagination of a man's own power and ability' (L 42). This is an 'exultation of the mind' (L 42), or in other words delight in status. Hobbes devotes a whole chapter of *Leviathan* (chapter 10) to the desire for honour, as a motive of human action. It drives people to attack for 'reputation' or in other words 'for trifles, as a word, a smile, a different opinion, and any other sign of undervalue' (L 88). In one form – 'vain glory' or overestimation by a person of his or her own abilities and power – it is also cited as a cause of crime, since vainglorious people are apt to regard themselves as being exempt from the criminal law (L 205).[1]

EXPLAINING CONFLICT

In fact, competition, diffidence and glory all have a common root: scarcity. The state of nature lacks the goods needed for what Hobbes calls 'commodious [i.e. pleasant] living' (L 90). Any good too scarce to go round will provoke competition. In the state of nature, physical security is a scarce good, because each person has a motive for pre-emptive attacks on others. And the good of honour, the desire for which Hobbes calls 'glory', is necessarily scarce because its value depends on being better than everyone else.

Why do these three motives bring about a state of 'war'? It is obvious how, in the absence of a supreme power that can enforce peace, the desire for goods that are scarce sparks competition between people and makes 'enemies' of them. Of course, this demands scarcity as an initial postulate. The argument from diffidence relies on the claim that people are roughly equal in offensive power.

We could speculatively represent Hobbes' implicit argument from 'competition' as follows. Take a person, A, in the state of nature. A knows that in the state of nature:

(1) Everyone is in competition for goods which are scarce.
(2) If two or more people compete for goods, each has a reason to attack the other(s).

Therefore,

(3) *A* has a reason to attack everybody else.
(4) Everybody else in the state of nature knows (1) to (3).

Accordingly, *A* can reason as follows:

(5). Everybody else in the state of nature has a reason to attack me, *A*.
(6) Being attacked destroys or threatens a prime good of mine, namely life.
(7) I, *A*, have reason to resist the attacks mentioned in (6).
(8) Given rough equality in offensive power, the best way to resist the attacks mentioned in (6) is by launching a pre-emptive attack of my own.

And, of course, everybody can reason along the same lines. So everyone has a reason to launch pre-emptive attacks. The mere fact that these reasons exist and hold a powerful rational grip on individuals' motivations is enough to make the state of nature into a state of war, in Hobbes' sense.

However, this argument from motives to the conclusion that the state of nature is a state of war cites two different motives – the motive of competition in (1) and diffidence in (8). If everybody knows that resources are scarce and that this scarcity gives everyone reason to attack everyone else, everyone will have reason to launch pre-emptive attacks. But this argument rests only on the fact of competition for scarce goods (which may, of course, include 'honour' as well as material resources). Since pre-emption will help me secure any scarce good (not just life), the reason for pre-emption is already implicit in (1). The argument doesn't need to rely on 'diffidence' at all.

Why then does Hobbes not simply rely on the motive of competition to generate the state of 'war'? The problem here is circularity. Resources are scarce in the state of nature, Hobbes seems to say in chapter 13, because it is a state of 'war'. But if (1) is doing the real work, he is also saying that the state of nature is a state of 'war' because resources are scarce. This prompts the thought that Hobbes needs the other motives as well, namely diffidence and glory.

However, the circularity problem affects the explanation from diffidence too, because that motive for aggression seems to depend on competition for scarce resources. Security is a scarce good in the state of nature, because it is a state of 'war'. But if the fact that the situation is one of 'war' explains why security is scarce, then scarcity cannot also explain why 'war' prevails. Once again a vicious circle looms. Only the explanation from glory escapes the circularity problem, because honour is a necessarily scarce good: it is in the nature of honour that not everyone can have it, so it is always scarce. And that means that its scarcity does not depend on whether or not we find ourselves in a state of 'war'. The trouble with this line of response, however, is that it does not rely on either of the other motives that Hobbes cites as causes of quarrel.

Hobbes could, in response, accept that there is circularity, but deny that this wrecks his explanation. The state of nature could be seen simply as a vicious spiral, whereby depleted resources provoke aggressive competition, which further depletes resources, which provokes aggressive competition and soon. As with other vicious spirals, the explanation seems circular, but each of the causal claims made may be true. Of course, we still want to ask how the vicious spiral gets started. But maybe that is unimportant. What matters is that in the spiral the to-and-fro of scarcity and competition is amplified with each successive cycle and unevitabily results in 'war'.

ACCUSING MAN'S NATURE

Because of his stress on self-interested motives, and his view that when a person acts, he always aims at some 'good to himself' (L 93, 105, 176), Hobbes is often described as a 'pessimist' about human nature, or as a psychological egoist, that is, someone who believes that the only motive on which people act is self-interest.

But he has an answer to those who think that his picture of human motivations is unduly gloomy: it is no more pessimistic than are people who take everyday precautions to secure their persons and possessions. Hobbes observes that a man making a journey,

> arms himself, and seeks to go well accompanied; when going to sleep, he locks his doors; when even in his house he locks his chests; and this when he knows there be laws, and public officers, armed, to revenge all injuries [which] shall be done him; what opinion he [i.e. someone who objects to Hobbes' depiction of the state of nature] has of his fellow subjects, when he rides armed; of his fellow citizens, when he locks his doors; and of his children, and servants, when he locks his chests. Does he not there as much accuse mankind by his actions, as I do by my words? But neither of us accuses man's nature in it.
>
> (L 89)

It does not follow that those who lock their doors regard everybody else as intruders or thieves. All that follows is that they treat strangers as *possible* intruders or thieves. If it is wise to do this even in a society where political authority and the rule of law already exist, it is likely to be all the wiser where there is no such authority.

The second reason why Hobbes is not accusing 'man's nature' is that the violence results from the need for pre-emptive action. On any sane view, I have a reasonable interest in securing the necessities of life. This hardly gets us as far as egoism, which says that each person is only motivated by his or her self-interest. But if vital resources are scarce, I will be driven willy-nilly to compete with others – perhaps to the death.

The bestial ethos of the state of nature shows not that humans are really brutish, but that in some circumstances, there is no reasonable alternative to behaving like a beast.

However, the motives of competition, diffidence and glory persist even under government. As we have just seen, Hobbes detects the state of nature's influence even in its absence, beneath the tranquil reveries of civil life. Prisoners are incarcerated and led

off in shackles to be executed, as there is no reasonable expectation that they will submit if unrestrained (L 208). Abroad, the
uncolonised native peoples of North America are in a state of
nature (L 89); around the globe, sovereigns remain in a state
of nature with respect to each other (L 90). The state of nature is
never entirely superseded, nor are the motives that produce
it. The persistence of the state of nature is under-remarked in
writing on Leviathan, but as I shall argue it has a profound
impact on Hobbes' account of sovereignty, law, punishment and
international relations.

NATURAL NORMS: LAW AND RIGHT

The second aspect of Leviathan's state of nature is normative.[2]
Rather than merely describing things as they are, normative
language aims to guide action – to tell us how to act, or how not
to act. Obligations and rights are normative in this sense: they
tell us whether or not we have the liberty 'to do, or to forbear', as
Hobbes puts it (L 91). To say that someone is under an obligation to
do something is to say that he is required to do it. To say that
somebody has a right to do something is to deny that she is under
an obligation not to do it.

THE LAW(S) OF NATURE

In common with many other works of political theory written in
the seventeenth century, Leviathan contains much discussion of
the laws of nature. These are not positive laws, that is, pieces
of legislation enacted by the governments of existing polities.
Rather they are to be thought of as existing before the political
authority does. Accordingly, they already exist in the state of
nature – though they also remain in force after sovereign power
has been instituted. Other seventeenth-century writers often
think of the laws of nature as being issued by God. At all
events, they are usually treated as having moral content, that is,
as providing moral guidance to human beings about how they
should act.

We can, accordingly, ask two main questions about the law of nature. The first question is:

(a) What did Hobbes think that the law of nature was in general?

Then we can also ask a question about what specifically the law of nature tells us to do, that is:

(b) What content do the particular laws of nature have?

Hobbes answers question (a) in a famous passage at the end of chapter 15. There he describes the laws of nature as 'dictates of reason'. He adds that

> men use [i.e. are accustomed] to call [them] by the name of laws, but improperly; for they are but conclusions, or theorems concerning what conduces to the conservation and defence of themselves; whereas law, properly is the word of him, that by right has command over others. But yet if we consider the same theorems, as delivered in the word of God, that by right commands all things; then are they properly called laws.
>
> (L 111)

So Hobbes thinks that

(i) the laws of nature are really a guide ('theorems') about humans' conservation;
(ii) they are not really (i.e. they are only 'improperly') called 'laws';
(iii) we can think of them as laws if we imagine them as commands by God.

A huge amount of critical commentary has built up around these claims, particularly (iii). The main bone of contention is whether Hobbes thought that God was the author of the laws of nature.

Hobbes' tone in the above passage seems to be, 'Well, the laws of nature are really only a guide to how to preserve ourselves, but if you want to call them commands by God, I suppose you can.' But some commentators, such as Howard Warrender and A.E. Taylor, have argued that Hobbes both believed in God and needs to cite God's existence to show that we are bound to follow the law of nature.

Further questions then arise. From where do the laws of nature derive their force and authority? If they are not really commands, why does Hobbes call them 'commands', and why should anyone take any notice of them? But if they are really commands, why does Hobbes go out of his way to say that they need not be seen as such (as in the passage from the end of chapter 15 just cited)? Commands are different from advice or counsel, since we can ignore advice if we so choose, whereas the point about commands is that we can't ignore them if we wish. I shall however suggest later that the imperative force of the laws of nature can be understood in a way that can dispense with any need for a divine commander.

As regards question (b) concerning the content of the laws of nature, they command us to seek peace. As Hobbes says, they require 'that every man seek peace, as far as he has hope of obtaining it; and when he cannot obtain it, that he may seek and use all helps and advantages of war' (L 92). Other laws of nature set out in chapter 15 include the obligation to perform valid 'covenants' (L 100), an obligation of 'gratitude' for non-covenanted benefits (L 105), that each man should try to accommodate himself to the rest (L 106).

Hobbes gives a list of nineteen laws in all. But he says that they can be 'contracted' to say that one 'should not do that to another, which you would not have done to yourself' (L 109). This is a negative variation of the well-known 'Golden Rule', sometimes encapsulated as 'do as you would be done by', or 'do unto others as you would have them do unto you', which Hobbes cites earlier (L 92) as 'whatsoever you require that others should do to you, that do you to them'. Thus for Hobbes the content of the laws can be summarised as a negative duty of reciprocity. This proves to be particularly important in relation to 'covenants', that is, the fulfilment of agreements where one side has already fulfilled its side of the bargain.

Defenders of the God-based reading of *Leviathan*, such as Warrender and Taylor, stress that these laws have normative, and indeed imperative, force. Their force, according to these writers, comes from God. The law of nature can be seen not merely as advising, but as commanding people to act in a certain way. These writers then assume that the laws' imperative force cannot derive purely from motivations that people may have in the state of nature. In itself, it may be observed, a motivation is simply a fact, and has no normative force at all. Hence the need for God, who steps in as the author of a set of commands to guide human conduct, the law of nature.

But it could be argued that the law's normative force results from a kind of practical necessity, rather than a command. That is, once we understand Hobbes' theory, our reason is compelled to assent to it. In fact, the appeal to God as commander does not obviously solve the problem. Why do God's commands carry normative force? This is a problem discussed 2,000 years earlier by Plato in the *Euthyphro*. If the commands carry normative force because God commands them, we can ask whether we would have to perform a quite different set of actions (including ones we might regard as morally depraved) if God had commanded us to do so. If, on the other hand, God commands us to perform the actions because they are good or right, the explanation has failed: God's commands are brought in to explain why the law of nature has normative force, but it turns out that God commands the actions because they have normative force independent of his commands.

There is also a risk that the explanation goes round in a circle. The question is why natural laws oblige, and the Taylor–Warrender answer is that they oblige as commands of God. But the imperative force of these commands is explicated in turn by assimilating the supposed pronouncements made by God to laws, that is, to the statutes and other human legal norms to which citizens are subject. Then the explanation seems to short-circuit itself. For natural law is law-like because it has the imperative force of divine command, but the latter's imperative force rests on its being law-like.

NATURAL RIGHT(S)

Again in common with other political theorists of his day, Hobbes includes an account of natural rights in the state of nature. He says that in the state of nature, everybody has a right to all things

> because the condition of man ... is a condition of war of everyone against everyone; in which case everyone is governed by his own reason; and there is nothing he can make use of, that may not be a help to him, in preserving his life against his enemies; it follows, that in such a condition, every man has a right to everything.
>
> (L 91)

It is important first to understand what Hobbes meant by talking of rights. Nowadays, when people talk about rights, they are often implicitly saying that other people owe duties to the right-holder: for example, people who hold that all human beings have a 'right to life' often take this to mean that others have duties to refrain from killing them (sometimes with certain exceptions, as in wartime or in self-defence). This is not the way in which Hobbes understands 'right'. For him, if you have a right in the state of nature, all that this means is that you are not under a duty or obligation. In his sense you have a right, for example, to buy a ticket for a film screening, but this right is not violated if you arrive too late and find that all the tickets have been sold. So, when he says that everyone has a right to all things in the state of nature, he means that nobody is under a duty to refrain from having or doing anything that might be useful in preserving their own life. But, by the same token, nobody has a duty to provide you with anything to which you have a right.

This enables us to see more clearly what Hobbes means by saying that everyone in the state of nature has a right to everything (cf. L 100, 214). There is no contradiction in the idea that more than one person – and in fact everyone – has a right to some specific thing (such as an item of food). He thinks that of no individual object is it true that it might not be of use to a person in trying to save his or her own life. The right to everything is derived from the right to self-preservation since, in Hobbes' view, if you have a right to something, you must have the right to whatever you think is an essential means to securing that thing. However, this does not mean that the right to use whatever means one thinks necessary to self-preservation has no limits.

The assertion from L 91 that everybody in the state of nature has a right to everything should be qualified in two respects. First, an individual's right in the state of nature is to whatever appears by the use of natural reason to be of assistance in preserving his or her life. It does not follow that the individual has a right to all things without restriction. For example, Hobbes notes that 'every man ha[s] a right to everything, and to do whatsoever he th[inks] necessary to his own preservation' (L 214). It might be thought on a casual reading that this states that the right of nature is wholly unqualified, as if the sentence ended with 'everything'. Indeed Hobbes' punctuation encourages this reading. It is however mistaken: the sense of the sentence distributes the phrase 'whatsoever he thought necessary' over both 'right to everything' and 'to do', so that it says, in effect, 'every man has a right to everything whatsoever he thinks necessary, and to do whatsoever he thinks necessary, to his own preservation'.[3] It is thus not, simply, a right to everything. It is a right to whatever is thought helpful to self-preservation.

The second qualification to the idea that everybody has a right to everything in the state of nature is that the right is an instrumental and conditional one. The right-holder must believe that the thing in question will help self-preservation. So I do not have a right to something that I know will not promote this (e.g. to administer weedkiller to myself). This is not the same as saying that I do not have a right to use the weedkiller to preserve myself, for example by poisoning the water supply of my enemies, and it is the fact that more or less anything might come in useful in preserving myself that makes the right of nature so extensive.

Moreover, there must be some restrictions on the rights people have in the state of nature, on pain of incoherence. For example, I cannot have the right to deprive you of your rights in the state of nature. I cannot unilaterally subject you to some obligation in the state of nature that deprives you of the relevant right, that is, the liberty 'to do or to forbear' in some respect. For, as already stated, that would be to limit your rights, and so in whatever sense I retained a right to everything, you would then have less than a right to everything. Nor, without authorisation of the sort described by Hobbes in *Leviathan* chapters 16 to 18 (see Chapter 7), do I have the right to act for you – that is, to behave in such a way that the actions that are naturally mine are taken as being yours. But the capacity to act for someone else results from the contract of civil association itself, which makes such relationships possible.

Hobbes conceives of the process of forming a political authority as essentially involving the renunciation of rights by each of the participants. He distinguishes the transfer of a right from the act of renouncing it. Essentially the difference is that I transfer my right to particular individuals (*L* 92) by relinquishing my right to prevent others from enjoying the benefit of their corresponding right, whereas renouncing the right involves relinquishing it in respect of everybody else. As Hobbes says, a person who renounces 'stands aside' for the other person(s) to enjoy their countervailing right. Thus the process of contracting, or 'covenanting' is one of removing rather than acquiring rights, and those that remain survive from the state of nature. The sovereign thus remains in a state of nature with respect to the subjects, even though they are bound with respect to him by agreements that transfer or renounce rights they had in the state of nature.

SORTING OUT OBLIGATIONS AND RIGHTS

I have argued so far that the law of nature is a fundamental rule of negative reciprocity. Its imperative force derives from natural reason, which dictates certain courses of action as inescapable. This leaves the question what status Hobbes regarded them as having and where their authority comes from. If everyone has a right to everything, that seems to imply that there can be no natural obligations or duties. For suppose that there were such a natural duty, which applied to some individual – say, to me. The duty must be a duty of mine to do or to refrain from doing something. But then I do not have a right not to do that thing (or not to refrain from doing it). So I do not have a right to everything, and so not everyone has a right to everything.

This means either that there is no natural law after all, or that if there is, it fails to impose any duties on anyone. And indeed Hobbes seems to say as much in chapter 14:

> though they that speak of this subject, use to confound *jus* and *lex*, *right* and *law*; yet they ought to be distinguished; because right, consists in the liberty to do, or to forbear; whereas law determines, and binds to one of them; so that law and right differ as much as obligation and liberty; which in one and the same matter are inconsistent.
>
> (*L* 91)

In fact, the mystery deepens when we add to this statement a remark Hobbes makes immediately before it, that a law of nature is that which forbids a person to act in a way that foreseeably destroys his own life. In a notoriously difficult passage at the start of chapter 14, Hobbes says that

> [a] law of nature (*lex naturalis*) is a precept, or general rule, found out by reason, by which a man is forbidden to do that which is destructive of his life, or takes away the means of preserving the same; and to omit that by which he thinks it may be best preserved.
>
> (*L* 91)

If we are forbidden to do that which is destructive of our own lives, how can we have a right (which is a liberty) to everything, and in particular a right to destroy ourselves?

So on top of the initial puzzle as to how there could be any duty-imposing laws of nature at all in the state of nature, we now have a question specifically relating to self-preservation. On the one hand self-preservation seemed to be a right, but on the other hand it is not something that one is free not to pursue. This makes it look not like a right, after all, but like a duty or obligation, which 'in one and the same matter' is 'inconsistent' with liberty or right.

As a first step towards the answer, we need to remember that Hobbes does not think that we have a right to destroy ourselves.

The fact that anything might be of use to us in preserving our lives is what grounds our right to all things in the state of nature, but clearly the (intentional) act of destroying ourselves cannot be of use in preserving our own lives. So we have no right to do this. But this is not the whole answer, since we do have the right of self-preservation, albeit one that it seems we have to exercise. However, since our understanding of a right usually includes a discretionary component – that is, a right is 'the liberty to do, or to forbear' – this looks more like an obligation than a right (see Tuck 1979).

Some writers try to solve these problems by adding to the natural impulse towards self-preservation a divinely imposed duty with similar content (see Warrender 1957, 212ff., and 1965; also Taylor 1938, 408). In other words, a divinely created natural law is super-imposed on the natural impulses that drive individuals towards self-preservation. On this view, our impulse towards self-preservation explains why we can follow the divine obligation, but the reason why I ought to submit to the sovereign, as a method of self-preservation, is that God commands it. This answers the question about the source and, presumably, the authority of the law of nature.

This interpretation fails, however, to explain how the state of nature can be so characterised that it both generates the problem – the war of all against all – to which political authority offers a solution, and also shows how nature furnishes the means by which we can escape from it. Warrender argued that the grounds of our obligation to seek peace (i.e. to escape from the state of nature) is that God commands us to do this, and therefore the reasons why we are obligated are moral. These are distinct, as Warrender argued, from the prudential or self-interested reasons we have for seeking peace. But then we are either insufficiently motivated to seek peace to get ourselves out of the state of nature, or else people are already sufficiently motivated in the state of nature by the thought of peace for the state of nature not to seem that bad. If these are people's underlying dispositions, then it hardly offers a horrific alternative to life under political authority.[4]

It is also not clear that Hobbes was saying in the passage quoted above from *L* 91 about the distinction between law and

right, that the law of nature imposes on us an obligation to preserve ourselves, or avoid destruction. The phrase 'precept or general rule, found out by reason, by which a man is forbidden, etc.',
is ambiguous: it is not clear whether 'which' refers to a precept or
general rule, or whether it refers to reason. In the Latin version at
this point, Hobbes states: 'But a law of nature is a precept or
general rule, worked out by reason, by which [that is, by reason]
everyone is prohibited to do that which seems to tend to his own
destruction.'[5] On this reading, Hobbes is not saying that the law
of nature is what prohibits people from doing what foreseeably
will tend to their own destruction, but saying rather that it is
reason that prohibits them from doing so.

So presumably 'which' in the English version also refers to reason.
This may seem to be a minor detail, but Warrender attached
considerable importance to this passage. The reading above gains
strong support from chapter 15, where Hobbes argues that keeping
covenants 'is a rule of reason, by which we are forbidden to
do anything destructive of our life; and *consequently* is a law of
nature' (L 103; emphasis added). The prohibitive force derives
from reason itself, rather than directly from the obligation of the
law of nature. In fact, as this passage makes clear, the binding
character of the law of nature itself derives from reason. It is the
natural force that reason has in making discoveries about what
best promotes one's own interests (the interests themselves being
given by nature), that is the basis of the prohibition (see Darwall
1996, ch. 4).

Here it is important to recall that the laws of nature are 'but ...
theorems' (L 111) that tell us, in general terms, how to preserve
our lives. Reason has a natural force of its own, which compels us
to assent to its conclusions. This is the source of the practical
necessity that can otherwise be understood as a law of nature. The
imperative force of the laws of nature, then, is derived from the
'right reason' that forces us to accept its conclusions. This is
supported by a passage in *De cive*, where Hobbes says that the law
of nature 'is the dictate of right reason about what should be done
or not done' to preserve life and limb for as long as possible
(Hobbes 1998, 33). This, then, is the source of the law of nature's
authority: the mind is naturally compelled to accept the conclusions

that reason hands down to it. This need not mean that we are invariably motivated to do what we have reason to do: we may be motivated to act irrationally.

The puzzling passage from L 91 can now be explained. In the state of nature I am free to pursue whatever I think I need for my own preservation. But I do not have a choice about whether I preserve myself or not. I am simply driven to seek my own preservation. Hobbes seems to have regarded people who seek their own deaths, for example by suicide, as insane or demented. Moreover, once I have concluded that something is necessary for my preservation, my reason compels me to pursue it. In this sense, I am no longer at liberty 'to do, or to forbear'.

Is it nature or reason for Hobbes that impels me to seek my preservation? If these can come apart, he faces a problem: maybe my nature forces me to act in ways that are contrary to reason, that is, irrational. Perhaps this could include the very impulse to self-preservation. Many people would say that someone who prefers euthanasia to a life of acute pain need not be thought of as irrational. If so, reason does not dictate self-preservation. With euthanasia, many would say that it is reasonable to choose death if reason declares that one's death is a greater good (that is, a lesser evil) than remaining alive. It seems that Hobbes can only say in response to this that in general reason will judge life preferable to death; it would clearly beg the question to argue that, if someone prefers death to life, he or she must therefore have lost the use of reason. With this qualification, Hobbes can still say that the overwhelming majority of people choose life over death, and that the force of reason compels them to assent to whatever is necessary to ensure self-preservation. What turns out to be necessary is, of course, political authority on the terms Hobbes lays down in *Leviathan*.

ENTER THE 'FOOL'

So far, then, Hobbes seems to say that 'reason' requires self-preservation, and will lend its force to the course of action that offers the best promise of achieving this. At this point we confront a passage in chapter 15 that has been much debated by

Hobbes' commentators. This concerns the 'Fool', who denies that there is any such thing as justice. Hobbes says that

> [t]he Fool has said in his heart there is no such thing as justice ... alleging that every man's conservation and contentment being committed to his own care, there could be no reason, why every man might not do what he thought conduced thereunto: and therefore also to make or not make, keep or not keep covenants [i.e. agreements], was not against reason, when it conduced to one's benefit. He ... questions, whether injustice, taking away the fear of God (for the same Fool has said in his heart there is no God) may not sometimes stand with that reason which dictates to every man his own good.
>
> (L 101)

Here the question is why Hobbes regards the Fool as foolish. If I have a right to all things, why do I not have a right to break my agreements? The answer to this question lies in Hobbes' view of natural reason.

Admittedly the 'Fool' passage contains obscurities, and this has encouraged commentators to graft their own preferred theories onto it. In the notoriously unclear passage where the Fool asks what follows if 'the Kingdom of God' could be secured not merely by violence, but by unjust violence (L 101), Hobbes seems to be saying that the sanction of divine punishment is not what makes it foolish to renege on covenants. Hobbes argues that it would be foolish to use unjust violence to seize the Kingdom of God, even though no punishment for the injustice would follow, given that a successful usurpation of God would make one omnipotent. Hobbes states clearly that 'this specious reasoning is ... false' (L 102).[6] But Hobbes' grounds for saying this seem to be not that it might be thought wrong in itself, but that the Fool would have no good reason to break his or her deal: it is simply a bad bet. Here, 'no good reason' can be read as 'no good self-interested reason, given the overwhelming interest people have in their own preservation'. Again this is not to deny that people could ever have non-egoistic, that is, altruistic, reasons for action. But the state of nature is too constrained for altruism to operate.

This suggests an answer to the question why it is foolish to deny that there is such a thing as justice, if the Fool has a right to everything in the state of nature. Hobbes makes it clear that the Fool is foolish not because he or she denies that there is such a thing as justice, but because he or she thinks it is a good idea to break his or her agreement, even when the other party has already performed: '[f]or the question is not of promises mutual, where there is no security of performance on either side ... [b]ut either where one of the parties has performed already, or where there is a power to make him perform' (*L* 102). The point is that failing to perform is irrational, even if in particular cases it may in fact pay off, because a rational calculation in advance would have shown it to be ill-advised. A bad bet is still irrational, even if you happen to win on it. On this showing the Fool is like a reckless gambler; what is wrong with him is not that he is self-interested, but that his actions fail to promote that interest in the most rational way.

However, this is not the last we shall hear from the Fool. In explaining how political authority might emerge from the state of nature, we still need to know in what conditions the Fool's bet is a bad one — that is, when failing to perform one's side of the bargain is irrational. In pursuing this issue in Chapters 5 and 6, we will find that the road out of the state of nature is less smooth than it may seem.

THE ROLE OF THE STATE OF NATURE IN *LEVIATHAN*

Beneath the questions we have pursued so far in this chapter lurks a more fundamental one. Why does Hobbes include a state of nature in *Leviathan* at all? Although the idea of a state of nature plays a role in many political theories, this role varies from theory to theory. There are a number of different ways in which the idea of the state of nature might be thought to justify the political authority, or (as Hobbes calls it) the 'commonwealth'. The first question, accordingly, is what role the state of nature is supposed to play in *Leviathan*. The second is whether it fills this role successfully.

How, if at all, does the state of nature do the job of justifying political authority? There is no consensus on this among Hobbes' commentators. A first and crude guess as to how it does so is set out below.

(1) The sole alternative to political authority is the state of nature.
(2) The state of nature is unbearably nasty.

Therefore,

(3) The sole alternative to political authority is unbearably nasty.

Therefore,

(4) Imposing political authority is justified,

which is the sought-after conclusion. The argument that purports to establish it, however, is not very convincing. Perhaps life under political authority is unbearably nasty too, and so no better than the state of nature. Of course, Hobbes himself did not believe this: his whole point is that subjection to authority is vastly preferable to anarchy. So we could add something like

(3') Political authority is much better than the state of nature,

in an effort to reach (4). Suppose we plausibly assume that, other things being equal, whenever something A is much better than something else B, there is reason to choose A over B. This might allow us to infer something along the lines of

(4') Other things being equal, we have reason to choose political authority over the state of nature.

But this would still not get us to (4), which draws on the notion of justification. For that we need to say,

(4″) If, other things being equal, we have reason to choose political
authority over the state of nature, then imposing political
authority is justified.

The nastiness of the state of nature – the fact that, as Hobbes
supposes, any sane person would want to get out of it – may give
us a reason to create political authority. But this fact does not, by
itself, obviously justify that authority. More generally, it is not
obvious that if you have reason to do something, then some other
person or agency is justified in imposing that course of action on
you. You may have reason to go to a lecture that I am about to
give, but it seems a further step to say that I am justified in
forcing you to do so, for example by frogmarching you into the
lecture hall. So the imposition of political authority – which
Hobbes accepts as a legitimate possibility – still raises questions
of justification.

So there is still a problem with (4″). Compare the following
example. Bank robbery is an enforced method of redistributing
money by transferring it from banks to robbers. If I am a cashier
in a bank, I have excellent reason to hand over money to robbers
in a hold-up if the alternative to my doing so is to be shot dead.
But the fact that I have, in the circumstances, excellent reason to
choose to hand over the money rather than being shot dead
does not show that the enforced redistribution is justified. The
robbers 'make me an offer that I can't refuse'. But if the question
concerns not the justification of my capitulation to their blackmail, but the justification of the blackmail itself, something more
needs to be said.

We have to pursue further the question of how the state of
nature justifies political authority. In *Leviathan*, the state of nature
is presented as a condition from which, in some way, the political
authority emerges, and this appears central to its justificatory role.
How does an account of its emergence help to show that the
political authority is justified?

Hobbes' answer seems to be that in order to be justified, the
political authority has to emerge in a particular way. It is clear that
Hobbes thought there was reason to choose political authority over
the state of nature: he remarks, for instance, that

the estate [condition] of man can never be without some incommodity or other; and that the greatest that in any form of government can possibly happen to the people in general, is scarce sensible [perceptible], in respect of [compared with] the miseries and horrible calamities that accompany a civil war.

(L 128)

But, as we have seen, this fact by itself is not enough to establish a legitimate government, at least if that means one that is justified in its use of coercion. What is required is that people give up their natural right to decide how best to achieve their own preservation. More specifically, it requires a form of agreement, which Hobbes refers to by the term 'covenant' (e.g. L 120, 141).

Hence Hobbes has to show two things. He needs to show that:

(I)   people in the state of nature would have reason to choose political authority over the state of nature; and
(II) the fact that they would have reason to choose political authority in the state of nature justifies that authority.

Investigating (I) further will be the main job undertaken in Chapter 5, while (II) will be considered in Chapter 6. One point that the investigation of (I) will have to clarify is whether it is enough for Hobbes to show that people have good reason to choose political authority, or whether he has to show that they do in fact choose it.

As regards (II), the arguments will have to show, in view of the bank robbery example given earlier, how the kind of reason that people have to choose political authority justifies that authority.

CONCLUSION

This chapter has presented what might be called a 'static' analysis of *Leviathan*'s state of nature: it has explained what the state of nature is like and the key concepts that Hobbes uses in presenting it. But the state of nature can also be considered 'dynamically', that is, as a condition from which we are to escape if political authority is to be justified.

Hobbes' account of the state of nature in *Leviathan* has generated a huge secondary literature. One reason for this is that the state of nature has both to set up the initial problem, while also containing the raw materials for its solution.

Hobbes has to make the state of nature look nasty enough to ensure we prefer life under government, while also showing that we do not have to make do with anarchy. Most commentators think that this means that Hobbes has to show how the state of nature can be escaped from. The trouble is that part of the nastiness of the state of nature is precisely that there seems to be no way out of it. I elaborate on this in the next chapter.

FURTHER READING

Leviathan, chapters 11 to 15

THE STATUS OF THE STATE OF NATURE

For the view that the state of nature in *Leviathan* is to be understood as a 'thought experiment', see A.P. Martinich, *Hobbes* (London: Routledge, 2005), 63ff.; Paolo Pasquino, 'Hobbes, Religion, and Rational Choice: Hobbes' two *Leviathans* and the Fool', *Pacific Philosophical Quarterly* 82 (2001), 406–19, at 406ff. (for a contrasting view, see Richard Tuck's Introduction to R.F. Tuck (ed.) and M. Silverthorne (trans.), *De cive* (Cambridge: Cambridge University Press, 1998), at xxv–xxvi). A useful discussion of the theoretical role played by the state of nature in justifying political authority generally (albeit with reference to Locke rather than to Hobbes) is Robert Nozick, *Anarchy, State and Utopia* (Oxford: Blackwell, 1974), chs 1 and 2.

For an interesting discussion of the theoretical uses of the state of nature, see W.R. Lund, 'The Historical and "Political" Origins of Civil Society: Hobbes on presumption and certainty', *History of Political Thought* 9 (1988), 223–35. For a discussion of how Hobbes derives the conclusion that life without government is a war of all against all from his initial account of the state of nature, see Gregory Kavka, 'Hobbes' War of All against All', *Ethics* 93

(1983), 291–310, and Kavka's *Hobbesian Political and Moral Theory* (Princeton, NJ: Princeton University Press, 1986).

Reason and the law of nature

On the law of nature, see Kinch Hoekstra, 'Hobbes on Law, Nature and Reason', *Journal of the History of Philosophy* 41, no. 1 (2003), 111–20. For an account of reasoning and the law of nature, see Gregory Kavka, 'Right, Reason and Natural Law in Hobbes' Ethics', *Monist* 66 (1983), 120–33. Accessible recent accounts of the state of nature (which however do not agree in all respects with the interpretation I have offered in this chapter) include Ross Harrison, *Hobbes, Locke, and Confusion's Masterpiece* (Cambridge: Cambridge University Press, 2003), ch. 3, and A.P. Martinich, *Hobbes*, 63–77. See also Noel Malcolm, 'Hobbes' Theory of International Relations', in Malcolm's *Aspects of Hobbes* (Oxford: Oxford University Press, 2002), ch. 13. Tom Sorell provides a good account of the law of nature in Hobbes' three major works of political theory in his *Hobbes* (London: Routledge, 1986), ch. 8. For a penetrating account of the role of the law of nature in Hobbes' account of the state of nature, to which the present chapter is indebted, see Stephen Darwall, *The British Moralists and the Internal 'Ought', 1640–1740* (Cambridge: Cambridge University Press, 1996), ch. 3; Howard Warrender's *Political Philosophy of Hobbes* (see below) sets out a contrasting view of the status of the laws of nature in *Leviathan*.

God and the Taylor–Warrender thesis

Advocates of the thesis. For the classic expression of the view that Hobbes needs to rely on the existence of God in order to underpin his political theory, see Howard Warrender, *The Political Philosophy of Hobbes: His theory of obligation* (Oxford: Clarendon Press, 1957). Further statements of Warrender's position can be found in Warrender, 'The Place of God in Hobbes' Philosophy', *Political Studies* 8 (1960), 48–57; 'Obligation and Right in Hobbes', *Philosophy* 37 (1962), 352–57; and 'Hobbes' Conception of Morality', *Rivista Critica di Storia della Filosofia* 17 (1962), 433–49. Warrender's reading of *Leviathan* was anticipated by A.E. Taylor earlier in the twentieth century. For Taylor's version of the thesis, see 'The Ethical Doctrine of Hobbes', *Philosophy* 13 (1938), 406–24. This essay is reprinted in K.C. Brown (ed.), *Hobbes Studies* (Oxford: Blackwell, 1965). See also Taylor's short monograph *Thomas Hobbes* (Bristol: Thoemmes Press, 1997). The view that the source of the obligation to obey the law of nature lies in God is also advanced in F.C. Hood, *The Divine Politics of Thomas Hobbes* (Oxford: Clarendon Press, 1964). A more recent statement of the 'theistic' interpretation of Hobbes is A.P. Martinich, *The Two Gods of 'Leviathan': Thomas Hobbes on religion and politics* (Cambridge: Cambridge University Press, 1992).

Critics of the thesis. For an important early criticism of Warrender's position on obligation, see Thomas Nagel, 'Hobbes' Concept of Obligation', *Philosophical Review* 68 (1959), 68–83. See also Brian Barry, 'Warrender and His Critics', *Philosophy* 43 (1968), 117–37. Further objections to the Taylor–Warrender thesis can also be found in Stuart M. Brown, 'The Taylor Thesis: Some objections', and in John Plamenatz, 'Mr Warrender's Hobbes' and 'The Taylor Thesis: Introductory note', all in K.C. Brown (ed.), *Hobbes Studies*.

A contextualist critique of Warrender, which relies heavily on the fact that Hobbes' political theory was widely received by his contemporaries as dispensing with any religious basis for political authority, is voiced by Quentin Skinner in 'Hobbes' "Leviathan"', *Historical Journal* 7 (1964), 321–33, which (savagely) reviews Hood's *The Divine Politics of Thomas Hobbes*; and Skinner's 'The Context of Hobbes' Theory of Political Obligation', in Maurice Cranston and Richard Peters (eds), *Hobbes and Rousseau* (New York: Doubleday, 1972), reprinted in Skinner, *Visions of Politics*, vol. III: *Hobbes and civil science* (Cambridge: Cambridge University Press, 2002), ch. 9. For a response to Skinner, see B.T. Trainor, 'Warrender and Skinner on Hobbes', *Political Studies* 36 (1988), 680–91; and Skinner's 'Reply' in the same volume, 692–95. A different defence of the view that Hobbes relies on a conception of moral obligation is in G. Schedler, 'Hobbes on the Basis of Political Obligation', *Journal of the History of Philosophy* 15 (1977), 165–70.

For a more recent view of the debate, see J. Curthoys, 'Thomas Hobbes, the Taylor Thesis and Alasdair Macintyre', *British Journal for the History of Philosophy* 6 (1998), 1–24.

The 'rational choice' interpretation of the laws of nature

As we shall see in more detail in Chapter 5, some readers of Hobbes take a purely 'game-theoretic'- or 'rational-choice'-based reading of the state of nature, and the obligatoriness of the law of nature. On the rational choice reading, the state of nature in *Leviathan* is to be understood as setting out a situation in which self-interested individuals have to calculate how best to achieve their overriding goal of self-preservation, rather than deciding how to obey the laws of nature as commands of God. See David Gauthier, *The Logic of Leviathan: The moral and political theory of Thomas Hobbes* (Oxford: Clarendon Press, 1969), ch. 2; for a critique of Warrender, Hood and other proponents of the theistic reading, see ch. 5. See also Kavka, *Hobbesian Moral and Political Theory* (Princeton, NJ: Princeton University Press, 1986), and Jean Hampton, *Hobbes and the Social Contract Tradition* (Cambridge: Cambridge University Press, 1986). See also the further reading section at the end of Chapter 5. Sharon Lloyd, *Morality in the Philosophy of Thomas Hobbes: Cases in the law of nature* (Cambridge: Cambridge University Press, 2010), argues that Hobbes commits himself to a reciprocity-based understanding of reasons for action that give a roughly constructivist basis for adherence to moral norms.

Hobbes' psychological claims

Do individuals in the state of nature act purely 'egoistically', that is, in their own interests, and if so, should we conclude that Hobbes thought that egoism was true of human behaviour generally? Discussion of Hobbes' psychological theories can be found in Bernard Gert, 'Hobbes and Psychological Egoism', in B. Baumrin (ed.), *Hobbes' Leviathan: Interpretation and criticism* (Belmont, CA: Wadsworth, 1969), and in Gert, 'Hobbes'

Psychology', in T. Sorell (ed.), *The Cambridge Companion to Hobbes* (Cambridge: Cambridge University Press, 1996). R.E. Ewin, *Virtues and Rights: The moral philosophy of Thomas Hobbes* (Oxford: Westview, 1991) also disputes the 'egoist' interpretation, arguing that Hobbes was concerned to set out the psychological traits that were necessary for human sociability. The traditional 'egoist' reading of Hobbes is defended in Richard Peters, *Hobbes* (Harmondsworth: Penguin, 1956), ch. 7. For an acute and nuanced dissection of the possible senses in which Hobbes might be seen as an egoist, see Tom Sorell, *Hobbes*, ch. 1. Also see Kavka, *Hobbesian Moral and Political Theory*, ch. 2, and F.S. McNeilly's 'Egoism in Hobbes', *Philosophical Quarterly* 16 (1966), 193–206.

NOTES

1 One example of conflict motivated by 'glory' which remained current in Hobbes' day was duelling. If, as sometimes happened, duels were approved by the sovereign, they opened up a contradiction in the law – the sovereign as lawgiver outlawed homicide, but turned a blind eye to this form of honour killing (*L* 211). Duels were clear indicators of the survival of the state of nature. Hobbes warns of the perils of duelling in a letter of 1638 to Charles Cavendish, brother of his pupil William Cavendish (Hobbes 1994a, vol. I, 53).

2 It might be said that the distinction between 'normative' and 'descriptive' aspects of the state of nature is not one that Hobbes himself made. Whether or not this is true, it does not prevent us now as readers of Hobbes from distinguishing aspects of the theory that seem to describe the world from those that aim to tell us what we should do about it.

3 This reading is corroborated by the Latin text, which states at this point 'ante civitatis constitutionem unicuique quidlibet agendi, quod ad conservationem sui videretur ipsi necessarium, jus erat naturale' (Hobbes 1841, vol. III, 223). That is, in the state of nature, everyone has the right to do whatever might seem necessary to his own preservation.

4 Warrender calls on Hobbes' distinction between two senses of obligation (*L* 110), which claims that in the state of nature we can be under a moral obligation without being obligated to act on it. If I find myself embroiled in a state of war, the 'validating condition' (in Warrender's terminology, e.g. Warrender 1957, 14) of the obligation to seek peace may be absent. The point, however, is that in the state of nature, even though – or precisely because – the validating condition is absent, there may be insufficient rational motivation for getting out of it.

5 'At lex naturalis præceptum est sive regula generalis ratione excogitata, qua unusquisque id, quod ad damnum suum sibi tendere videbitur, facere prohibetur' (Hobbes 1841, vol. III, 102).

6 It is far from clear why Hobbes thinks this is true in the case of someone who successfully usurped God. His reason for thinking the Fool foolish seems to be that the Fool in effect declares that he will break agreements whenever it suits him, and this makes him an enemy to his fellow human beings, and liable to be destroyed by them. But – as the Job passage in which the Leviathan appears underlines – this is hardly true of God, or someone in God's position. Presumably the point, again, is that nobody would have a reasonable prospect of successfully usurping God.

5

STATE OF NATURE TO COMMONWEALTH

INTRODUCTION

The last chapter left us with the following question. How does *Leviathan*'s state of nature help Hobbes to show that political authority is justified? I suggested that his answer needs to show two things:

(I)   people in the state of nature would have reason to choose political authority over the state of nature; and
(II) the fact that they would choose political authority in the state of nature justifies that authority.

As I argued in the last chapter, there is an explanatory gap between (I) and (II). Hobbes needs to tell a plausible story not just about how people would have reason to choose political authority, but that they would choose it in a way that justifies that authority.

Most commentators on *Leviathan*, though by no means all, think that Hobbes tries to justify political authority in the following way. They argue that Hobbes tries first to show that people in the state of nature would recognise that they had good reason to get out of it; and second, that once people recognise this, they would bind themselves to obey the political authority that came about as a result of their decision. Hobbes is taken to be offering a story or narrative about how political authority is created.

JUSTIFICATION AND THE STORY OF AGREEMENT

This story could take one of several forms, depending on how we decide to interpret *Leviathan*. On the first reading, Hobbes may think that political authority is justified because

(i) people who are now citizens or subjects did, as a matter of fact, agree to leave the state of nature and form a political authority.

This is the view that Hobbes intended the state of nature to be seen as historically real. I have already indicated ways in which traces of the state of nature survive in or alongside the political authority. But it is fairly clear that Hobbes does not think that the state of nature persisted in England at the time he was writing. He also says that the state of nature 'never generally' existed (*L* 89). We do not know when, or even whether, our distant forebears decided to leave the state of nature by making an agreement. It seems implausible that they did. Even if they did, we can ask why an agreement that they made should bind us now.

On two further possible readings of *Leviathan*, Hobbes is saying either that

(ii) though our ancestors did not actually agree, they would have agreed, had they found themselves in the state of nature; or that

(iii) as (ii), but they would now agree if the alternative that was offered to them were the state of nature.

Rather than seeing it as an actual historical situation, we might regard the state of nature as a hypothesis or 'thought experiment'. If the state of nature is a thought experiment, we can imagine the agreement as either having occurred in the hypothetical situation (as in (ii) above), or as being presented to us here and now (as in (iii)).

It is a mistake to think that these are two ways of saying the same thing. The justificatory power of (ii) is greater than that of (iii) in at least one respect. Suppose that what we are offered is a choice now as citizens, or as individuals who imagine that we are neither citizens nor inhabitants of a state of nature, and we rationally choose to live under government rather than in the state of nature; this is quite consistent with our having rationally chosen to remain in the state of nature, had we found ourselves there to start with. What I rationally choose in certain circumstances may depend on where I am when I make the choice. The fact that I, as a UK native, rationally prefer living in the United Kingdom to (say) Belgium does not show that, had I been a Belgian native, I would not rationally prefer living in Belgium to the United Kingdom.

The main problem with this is that Hobbes does not say much to suggest that either (ii) or (iii) is what he has in mind. At the end of chapter 17, Hobbes describes the process by which a 'commonwealth' is set up. He says that the sovereign is *one person, of whose acts a great multitude by mutual covenants with one another, have made themselves every one the author* (L 121; emphasis in original). He goes on to say that the circumstances in which political authority is set up can either involve actual power, or 'when men [actually] agree amongst themselves' (L 121). Admittedly Hobbes also says that it is 'as if' every man had said that he would give up his right of self-government to the sovereign (L 120), but here he means only that it would be practically impossible for each person literally to make an agreement with everyone else. His point, though, is that everyone is bound just as if they had made such an agreement.

It may seem that this returns us to the historical interpretation of the state of nature. But it is also possible to argue that the crucial move is not to regard the state of nature, or the agreement to leave it, as historically real, but rather to think of the obligation to agree to political authority as real:

(iv) whether or not they would agree, even hypothetically, to accept political authority, people are under an obligation (e.g. a moral one) to accept such an authority.

So (iv) says that there are independent reasons for entering or remaining in the political authority. What bears the justification is not any account of how individuals subjected to the power of the political authority understand their own reasons for action. Though they will, if they are fully informed and rational, come to see that they have reason to obey authority, this recognition itself is not part of the justification for their doing so. The reasons justifying political authority have independent force. Moral reasons are the most obvious, but not the only candidates for this role. The interpretation of *Leviathan* offered by writers such as Howard Warrender fits this pattern (Warrender 1957). Like other writers, Warrender in effect offers a story about how justified political authority comes into being in *Leviathan* – it is just that, for him, what carries the burden of justification is not agreement itself, but the independent moral obligation to reach agreement. The story then explains how the 'validating condition' of the obligation can be realised.

I believe that none of the possibilities (i) to (iv) offers the best account of Hobbes' views, though advocates of each one can point to passages from *Leviathan* that seem to support their case. It is important for the time being to bear in mind that there are these different ways of understanding the theory. Which one is right will affect not just how Hobbes' 'commonwealth' is justified, but what sort of organisation a justified political authority is.

The underlying question is whether the agreement that justifies political authority in *Leviathan* needs to take the form of a story at all. As we have seen, the story shows how individuals discover reasons for agreeing to political authority, which stem from features of the state of nature such as its nastiness, or the natural obligations to which they as human beings are subject within it. I shall return to these general questions later, and eventually cast doubt on whether the story-based form of justification best captures what Hobbes seems to have in mind. First, however, we consider a particularly influential version of the narrative reading of *Leviathan*. This is game theory.

LEVIATHAN AND GAME THEORY

Game theory, a branch of economics developed in the twentieth century, studies the behaviour of individuals acting together in circumstances of partial uncertainty, where they are faced with a number of possible outcomes. Typically, for each outcome, the individuals know what they will get if it occurs, but they do not know which outcome will occur, and this itself depends on what the individuals do.

A number of commentators have applied game theory to Hobbes' political theory (Gauthier 1969; Watkins 1973; Hampton 1986; Kavka 1986; Kraus 1993; Slomp 2000). It has often been supposed that it is possible to see the individuals in Hobbes' state of nature as being caught in a practical decision problem, much discussed by game theorists, known as the prisoner's dilemma. Many interpreters of Hobbes dismiss it as unhistorical, since they think that the assumptions on which it is based were only developed much later than *Leviathan* (for discussion of this point, see further reading, 'Contextualism and Interpretative Method', below). However, the interpretation is widely discussed, and needs to be considered partly for this reason.

The standard example of the prisoner's dilemma is that of two persons accused of joint involvement in a crime. After being arrested, they are interrogated separately and cannot communicate with each other: each prisoner can either keep quiet, or turn state's evidence against the other – that is, 'grass' him or her up to the authorities. Figure 5.1 illustrates the outcomes, which can be thought of as the number of years in jail that each prisoner can expect to get, depending on how they both decide to act. It is also assumed that all either prisoner wants is to minimise the amount of time in jail for him- or herself. In particular, neither

		Prisoner 2	
		Grass	Keep quiet
Prisoner 1	Grass	3rd best; 3rd best	Best; worst
	Keep quiet	Worst; best	2nd best; 2nd best

Figure 5.1 The prisoner's dilemma

prisoner is bothered what happens to the other. Neither is motivated by feelings of altruism or vindictiveness towards his or her partner in crime.

In the figure, the first outcome listed in each square is the outcome for Prisoner 1, and the second outcome is that for Prisoner 2. So, for example, if Prisoner 1 opts for 'Keep quiet' and Prisoner 2 for 'Grass' (bottom left-hand square), the outcome is worst for Prisoner 1 and best for Prisoner 2.

The fundamental feature of the prisoner's dilemma, as thus presented, is that if each prisoner does what he or she apparently has good reason to do, each will end up worse off than he or she would have been by acting otherwise.[1] Suppose each prisoner asks what the best thing to do is, given an assumption about what the other prisoner does. It turns out that each prisoner is better off grassing whatever the other one does, since each will get a lower sentence by grassing whether the other also grasses, or keeps quiet. In the language of game theory, grassing in this situation is dominant, that is, it is the best thing to do regardless of what the other person does. But if each prisoner follows this through and talks, then we land in the 'Grass'/'Grass' quadrant (top left), and each will end up worse off than he or she would have been had both kept quiet.

Despite the artificial air of this example, the prisoner's dilemma seems to be a part of our world. Here we can generalise from the 'Grass' option to speak of 'defecting' – that is, engaging in non-cooperative behaviour in order to maximise one's own outcome, given how other people will behave. Similarly, for 'Keep quiet' we can speak of 'cooperating'. Possible real-life examples, which of course involve many individuals rather than just two, include environmental pollution, the nuclear arms race, fisheries depletion and over-congestion on the roads. In each case it can be argued that each individual is better off defecting, given that everyone else is doing it, even though that course of action, when pursued by everyone, makes each person worse off than they would have been had everyone cooperated.

So, for example, in the fisheries case, if country A is defecting by fishing stocks to exhaustion in international waters, then, in the absence of any effective regulation to guarantee cooperation, country B may as well defect too, trying to grab as many fish as it can; but this will leave each country worse off than it would have been had neither adopted this policy, since no fish stock exists to provide supplies for the future.

The key feature of the prisoner's dilemma is as follows. There is a course of action that gives the best outcome for each individual, regardless of what the other does; but if each individual performs that action, each does worse than they could have done by acting otherwise. One of the disconcerting features of real-life examples of the dilemma (hereafter 'PD') may be that where many individuals are involved, it may take only a few individuals to defect for everyone else's lot to be dramatically worsened. Panic buying in times of anticipated scarcity, or panic selling of shares when it is feared that their price may be about to fall, are further examples of defecting. And the very possibility that someone will defect to take advantage of general cooperation, as in secret nuclear weapons proliferation – the 'free-rider' problem – makes general cooperation itself unstable.

Jean Hampton (1986, 58–59) considers two readings of Hobbes' state of nature. One, the 'rationality' account, holds that the state of nature is a state of 'war' because it is like a PD. Defection is the dominant strategy, and getting out of the state of nature therefore proves impossible. The second, the 'passions' account, holds by contrast that though it is rational to leave the state of nature, human beings happen to be driven by irrational 'passions' that prevent them from doing what it is rational for them to do.

		Player 2	
		Defect	*Cooperate*
Player 1	*Defect*	3rd best; 3rd best	2nd best; worst
	Cooperate	worst; 2nd best	best; best

Figure 5.2 The assurance game

In the latter case, the structure of the state of nature may correspond not to a PD, but to an 'assurance game', or AG (Figure 5.2). Some writers (e.g. Hampton 1997, 45–46) think that a PD turns into an AG if the original PD is repeated often enough: while it was rational to defect in the one-off PD, over time there is reason to cooperate as long as others do so as well (recall that in the one-off PD, it was still rational to defect even if the other person cooperated). Here it is no longer rational to defect whatever the other person does. It is rational if, but only if, the others defect as well.

Here there is no dominant strategy, but each party has good reason to cooperate as long as the other does so. This would make the state of nature very different from one modelled by means of a PD, since people would have a conditional reason for cooperating, rather than an unconditional reason for defecting. It would still not guarantee peace. For in a climate of fear, any given person may doubt that the others will cooperate, because the others in turn each fear that everyone else will not cooperate. And this is one way to interpret the uncertainty that makes the state of nature into a state of 'war'.

An example of an AG is driving. Given that we want to avoid death, it makes sense for everyone to drive on the same side of the road (cooperate): if everyone else is driving on the left, I get no advantage – quite the opposite – from driving on the right. But if others drive randomly, weaving all over the road, it makes no sense for me to stick to the left. I have to be ready to weave around too, if I want to avoid the other cars. In fact, the cooperative alternative of sticking to one side of the road will then prove worse than weaving around.

RATIONALITY IN THE STATE OF NATURE

The main question is whether – assuming that the game-theory reading of the state of nature is correct – it is more like a PD or an AG. In *Leviathan* there are at least the following possibilities concerning the state of nature:

- Clearly, if the state of nature resembles a PD, the news is bad: rational individuals will defect (i.e. choose the equivalent of the 'Grass' option), and will not rationally act on any reason to cooperate.
- On the other hand, if the state of nature is more like an AG, rationality will not preclude cooperation – that is, it will not be irrational to seek peace. But peace will still not be guaranteed, because people may lack the assurances they need in order to seek peace.

Which of these interpretations offers the most convincing picture of Hobbes' state of nature? Let us start with AG. The strongest evidence for thinking that Hobbes regarded the state of nature as being like an AG is the 'Fool' passage that we considered in Chapter 4 (*L* 101–3). There Hobbes says that it is foolish to renege if others have shown their willingness to seek peace, and his argument tries to establish that reneging is worse for the Fool. If it really is true that mutual cooperation is better for all than unilateral defection, the state of nature looks like an AG rather than a PD.

But matters are more complex than this. If the state of nature is an AG, it ought to be fairly easy to get out of it, since everyone's interests coincide. Hobbes goes out of his way, though, to stress how bad life is in the state of nature. And the problem with AGs in general is that, since it's better for me to defect if others defect as well, I need assurances that they will indeed cooperate. It is no good saying that, because cooperation is best for them, they will, since they will have the same worry about me – whether I will cooperate. So it seems we cannot rule out the possibility that, though we are in an AG, it still may be irrational to cooperate.

Can we at least rule out PD? On the PD reading, the problem in the state of nature is that, although it would be better for each individual to escape the 'war' of all against all, defection (i.e. refusal to lay down natural rights and submit to a political authority) seems to be the dominant course of action. It is sometimes thought (McLean 1981, 339–40; Zaitchik 1982, 248ff.; Hampton 1986, 90) that this interpretation is supported by a distinction that Hobbes draws in chapter 15 between two kinds of obligation, namely obligation *in foro interno* ('in the internal court'), and *in foro externo* ('in the external court'). Hobbes sets out the distinction as follows:

> The laws of nature oblige *in foro interno*; that is to say, they bind to a desire they should take place: but *in foro externo*, that is, to the putting them in act, not always. For he that should be modest, and tractable, and perform all he promises, in such time and place where no man else should do so, should but make himself a prey to others, and procure his own certain ruin, contrary to the ground of all laws of nature, which tend to nature's preservation. And again. he that having sufficient security that others shall observe the same laws towards him observes them not himself, seeks not peace but war.
>
> (*L* 110)[2]

Thus, I am always obligated to desire the fulfilment of the laws of nature – the most important of which commands me to 'seek peace' with other human beings. But, in some circumstances, I may not be obligated to act on this desire. In fact, I may be obligated to make war, if this happens to be the best way of preserving my life: the second law of nature commands that we should all 'defend ourselves', using 'all helps and advantages of war' (*L* 92). This means not merely that it is not against the law of nature to choose 'war' if others are doing so, but that the law of nature requires me to continue hostilities in these circumstances. For the 'ground' of the law of nature is 'preservation' (*L* 110).

However, the last sentence seems to rule out the PD interpretation. Someone who defects while others cooperate violates the law of nature, which commands self-preservation. This is because it is a worse bet, if the necessary assurances exist, to defect – that is, remain in a warlike posture – than to seek peace. A person who does this seeks 'the destruction of his nature by violence' (*L* 110). But if the state of nature is a PD, defection is still the rational, because dominant, action. As we have seen, Hobbes denies that if others are cooperating, it still makes sense to defect oneself by disobeying the law if one can get away with it.

Some commentators have suggested that the state of nature could be seen as an iterated PD (e.g. Hampton 1986). Here the idea is that instead of a one-off encounter between two individuals, PDs are repeated indefinitely often in the state of nature, including rematches between the same individuals. As investigation has shown, more cooperation-friendly strategies become possible with iterated PDs. It turns out that the most rational strategy is 'tit for tat', that is, my best strategy is to copy whatever you did in the previous round of the game (Axelrod 2006). In the iterated PD, then, 'Grass' is no longer dominant, and I have a conditional motive to seek peace if you have given evidence previously of a desire to do the same.

However, it is hard to fit the iterated PD into Hobbes' state of nature. It is true that this kind of expectation is often justified in small communities, and thus game theory can explain the prevalence of cooperative behaviour there as contrasted, for example, with cities, where the population is larger and more mobile. But this is the case only where a significant degree of social life already exists, which is of course not the case in *Leviathan*'s state of nature (*L* 89–90). As Hobbes describes it, the state of nature will lack the stability needed to justify the expectation that encounters with specific individuals will be repeated (let alone repeated indefinitely often). Hobbes seems indeed to envisage that many if not most of the two-person encounters in the state of nature will result in the death or one person or the other (e.g. *L* 70, 87).

What has been said so far seems to rule out the idea that the state of nature is a PD, since Hobbes explicitly says that defection when others cooperate is irrational (*L* 110). Hobbes does seem to endorse the view that humans behave irrationally by failing to seek peace when the opportunity for it arises. If so, his view must be something like this: if people were reasonable, they would see that they are in an AG; but in fact they behave as if they were in a PD, that is, they defect – make 'war' – when they in fact have reason to cooperate by seeking peace (Hampton 1986, 80–92).

On the evidence so far, Hobbes upholds the following claims about the state of nature:

(1) Ideally, humans seek peace, not war.
(2) If I know that others seek peace, it is irrational not to seek peace myself.
(3) If others make 'war', it is not irrational, and in fact is rational, for me to make 'war' as well.

Unfortunately, this is not the end of the story. The problem for people in the state of nature, as Hobbes says in chapter 13, is that they do not know what everybody else intends to do. Even if I believe that everyone has a conditional reason to seek peace, I cannot assume that others will behave rationally. So the condition itself – that others are known to be seeking peace – may not be met. So I run the risk that others will make war. And of course, as we have seen, 'war' on Hobbes' definition just is the absence of any rational expectation that others will behave peaceably.[3]

I have reason to seek peace if I know others are committed to seeking it. But I do not know this, and may have good grounds for believing the opposite. Hobbes himself stresses the uncertainty of the state of nature in chapter 13. So we can say that in the state of nature,

(4) Nobody knows whether others are seeking peace.

What should I do in this situation? If I do not know whether others are seeking peace, it might seem that no action is dominant: for I may be in an AG, where no action is dominant. In particular, making 'war' is not dominant. But of course the stakes could hardly be higher: my life is on the line. In these conditions I will want cast-iron evidence that others seek peace before I lay down my arms. Without this evidence, I will probably play safe and assume warlike dispositions in others. This suggests that

(5) Seeking peace is rational for me if, and only if, I know that others are committed to seeking peace.

But, given the uncertainty of the state of nature,

(6) I do not know that others are committed to seeking peace.

So,

(7) It is not rational for me to seek peace.

And, since everyone else can reason the same way, the state of nature remains a state of 'war'. So it seems that even if it is an AG, the state of nature cannot overcome the assurance problem. All this is consistent with Hobbes' view that it is rational for me to seek peace if I know that others do so. If someone has laid down his arms, this provides the necessary assurance. But on the argument above, laying down one's arms first is irrational. Hobbes is explicit that it is not irrational to follow suit if others have already laid down their arms. But the first party to lay down its arms lacks the assurance that others will follow suit. It is not enough simply to say that following suit is not irrational. Even if this is true, given the stakes, someone who gives up their means of self-defence will not wish to gamble that others will behave rationally.

Hobbes spells this out in chapter 14:

> [i]f a covenant be made, wherein neither of the parties perform presently, but trust one another; in the condition of mere nature (which is a condition of war of every man against every man) upon any reasonable suspicion, it is void. But if there be a common power set over them both, with right and force sufficient to compel performance, it is not void. For he that performs first has no assurance the other will perform after ... And therefore he who performs first, does but betray himself to the enemy.
>
> (L 96)

Of course, I may decide to make a bold gesture of cooperation. But even if I accept Hobbes' views about the Fool, this does not mean I have acted rationally. That depends not only on whether I think you will act rationally in response, but also what I think you will yourself regard as rational. A lot of political life, like personal life, involves planning for others' failure to do what one regards as rational. If I predict that you will think it rational to defect, I have to act accordingly – defend myself – even if I think that it would be rational for you to cooperate. So it seems that peace cannot get started.

JUSTIFICATION AND THE NARRATIVE STRATEGY

To sum up so far: even if the state of nature is an AG in the sense that it is rational to repay peacemaking with peacemaking, there is no secure pathway to peace. The situation looks like a classic catch-22. We can generate the cooperation needed for peace only if those who first lay down their arms have assurances that others will do likewise. These assurances can only stick if there is a person or body who wields supreme power, the sovereign. But the sovereign exists only if there is peace, that is, if others have followed suit in laying down their arms. In short, it seems we need assurances in order to underwrite peace, but also need peace to underwrite the assurances. By themselves, promises or 'covenants' lack the power to force people to act pacifically. In a famous passage, Hobbes says that 'without the sword', covenants 'are but words, and of no strength to secure a man at all' (L 117; cf. 94, 102, 123). So Hobbes' remarks about the Fool, which suggest that the state of nature is an AG rather than a PD, offer scant comfort. Rational individuals will still make 'war' rather than seeking peace.

Life in the state of nature is certainly disagreeable. People in it may well think that anything else would be preferable, and specifically life under political authority. But that recognition is not enough to propel them out of the state of nature, because one of the nasty aspects of the state of nature is that it offers no stable basis for cooperation. As a result, nobody can be confident that laying down one's arms will be rewarded rather than being punished. That confidence will come about only when there is a 'sword' that makes others reciprocate when someone lays down their arms. But the sword – at least in the form of a supreme power created by all for mutual defence – itself requires cooperative behaviour.

This catch-22 can be reformulated to apply to the narrative strategy itself; that is, the project of justifying political authority by telling a story that shows how people in the state of nature come to see that they have good reason to leave it. The state of nature has to be very bad in order to do its job of justifying political authority. But it is bad precisely (though not only) because cooperation in it is impossible. It seems that Hobbes has stated his case too well. In making the state of nature bad enough to ensure that nobody would choose it, Hobbes makes it so bad that nobody can escape it. The pathway out of the state of nature proves to be a dead end.

If so, it seems we have to choose one of the following alternatives: either Hobbes failed in his attempts to justify political authority by showing how people would decide to escape the state of nature; or he was not following a narrative strategy in *Leviathan* after all. Let us consider this second possibility. Part of the case for thinking that Hobbes was not following the story-based strategy is negative.

We first need to bring out the motivational assumption that underlies the narrative strategy. This assumption is in fact a standard one in modern political theory. It can be set out as follows:

> *The motivational assumption.* If the story about how people leave the state of nature is to justify political authority, it needs to give them reasons to create an authority that, if acted upon, will generate a basis for the authority in people's consent.

The important idea here is that the story gives people reasons for creating political authority, reasons on which they can act. Fairly obviously, a further supposition underlies the motivational assumption: that a necessary condition for justifying political authority is that people consent to it, which is a standard liberal claim.

> *The liberal claim.* If political authority is justified, then people must consent to it.

Now, although Hobbes does give a very strong reason for wanting a political authority – that the state of nature is so grim – this seems to fall short of providing a compelling reason for creating an authority. It is not compelling, because 'war' pervades the state of nature, and I seem to have stronger reason for remaining in a warlike posture when others are making 'war'. So the demand posed by the motivational assumption – that the story gives reasons for people to act on, and create a political authority in the state of nature – cannot be satisfied. And this is why game-theoretical descriptions of the state of nature in *Leviathan* seem to hit a brick wall.

As a first step towards solving these problems, we should unpick the key idea in the motivational assumption, that a justification of political authority needs to give people reasons in the state of nature for creating the authority. However, the phrase 'give people reasons' is ambiguous. Reasons may be compelling, that is, in the circumstances they may provide an overriding ground for acting in a certain way. But the reasons in question may not be so decisive. I may give you a reason simply by referring to some consideration that could in principle provide a reason for someone to act in a certain way. So in this sense I might be said to give you a reason to jog, for instance, by citing the health benefits of jogging, even if you couldn't care less about healthy living, or have only a mild interest in health that is not strong enough to override your indolence. Health is still, in a sense, a reason for acting – but it is not a reason on which you do act.

Now we can see that the motivational assumption is ambiguous. It talks of 'reasons to create a political authority' as a way of generating consent to that authority. In one sense, Hobbes' state of nature clearly does give us strong reason to create political authority – the reason being the grimness of the state of nature. But the fact that there is reason to escape the state of nature by creating political authority will not make it rational, all things considered, for us to try to do it. If I have reason to think that others will act irrationally, or will think that I will act irrationally, then the grimness of the state of nature will not suffice to lead me to seek peace.

As a rough parallel, consider addiction. If I am a helplessly addicted cigarette smoker, I may or may not recognise the health benefits of quitting. I may find the reasons compelling. But even if I do recognise them, the very fact that I am addicted may mean that I cannot in fact quit. Moreover, someone who is not addicted, but witnesses my pitiful wheezing, may well think not only that health gives reasons for not starting to smoke, but also that since nicotine is highly addictive, a further reason for not doing so is that one is liable to get hooked. So deciding to smoke now may impair one's ability to act on certain reasons later on. Leaving aside the cost, it would not matter so much that smoking is unhealthy in itself if it were not addictive. But given that it is addictive, I have further reason not to start.

This is only a rough parallel, because for the addict the reasons do at least point in the right direction, whereas in the state of nature, as I have argued, they point the other way. The addict may well recognise that there is good reason to quit, despite being unable to do so, and think there is no good reason – just the force of habit – for going on with it. However, despite the awfulness of the state of nature, each individual in it has reason to choose 'war' rather than seeking peace: it is this that makes the state of nature so hard to escape.

What the addict and the person in the state of nature have in common is that both would like to be in a situation where they do not have to act as they currently find themselves constrained to act. The reasons on which they wish to act are inoperative in their current circumstances. Having compelling reason to create political authority does not make it possible to create it in the state of nature.

So either we have to drop the motivational assumption, or else interpret it so that the justification of political authority does not require that individuals act on reasons for seeking peace. It is important to see that this does not, in itself, require us to drop the liberal claim. We can still require that political authority rest on consent, without demanding that the justification for it gives reasons on which people in the state of nature can act.

But, in doing so, we have abandoned the narrative strategy. We no longer tell a story in which people in the state of nature escape from it by realising they have good reason to seek peace. They still have a good conditional reason to do so, if there is good reason to think that others are seeking peace. But either they fail to realise that this reason exists, or they do realise it, but they cannot act on it, because the condition is not satisfied. In their situation, they have other and stronger reasons for choosing 'war'.

VARIETIES OF POLITICAL AUTHORITY

The story-based approach to justification faces a further problem. In chapters 18 to 20, Hobbes discusses the different ways in which a commonwealth or sovereign power may be brought into being. In these chapters Hobbes distinguishes between what he calls a 'commonwealth by institution' and a 'commonwealth by acquisition'. The distinction is between political authorities that arise through conquest by a single dominant power, and those that come about by mutual agreement. In a commonwealth by institution, 'the men who choose their sovereign, do it for fear of one another' (L 138). He amplifies this by saying that '[a] commonwealth is said to be instituted, when a multitude of men do agree and covenant, every one with every one' to appoint a person or body as their political representative (L 121). By contrast, in a commonwealth by acquisition, people 'subject themselves to him they are afraid of'; in this case, 'the sovereign power is acquired by force' (L 138).

So far this may simply look like a classification of different ways in which the commonwealth can arise. People – the future subjects – either agree to institute a sovereign through fear of one another, or else they submit through fear of a powerful conqueror. The oddity, though, is that despite Hobbes' evident concern that people may think that they have good reason to choose 'war' rather than peace in the state of nature, in chapter 19 he readily allows that people may come together in the state of nature when they agree to set up a sovereign by promising – that is, they may create a 'commonwealth by institution'.

But, as I have argued, it is very hard to extract from Hobbes' theory a coherent account of how this happens, if people act rationally. If the state of nature is a PD, or even if it is an AG, the very fact that it is a state of 'war' makes it impossible to create the trust needed for cooperation. Moreover, Hobbes introduces the notion of a commonwealth by institution only a couple of pages after he insists that unless promises are backed up by force, they are 'mere words'. It is true that Hobbes says that if a political authority is instituted, the operative motive is men's 'fear of one another' (L 138). But this fear, in the state of nature, puts men on a warlike footing rather than impelling them to seek peace. So we are still left with a puzzle about why Hobbes is ready to accept that a political authority can be instituted, as well as forged by conquest.

There is a further reason to question the story-based approach to justification. According to it, the difference between a commonwealth by acquisition and one by institution should be fundamental, since there is a force that can compel the performance of agreements in the one case, but not in the other. If so, Hobbes should have thought that political authority could be set up by acquisition, but not by institution, since only when people face overwhelming force will they be scared into keeping their agreement. The commonwealth by institution ought to be an idle wheel in Hobbes' theory. His argument about the irrationality of the Fool in chapter 15 shows only that if others are cooperating, it is not irrational to follow suit. But this is far from saying that it is rational for me to take the lead in laying down my arms, even if I believe with Hobbes that others would have rational grounds for following me if I did so.

Nonetheless, Hobbes gives no sign of thinking that it makes any difference to the justification of the commonwealth, whether political authority is instituted or acquired. He explicitly states, moreover, that the rights of the sovereign are the same, regardless of which form the commonwealth takes: 'the rights and consequences of sovereignty are the same in both' (L 139). Hobbes goes on to say that 'the rights and consequences of both paternal and despotical dominion [i.e. forms of commonwealth by acquisition] are the very same with those of a sovereign by institution ... [f]or the sovereign is absolute over both alike' (L 142). These claims rest, in turn, on Hobbes' views about the nature of consent, as we shall see in Chapter 6.

His underlying aim here is to block those who argue that certain kinds of political authority are legitimate whereas others are not. In particular, he wants to refute the claim that a political authority instituted by the consent of each individual is more legitimate than one founded on conquest. This claim assumes that it matters for legitimacy how the political authority began. But Hobbes dismisses this as irrelevant. The 'rights and consequences of sovereignty' are the same, irrespective of how the political authority came into being, since they have to be absolute if we are to avoid relapsing into a state of 'war' (L 142). And, in any case, if legitimacy depends on consent as is claimed, those who submit through fear of a conqueror have consented, as have those who seek peace through fear of one another (L 138).

For Hobbes, then, it makes no difference at all to the juris-prudential relation between the sovereign and the subjects which pathway has been followed. His rhetorical move is to argue that the means by which authority arises matters less than the form of political order that it inaugurates. The point may be taken as a counterfactual one, which attempts to reduce to absurdity the claim that it matters how the authority comes into being – matters, that is, for the resulting parcels of rights and obligations held by sovereign and subjects. It is because the parcels are exactly the same regardless of how the commonwealth arises that it makes no difference even if it could come about through institution.

So, since 'the rights and consequences' are the same regardless of whether the political authority comes about by conquest or agreement, it cannot matter greatly to Hobbes how that authority arises. The justification of political authority cannot depend on the story we tell about its origins. However, it may be said that we cannot infer, from the fact that different political authorities have the same rights and consequences, that it does not matter for their justification how they came into being. We should distinguish what justifies authority in general from what rights and consequences particular political authorities may have. So the authorities' justification may still depend essentially on how they originated, even if the same bundle of rights and consequences follows in each case.

It is true in principle that political authorities could have the same set of rights but different justifications. Of course, if the justification fails, they presumably will lack any rights. But Hobbes is in any case offering a functional justification of political authority. What matters if subjects' obedience to the authority is to be justified is, first, that it serves the end of protecting them and, second, that they agree to it, whether this agreement is thought of as having been given in advance or retrospectively. The agreement is real, even though it may be couched in hypothetical terms. The hypothesis is that we as subjects are bound as if we really had met and exchanged contracts (L 120), each person with everybody else – though, of course, we never did.

In other words, the political authority is founded on a collective act of imagination. It is imagined that our real consent to be subject to political authority is grounded in an agreement made by each person with everybody else. The subjects really are bound to obey the political authority. As Hobbes stresses, 'it is a *real unity* of them all, in one and the same person' (L 120; emphasis added).

In imagining that we renounce our rights, and authorise the sovereign to act on our behalf, we really do perform the acts of renunciation and authorisation. It belongs to our power as political agents that we can make the imaginary real. Because of this, it no longer makes sense for the purposes of justification to ask whether the hypothesis on which the justification rests is really true or not. The actions of political agents give the agreement the reality it needs.

As Hobbes says in chapter 18, it is

> vain to grant sovereignty by way of precedent covenant ... covenants being but words and breath, have no force to oblige, contain, constrain or protect any man, but what it has from the public sword ... when an assembly of men is made sovereign, then no man imagines any such covenant to have passed in the institution, for no man is so dull as to say, for example, 'The people of Rome made a covenant with the Romans to hold the sovereignty on such or such conditions' ... [M]en see not the reason to be alike in a monarchy.
>
> (L 123)

In other words, there never was an agreement to establish a government. In Hobbes' description of 'commonwealths by institution' in chapter 19, he does indeed envisage a 'covenant' of individuals with one another, such as could fit the description 'the people of Rome made a covenant with the Romans'. But he explains in the above passage that this description should not be taken literally, either in the case of sovereign assemblies or monarchies. There is no point in making such an agreement because it antedates the forging of the 'public sword', and hence individuals cannot at the time be held to it.

What does make sense, however, is that individuals can be thought of as bound to an agreement they have made, expressly or tacitly, when the 'sword' already exists. He does say that the folly of the Fool lies in failing to respond cooperatively to the cooperative actions of others. But this is far from saying that the basis for cooperation already exists – or can exist – in the state of nature.[4]

For Hobbes, then, what justifies authority, and distinguishes it from brute force, is the fact of renouncing or transferring rights.[5] The crucial thing is the fact that the rights are renounced or transferred, not the process by which people are thought of as doing this.

CONCLUSION

The argument of this chapter has been rather tortuous, and I will briefly review it. I began by distinguishing various ways of reading the role of agreement in *Leviathan*'s justification of political authority, each of which relies on the idea that Hobbes is telling a story, about how people in the state of nature come to see that they have good reason to agree to set up a sovereign. We then looked at the difficulties that face the game-theoretic version of this story. I distinguished between seeing the state of nature as a prisoner's dilemma or PD, in which non-cooperation in the form of warlike behaviour is rational, and an assurance game or AG, where individuals have good reason to cooperate by seeking peace, provided that others do the same.

Some textual evidence supports the view that Hobbes saw the state of nature as an AG instead, particularly the 'Fool' passage in chapter 15. But this is not conclusive, because Hobbes appears to acknowledge (perhaps reluctantly) that it is an AG only if there is already a common power – the very thing the agreement to leave the state of nature was meant to bring about. So it looks as though without a sovereign, people lack sufficient assurance to make peace rather than continue in 'war'. I can acknowledge that it would be better for all if everyone behaved peaceably – this is the force of Hobbes' claim that the law of nature, which commands us to seek peace, does not always obligate us *in foro externo*. But this is not enough to make people rationally seek peace. And, if I do not think that others will rationally seek peace, it becomes irrational for me to do so.

The fact that it might be rational to seek peace would not, in any case, show that people will behave rationally. Even if rationality dictates that the schedule of rewards contained in the AG correctly describes the state of nature, it does not follow that people will behave as if they are in one, rather than in a PD.[6] But if they do seek to continue 'war', when they are really in an AG, then it is rational for me to do what it would be rational to do if I really were in a PD: defect. This may not even (contrary to what Hampton implies (1986, 64)) be because anyone is acting irrationally: a person has rational grounds for defecting if there are rational grounds for believing that others will defect, even if defecting would not otherwise be rational. But if it is rational to defect, we will indeed be stuck in the state of nature. So people may well have insufficient rational grounds for cooperation even if they are in an AG, and know that they are.

Hobbes' distinction between a 'commonwealth by institution' and a 'commonwealth by acquisition' is hard to make sense of if we assume that he was trying to map a route out of the state of nature. This route is clear enough in the case of acquisition, that is, conquest, but not at all in the case of institution, that is, agreement. But Hobbes is emphatic that it makes no difference to the resulting bundle of rights and obligations how sovereignty comes into being. The upshot of his argument is that it is irrelevant how the political authority comes about.

The disturbing thing about the state of nature is that it seems that we cannot do what we have good reason to do. Hobbes' argument stakes out the limits of reason in humans' collective life. And when reason vacates the scene, power steps in to take its place.

FURTHER READING

Leviathan, chapters 14, 15

PROPONENTS OF THE GAME-THEORY INTERPRETATION

The game-theory (also known as rational choice theory) interpretation of *Leviathan* has been much discussed. For classic statements, see: David Gauthier, *The Logic of Leviathan* (Oxford: Clarendon Press, 1969); Jean Hampton, *Hobbes and the Social Contract Tradition* (Cambridge: Cambridge University Press, 1986); Gregory Kavka, *Hobbesian Moral and Political Theory* (Princeton, NJ: Princeton University Press, 1986). See also Gabriella Slomp, *Thomas Hobbes and the Political Philosophy of Glory* (Basingstoke: Macmillan, 2000).

Of these works, Hampton's interpretation has perhaps been the most extensively debated in recent years. She concludes that individuals in the state of nature are kept there because some people are too 'shortsighted' to realise that cooperation is the rational long-term strategy, and therefore the rational response to this is to pre-empt rather than cooperate (Hampton 1986, ch. 3). As I argued earlier in this chapter, it is unclear that the state of nature would have even the minimally structured interaction needed for two-person PDs to be repeated.

Gauthier provides an updated restatement of his views in his 'Hobbes' Social Contract', in G.A.J. Rogers and Alan Ryan (eds), *Perspectives on Thomas Hobbes* (Oxford: Oxford University Press, 1988), where he argues that the state of nature is not, after all, a PD. See also Gauthier's *Morals by Agreement* (Oxford: Clarendon Press, 1986). For Kavka's interpretation of the state of nature as a state of war, see his 'Hobbes' War of All Against All', *Ethics* 93 (1983a), 291–310.

CRITICAL DISCUSSION OF THE GAME-THEORY INTERPRETATION

Jodie Kraus, *The Limits of Hobbesian Contractarianism* (Cambridge: Cambridge University Press, 1993) has a detailed discussion and comparison of the views of Gauthier, Hampton and Kavka. For further discussion, see Russell Hardin, 'Hobbesian Political Order', *Political Theory* 9 (1991), 156–80. For critical discussion of Hampton, see Ishtiyaque Haji, 'Hampton on State-of-Nature Cooperation', *Philosophy and Phenomenological Research* 51 (1991), 589–601. See also Hampton's reply in the same issue, pp. 603–9.

For a full critical discussion of Hampton's and Kavka's books, see David Gauthier, 'Taming *Leviathan*', in *Philosophy & Public Affairs* 17 (1987), 280–98. Another valuable discussion of the interpretations of Kavka and Hampton is Edwin Curley, 'Reflections on Hobbes: Recent work on his moral and political philosophy', *Journal of Philosophical Research* 15 (1990), 169–250, see especially 192–211. See also chapter 2 of Hampton, *Political Philosophy* (Boulder, CO: Westview Press, 1997), for a briefer discussion by her of Hobbes' contract. Older discussions are contained in Iain McLean, 'The Social Contract in *Leviathan* and the Prisoner's Dilemma Supergame', *Political Studies* 29 (1981), 339–51, and Alan Zaitchik, 'Hobbes' Reply to the Fool: The problem of consent and obligation', *Political Theory* 10 (1982), 245–66.

Pasquale Pasquino, 'Hobbes, Religion and Rational Choice: Hobbes' two *Leviathans* and the Fool', *Pacific Philosophical Quarterly* 82 (2001), 406–19, argues (as I have) that the significance of the game-theoretic elements of the state of nature is not to provide a basis from which individuals in it can exit from it, but precisely to show that the state of nature is inescapable. Pasquino accordingly denies Hampton's claim that unless Hobbes can show how one can escape the state of nature, Hobbes' 'argument collapses', as Hampton argues in Hobbes and the *Social Contract Tradition* (132).

For the view that the state of nature is an AG rather than a PD, see Alan Ryan, 'Hobbes' Political Philosophy', in Tom Sorell (ed.), *The Cambridge Companion to Hobbes* (Cambridge: Cambridge University Press, 1996). Ryan argues that Hobbesian individuals are not utility-maximisers; instead they are 'disaster-avoiders' (224), and this means that they will cooperate if they are given sound reason for believing that the other party will cooperate.

BACKGROUND ON GAME THEORY/RATIONAL CHOICE THEORY

For a useful overview of game theory and rational choice, see J. Morrow, *Game Theory for Political Scientists* (Princeton, NJ: Princeton University Press, 1993). An accessible brief introduction is Michael Allingham's volume in the *Very Short Introductions* series on *Choice Theory* (Oxford: Oxford University Press, 2002). Brian Skyrms, *The Evolution of the Social Contract* (Cambridge: Cambridge University Press, 1996) gives a useful and concise general account of the relevance of game theory to the idea of the social contract. A classic exposition of the game-theoretic path to cooperative behaviour is Robert Axelrod, *The Evolution of Cooperation*, revised edition (New York: Perseus, 2006), which explores rational action under repeated PDs.

SCEPTICS ABOUT THE GAME-THEORETIC INTERPRETATION

Many writers on Hobbes display their scepticism about the game-theoretic approach to *Leviathan* simply by ignoring it. This is true of the Cambridge school (see next section). Others, however, address it only to repudiate it. For a sceptical view about the applicability of game theory, and the PD in particular, to Hobbes' state of nature, see Richard Tuck, 'Hobbes' Moral Philosophy', in T. Sorell (ed.), *The Cambridge Companion to Hobbes*, especially 193ff., though Tuck's reasoning here is clearly influenced by his wider reading of *Leviathan*. For further doubts about the applicability of game theory to *Leviathan*, see Patrick Neal, 'Hobbes and Rational Choice Theory', *Western Political Quarterly* 41 (1988), 635–52; R. Rhodes, 'Hobbes' Unreasonable Fool', *Southern Journal of Philosophy* 30 (1992), 177–89; and Andrew Alexandra, 'Should Hobbes' State of Nature Be Represented as a Prisoner's Dilemma?', *Southern Journal of Philosophy* 30 (1992), 1–16.

CONTEXTUALISM AND INTERPRETATIVE METHOD

There is a lively debate as to how best to approach the interpretation of historical texts, in which *Leviathan* has often been cited as an example. The contextualist or Cambridge School of interpretation, of which Quentin Skinner is the doyen, argues that interpreting texts is an irreducibly historical enterprise. Broadly, for contextualists, interpretation is a matter of understanding not only what the text means, but what its author intended in writing it, and it is held that intentions are fixed or bounded by the local historical context. For the classic statement of this view, see the essays collected in Quentin Skinner, *Visions of Politics*, vol. I: *Regarding method* (Cambridge: Cambridge University Press, 2002), especially essays 1, 3, 4, 5, 6 and 7.

Others question the contextualists' faith that 'the' meaning of texts such as *Leviathan* is historically bounded. For a good critical discussion of contextualism, see David Boucher, *Texts in Context: Revisionist methods for studying the history of political theory* (Dordrecht: Martinus Nijhoff, 1985).

The obvious objection for contextualists to make against the game-theoretic reading is that it is anachronistic, because game theory was invented 300 years after *Leviathan* was published, in the mid-twentieth century (by the mathematicians Morgenstern and von Neumann). The trouble with this claim is that it is question-begging: it affords no leverage against someone who claims that some aspects of Morgenstern and von Neumann's work were anticipated by Hobbes. To argue that game theory hadn't been invented in the mid-seventeenth century thus assumes what is to be proved.

NOTES

1 It might be thought that there is a key difference between the prisoner's dilemma and the state of nature, since in the former but not the latter, there is an authority that lays down the tariff (i.e. the number of years in jail) for each outcome. However, this is incidental. What matters is that the prisoners have subjective preference orderings which are assumed to be of a certain form – that is, each prefers to get fewer years in jail rather than more.

2 Hobbes repeats the *in foro interno/externo* formulation in the Latin text (Hobbes 1841, vol. III, 121).

3 Note, however, the slipperiness of the term 'rational'. What it is rational to do depends on what I know that others are doing, even if their behaviour is itself irrational. So it may be rational to continue to make war giver that others do so, even if their doing so is irrational.

4 For further discussion, see Chapter 6.

5 Whether we should think that individuals transfer or renounce their rights when they set up the sovereign is a major bone of contention between Hobbes' interpreters. I address this question in Chapters 6 and 8.

6 I ignore the fact that, on revealed preference theory, the only basis on which the schedule of rewards is itself identifiable is agents' behaviour, so a gap between rationality and actual behaviour could not arise. On this point see Blackburn 1998, ch. 6.

6

CONTRACT AND CONSENT

INTRODUCTION

In the last couple of chapters we have puzzled over *Leviathan*'s state of nature. In Chapter 5, we asked how the nastiness of the state of nature furthers Hobbes' aim of justifying political authority, given that people have good reason to prefer that authority to the state of nature. I argued that it is hard to make sense of the justification as a story about how people come to leave the state of nature and set up political authority. Rather, the state of nature proves to be unleavable, at least by rational decision. It is not that we actually were in the state of nature, and agreed to leave it, because there is no rational pathway from it to political authority. In the absence of such a pathway, we cannot think of ourselves as leaving it even hypothetically.

At the same time, Hobbes does not think that political authority is justified simply because there is some common power that dominates everyone else. Rather authority requires agreement: it is not that someone who is 'vanquished' in battle is 'obliged because he is conquered, that is to say beaten and taken, or put to flight; but because he comes in and submits to the victor' (*L* 141).

In this chapter we shall see what Hobbes takes 'submission' to involve.

CONTRACT AND JUSTIFICATION

Many modern and past political theorists have thought that political authority can be justified by means of a contract. A contract is a formal promise or undertaking, which creates an obligation to do something that did not previously exist. Hobbes seems to propose a contract of sorts in *Leviathan* when he explains how political authority is justified. But what sort of contract is it? What role does it play in his theory? And does it in fact justify political authority?

Because contracts create obligations, they have proved attractive to political theorists who are trying to justify political authority, particularly when they ask how such an authority could legitimately arise from the state of nature. As we saw in Chapter 5, they have thought that the way to justify political authority was by explaining how a legitimate political authority could come into existence from an initial situation in which it did not exist. Most theorists assume that if a political authority is legitimate, then it must impose on its citizens obligations that did not exist before the authority itself did. So, on this view, we need to justify obligations in order to justify political authority.

A contract is attractive to these theorists, accordingly, because it creates obligations where none previously existed. The most obvious example is that of promising. Most people believe that if I promise to do something, I thereby assume an obligation to do that thing.[1] For example, if I promise to look after your dachshund for the afternoon, I have taken on an obligation where none existed before. Admittedly the issue is often muddied in modern discussions when writers assume either that we are already under an obligation to contract, or at least that the fact that we would agree to contract in some imaginary situation means that we are bound as if we really had contracted.[2] Once this move is made, the initial attraction of contract – that it bases obligation on a voluntary agreement – threatens to vanish, because the agreement concerned need no longer be one that people actually make. One reply is to say that the contract is just a picturesque way of justifying the obligations to which we are subject anyway. But then it seems that agreement drops out of the picture. The point is not that people really agree – it is just that they should, or would do if they were rational.

Nonetheless, contracts remain attractive to political theorists who want to explain how we could become obligated to obey political authority. Contractual devices also appeal because they offer the prospect of harmonising distinct kinds of normative concern or interest. Once I have promised or contracted to do something, the very fact that I have thereby assumed an obligation creates a distinct reason for doing that thing. That reason, more-over, is of a binding kind: it is not just that it is nice, or a good idea, to do the thing – rather it becomes a matter of obligation. This seems to many political theorists a good way of capturing the obligatory force of law. It tells us what we must do, or must avoid doing.

At the same time, the promise or contract itself needs a rationale. The promiser or contractor has to be represented by the theory as acting with good reasons. The reason will often be that the contract benefits the contractors. For example, an insurance policy provides the policyholder with a financial guarantee against losing his or her property, and the insurance company with profits. House-buying contracts serve to give the vendor and purchaser assurance, by giving each party reason to expect that an offer or acceptance, once made, will be honoured. Where they can be made to stick, contracts are a good way to stabilise expectations, especially in relation to funda-mental interests. Reasons grounded in these interests can then yield a rationale for contracting.

COLLECTIVE IMAGINING

An important aspect of Hobbes' theory is that power is exercised by a single agent, whether that agent is one individual, or one organisation composed of a number of individuals. The sovereign – as Hobbes calls this agent – exercises power that is undivided, though not wholly unrestricted. There are certain respects in which the sovereign's power must be limited for Hobbes.

In his account of the family in chapter 20, Hobbes insists that the 'right of dominion' rests on consent, and that consent can be given non-contractually. Obviously, a babe in arms is incapable of signing a contract, so the basis of the father's or mother's right of dominion over it cannot lie in any actual contract. But paternal dominion derives from 'the child's consent, either express, or by other sufficient arguments declared' (L 139); for example, an infant that takes its mother's milk has submitted to her authority because it owes her its life (L 140). Of course, even the notion of 'agreement' sounds rather strained when it is applied to newborn infants, as it is natural to think that babies are not yet capable of agreeing to anything. But Hobbes makes it clear that he thinks that 'if she [the mother] nourish it, it owes its life to the mother; and is therefore obliged to obey her' (L 140).

Thus the obligation to obey arises from the fact that the infant's life is protected. So it is not necessary, for the incurring of obligations, that they rest on any explicit contract. Hobbes insists that the right to dominion, both in the family and under government, derives not from the brute fact of power, but from the agreement to submit to it: 'the right of sovereignty ... is acquired in the people's submission, by which they contract with the victor, promising obedience for life and liberty' (L 486). The baby is taken to have submitted by the act of taking its mother's milk.

How is the right of sovereignty to be understood? Recall that in the state of nature, each person has a right to whatever he or she needs for self-preservation, which Hobbes sometimes interprets as a right to anything (e.g. L 92). This means that the act of 'transferring' a right reduces to 'renouncing', that is, standing aside so that the other person 'may enjoy his own original right without hindrance' (L 92). The general idea here is clear enough: no new rights are acquired if one person simply agrees to waive his or her right to something so that the other can enjoy that thing. Since to have a right to something, in this sense, means lacking the obligation not to pursue it, the act of waiving such a right must involve the taking on of an obligation.

The crucial thing that people set aside in creating a sovereign is their right to judge what is and is not conducive to self-preservation. Hobbes makes it clear in chapter 17 that the contract that sets up the political authority is 'a real unity' of all the people in it (*L* 120). But even here Hobbes qualifies the force of this claim. He goes on to say that this unity is created

> in such manner, *as if* every man should say to every man, 'I authorise and give up my right of governing myself to this man or to this assembly of men, on this condition, that you give up your right to him, and authorise all his actions in like manner [i.e. in a similar way].'
>
> (*L* 120; emphasis added)

This 'as if' language, and other formulations like it, are quite common in *Leviathan*, particularly when Hobbes is discussing the setting up of the sovereign, or the relation of the sovereign to the subjects. The sovereign's actions are said to be authorised by each man 'as if they were his own' (*L* 121), though Hobbes is also prepared on occasion to dispense with this form of words and say that the sovereign's actions simply are those of the subjects. That is, though it is imagined that we contract 'in such manner, as if' every person were uttering the quoted formula to every other person, this does not really happen.

What we have is an imaginary contract, but a real agreement, with real obligatory force. Unlike the hypothetical contract, the agreement concerned is real and, since agreement creates obligations, the obligations created by the agreement are real as well. The contractual elements in Hobbes' theory then become a metaphorical redescription of the actual undertakings we have made. The idea is not that someone needs to have read *Leviathan* in order to make the agreement, but that it offers a way of understanding the political relationships in which people already find themselves, including their obligation to obey the sovereign.

The creation of the sovereign involves a collective act of imagination. There are two stages to this act: first, the subjects imagine themselves as a 'real unity', that is, as one person; and second, they imagine that the acts of one individual or organisation will be taken for the acts of them all. The contract is imagined as being agreed among the subjects, not between the subjects and the sovereign. This is because the sovereign cannot be a party to the contract, since this would involve a kind of self-contradiction:

> That he which [i.e. who] is made sovereign makes no covenant with his subjects beforehand is manifest, because either he must make it with the whole multitude, as one party to the covenant; or he must make a several [i.e. separate] covenant with every man. With the whole, as one party, it is impossible, because as yet they are not one person. And if he make so many several covenants as there be men, those covenants after he has the sovereignty are void, because what act soever can be pretended for [i.e. alleged to cause the] breach thereof, is the act both of himself and of all the rest.
>
> (L 122–23)

Before the contract is made, the 'people' as a single body does not exist, so the sovereign cannot breach (or indeed make) a contract with it. On the other hand, the sovereign cannot breach a contract made with each person separately either, since by the contract the sovereign is authorised to act for each person: so to sue for breach would, in effect, be to sue oneself. Hobbes adds that there is no superior judge, so the sovereign would be judge in its own case (L 123).

CONSENT

We saw in Chapter 5 that Hobbes believes political authority is justified because people agree to it, although it remained unclear exactly how the agreement confers justification. Although Hobbes is not usually understood as a 'consent' theorist (unlike the seventeenth-century political theorist John Locke), he does state clearly in *Leviathan*: 'the point of time, wherein a man becomes subject to a conqueror, is that point, wherein having liberty to submit to him, he consents, either by express words, or by other sufficient sign, to be his subject' (L 484). This was a pertinent question for the defeated supporters of Charles I at the time when *Leviathan* was being written. Hobbes reiterates his view that it is not the fact of victory, but the willingness of those who are defeated to submit, in which the rights of sovereignty consist. He goes on to say that

> he that upon promise of obedience, has his life and liberty allowed him, is then conquered, and a subject ... But this promise may be either express, or tacit: express, by promise; tacit, by other signs. As for example, a man that has not been called to make such an express promise (because he is one whose power perhaps is not considerable), yet if he live under their protection openly, he is understood to submit himself to the government.
>
> (L 485)

Hobbes is fairly relaxed about the means by which an individual indicates his or her consent to the coercive power of the sovereign. The tokens of consent need not be very demonstrative: 'silence is sometimes an argument of consent' (L 184). This is more obviously true in the case where political power is 'acquired' by a conqueror. But it also applies when political authority is thought of as originating with a collective agreement among agents who are motivated by fear of one another: 'where testament and express words are wanting, other natural signs of the will are to be allowed: whereof the one is custom' (L 137).

Consent follows from 'submission', and a person can submit merely by living openly within the sovereign's jurisdiction. Elsewhere in *Leviathan*, as we have seen, Hobbes affirms that consent – and tacit rather than express consent at that – suffices for the transfer of right. Above all, I consent to the sovereign's dominion over me even if I act out of fear. Those who think that agreements entered into for fear of death are void, Hobbes scoffs, must believe that 'no man, in any kind of commonwealth, could be obliged to obedience' (L 139). More generally, the act of accepting protection from a dominant power signals consent to it (L 153, 230, 485).

The crucial point is that if I am subject to a superior power, then I have, merely by accepting its protection, consented to its authority over me, and this is enough in Hobbes' view for it to be justified. Once this is granted, it does not matter any more how that power came into being.[3] We can imagine if we prefer that it came about as the result of spontaneous decision by everyone acting individually, or by some other route. It does not even seem to matter for Hobbes whether the political authority came to power by actions that are unjust, as Hobbes thought of the Parliamentary rebellion against Charles I. All that matters is consent, and consent is granted 'when the means of [one's] life is within the guards and garrisons of the enemy' (L 484).

This also helps to explain the status of contracting within the theory. On the one hand, Hobbes is very insistent, as we have seen, that 'covenants without the sword, are but words' (L 117), and that in themselves they 'have no power to oblige, contain, constrain, or protect any man' (L 123). On the other hand, though, it is the agreement itself, and not the physical force behind it, which creates a 'transfer' of rights, and sets up obligations: promises extracted through fear of death within political society are void, because the promisor has no right in the thing promised (L 139). For example, a robber who makes me promise to hand over my belongings by threatening me at knifepoint has no right to do so if the political authority is already in place, and therefore cannot extract a valid promise from me in this way. The agreement always stands in the background as the justification for the rights and obligations that exist under political authority. But it is not the agreement itself that exercises a grip on individuals' motivations: it is ultimately the threat of force.

As Hobbes famously says, 'the passion to be reckoned upon is fear' (L 99). This is what makes Hobbes look like a 'de facto' theorist, who claims (in the simplest form of the theory) that 'might makes right'. Though this is too simple a summary of Hobbes' views, on his theory, right does always closely shadow might.

FREEDOM AND ITS OPPOSITE

Hobbes believes that consent is necessary to justify political authority (L 120). He thus accepts the liberal claim set out in Chapter 5. In chapter 21, Hobbes says that a person on a ship who is forced to throw his belongings overboard to keep the ship afloat nonetheless 'does it very willingly' (L 146). It makes no difference, in Hobbes' view, if the compulsion comes from an individual, or from some corporate body. As we have seen, he also thinks that if I submit to somebody's power in the state of nature purely from fear, I nonetheless consent to that power. A person who consents acts freely. Your freedom is not compromised simply because you act from the fear of another's greater power. 'Fear and liberty are consistent' (L 146): if you act out of fear, you nonetheless act freely.

This squares with Hobbes' wider view that 'liberty and necessity are consistent' (L 146). Hobbes was a determinist, that is, he believed that every event, including all human actions, is the necessary causal result of earlier states of the universe. Here Hobbes' materialism surfaces in his view that everything that happens, including acts of will, is determined by a prior cause, which is itself caused, and so on 'in a continual chain' (L 146). But he also thought that liberty could be reconciled with determinism. So if through fear during a storm at sea I throw my belongings overboard, my action is free (I throw them willingly) even though it is necessitated by the circumstances. He identifies liberty with action initiated by the will: to be free with regard to some action is to will the doing of that action. So, in willing to throw my belongings overboard, or to submit to the sovereign, I act freely. Someone might then ask whether the will itself is free. But in his dispute over free will with Bishop John Bramhall, Hobbes dismisses the question whether I am free to will, that is, whether I will to will, as 'an absurd speech' (Hobbes 1999, 16).

It is fair to say that these views of Hobbes about freedom are not widely shared among philosophers. The main political use to which he puts his claim about the compatibility of liberty and necessity is to argue that those who submit to the sovereign, through fear of it or of one another, do so freely, with the implicit further premise that what one freely does cannot be an injury. However, this does not seem to *justify* the political order to which submission gives rise, any more than a gunman's threat of violence justifies the surrendering of cash that it elicits. The argumentative leverage here must come from the thought that, unlike other valuables such as cash, one's life has an infinite or absolute value, and so one would undertake any trade, no matter how otherwise onerous it is, in order to secure it, if no alternative to this trade exists. Hence Hobbes' view on the compatibility of freedom and necessity, if it is to perform its justificatory task, needs to exclude other alternatives to the plenipotentiary sovereign. I examine this side of the argument in the next chapter.

The more intrinsic problem with Hobbes' theory of freedom is that the bar for consent seems to be set very low. Most people would argue that someone whose agreement is extorted under threat of death has not acted freely, but Hobbes' theory of obligation seems to imply just this. After all, the law of rape holds that a woman does not consent to sex if she is subject to physical duress: force, or the threat of force, annuls the possibility of consent.

Hobbes' response, if he has one, must distinguish sharply between consent in the state of nature and consent under government. The reason why a person who submits to rape does not consent to sex, or the victim of robbery does not consent to handing his valuables over, is that they have already given up their natural freedom in order to secure protection, including against violent assault, so they cannot be understood as consenting to submit to the assaulter. Once under government, it is part of the deal that one cannot consent to submit to *force majeure* unless it is wielded by the sovereign. By contrast, being prey to violent assault is part and parcel of life in the state of nature. In such circumstances, Hobbes thinks, you would choose rape or robbery in preference to death. So, if you agreed to live in the state of nature, you would agree that your choosing rape or robbery in preference to violent death would amount to consenting to these assaults. And the very fact that the bar for consent would then be set so low is an excellent reason, here and now, for not agreeing to live in the state of nature. Or at least, so Hobbes may be taken to argue.

Hobbes also differs from many philosophers who have written about freedom because he does not believe that 'I did x freely' entails 'I could have done something other than x.'[4] Hobbes denies that it is really possible to have done otherwise. Of course it may seem possible to those who lack perfect knowledge. If I am free, I have the liberty 'to do or to forbear' (L 152). What this means is not that there was a real possibility that I can do something if I am causally necessitated to act in some other way, but that no 'external impediments', that is, obstacles, get in my way when I try to do something (L 91). On Hobbes' view, I am free to have an ice cream if nothing stops me following through on my will to do so. It does not, however, follow that I could have willed not to seek an ice cream.[5]

So far, then, Hobbes claims that to be at liberty or free is to will an action and to encounter no external obstacle to performing it. At the same time, though, he seems to acknowledge that obligating oneself in this way must involve a repudiation of the freedom people enjoy in the state of nature (e.g. L 147). In chapter 21 of *Leviathan* he notes that condemned men may band together to resist the execution of their sentence, and goes on to say that

> [a]s for other liberties, they depend on the silence of the law. In cases where the sovereign has prescribed no rule, there the subject has the liberty to do, or forbear, according to his own discretion. And therefore such liberty is in some places more, and in some less.
>
> (L 152)

Hobbes then comments that the right forcibly to take back illegally occupied property, or to engage in polygamy, are examples of how liberty may be more or less extensive in particular societies. We can recall also that in chapter 14 he remarks that 'law and right differ as much as obligation and liberty; which in one and the same matter are inconsistent' (L 91). Thus, for Hobbes, as long as the sovereign keeps the peace, my liberty may be promoted by legal regimes that differ greatly in how far they restrict my actions. The sovereign's peacekeeping restricts my own freedom but at the same time, within the civil state, the laws may be more or less restricted.

But Hobbes also contends that the subjects' liberty depends on the silence of the civil laws. Indeed, he says that 'right is liberty, namely that liberty which the civil law leaves us: but civil law is an obligation, and takes from us the liberty which the law of nature gave us' (L 200). This may sound rather odd, since we might expect liberty to be identified with the right rather than the law of nature. But Hobbes means that the right to everything that exists in the state of nature is a product of the law of nature that commands self-preservation. It allows us to use whatever we see fit to use in order to preserve ourselves.

So, alongside the no-obstacle view of freedom, there is this no-law account of freedom too. We might think that the two notions can be brought together by imagining that the law imposes obstacles on wrongdoers, in the form of police and so on. But in fact Hobbes also denies that the law infringes liberty, arguing that it is 'absurd' to think that under political authority we lose our liberty, when in a state of nature 'all other men may be masters of [our] lives' (L 147). Equally, I may ask you to restrict my actions in certain ways so as to promote other goals of mine. As Hobbes says, 'in the act of our submission consists both our obligation and our liberty' (L 150). In any case, for Hobbes it is not true that I am not free to break the civil law, since 'all actions which men do in commonwealths for fear of the law are actions which the doers had liberty to omit' (L 146). It is hard to reconcile this with his earlier claim that my liberty varies inversely with the extent of the civil law.

The best way to make sense of Hobbes' views is to contrast natural and civic freedom. I have natural freedom insofar as I meet with no obstacles to doing what I want. But under political authority, I act so as to place obstacles in my own path by agreeing to a sovereign who will restrict my actions in various ways. However, the civic freedom I enjoy there consists in my securing what is most valuable to me – my life – and is the condition of my getting anything else I value. In other words, laws may curtail specific freedoms of mine, and the fewer laws there are, the more natural freedom remains to me. But legal restriction is necessary for the civic freedom that I express by consenting to the sovereign's power over me.

The implication of this theory is that a people who subject themselves to political authority through fear of a conqueror (such as the victorious republican regime) is not for that reason less free than one that is instituted by mutual agreement (L 149). Hobbes' point, again, is that no distinction in point of freedom can be drawn between commonwealths by conquest and by institution. The whole point of consent-based arguments for 'political obligation' is that the citizens or subjects have obligated themselves freely. For, on Hobbes' view of the matter, I remain free in my decision to submit myself to the political authority regardless of whether or not my reason for doing so is that it (or more precisely, whoever will become the sovereign) can threaten me with overwhelming force if I do not.

A further consequence of this view is that republican regimes were not, just by being republican, necessarily freer than monarchies: '[w]hether a commonwealth be monarchical or popular, the freedom is still the same' (*L* 149). The same goes for commonwealths formed by 'acquisition' (i.e. conquest) and those formed by 'institution' (i.e. agreement). The 'obligation and liberty of the subject is to be derived' from the act of authorisation (*L* 150). However, this is a conjectural history rather than one that has really played out in the past.

The rational ground for submitting oneself to political authority is that the sovereign can offer protection. Hobbes' famous remark about the 'mutual relation between protection and obedience' (*L* 491), which he highlights as the main conclusion of *Leviathan*, entails that subjects are no longer bound to obey once the sovereign can no longer protect them. But Hobbes does not take this to mean that subjects may try to bring it about that the sovereign is no longer capable of protection. The 'Review, and Conclusion' explicitly rules this out: a subject's allegiance can be transferred from a sovereign to a usurper only when 'the means of his [the subject's] life is within the guards and garrisons of the enemy' (*L* 484).

For Hobbes, what counts above all is that I promote the ends that I am naturally impelled to seek, prime among which is self-preservation. I am free to the extent that I do not encounter obstacles in willing what is necessary to obtain this end. It is clear that I can be interfered with in this process – indeed, I can will that this be so, if I think this will promote my ends more successfully. This would be true, for example, if I thought that others had a better idea of how to promote my own preservation than I did.

This creates problems for Hobbes regarding the scope for subjects to exercise their own political judgement, about which he is generally scathing (e.g. *L* 118). He thinks that leaving people to make up their own minds about politics or religion is a recipe for chaos. But he is equally adamant that each person must retain his or her right to defend him- or herself if in mortal danger. The obvious problem is that everyone must rely on their private judgement to decide when mortal danger threatens. Then they can resist willy-nilly the dictates of the sovereign. Private judgement thus survives into the political authority, with its potential for instability. Those who 'dare take up arms to defend or introduce an opinion are still in war; and their condition [is] not peace, but only a cessation of arms' (*L* 125). Hobbes might reply that subjects' private judgement can only be mobilised in the face of clear and present danger. But when clear and present danger threatens is itself a matter on which private judgements will differ.

MORALITY AND CONTRACT

One of the major bones of contention between interpreters of *Leviathan* concerns the role, if any, played by morality in the book, and in particular its bearing on the contract or, as Hobbes often calls it, the 'covenant', which sets up the political authority. Hobbes' use of 'covenant' is not consistent. At times he uses the term in a special sense, to refer to a situation where one party has performed its side of the bargain but the other has yet to do so (*L* 94); elsewhere, however, he seems to treat it as synonymous with 'contract' (e.g. *L* 120). Since we are concerned with agreement generally, we will stick to the more general term 'contract' in what follows.

On one view, the state of nature is morally evacuated – in other words, no moral norms have any applicability in it. The contract itself makes the moral laws effective, by forming a union of the people and delegating some person or persons to act as their sovereign, taking people out of the state of nature and into the political authority. Before the contract comes into existence, the moral law is empty.

Some commentators reject the idea that the state of nature is morally empty. For Howard Warrender and A.E. Taylor, the law of nature, which prevails in the state of nature, is a moral law that follows from God's commands, as we discussed in Chapter 4. Hence, the advocates of this 'theistic' interpretation argue, the overriding reason why people have to set up a political authority is that it is the only way to comply with the divine command to seek peace. The theistic interpretation rests on the central contention that Hobbes distinguishes between people's motives, such as the desire for self-preservation, and the basis for the law of nature, which commands people to seek peace – which exponents of this interpretation see as a command issued by God.

A related question concerns the motivations of those, the subjects, who are obligated to obey authority. These two issues come together when we ask how Hobbes can provide a satisfactory argument for the obligation, while also explaining how the subjects can be consistently motivated to fulfil it. Part of the concern here, which bothered philosophers when Warrender was writing in the 1950s, was how to derive an ought-statement from a factual one: how could Hobbes get from the factual claim that humans desire self-preservation to the statement that they therefore ought to follow the law of nature?

Warrender concluded that the normative force of the law of nature, which tells us to seek peace, could not be derived from the fact that we all desire to preserve ourselves. But Hobbes uncompromisingly states that contracts without the 'sword' not only fail to motivate us; they also fail to obligate us. '[C]ovenants being but words and breath, have no power to oblige, contain, constrain, or protect any man, but what it has from the public sword' (L 123; cf. 117). Later, Hobbes says that nobody in their right mind 'believes the law can hurt him – that is, words and paper, without the hands and swords of men' (L 471). The laws of nature 'oblige ... only then where there is security' (L 110). The way to get from the factual claim to an ought-statement is to use a conditional claim, as follows:

(1) If you want to preserve yourself, you ought to do what the law of nature tells you to do.
(2) You do want to preserve yourself.

So,

(3) You ought to do what the law of nature tells you to do.

The law tells you to seek peace when, but only when, doing so promotes self-preservation, which is the 'ground' of the law of nature.

The passages just quoted make it clear that the contract cannot 'oblige' without the 'sword' of physical force to back it up. 'Oblige' and 'obligate' are usually distinguished in modern English, at least by philosophers: whereas 'oblige' is taken as synonymous with 'physically force' or 'compel', the word 'obligate' means 'place under a [moral, legal, etc.] obligation'. If this is what Hobbes means by 'oblige' here, then he is only stating the obvious – that since contracts have no physical force in themselves, they cannot in themselves physically force us to do anything.

But he seems to have something less obvious in mind. This becomes apparent when Hobbes discusses 'Those Things that Weaken or Tend to the Dissolution of a Commonwealth' in chapter 29:

> when in a war (foreign or intestine [i.e. civil]) the enemies get a final victory, so ... there is no further protection of the subjects in their loyalty, then is the commonwealth dissolved, and every man at liberty to protect himself by such courses as his own discretion shall suggest unto him.
>
> (L 230)

An even clearer statement appears in chapter 21, where Hobbes coolly remarks that

> [t]he obligation of subjects to the sovereign is understood to last as long, and no longer, than the power lasts by which he is able to protect them. For the right men have by nature to protect themselves, when none else can protect them, can by no covenant be relinquished.
>
> (L 153)

Hobbes means by this not merely that, when the sovereign is crippled by war, people will not be motivated to do what they have contracted to do. The obligation itself will either dissolve, or proves not to apply in these circumstances, because you cannot contract to give up your right to protect yourself when nobody else can protect you. This is not to say that the obligation to obey the sovereign is nothing but the motivation that subjects feel (that is, fear) when confronted with the sovereign's power. But it suggests that the subjects' obligation to obey cannot outlast the sovereign's ability to protect them.

Hobbes says that overwhelming physical force is the occasion for contracting, but he is unambiguous that the ground of the obligation is the mutual transfer of right that occurs when the contract is signed. In the 'Review, and Conclusion' he asks what happens if a person is abroad when his country is conquered. His answer is that the person 'is not conquered, nor subject; but if at his return, he submit to the [new] government, he is bound to obey it' (L 486). This makes it clear that the act of submission is what counts in grounding the obligation. Hobbes underlines this point in chapter 20, where he notes that '[i]t is not ... the victory that gives the right of dominion over the vanquished, but his own covenant' (L 141).

It is important to understand what is involved here. Some commentators have concluded from the distinction I have just drawn between the occasion and the ground of an obligation, that Hobbes' theory is a pure duty-based theory – where the duties, or obligations, are owed to God (Warrender 1957; Taylor 1965). Hobbes certainly says that '[t]he laws of God ... are none but the laws of nature' (L 404), and this claim can be given a theological as well as a secular interpretation, depending on what is held to be reducible to what. There is also an acknowledged analogy that I mentioned at the start of Chapter 2, between the civil sovereign or 'mortal God' (L 120), whose commands are the laws of the political authority, and the immortal God in heaven, whose commands are the laws of nature. Both can compel action through sheer physical force.

But all that this implies is that if the laws of nature are the laws of God, then whatever we are required to do because the law of nature demands that we perform our contracts is also the law of God. It does not follow, even if Hobbes did think that the laws of nature were the laws of God, that this is the reason why the subjects should obey them. The reason why they should obey the laws of nature, and the civil laws that result when subjects follow them, is that they tell us how to secure our preservation through peace.

As we have seen, Hobbes is clear that the subjects' obligation to obey the sovereign lasts only for as long as the sovereign retains the power to protect them. '[T]hough the right of a sovereign monarch cannot be extinguished by the act of another, yet the obligation of the members may. For he that wants [i.e. lacks] protection may seek it anywhere' (L 230). This emphatically does not mean that the subject is entitled to bring about the failure of protection by inciting rebellion – this was precisely Hobbes' charge against the Parliamentarian rebels against Charles I. The subject 'is obliged ... to protect his protection as long as he is able' (L 230).

But equally the claim that there is a mutual relation between protection and obedience does not require that subjects are bound to a lame-duck sovereign once it becomes advisable to switch their allegiance. Obligations are contoured to fit in with the natural facts about human motivation, and are dissolved when, as a matter of brute fact, we cannot be motivated to act on them. Hobbes thinks that no man can be obligated to kill himself (L 151); a condemned prisoner cannot but resist, so (assuming that 'ought implies can') his obligations cannot extend to submission if he faces death (L 152). Hobbes asks, 'have they [i.e. criminals who expect to be condemned to death] not the liberty then to join together and assist and defend one another?' He answers: '[c]ertainly they have' (L 152). Similarly, '[i]f a man by the terror of present death' is forced to break the law, 'he is totally excused' (L 208). In all these respects, the state of nature survives within the political authority, facing citizens with the constant choice whether to remain in a civil state, or to plunge into war.

In the right circumstances, citizens have good reason to accept political authority. But this is far from saying that they are under an obligation to accept it. They are free to refuse, in the sense that they are not bound by 'antecedent covenant' to accept the authority. They not only can, but will resist, if the authority threatens their lives. Defenders of the view that Hobbes thought the laws of nature had independent moral force rightly point out that Hobbes distinguishes the motive to preserve oneself from the ground of the law of nature. But the ground of the law of nature is itself 'nature's preservation' (*L* 110). Political authority is justified because we consent to it (*L* 141) from the desire for self-preservation.

CONTRACTS REAL, HYPOTHETICAL AND IMAGINARY

As we saw in Chapter 5, it is possible to view the agreement to accept political authority as hypothetical rather than actual. The idea is that Hobbes is laying down the conditions under which individuals would have good reason to submit themselves to the political authority, and it is then hoped that the benefits of the contracting device will follow. But, as has often been pointed out, a hypothetical contract is not a real contract. Any obligations supposedly created by it remain as hypothetical as the contract itself.

It may be said in response that the hypothetical contract is not meant to justify actual political relationships. Instead it is a device that aims to identify the conditions in which a political authority would be justified. Is this what Hobbes is up to in *Leviathan*? There is reason to doubt it, not least because Hobbes himself says that his aim is to persuade real people of their real obligations (*L* 484–85).[6] If so, Hobbes was aiming to justify not a hypothetical agreement, but a real one – or, at least, to justify real obligations.

One way of consenting, of course, is via a real contract. But we should not lose sight of a more subtle possibility – that though the contract is not itself real, there are real actions of ours that can be taken as proxies for it. Even if we do not contract, it may be that certain actions of ours can do duty for contracting. This follows, for instance, if I am faced with a situation in which obligations are imposed on me and I do nothing to demur from accepting these obligations. A possible formalisation of Hobbes' argument runs as follows:

(1) Anyone who knowingly fails to resist a dominant power, submits to it (*L* 485).

(2) Submission is a token of consent (*L* 328).

(3) Anyone who consents to the power of another (e.g. by accepting their protection), undertakes not to resist that power (*L* 140, 153).

So,

(4) Anyone who knowingly fails to resist a dominant power undertakes not to resist that power (*L* 484–85).

(5) Anyone who undertakes to do something, freely accepts the obligation to do that thing (*L* 150).

(6) Any obligation that is freely accepted is valid (*L* 373).

So,

(7) Anyone who submits by failing to resist a dominant power accepts a valid obligation not to resist that power (*L* 140).[7]

Consent is actual, and creates obligations. So we should not think of political authority as justified by a hypothetical contract. It is more accurate to say that the obligation actually to obey has the force it would also have in some hypothetical situations, as for example if everyone had really come together to sign a contract. Hobbes' point is that they have agreed. Agreement is necessary to justification, but it does not follow that subjects' agreement to political authority is hypothetical. This is the truth in the historical reading of the state of nature: it rightly stresses actual agreement, but wrongly displaces that agreement to the state of nature. The point is rather that the state of nature is a way of making vivid the agreement that subjects make here and now to submit themselves to political authority.

RETURN TO GAME THEORY

I argued in Chapter 5 that the story-based reading of the state of nature and justification of political authority fails.[8] But it does not follow that a game-theoretic interpretation of the state of nature is redundant. Actual consent may be grounded on the danger of relapsing into a full-blown state of nature. I may have to decide now between getting into a situation where a PD-like structure prevails, and one where it does not. If I have good reason now for thinking it would be worse for me to have to make a future decision within a PD (prisoner's dilemma), I have good reason now for avoiding that situation. For example, if I have to choose now between taking my second-best outcome on the one hand, and getting into a PD on the other – where, I conclude from reasons of dominance, I will do no better than getting my third-best outcome – I have good reason to avoid getting into the PD.

This is prospective, or future-orientated reasoning. But the reasoning can just as well operate retrospectively. I may justify some past decision of mine on the basis that by doing so, I avoided getting into a situation that would have been worse for me precisely because my options, or my decision-making abilities, would have been depleted. So, for example, I might decide to act to ensure that my subsequent decision-making abilities were not impaired, for example through drunkenness, or because I would lack relevant knowledge in that situation. Equally, I can justify a present decision by thinking that if I took some alternative course of action, it would land me later on with a decision whose outcome would be worse for me. Here there really is a decision that I now have to make. But whether or not a later decision remains hypothetical depends on what I decide to do now.

Maybe the state of nature in *Leviathan* can be seen as having this structure. Citizens of an already existing political authority can justify abiding by the status quo by thinking that if they were to rebel, the basis on which they would then have to make decisions would be worse for all. Despite this conditional element, the decision that is justified is a real one – whether, here and now, to rebel. If the state of nature is a PD, its theoretical role has to be understood conditionally if the rational choice elements are to work. So the state of nature could justify the political authority by showing how, without political authority, we would feel we had to defect – that is, make war. This would be worse for us.

It would be worse precisely because we would, by each acting rationally, all end up worse off than we would be under government.

An advantage of this interpretation is that it enables us both to explain why the state of nature is bad, and to justify the political authority without assuming that people have to exit from the state of nature via the narrative of reasons. The PD aspects of the state of nature work not to propel us from the state of nature to the political authority, but in giving us good reason not to depart from obedience once we have bound ourselves to it. The fact that defection may be rational in the state of nature is a good reason for not getting back into that state, once one is out of it.

This interpretation also suggests a response to the problems raised in the last chapter about the lack of any rational deliberative path from the state of nature to political authority. The answer is that we need not think that Hobbes believed that there is any such path. What matters is consent, not prior deliberation. Equally, the objection to hypothetical agreements no longer applies, since Hobbes is talking about actual agreements – the submission by subjects, here and now, to a superior power. Hobbes replies to someone who receives the benefits of protection, but asks 'Why should I agree to authority?' is, in effect, 'You already have.'

THE 'FOOL' REVISITED

If we look again at the 'Fool' passage (*L* 101), Hobbes does not simply say that it would be wrong or immoral for the Fool not to keep his side of the bargain when the other person has already done his side. His claim is that the Fool has a self-interested reason for keeping his agreement, on the following grounds: the Fool will not be trusted by others, and will therefore not be defended by them; it is irrational to risk disaster by defecting (*L* 102) or attempting to assassinate the sovereign (*L* 103), even if in some cases defection is not detected; and it is no way to get to the Kingdom of Heaven (*L* 103).

It may look as if Hobbes is taking a strong line on the rationality of performing even when there may appear to be solid self-interested reasons for defecting. But it is a mistake to infer from this that Hobbes is pointing to a way out of the state of nature. Rather he is talking about what is rational when a political authority, or at least an embryonic 'common power', already exists. Hobbes' distinction between 'promises' and 'covenants' is crucial here. At first sight it seems fundamental to this distinction that he holds it to be reasonable to break promises, but not covenants. Hobbes states that promises made where there is no civil power 'are no covenants; but [that is, except] *either* where one of the parties has performed already, *or* where there is a power to make him perform' (L 102; emphasis added).

The 'either ... or' may seem clearly to allow for the possibility that a promise may be transformed into a 'covenant' – that is, a contract where one side has already performed – even before the establishment of the 'civil power'. And if there are indeed covenants in the absence of the civil power, and it is in the nature of covenants not merely that one is not irrational to keep them, but also that one is irrational to default on them, this would provide a clear example of the irrationality of defection. But it is far from clear that Hobbes did mean to say this.

For one thing, 'or' does not have to be read as making out that these possibilities are alternatives, that is, that they exclude one another: 'or' may have the force of 'and/or'. It is instructive to compare the Latin text at this point, where Hobbes clearly says that there must be a constituted power to compel performance, rather than the simple fact that the other party has already performed. The Latin passage, translated, runs as follows:

> But with an existing power which enforces [agreements], *and* if the other fulfils his promise, then the question is whether he who defaults, does so with reason and in accordance with his own good. I say that he does indeed act against reason, and imprudently.
>
> (Hobbes 1841, vol. III, 113; emphasis added)[9]

This may not alter the claim that reasons of self-interest explain why the Fool is foolish, but it does alter (by making more stringent) the conditions that have to be met if I am to have a self-interested reason not to break my word. Latin, unlike English, does have an exclusive 'or', namely 'aut', which Hobbes often uses, and could have used at this point, but does not. He says instead that if the other performs, and there is an existing power, the Fool will behave irrationally in failing to do what he promised. Clearly this is different from claiming that if the other person has performed, it is irrational not to follow suit if no such power exists.

It is not certain anyway that the passage refers to actions before the political authority exists. Hobbes makes it plain both that the Fool's actions contravene rules of justice, and that these rules only come into being with such an authority (L 90; cf. 469). This, of course, corroborates the reading of the passage from L 102 given above. Hobbes assumes that society already exists, when he talks of a 'power' to make people 'perform' their agreements, although the Fool still thinks it a good idea to renege on them.[10]

The Fool passage, accordingly, can be taken as saying that only a Fool would abandon the security of the political authority for a resumption of the state of nature. In fact, Hobbes says explicitly that 'the validity of covenants begins not but with [i.e. only with] the constitution of a civil power, sufficient to compel men to keep them' (L 101). Similarly, though the *in foro interno/in foro externo* passage certainly does not say that a rational person will defect even if the other has already performed, it also stops short of saying that it is rational to perform in these circumstances without a supreme power.

Early in the notoriously obscure passage that begins, 'The Kingdom of God is gotten by violence' (L 101), Hobbes does seem to wobble about this. He is worried that self-interested rationality may well urge us to break promises and otherwise behave unjustly if we can get away with it. The examples he considers in this passage, which involve rebellion in earthly kingdoms (such as the usurpation of a reigning monarch by his son), give rise to the troubling thought that sometimes people who behave unjustly can escape scot-free because there is no power to which they are answerable for their actions. And if this could be true equally of the Kingdom of God, there is no hope that justice will even impose sanctions on such people in any life that may come after death. So Hobbes' worry here is that those who usurp God, as the supreme power in the universe, by unjust actions, will not get their just desserts: in such a situation, the unjust themselves would wield supreme power. But then he dismisses this thought by saying that he is not, after all, talking about situations where there is no 'common power' to compel me to perform when you have already done so. I have a good self-interested reason to perform precisely because there is a common power. The upshot of the 'Fool' passage, then, is that only a fool would renege on agreements that are enforced by a common power, not that it is foolish to renege where no such power exists.

CONCLUSION

The conclusion we have reached is that the consent that justifies political authority is actual rather than hypothetical for Hobbes. Transfer of right is the token of consent, but Hobbes thinks that anyone faced with overwhelming power will consent in this way, whether explicitly or tacitly. He seems to think that the Fool is foolish only when there is an overwhelming power that can enforce contracts, so that in a full-blown state of nature it will be rational not to seek peace. The state of nature is nasty in part because its nastiness is inescapable.

At the same time, some aspects of the state of nature persist into political society. It exists wherever someone is an enemy of the sovereign, which includes not only foreign nationals or stateless persons, but all those faced with the choice between submission and resistance. That choice faces all subjects of an overwhelming power. As subjects we are still in a state of nature as regards our unrenounceable right of self-defence. On the whole, life under political authority is a better bet than taking our chances against the overwhelming power of the sovereign. But it is still a bet. Sovereignty is perishable. It is 'subject to violent death by foreign war' and 'through the ignorance and passions of men, it has in it, from the very institution, many seeds of a natural mortality, by intestine [internal] discord' (L 153).

FURTHER READING

Leviathan, chapters 14–15; chapter 21

LEVIATHAN AND THE CONTRACT

There is a large body of literature on Hobbes' contract. Some of the major contributions are listed in the further reading in Chapters 4 and 5. Particularly important is Jean Hampton, *Hobbes and the Social Contract Tradition* (Cambridge: Cambridge University Press, 1986).

Other good general treatments include Ross Harrison, *Hobbes, Locke, and Confusion's Masterpiece* (Cambridge: Cambridge University Press, 2003), ch. 4. See also Alan Ryan, 'Hobbes' Political Philosophy', in Tom Sorell (ed.), *The Cambridge Companion to Hobbes* (Cambridge: Cambridge University Press, 1996). For a traditional reading of Hobbes as the prophet of an anti-liberal 'absolutist' state, see Gordon Schochet, 'Hobbes and the Voluntary Basis of Society', in Mary Dietz (ed.), *Thomas Hobbes and Political Theory* (Lawrence, KS: University Press of Kansas, 1990). See also F.S. McNeilly, *The Anatomy of Leviathan* (London: Macmillan, 1968).

THE THEISTIC INTERPRETATION (THE 'TAYLOR/WARRENDER THESIS')

Defenders

The 'Taylor/Warrender thesis' claims, in essence, that Hobbes argues in *Leviathan* that subjects are required to exit from the state of nature and submit themselves to the authority of the sovereign because God requires this of them. That is, the laws of nature, the most fundamental of which commands people to seek peace, should be regarded as divine commands.

Some of the most important statements of the thesis have already been listed in the further reading section in Chapter 4. Of particular importance for the thesis are the works by Howard Warrender, *The Political Philosophy of Hobbes: His theory of obligation* (Oxford: Clarendon Press, 1957); and A.E. Taylor, 'The Ethical Doctrine of Hobbes', *Philosophy* 13 (1938), 406–24, as well as the same author's *Thomas Hobbes* (Bristol: Thoemmes Press, 1997). For further defences of this view see F.C. Hood, *The Divine Politics of*

Thomas Hobbes (Oxford: Clarendon Press, 1964); Brian Trainor, 'The Politics of Peace: The role of the political covenant in Hobbes' *Leviathan*', *Review of Politics* 47 (1985), 347–69; and Trainor's 'Warrender and Skinner on Hobbes', *Political Studies* 36 (1988), 680–91. For a further statement of the view that the normative force of the laws of nature derives from God's commands, see A.P. Martinich, *The Two Gods of Leviathan* (Cambridge: Cambridge University Press, 1992), chs 4 and 5; and Martinich, *Hobbes* (London: Routledge, 2005), chs 3 and 4.

Critics

Criticism of the Taylor/Warrender thesis can be found in Thomas Nagel, 'Hobbes' Concept of Obligation', *Philosophical Review* 68 (1959), 68–83. See also John Plamenatz, 'Mr Warrender's Hobbes', in K.C. Brown (ed.), *Hobbes Studies* (Oxford: Oxford University Press, 1965), and J.N.W. Watkins, *Hobbes' System of Ideas*, 2nd edn (London: Hutchinson, 1973), ch. 5. For further doubts on the thesis, see Quentin Skinner, 'Hobbes' Theory of Political Obligation', reprinted in Skinner, *Visions of Politics*, vol. III: *Hobbes and civil science* (Cambridge: Cambridge University Press, 2002); and Brian Barry, 'Warrender and His Critics', *Philosophy* 43 (1968), 117–37. For a restatement of the secular interpretation of the force of the laws of nature, see David Gauthier, 'Hobbes: The laws of nature', *Pacific Philosophical Quarterly* 82 (2001), 258–84.

CONTRACT AND COVENANT IN GENERAL

For a rational choice interpretation of Hobbes' contract, see David Gauthier, 'Hobbes' Social Contract', *Noûs* 22 (1988), 71–82, reprinted in G.A.J. Rogers and Alan Ryan (eds), *Perspectives on Thomas Hobbes* (Oxford: Oxford University Press, 1988). See also M.T. Dalgarno, 'Analysing Hobbes' Contract', *Proceedings of the Aristotelian Society* 76 (1976), 209–26; for the legal background to Hobbes' theory see Robinson Grover, 'The Legal Origins of Thomas Hobbes' Doctrine of Contract', *Journal of the History of Philosophy* 18 (1980), 177–94. See also the essays collected in

Claire Finkelstein (ed.), *Hobbes on Law* (Aldershot: Ashgate, 2005), including Larry May, 'Hobbes' Contract Theory', *Journal of the History of Philosophy* 18 (1980), 195–207. For a further argument that the 'covenant' of civil government is superfluous if individuals are already minded to keep to their agreements, see Robinson Grover, 'The Legal Origins of Thomas Hobbes' Doctrine of Contract'.

CONSENT, FREEDOM AND NECESSITY

For Hobbes' views on freedom, see his controversy with Bishop John Bramhall about free will and determinism, reprinted in the Vere Chappell (ed.), *Hobbes and Bramhall on Liberty and Necessity* (Cambridge: Cambridge University Press, 1999). See also David van Mill, 'Hobbes' Theories of Freedom', *Journal of Politics* 57, no. 2 (1995), 443–59, and his *Liberty, Rationality and Agency in Hobbes' Leviathan* (New York: SUNY Press, 2001). Van Mill's major claim is that Hobbes' view of liberty is considerably more complex than is implied by the status that Isaiah Berlin assigned to him as a classic exponent of 'negative' liberty (see 'Two Concepts of Liberty', in Berlin, *Four Essays on Liberty* (Oxford: Oxford University Press, 1969), e.g. 123 n. 2). According to van Mill, Hobbes does espouse elements of the 'negative' theory of liberty as non-interference, but supplements this with a much richer account of autonomy under political authority that bears a closer affinity with Berlin's 'positive' liberty.

For criticism of van Mill's thesis, see John D. Harman, 'Liberty, Rights, and Will in Hobbes: A response to David van Mill', *Journal of Politics* 59 (1997), 893–902. An attempt to make Hobbes' views consistent can be found in Maurice Goldsmith, 'Hobbes on Liberty', *Hobbes Studies* 2 (1989), 23–29. For a more traditional view of Hobbes as the archetypal exponent of 'negative' liberty, see Quentin Skinner, 'The Paradoxes of Political Liberty', *The Tanner Lectures on Human Values*, vol. VII (Cambridge: Cambridge University Press, 1986), 227–50, reprinted in David Miller (ed.), *Liberty* (Oxford: Oxford University Press, 1991). In addition, see Skinner, 'Hobbes on the Proper Signification of Liberty', *Transactions of the Royal Historical Society*, 5th series, 40

(1990), 121–51, reprinted in Skinner, *Visions of Politics*, vol. III: *Hobbes and civil science*, ch. 7; and Annabel Brett, *Liberty, Right and Nature: Individual rights in later scholastic thought* (Cambridge: Cambridge University Press, 1997), ch. 6.

See also A.G. Wernham, 'Liberty and Obligation in Hobbes', in K.C. Brown (ed.), *Hobbes Studies*; F.C. Hood, 'The Change in Thomas Hobbes' Definition of Liberty', *Philosophical Quarterly* 17 (1967), 150–63; Cees Leijenhorst, 'Hobbes' Theory of Causality', *Monist* 79 (1996), 426–47. For an account that, like the present chapter, emphasises the importance for Hobbes' argument both of de facto power and the subjects' consent to government, see Kinch Hoekstra, 'The De Facto Turn in Hobbes' Political Philosophy', in Tom Sorell and Luc Foisneau (eds), *Leviathan after 350 Years* (Oxford: Clarendon Press, 2004). Don Carmichael, 'Hobbes on Natural Right in Society: The *Leviathan* account', *Canadian Journal of Political Science* 23 (1990), 3–21, emphasises how the sovereign's rights are restricted by the remaining rights of the subjects. For an argument that the residual right to self-preservation that is retained by subject does not support a general right to resistance against the sovereign, see Patricia Sheridan, 'Resisting the Scaffold: Self-preservation and the limits of obligation in Hobbes' *Leviathan*', *Hobbes Studies* 24, no. 2 (2011), 137–57. Susan Sreedhar, *Hobbes on Resistance* (Cambridge: Cambridge University Press, 2010), argues, on the contrary, that Hobbes envisages a wide-ranging right to resist in *Leviathan*.

NOTES

1 That is, an obligation if there is no countervailing obligation not to do the thing I have promised to do. For example, I can't create such an obligation by promising to murder somebody if I have no right to murder them in the first place. This restriction is important to Hobbes' theory of punishment (see Chapter 8).
2 Major examples include Rawls 1971 and Scanlon 1999.
3 As Hobbes' contemporaries, including his one-time royalist friends such as Edward Hyde, saw. They particularly disliked the implication that, since Parliament was now the effective protector following the defeat of King Charles I, its rule over the people of Britain was justified. See Burgess 1990.
4 Note, however, that Hobbes could still say that 'I did x freely' entails 'I could have done something other than x, if I had chosen to' (I am indebted to John

Rogers for this observation). This is because freedom results from choice. For Hobbes it does not matter, as far as this goes, that because my actual choice was predetermined, I could not have chosen differently.

5 So, for Hobbes, it does not follow that if I have liberty, I am metaphysically free, if this requires that it was possible for me to will to do something other than what I actually will. All it means is that when I will to do something, nothing external stops me.

6 Those who believe Leviathan was published as a response to immediate political conditions (Skinner 1972a; but cf. Burgess 1990; and see Chapter 1 above), contend that the book was hurried out partly to justify the Oath of Engagement to the new republican regime in England. There was still good reason to believe that the wars were not over when Hobbes was writing *Leviathan* – the royalists staged their last stand at the battle of Worcester in September 1651.

7 Hobbes thinks that children submit by accepting nurturing by their parents (L 140). It might be thought that this extorts consent from those who are too young to be capable of it. Hobbes might say that once in control of his or her faculties, a person still faces the decision whether to accept obedience or to make him or herself an 'enemy' by withholding consent.

8 The argument of this section follows up a brilliant suggestion first put to me a number of years ago by my then colleague at the University of Sussex, Dr Andrew Chitty, to whom I am indebted.

9 'Sed existente potentia quæ cogat, et si alter promissum præstiterit, ibi quæstio est, an is, qui fallit, cum ratione et ad bonum proprium congruenter fallat. Ego vero contra rationem, et imprudenter facere dico.' The Latin text could support the view that the two conditions – that the other party has already fulfilled its promise, and that there is a common power – were jointly sufficient for it to be rational for me to do what I have promised, but also that each condition was necessary by itself. But this would still not make either condition severally sufficient for my performing to be rational.

10 Of course, this also casts doubt on whether the state of nature can be seen as an AG (assurance game) in the first place, since the 'Fool' passage is the main evidence for this interpretation.

7

SOVEREIGNTY, STATE, COMMONWEALTH

INTRODUCTION

In chapters 16 and 18 of *Leviathan*, Hobbes develops an elaborate account of political representation with far-reaching implications for his political theory as a whole. The theory of representation, unlike many other aspects of *Leviathan*, has no real precedent in Hobbes' earlier political works, *De cive* and the *Elements of Law*.[1]

Why does Hobbes need a theory of political representation? The first answer is that he needs it to make sense of the idea that the sovereign acts for the subjects over whom power is exercised. But of course this raises further questions. How can the sovereign take decisions and act in ways that represent those who make up the polity? How does the sovereign represent something that seems shadowy or even an outright figment, namely the collective will of the people? How can the sovereign perform actions that private individuals cannot do at all, such as declare war, or dissolve parliament? Any satisfactory theory of political representation needs to answer these further questions.

The second reason why Hobbes needs such a theory is to transmute power into legitimacy. When we consent to the power of the sovereign over us, we agree that he, she or it will act on our behalf. The transfer of right legitimates the sovereign's actions. In acting on our behalf, the sovereign takes over, with our agreement, our right to determine what we do. By the same token, in representing us, the sovereign takes over our powers of acting. Hobbes concludes from this that we cannot object to what the sovereign does because they are our own actions, carried out by our representative.

To understand Hobbes' theory, we need to grasp his terminology. Although the sovereign acts as our representative, it does not represent each individual taken separately. Rather, according to Hobbes, the individual subjects form themselves into a single corporate person, which Hobbes calls the 'state', and it is that corporate person whom the sovereign represents. Of course the individuals in some sense compose the person of the 'state', as is graphically shown in the famous title-page of *Leviathan* (see Figure 2.1). But, strictly speaking, it is the corporate person, the 'state' whom the sovereign represents.

REPRESENTATION: PERSONS AND AUTHORS

As is often true in political theory, the novelty of Hobbes' approach lies partly in exposing awkward problems in concepts and practices that we take for granted. This applies to the familiar situation where we, as citizens of democratic states, get politicians to act on our behalf, for example by voting them into office at an election. Hobbes is no democrat. But he still needs a notion of representation.

He starts by asking what it means for somebody to represent someone, and focuses on the case where one person represents another. His underlying assumption is that this will provide a clue to understanding political representation. His initial question is this: in what circumstances is it possible to regard the actions of a person as representing those of another? In *Leviathan*, chapters 16–18, Hobbes says that action, with its associated notions of responsibility, blame, purpose and so on, can be attributed to a person acting in a representative capacity. This is the familiar circumstance in which we authorise someone such as a lawyer or estate agent to act on our behalf. There is also the even more familiar case – so familiar that we hardly notice it – when a person acts as his or her own representative.

> A person, is he, whose words or actions are considered, either as his own, or as representing the words or actions of another man, or of any other thing to whom they are attributed, either truly or by fiction. When they are considered as his own, then is he called a natural person. And when they are considered as representing the words and actions of another, then is he a feigned or artificial person.
>
> (L 111)

For Hobbes, the concept of a person is the basis for attributing moral or legal responsibility. And such attributions are made when actions are performed by those representing other people, who are held responsible for the actions. Persons are both potential representatives, and can at the same time be represented. Hobbes sometimes refers to the one who represents as the *actor*, and the one represented as the *author*. When, as in the most familiar case, these roles are combined in a single agent – that is, the actor and author are one – that agent is in Hobbes' terminology a 'natural person' (L 111). This is the everyday situation where I act on my own behalf and am held accountable for what I do.

Hobbes sometimes uses the term 'bear the person' (e.g. L 114) to describe the relation between the representative and the represented; this is the relation of personation.[2] All attributions of responsibility make a claim about representation, which determines who is to be held responsible for a given action or actions performed by a representative. This enables Hobbes to describe natural persons as the limiting case, in which the person who is to be held responsible is the same as his or her representative. It is an insight of Hobbes' in *Leviathan* to see in natural personation an instance of a more general representational relationship. This account of natural personation can then be used to generate the notion of artificial personation laid out in chapter 16 (L 112–14).

An artificial person comes into being when one natural person acts on behalf of another one, with the latter's authorisation, or on behalf of some other thing, with the authorisation of a natural person. Where one natural person represents another, the actions of the actor will be taken to be actions of the author – but not the actions of the actor as a natural person. This may sound convoluted, but is in fact exemplified by quite familiar forms of representation. For example, when a client is represented in court by a barrister, the barrister's actions are taken as authorised by the client, and this has a direct impact on who is held responsible for them. If the barrister enters a plea of 'Not guilty', the author of the plea is taken to be the client, who will then be held responsible for it – for instance, it may result in a longer jail sentence for him or her, if he or she is duly convicted of the crime, than if (again through his or her barrister) he or she had pleaded guilty.

Similar considerations apply to fictional persons, such as Agamemnon, the character from Greek mythology – the example that Hobbes uses in his 1658 work *De homine*. Agamemnon can be played by an actor, and in this way represented on stage. A fictional person is borne by a representative of someone who is not a natural person at all. This is clearly true of Agamemnon, who is a product of fiction, and thus not a natural person; but it applies equally to inanimate objects such as hospitals and bridges.

This may sound odd, but Hobbes' idea is that bridges and hospitals (or their owners) can be thought of as having interests, which will be served for example by taking care of their upkeep. We can then think of the person charged with doing this as bearing the person of these objects. Fictional persons, then, arise when the actor represents something that is not a natural person, whereas in the case of artificial persons the actor represents a natural person.

So far, then, we have the following scheme:

Natural persons represent themselves.
Artificial persons are natural persons who represent either other natural persons, or things that are not natural persons.

We can also distinguish among artificial persons: between non-fictional artificial persons, where the agent that is represented is a natural person, such as a barrister's client; and fictional artificial persons, such as Agamemnon and hospitals, where this is not the case – we might (though this is not Hobbes' terminology) call those falling into this latter possibility *fictional* persons. Obviously an actor playing Agamemnon and the overseer of a hospital are rather different kinds of personation as well – the point being that though neither is really a person, Agamemnon, unlike a hospital, is thought of as being a person in his own right.

Hobbes' scheme is set out in Figure 7.1.

After having sketched this typology of persons in chapter 16, Hobbes models political representation on personation. An obvious question arises. Is the political representative in Hobbes' model a natural or artificial person?

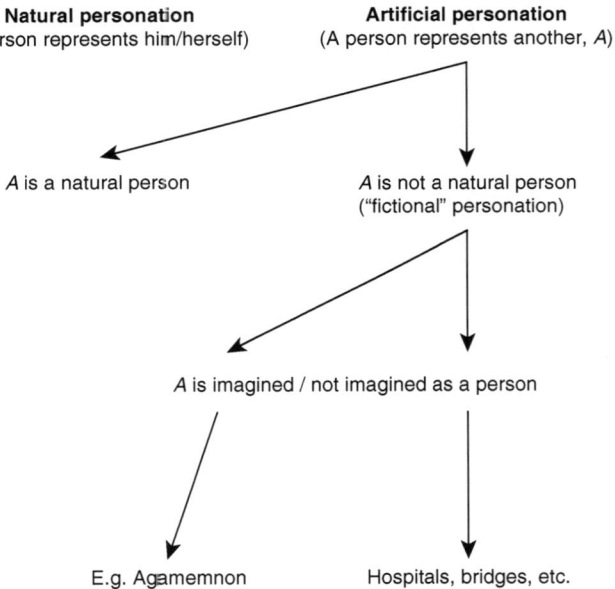

Natural personation
(A person represents him/herself)

Artificial personation
(A person represents another, *A*)

A is a natural person

A is not a natural person
("fictional" personation)

A is imagined / not imagined as a person

E.g. Agamemnon

Hospitals, bridges, etc.

Figure 7.1 Personation in Hobbes' *Leviathan*

PERSONS AND REPRESENTATION

Suppose we start with the familiar situation, where one group of people represents another politically. It might seem that this was a case of artificial personation, the sole difference from the examples given so far being that actor and author are groups of persons rather than individuals. Unfortunately, Hobbes' theory of representation in *Leviathan* is more involved than this. There are also some false trails, which can lead the reader away from the main outlines of the theory. One of these is whether the artificial person is to be identified with the representative or the represented. I deal with this first.

As Hobbes remarks earlier, it is 'the unity of the representer, not the unity of the represented, that makes the person one' (*L* 114). The identity of artificial persons comes from the representative. This is still clearer with what I have called fictional personation, where the author is not a natural person at all. In chapter 29 Hobbes bemoans the idea of 'mixed monarchy', in which the powers of legislation, taxation and military command are divided between different agencies. '[T]he truth is', Hobbes says, 'that it is not one independent commonwealth, but three independent factions; nor one representative person, but three' (*L* 228). It is precisely because the person's identity depends on the 'representer' that dividing powers between (say) monarch, parliament and judiciary – three competing representatives of the people – creates three persons, even if the group they represent – the people taken as a whole – is the same in each case. If the identity of these representers were determined by the represented, the subjects, they would be the same person. More important, Hobbes' polemical point against dividing sovereignty would lose its force.

Conversely, distinct representatives create distinct artificial persons. This is so even if they represent the same natural person. So the artificial person created if I am represented by my lawyer, say, is different from the one created if I am represented by an estate agent. In chapter 16 Hobbes says that 'it is the representer that bears the person, and but one person: *and unity cannot otherwise be understood in multitude*' (*L* 114; emphasis added). It would be disastrous for Hobbes' theory if the identity of artificial persons were to derive from the person represented, since this would mean that any number of different representatives could be separately authorised by the same individual and then be the same artificial person. This enables Hobbes to escape an otherwise baffling problem in his theory, as we shall see.

So, given the classification of persons as natural and artificial in chapter 16, what kind of person is involved in political representation? Hobbes may have found this a hard question to answer. On the one hand it seems clear that the person in political representation cannot be a natural person. The main reason for this is that the representative and represented are not identical with one another, as they are in the case of natural personation – or at least they need not be, and in most cases will not be: the sovereign and the people are not identical with one another, except in the limiting case where the sovereign consists of the people taken together – that is, the people represents itself. So, it would appear, the sovereign cannot be seen as a natural person, that is, as a self-representer.

On the other hand, the remaining possibility, that the sovereign is an artificial person, also faces difficulties. If the sovereign as political representative is an artificial person, the represented must, on the definitions given above, be either a natural person or some other thing. With what might be called *direct* artificial personation, one natural person represents another such person. But we have already seen that the 'state' is not a natural person: it is itself an artificial construction, created by the individual wills of those who submit to the sovereign. So, it seems, the 'state' cannot be an artificial person.

However, there is the further possibility that the 'state' itself is not a natural person but a fiction. If so, then what is represented, the 'state', is not a person at all. It is rather an imaginary object, perhaps one that is imagined to be a person in an analogous way to that in which Agamemnon is imagined to be one. But difficulties persist. As we have seen, we can regard what is represented in fictional personation as something that is real but not a person, such as a bridge, or as something that is thought of as a person but is not real, such as Agamemnon. But either way, the represented or 'author' whom the sovereign represents is not a real, i.e. a natural, person. This means that what is represented in fictional personation is not capable of doing the things that only real persons do. But Hobbes' account of authorisation requires that the people as a collectivity – that is, the 'state' – is thought of as acting in certain ways, primarily by authorising its own representation by the sovereign.

So it seems Hobbes is in trouble whether we see political representation as involving natural, artificial or fictional personation. Is there any way out?

UNRAVELLING THE KNOT

It may be that Hobbes was aware of these difficulties and could not see a way through them; perhaps, on the other hand, he did not see political personation as problematic. At any rate, he returned to the subject of personation in *De homine*, where he presented a simplified version of the English *Leviathan* account. There he distinguishes between natural and fictional persons, and the latter now subsumes the category of artificial persons. In the Latin *Leviathan* of 1668, he seems to streamline the theory further, dropping the talk of artificial and fictional personation completely:

> A person is he who acts in his own name, or another's: if in his own name, he is his own, or a natural person; if in another's name, he is a person representative of him in whose name he acts.[3]

So now Hobbes simply distinguishes acting in one's own name, or in the name of another. The most obvious explanation for this is that Hobbes came to believe that his earlier account was unsatisfactory. However, the problem remains, given that none of the varieties of personation distinguished in the English *Leviathan* seems fitted for the task of modelling political representation.

Natural persons are self-representers, individuals acting on their own behalf. They have two aspects: as representative and as represented. But how can the 'state' authorise its own representation by the sovereign, if it does not exist as a real, that is to say a natural, person? The key to unravelling the problem is to abandon the attempt to identify the person with either the represented or the representative. Recall that according to the theory,

> *Artificial persons* are natural persons who represent either other natural persons, or things that are not natural persons.

That is, in cases of artificial personation both representative and represented are natural persons, as when I am represented in court by a lawyer. We can amplify the definition of artificial persons as follows. If something is an artificial person, then there are two natural persons P and A, such that P represents A. In artificial personation, one natural person represents another.

But, of course, each natural person is, in other contexts, a self-representer, that is, someone who represents him- or herself. So we can say that in artificial personation, one self-representer is represented by another. Artificial persons thus embody a dual level of representation. But we should note that in Hobbes' reformulation above from the Latin text, he no longer states that the represented is a person: all he says is that there is a representative, who is a person, and that there is 'another' (*alienum*), whom this person represents. This does not commit itself on whether 'another' is also a natural person. The problem in the case of political representation is that it is far from clear in what sense the 'state' itself can be said to be a natural person. Rather it seems like an artefact, constructed from the distinct wills of individuals who agree to submit to the sovereign.

Suppose then that political representation is an example of what I have called 'fictional' personation. That is, the sovereign, a natural person, represents something that isn't a person, namely the 'state'. But this faces several problems. One is that, as Hobbes makes clear in chapter 19, the sovereign need not be a natural person: it may equally be a 'sovereign assembly'. In this case neither the representer nor the represented is a natural person. And, as already mentioned, if the author is not a natural person it is incapable of doing what only a natural person can do, such as authorising others to act on one's behalf.

However, one should hold onto the idea that the state may be imagined or thought of as a person, in the same way that one can imagine that a fictional character such as Agamemnon is a person. Where the represented is not a natural person, the representative can provide the attributes of thought and action, with their attendant ideas of responsibility, which would otherwise be absent. In other words, the representative – that is, in political representation, the sovereign – gives the state personality. By acting in certain ways, the sovereign behaves as if it had been authorised by someone else, an author.

Instead of seeing the 'state' as given in advance of the agreement to submit to the sovereign, we should think of it as something that becomes a person in the very act of representation. It is not that the person of the commonwealth, the political association seen as a single agent – in other words, what Hobbes calls the 'state' – already exists and then authorises the sovereign to represent it. Instead, we infer the existence of the person of the 'state' from the fact that there is a sovereign who represents it. In a passage that I have already quoted, Hobbes says that it is 'the unity of the representer, not the unity of the represented, that makes the person one' (L 114). The person of the 'state' is created in the act of being represented by a sovereign. Once again we find that it makes more sense not to imagine that everyone first comes together, and then authorises the sovereign to act for them: instead, the theory works retrospectively. Hobbes is offering a way of re-imagining an existing political reality, where the sovereign already wields power.

The key idea is a familiar one. We can see this from the analogy with an actor who represents Agamemnon, or some other fictional person. Of course Agamemnon is a figment of the imagination, and so in reality he has no thoughts, feelings or actions. But in the theatre we take the words and deeds of the actor playing him to represent Agamemnon's own thoughts, feelings and actions. We have no trouble in understanding – and even in believing for the duration of the performance, by the process known as the suspension of disbelief – that this non-existent person is given life by a dramatic representation. There is in fact a dual fiction here: it is imagined, first, that a person, Agamemnon, who in fact does not exist, is a real person; second, that the person, who is in fact an actor playing the part of Agamemnon, is that real person.

But the dramatic representation achieved by actors in plays only offers an imperfect analogy with political representation. The difference is that the dramatic character Agamemnon remains a fiction, and we suspend our disbelief only for the duration of the play. His thoughts and actions are not real. By contrast, Hobbes is urging that we really believe that, through the sovereign, we as the people think and act. The 'people' is created in the very act of being represented politically, whereas actors do not create the personae they represent on stage, as Hobbes makes explicit by saying that the commonwealth is 'a real unity' of all the people who are represented.[4]

The people as a distinct agent – the one that Hobbes calls the 'state' – does not exist until the sovereign comes to represent it. More specifically, it is brought into being by the resolution of individuals to submit to a sovereign who represents the people. The person represented by the sovereign could thus be thought of as an imputed person, one whose existence is inferred from the fact that there is a representative, for whose actions this imputed person is to be held responsible. The fact that this latter person does not exist before the agreement to form a commonwealth does not create any special problems. The representative relation comes into being with the persons between whom it holds. So it seems Hobbes can say that the sovereign bears the person of those whom it represents, despite the fact that this person does not exist before the agreement that sets up this representative relation.

Political representation thus involves an act of collective imagination, by which the 'people' is thought of as coming into being through the very fact of being represented. The reason for engaging in such an act is that it enables us to make sense of things that would otherwise be incomprehensible. Of course the person of the 'state' is an imaginary being, in the sense that it exists only insofar as it is imagined to do so. But this is true of many other things that naturally do not exist – at least if that means that they exist only because humans have invented them, such as rights of way, exchange rates, the 24-hour clock, or the rules of chess.

This also means that we can dispense with the idea that sovereign power must be a relation in which one natural person represents another, as in the direct form of artificial personation. One could of course insist that what is represented is not a person at all, as in Hobbes' definition of fictional personation. But whether we think of the represented as one aspect of a natural person, or of a fictional person, its status as represented depends on its will being articulated by a representative. By itself, purely as represented, it is not a natural person. But we can think of the amalgam, the representative plus represented, as a natural person – as it might be called, the-people-as-represented-by-the-sovereign. Just as one can think of individual human adults as natural persons because they are self-representing, one can think of the authorisation of the sovereign to act for the people as an act of self-representation. In the terminology I used earlier, sovereign and people are two aspects of a single being. It is not that the sovereign represents the people, as a separate natural person; the sovereign is the people, providing it with the only identity it has.

If this is what Hobbes is doing, it is an astonishing move. It marks the fruition of the seemingly throwaway comment made by Hobbes at the very start of *Leviathan*, which I noted in Chapter 3. There, the very distinction between the natural and the artificial dissolves, as Hobbes describes nature itself as artificially created (by God). By allowing itself to be represented by the sovereign, the people makes itself into a natural person, identical with its political representative. It makes the decision to regard itself as naturally one with the sovereign. So sovereign and 'state' are two aspects of a unitary natural person, just as we can think of an adult human being as at once representer, and represented. As a result, the authorisation of the sovereign by the people acting as a collectivity is in fact a case of self-representation. Despite appearances, we can think of the-people-as-represented-by-the-sovereign as a natural person. Thus what might seem a quite artificial act – the joint agreement of individuals to accept somebody as their representative – creates something that can be seen, according to Hobbes' schema, as natural. Artifice becomes nature, and the line between the natural and the artificial dissolves, just as Hobbes in effect promises at the start of the book.

This novel theory of political representation parallels a revolutionary account of the Christian doctrine of the Trinity, which is dealt with in passing in the English *Leviathan* but figures directly in the Appendix to the Latin version of the book. In the Appendix to the Latin *Leviathan*, Hobbes seems to compound the offence by reinterpreting the Christian doctrine of the Trinity using the theory of personation – so that Jesus Christ is 'one person' with God in much the same sense that a legal representative is 'one' with his client. Since, as we have seen, persons are differentiated by those who 'bear' them – that is, when *P* represents or bears the person of *A*, this person is distinct from the one borne by a second representer, *P**, even if *P** is also representing *A* – God is one person as represented by Jesus, and another as represented by the Holy Spirit. Unfortunately for Hobbes, he also says that God is a separate person as represented by Moses, as well, and by other biblical prophets, with the consequence that God is not merely three persons, as Christian orthodoxy requires, but as many persons as can be said to have 'borne the person' of God in scripture through prophesy or other signs of having received a commission from the Almighty.

The theory of sovereignty creates other theological problems, from an orthodox Christian standpoint. Hobbes' blurring of the line between the natural and the artificial is something only God, as the creator, can do. One might say that the people creates itself by creating its own creator, the Leviathan or 'mortal God' (*L* 120). In so doing it imitates – or indeed usurps – the immortal God. Indeed, Hobbes, says in chapter 17 that to describe the sovereign as a 'mortal god' rather than as 'Leviathan' is 'to speak more reverently' of it, but in fact (as Hobbes probably realised) the reverse could well be said to be true: mere humans commit the sin of hubris or pride in thinking that they have the powers that, for orthodox Christians, only God can command. It is little wonder that Hobbes' Christian contemporaries took offence at his presumption.

To sum up, the 'people' is indeed a figment, a fiction, before it is created through the act of political representation. This might naturally lead one to conclude that sovereignty in *Leviathan* must exemplify fictional personation.[5] It is indeed true that, as Hobbes says, the people has no identity before it is represented by the agent or agency that bears its person, namely the sovereign. But, once the people is represented by the sovereign, it comes into being as the 'state' – the person whom the sovereign bears. And, since sovereign and people, representative and represented, are dual aspects of one and the same person, we can think of the people as represented by the sovereign as a natural person.

UNITARY SOVEREIGNTY

Hobbes thinks of the people not just as authorising the sovereign to act on their behalf, but as identical with the sovereign under the category *person*. This does not mean, as we shall see in Chapter 8, that the people and sovereign are identical in all respects, any more than a lawyer and the lawyer's client are identical in all respects. Given Hobbes' general account of responsibility and representation, however, it does mean that the people is ultimately responsible for the sovereign's actions, just as a natural person is generally taken to be responsible for his or her actions. For this reason, the acts of the sovereign are in fact acts of the people, as Hobbes is keen to stress.

As we have seen, the sovereign does not directly represent each of the people taken separately. Instead, the agreement to establish civil government merges each individual into a single, corporate person. The sovereign does not represent each of us taken individually. What the sovereign represents, according to Hobbes, is a single collective individual, composed of all the persons who submit to the power of the sovereign. So the author could be called a logical individual, which can be thought of as authorising the sovereign to act on its behalf, in much the same way as that in which corporations have legal personality. At the same time, we can talk of it as if it were a real individual, which has certain intentions and interests, certain rights and obligations, which takes responsibility for its actions, and so on.

The introduction of the 'state' as an intermediary between the individuals and sovereign might appear pointless. Why not just say that the sovereign represents individuals – which Hobbes sometimes refers to as 'the multitude' (e.g. *L* 73)? The answer is that he had to find a way of bringing together the different wills of individuals into the unified political will implemented by the sovereign. Hobbes remarks of the interlocking set of agreements by which the sovereign is thought of as being created that

> [t]his is the generation of that great Leviathan ... and in him consists the essence of the commonwealth; which (to define it) is *one person, of whose acts a great multitude, by mutual covenants, have made themselves every one the author* ... And he that carries this person is called sovereign, and said to have sovereign power; and everyone besides, his subject.
>
> (*L* 120–21)

This offers an elaborate conception of political agency. We can begin from the undifferentiated mass or 'multitude', and note that, if it is viewed as a mass, it is not a person at all, though it is obviously composed of persons. Then there is the possibility that this mass becomes a single person – a corporate individual. But Hobbes is careful not to say simply that the sovereign directly represents this mass. He says instead that the mass becomes a single person through the act of covenanting or agreeing to do so, and *that* person authorises the sovereign to represent it.

The two-stage theory of representation is fundamental to *Leviathan*'s conception of sovereignty, and marks an advance on earlier published versions of his political theory. Hobbes infers from this conception that the people cannot object to the sovereign's actions, since this involves a kind of contradiction. The sovereign's actions are really the people's actions, so if I as a member of the people object to what the sovereign does, I object, effectively, to myself. That is, I contradict my own will: 'because every subject', Hobbes says, is 'author of all the actions and judgments of the sovereign instituted, it follows that whatever he does, it can be no injury to any of his subjects' (*L* 124).

This is a very controversial feature of the theory. It says, in effect, that nobody who has accepted the sovereign's power can object to anything that the sovereign does in his or her name. Hobbes' reasons for thinking this may be presented as follows:

(1) Whatever you freely consent to cannot be an injury to you.
(2) You authorise the sovereign to act for you, so that whatever the sovereign does is authorised by you.
(3) To authorise something is to consent to it.
(4) You consent to whatever the sovereign does (by (2) and (3)).
(5) Whatever the sovereign does cannot be an injury to you (by (1) and (4)).

Some people would dispute (1), sometimes referred to by its Latin translation, *volenti non fit iniuria*, a principle in common law, for example in defences against tort proceedings. Many people, moreover, would dispute that legitimate government requires authorising each and every act of the sovereign, as (2) claims. Even Hobbes himself needs to allow some exceptions to (2), since I am not bound not to resist if the sovereign tries to kill me, for example as punishment for a capital crime – or at least, my having consented to the relevant capital statute, by authorising the sovereign who enacted it, does not preclude my withholding my consent to its implementation. Hobbes relies in other cases on the idea that to oppose the sovereign, having earlier authorised it, amounts to a contradiction; but it seems this is not so when it comes to implementing capital punishment. It would be possible to argue that since the right to resist violent death has not been transferred, it lies outside the set of powers that are granted to the sovereign on authorisation. But Hobbes does not in fact deny that the sovereign may legitimately inflict capital punishment.

It is important to Hobbes' account that all cases of personhood, natural or otherwise, involve the giving up of rights. The underlying thought is that I cannot authorise you to do something on my behalf if I am not entitled to do it myself. For example, I cannot give you an admission ticket to a film, that is, a right to see the film, unless I possess the ticket in the first place (of course, I could have stolen the ticket, but then I will not be entitled to it, and I cannot transfer the entitlement to someone else by giving them the ticket). The most obvious case, again, is that of natural persons. Where A and B are identical (that is, "A" and "B" are two names for the same person), A cannot authorise B to do what A has no right to do, since B cannot then acquire the right from A. Hobbes says:

'by "authority" is always understood a right of doing any act: and "done by authority", done by commission or licence from him whose right it is' (*L* 112).

The person represented by the sovereign is thought of as coming into being via a covenant or agreement between the subjects. As already noted, Hobbes is very clear that the sovereign makes no contract with the subjects: 'the right of bearing the person of them all, is given to him they make sovereign by covenant only of one to another, and not of him to any of them' (*L* 122). Hobbes goes on to argue that no agreement can be made with the sovereign, because any person who, having made such an agreement, later accused the sovereign of breaching it, would in effect be accusing himself, since the sovereign's actions are his own (*L* 123). More obviously, agreements have no force without the 'sword', so since the sovereign has a monopoly of force, no breach by the sovereign would be actionable.

Hobbes aimed to repudiate the idea that government must rest on a contract between ruler and ruled. He does not dismiss the idea that there may be an agreement, in the form of submission, between conqueror and conquered. But Hobbes' main objection to this idea is that it leaves the door open to voiding the contract when the ruled think that their rulers have breached its terms. Even when the sovereign agrees to give protection in exchange for submission, this undertaking is not subject to any external authority who could determine whether the sovereign is in breach of the agreement: if there were, this other authority would effectively be sovereign instead. Since for Hobbes the author is a purely imputed person whose existence depends on the contract itself, this possibility cannot arise: the person in question disappears at the moment of breach. To void a supposed contract between ruler and ruled would, then, be an act of self-destruction by the 'people': it would annihilate the very thing that gives the people its unity.

It is important to appreciate that the agreement need not be thought of as occurring prospectively, rather than retrospectively. As I argued in Chapter 6, the state of nature makes prospective agreement more or less impossible. For example, the agreement is supposed to be one made by 'every man with every man' (*L* 120), but this could hardly occur literally even in the most favourable circumstances, let alone the state of nature. However, Hobbes takes care to stress that it is 'as if' everyone agrees with everybody else to set up a sovereign, not that they really do so. Indeed, by imagining that this is the case and acting accordingly, everyone can make it true that they are agreeing to this arrangement.

So the sovereign can 'bear the person' of the state without entering into an agreement to do so. It is just that the sovereign's actions are, according to the terms of the agreement, taken as those of the people. As I have argued, the represented person comes into being at the very moment that a sovereign represents that person. It may of course be unclear when that point has been reached. But Hobbes clearly thinks that in many cases it is obvious both that there is a sovereign, and who that sovereign is:

> I know not how this so manifest a truth should of late be so little observed; that in a monarchy, he that had the sovereignty from a descent of 600 years, was alone called 'sovereign', had the title of 'majesty' from every one of his subjects and was unquestionably taken by them for their King, was notwithstanding never considered as their representative.
>
> (L 130)

The question now is why Hobbes introduces into his theory an elaborate theoretical apparatus that was absent from *De cive* and the *Elements of Law*. He was certainly concerned to produce a unified account of sovereignty. Against 1640s Parliamentarian writers such as Henry Parker, who believed that sovereignty should be shared between the monarch and Parliament, Hobbes was concerned to show that sovereignty could not be divided between different individuals or bodies. And the account of representation is meant to show why this must be so: whoever bears a person (whether natural or otherwise) must be regarded as a logical individual, incapable of subdivision. So the fact that the bearer of the person of the commonwealth is a person is what invests political authority with unity – with the unity of the representative, not the represented.

In both the English and Latin versions of *Leviathan* Hobbes is careful throughout to leave it open whether the sovereign is an individual, or an assembly.[6] He argues against the widely held view that though the sovereign is greater than each of the subjects taken individually, the sovereign is less than the mass of subjects taken as a whole. The absurdity of this view only remains obscured when the talk is not of 'an assembly' (*L* 128). The assembly may be the people as a whole, viewed under a certain aspect, rather as the modern House of Commons in the United Kingdom Parliament appears under a different aspect when it transforms itself for certain legislative purposes into a Committee of the Whole House. There also remains the theoretical possibility not merely of representative, but of direct democracy.

As Hobbes says, with reference to the then-recent civil wars:

> a kingdom divided in itself cannot stand. For unless this division [of powers, regarding e g. church government, judicial decisions, tax-raising, etc.] into opposite armies can never happen. If there had not first been an opinion received of the greatest part of England that these powers were divided between the King, and the Lords, and the House of Commons, the people had never been divided, and fallen into this civil war.
>
> (*L* 127)

In support of the claim that sovereignty must be indivisible, Hobbes gives what Jean Hampton (1986, 98) calls the 'regress' argument.[7] The argument goes as follows. In a political system, the power wielded by any person or body is either unlimited or limited: if it is unlimited, it is absolute; but if it is limited, it can only be limited by the power of another agent; when we ask about this other agent's power, it will either be unlimited, or ultimately limited by some yet other agent whose power is unlimited. So in this chain, we always end up with an agent whose power is unlimited, namely the absolute sovereign.

Hobbes gives what may be a compressed version of this argument in chapter 19:

that king whose power is limited is not superior to him or them that have the power to limit it. And he that is not superior, is not supreme – that is to say, not sovereign. The sovereignty therefore was always in that assembly which had the right to limit him.

(L 134)

For any agent exercising political power, we can always ask whether that power is limited, and if so by whom; by which process we must eventually arrive at an unlimited power, that is, the sovereign power.

This looks like a necessary truth. We must come to a point where, at the end of the chain, the sovereign power is unlimited. However, Maurice Goldsmith argued that Hobbes' theory of sovereignty contains a 'fallacy' (1980). His argument is based on a distinction between what is involved on the one hand in sovereignty's being absolute, and in its being embodied in a 'closed' system on the other. A political system may be closed – it yields a determinate and final outcome – even though no single person or body within the system wields absolute power. We could compare systems for the administration of justice: while it is true, once the legal processes, including for example appeal or retrial, have been exhausted, the outcome of the process is final, this does not mean that any one individual or body within the process, such as a judge or court, has dictatorial control over the outcome.

Goldsmith's point is that while it is a necessary or 'analytical' truth that a sovereign system is closed, it is much more contentious to say that political instability will follow unless a single person or body monopolises power. In effect Goldsmith accuses Hobbes of smuggling in the second, contentious claim in the guise of the first, necessary one.

The regress argument says that we have to go up the chain of command to find where power lies, and it is a necessary truth that the chain must have an end. Whatever lies at the end of the chain is sovereign, with absolute power. In effect, Goldsmith replies: 'Yes, but that doesn't mean that any one person or body necessarily stands at the end of the chain. There may be procedures regulating the interactions of several or many such agents, none of which has unlimited power.' Political systems such as that of the

US aim to balance different branches of the constitution, such as the legislature and judiciary, are sometimes described as having these countervailing elements, in order to ensure that no single branch monopolises power.

In response to this objection, Hobbes can, it seems, offer three possible replies:

(a) to identify the absolute sovereign with some particular agent within the system, who shares power with other agents;
(b) to identify the sovereign with the system as a whole;
(c) to reject both of these identifications, and insist that without any unlimited power, we have a state of war, in Hobbes' special sense of that term.

Possibility (a) seems to be untenable on the grounds that it runs directly counter to what Hobbes says. He repeatedly argues that the sovereign must be all-powerful within the system, and not simply one who shares power with others. So to identify the sovereign with an individual, such as the modern US president, who works within a system as an extremely powerful but not omnipotent individual, seems to fly in the face of Hobbes' insistence that the sovereign must be all-powerful.

The second possibility, (b), also fails to give Hobbes what he wants, since a US-like system internalises the very checks on power that he aims to rule out. For example, Hobbes emphasises that 'the right of judicature' (*L* 125), that is, the right to resolve disputes about law, remains with the sovereign, whereas in the US system this right ultimately lies in the hands of the US Supreme Court. So, although outputs from the system are 'closed' in the sense of being final, this does not preclude the balancing of power between different agencies within the system.

It may seem that possibility (c) is hard to swallow, but Hobbes might press the question whether the procedural rules really do determine how outcomes are produced. Who enforces the rules? If there is really nobody who does this, then the different constituents of the constitution are in a state of war. On the other hand, if there is someone who enforces them, there is an absolute ruler after all. The cost of accepting this, for Hobbes, would be that the absence of a sovereign in his sense would be consistent with a high level of political stability: it would not necessitate the dire consequences set out in *Leviathan* chapter 13.

But, as we saw in Chapter 4, aspects of the state of war persist in any case at all times, even within an established political authority. This is because of the natural limits on political power. These limits apply even to certain features of the relation between sovereign and subjects, in the fact that the latter cannot be made to renounce their right to self-preservation, and that there is no contract between sovereign and subjects. One possibility is that the subjects may be in a state of war even though they believe that they are subject to government. The effects of the state of war are felt in international relations, in stateless territories and in a multitude of circumstances where the political authority cannot impose its will.

The state of nature, as a state of 'war', thus continues in the commonwealth. Life under the sovereign – the civil state, or state of peace – is temporary and frail. In his discussion of the commonwealth, Hobbes displays a constant awareness of its mortality. Leviathan is 'a mortal God' (L 120); without its fundamental laws, 'the commonwealth fails, and is utterly dissolved' (L 200), and in fact 'nothing can be immortal, which mortals make' (L 221). Chapter 29 pursues an extended metaphor of illness in identifying the 'infirmities' or 'diseases' of commonwealths (L 221; 228). The commonwealth dies when it succumbs to civil or foreign war, 'which expiring, the members are governed by it [the sovereign] no more than the carcass of a man by his departed (though immortal) soul' (L 230).

Prime among the infirmities to which political authority is prey is the idea that 'the sovereign power may be divided' (L 225). But, it may be said, it is a fact of history that power may be divided without precipitating political breakdown. In the constitution of ancient Sparta, for instance, power was partitioned between two kings, who reigned simultaneously. How far different persons or bodies within a constitution can share power seems to be an empirical question. If so, it may be said, the possibility of sharing power cannot be ruled out by the regress argument.

In response, Hobbes would presumably counter that trying to 'balance' powers is tantamount to triggering a 'war' between the elements of the constitution. And then he has to say either that one of the elements must come out on top, or else that the war between them will in the long run cause political collapse. '[W]hen men ask, where and when such [supreme] power has by subjects been acknowledged ... one may ask them again, when or where has there been a kingdom long free from sedition and civil war[?]' (L 145). This exemplifies not peace but 'only a cessation of arms ... they live as it were, in the precincts of battle continually' (L 125).

REAL POLITICS?

What room does the theory of sovereignty, and indeed *Leviathan* as a whole, leave for politics? On the face of it, Hobbes has rubbed out politics as we know it in liberal democratic states in its entirety. The sovereign, whether it is a monarch or an assembly, wields absolute power. There is no scope for dissent, let alone organised political dispute. Religion is dictated by the sovereign, as is the content of the law. Nor is there meant to be room for disputes over tax-raising – a long-running bone of contention between Parliament and Charles I. And there would seem to be little space for the notion of a 'loyal opposition' – that is, a party or group that, though opposed to the government, nevertheless upholds the national interest, rather than being a 'fifth column' or 'enemy within'.

However, the picture is slightly more complex than this. It is true that Hobbes does not envisage party competition as we know it in multiparty democracies. But such a model is to some extent anachronistic anyway, since in Hobbes' day politics was not organised along formal party lines. Even so, politics, as a working-through of the colliding interests of different individuals and groups who hold distinct and often conflicting schemes for public policy, was a fact. And, although as we have seen Hobbes concentrates sovereignty in a single assembly or individual, this still leaves room for debate over policy.

He is certainly hostile to 'leagues' (i.e. associations or coalitions) of subjects, regarding them as a danger to the commonwealth

(*L* 164). But at an informal level, at least, Hobbes is prepared to allow for some forms of political activity. An important test case concerns freedom of assembly: if individuals are denied the liberty to assemble to debate questions of policy, politics itself barely exists as part of public life. But Hobbes' stance on freedom of assembly is fairly permissive: '[i]f the occasion be lawful and manifest, the concourse [meeting] is lawful' (*L* 164). He is mindful of the threat posed to public order by large gatherings of people. But he still allows that '[i]t may be lawful for a thousand men to join in a petition to be delivered to a judge or magistrate' (*L* 165).

Leviathan contains a good deal of discussion of political issues, most obviously religious politics. Hobbes also provides, for instance, numerous passages on taxation (e.g. *L* 167, 173, 238–39). Hobbes has his own controversial views on fiscal policy: taxes should be levied at equal rates on all, because everyone equally enjoys the benefits of life under the commonwealth (*L* 238). He also discusses the distribution of wealth, especially land, in chapter 24, arguing that no subject has a right to private property that may not be overridden by the sovereign. He rests his case on the claim that the public good takes precedence over private ownership.

So, contrary to some views (e.g. Macpherson 1962), Hobbes does not envisage a free-for-all in which the market goes more or less unchecked. In fact, he makes express allowance for central intervention in the economy, for example in the regulation of foreign trade (*L* 173). By contrast, insofar as any template for the free market is presented in *Leviathan*, it is the state of nature, where there is no government to regulate economic activity. Admittedly, the state of nature as Hobbes describes it lacks the minimal social cohesion needed to make many market exchanges possible. But he does not think that central intervention is unjustified: on the contrary, it is justified whenever it promotes the common good. For example, Hobbes argues that 'it is necessary that men distribute that which they can spare, and transfer their property therein' (*L* 174); he envisages collective property, that is, the public ownership of assets such as land (*L* 172); ultimately the distribution of private property is made by the sovereign (*L* 125, 172, 173, 225).

By contrast, the sovereign is meant to take a leading role in encouraging commerce and industry (*L* 239). Hobbes says that under the commonwealth, the 'first law' of distributive justice concerns the ownership of land, whereby 'the sovereign assigns to every man a portion, according as he [i.e. the sovereign] and not according as any subject, or any number of them, shall judge agreeable to equity and the common good' (*L* 171). This is, at least in theory, consistent with communism, since individual freehold rights are made subservient to the collective good. Subjects cannot complain about the distribution because the sovereign who makes it 'is understood to do nothing but to the common peace and security' (*L* 172). If everyone has an absolute freehold right in property, 'the sovereign … cannot perform the office they [the subjects] have put him into' (*L* 224; cf. 228).

In *Leviathan* Hobbes also devotes some space to political advice or 'counsel' (chapter 25). First he distinguishes counsel from 'command', which is the mark of law-giving, and accordingly the province of the sovereign (*L* 176–77; see Chapter 8 below). The mark of counsel is that, while also in the imperative mood, it aims only at the good of the person to whom it is given (*L* 176). It requires 'great knowledge of the disposition of mankind, of the rights of government, and of the nature of equity, law, justice, and honour … and of the strength, commodities, place, both of their own country, and their neighbours' (*L* 180). Again here Hobbes is troubled by the danger that advice will be tainted by self-interest and factionalism. This is the charge, familiar from modern politics, that arguments purportedly based on the public interest are in fact self-serving.

Beyond these manifestations, however, Hobbes seems to allow scope only for administration. Even in a monarchy, there need to be 'public ministers' (*L* 166), who are charged with such duties as regional government, tax collection, levying militias, instructing people about their duty to obey the sovereign, administering justice and representing the commonwealth abroad (*L* 167–69). All these tasks however involve what would be regarded as administration rather than political activity, at least if that means deliberating over policy.

It is fair to say that for Hobbes, as for many other political philosophers, the aim of theory is as far as possible to close down the space for politics.[8] Individuals are swayed by passion rather than reason (L 131), by bad definitions or by reasoning from false premises (L 73). Hobbes makes a sustained attempt to banish most features of politics from human life, by quashing the dissension that inevitably results from free thought and discussion. At the same time, politics continually intrudes, or threatens to intrude, into the settled order of the commonwealth. For Hobbes, politics treads a precariously thin line between security and war.

This ambivalence towards politics is reflected in his double-minded attitude towards rhetoric. In the 'Review, and Conclusion', for instance, Hobbes says that '[t]here is nothing I distrust more than my elocution [i.e. eloquence, or verbal facility]' (L 490). In politics, rhetoric is not merely harmlessly absurd, but also liable to foment civil unrest by disseminating opinions as if they were truths. Among the failings of 'sovereign assemblies' is that their members are 'not moved by their own sense, but by the eloquence of another' (L 181). He often expresses his distrust of rhetorical figures such as metaphor (e.g. L 35, L 54).

Despite these strictures on rhetoric, Hobbes finds he cannot disown it. He is caught in a kind of pragmatic contradiction in *Leviathan*. His civil science aspires to the demonstrative certainty of geometry, and ideally would attain this. But unlike the subject matter of what we now call the natural sciences, the theory applies to persuadable beings who can reason as to how they should act – and can therefore falsify the theory by failing to do what the theory predicts. Hence the need to augment scientific demonstration with persuasion.

As Tom Sorell remarks, 'Hobbes' use of cause-effect reasoning is [such] that at the same time as it tells us something about the effects of the passions, it engages our passions and motivates us to inhibit those effects' (Sorell 1990b, 107). That is, the need for persuasion means that rhetoric is indispensable. Even a political philosophy avowedly based on reason, like Hobbes', cannot abjure it. And indeed *Leviathan* is replete with rhetorical devices (Skinner 1996). So we find Hobbes confessing that 'reason and eloquence (though not perhaps in the natural sciences, yet in the moral) may stand very well together' (*L* 483–84). Even political philosophy has to rely on the political methods of persuasion – that is, rhetoric. The ineliminability of politics reaches back into political philosophy itself.

CONCLUSION

In this chapter we have examined *Leviathan*'s theory of political representation. We have trodden a rather winding path, so I shall summarise the main landmarks in the journey. Hobbes stipulates that the sovereign – the person or body who wields supreme political power – represents individual subjects not directly, but by representing a corporate individual, which he calls the 'state'. In chapter 16 he distinguishes two main varieties of personation, corresponding to different ways in which the relation of representation can be understood: natural persons, where somebody represents themselves, and artificial persons, where one natural person represents another, or a thing other than a natural person.

We can then ask which of these forms of personation applies to the sovereign's representation of the people. I argued that we can rule out artificial personation where that requires that what is represented is a natural person, as the 'state', the thing represented, is not a natural person, but a construct. It might seem, therefore, that what I earlier called 'fictional' personation captures the relation we are seeking, since on the argument just given the 'state' is a represented thing, which taken literally, is a fiction. However, there is no pre-existing thing that the sovereign represents: what is represented, the people, is created in the very act of creating the representer or sovereign.

Of course, this leaves it open that what is represented is a fiction, just as a stage actor who plays the part of Agamemnon represents a fiction. But Hobbes insists that what is represented is real: the person of the 'state' is 'a *real* unity of them all, in one and the same person', as he stresses (*L* 120; emphasis added). I suggested that there is no insuperable obstacle to seeing political representation as an instance of natural personation. The sovereign-and-people, taken together, is a natural person, seen from one aspect as the representative, and from another as represented. It is, in the image with which Hobbes opens *Leviathan*, a person that we create, through a collective act of imagination. Political authority involves self-representation. Unlike a fictional object, the political author is thus self-created by the very act of being represented, just as natural persons create themselves through acting as their own representative.

Finally, I argued that sovereignty must be indivisible for Hobbes, but that the 'regress' argument has to bear too much weight. His argument must be that with divided powers, there is no reasonable expectation that constitutional breakdown will not occur, and thus the state of 'war' persists. This is why he is at pains to exclude politics, as we would recognise it. Nonetheless, Hobbes knows the risk of 'intestine discord' remains ineradicable.

FURTHER READING

Leviathan, chapter 16; chapters 18–19; chapters 22–24; 'Review, and Conclusion'

HOBBES AND REPRESENTATION

Pioneering work on Hobbes' theory of representation is contained in Hanna Pitkin, 'Hobbes' Concept of Representation – Part I', *American Political Science Review* 58 (1964), 328–40; and 'Hobbes' Concept of Representation – Part II', *American Political Science Review* 58 (1964), 902–18. See also Pitkin's *The Concept of Representation* (Berkeley, CA: University of California Press, 1967). A more philosophical treatment of the concept of representation, both in general and in specific relation to Hobbes, appears in two articles by David Copp: 'Collective Actions and Secondary Actions', *American Philosophical Quarterly* 16 (1979), 177–86; and 'Hobbes on Artificial Persons and Collective Actions', *Philosophical Review* 89 (1980), 579–606.

SKINNER ON SOVEREIGNTY

I have interpreted Hobbes in a way that casts doubt on Quentin Skinner's interpretation of *Leviathan*'s theory of sovereignty, the main point of difference being that in my view Skinner is mistaken in thinking that Hobbes regarded the person in personation as identifiable determinately with either the representer or the represented, and further mistaken in reading certain passages in *Leviathan* as making the relevant identification with the represented; Hobbes in my view is less concerned with identity than with differentiation, and what differentiates persons is distinctness of representers.

See Skinner, 'Hobbes and the Purely Artificial Personality of the State', *Journal of Political Philosophy* 7 (1999), 1–29, reprinted in Skinner's *Visions of Politics*, vol. III: *Hobbes and civil science* (Cambridge: Cambridge University Press, 2002), ch. 6. See especially p. 189: 'Hobbes ... makes it clear that his preference is for using the terminology of artificial persons to describe persons who are represented'. Although Skinner cites the passage in his own support, Hobbes says what amounts to the opposite at *L* 338, where he says that 'God is one person as represented by Moses, and another person as represented by his son the Christ.' Another decisive statement of the same view of personation appears at *L* 228, where Hobbes is discussing the evils of dividing political representation among different agencies:

> if the King bear the person of the people, and the general assembly bear also the person of the people, and another assembly bear the person of a part of the people, they are not one person, nor one sovereign, but three persons, and three sovereigns.

But Skinner's work on Hobbes' theory of sovereignty remains of fundamental importance. Skinner re-examines more sympathetically than Pitkin or Copp Hobbes' conception of representation, arguing that for Hobbes the person of the state must be seen as 'purely artificial'. I believe however that the text of *Leviathan* decisively refutes Skinner's claim that the identity of artificial persons for Hobbes was reducible to that of the person represented rather than the representer.

The most illuminating commentator on Hobbes' theory of personhood, as it features in the theory of representation given in *Leviathan*, is David Runciman; see *Pluralism and the Personality of the State* (Cambridge: Cambridge University Press, 1997), ch. 2. For Runciman's critique of Skinner, see 'What Kind of Person Is Hobbes' State? A reply to Skinner', *Journal of Political Philosophy* 8 (2000), 268–78. See also Runciman, 'The Concept of the State: The sovereignty of a fiction', in Quentin Skinner and Bo Stråth (eds), *States and Citizens: History, theory, prospects* (Cambridge: Cambridge University Press, 2003), ch. 3. Christine Chwaszcza argues that the sovereign is to be seen as an office rather than as an abstract person in her 'The Seat of Sovereignty: Hobbes on the artificial personality of the commonwealth or state', *Hobbes Studies* 25, no. 1 (2012), 123–42.

CRITICS OF HOBBES ON SOVEREIGNTY

For a critique of Hobbes' theory, see the Pitkin and Copp articles cited above, and Maurice Goldsmith, 'Hobbes' "Mortall God": Is there a fallacy in Hobbes' theory of sovereignty?', *History of Political Thought* 1 (1980), 33–50. Deborah Baumgold defends Hobbes' position in her *Hobbes' Political Theory* (Cambridge: Cambridge University Press, 1988), ch. 4.

Further discussion of Goldsmith's criticisms can be found in Jean Hampton, *Hobbes and the Social Contract Tradition* (Cambridge: Cambridge University Press, 1986), 98ff.; see also Edwin Curley, 'Reflections on Hobbes: Recent work on his moral and political philosophy', *Journal of Philosophical Research* 15 (1990), 169–250. For further criticism, arguing that Hobbes must see that contract as being made with the sovereign if he is to be consistent, see S.W. Wood, 'Confusions in Hobbes' Analysis of the Civil Sovereign', *Southwestern Journal of Philosophy* 2 (1971), 195–203.

HOBBES AND POLITICS

On the details of political and institutional organisation, see Baumgold, *Hobbes' Political Theory*, especially chs 5 and 6. See also her 'Hobbes' Political Sensibility: The menace of political ambition', in Mary Dietz (ed.), *Thomas Hobbes and Political Theory* (Lawrence, KS: University Press of Kansas, 1990). For further details on Hobbesian politics, see Jeremy Waldron, 'Hobbes and the

Principle of Publicity', *Pacific Philosophical Quarterly* 82 (2001), 447–74; and Susan Okin, '"The Soveraign and His Counsellours": Hobbes' re-evaluation of Parliament', *Political Theory* 10 (1982), 49–75. Johann Sommerville, *Thomas Hobbes: Political ideas in historical context* (Basingstoke: Macmillan, 1992), chs 3 to 5, refers the doctrines of *Leviathan* and Hobbes' other political writings to contemporary debates over the locus and divisibility of sovereignty.

LEVIATHAN'S RHETORIC

Skinner

The doyen of the revival of interest in Hobbes' rhetoric has been Quentin Skinner. See Skinner, *Reason and Rhetoric in the Philosophy of Hobbes* (Cambridge: Cambridge University Press, 1996). As noted above, Skinner argues that *Leviathan* marks a dramatic shift from an outright rejection of rhetoric to a qualified espousal of its methods. A useful shorter statement of the main thesis of Skinner's book may be found in Skinner, 'Thomas Hobbes: Rhetoric and the construction of morality', *Proceedings of the British Academy* 76 (1991), 1–61, especially 31–61.

Others

On the rhetoric of *Leviathan*, see also Tom Sorell, 'Hobbes' Persuasive Civil Science', *Philosophical Quarterly* 40, no. 3 (1990), 342–51. An important early statement of the revisionist treatment of rhetoric in *Leviathan* was David Johnston, *The Rhetoric of Leviathan: Thomas Hobbes and the politics of cultural transformation* (Princeton, NJ: Princeton University Press, 1986). F.G. Whelan, 'Language and Its Abuses in Hobbes' Political Philosophy', *American Political Science Review* 75 (1981), 59–75, rejects the view later upheld by Skinner that Hobbes abandons his earlier hostility towards rhetoric in *Leviathan*.

Terence Ball's *Reappraising Political Theory: Revisionist studies in the history of political thought* (Oxford: Clarendon Press, 1996), focuses on Hobbes' attempts to generate a transparent language for philosophical argument and his conventionalist account of the meaning of normative terms.

NOTES

1 See Tuck 1993a, 327. Hobbes does foreshadow a representational theory of roughly this form in *De cive*, ch. 5, §9, where he says (Hobbes 1998, 73) 'a commonwealth then (to define it) is one person whose will by the agreement of several men be taken as the will of them all'. This unitary person seems to be identified with the sovereign. In *Leviathan* however Hobbes says instead that the mass becomes a person, and that person is the one whom the sovereign represents. It could thus be said that the title-page illustration depicts, not the sovereign, but the corporate person (in Hobbes' terminology, the 'state') whom the sovereign represents (recall Figure 2.1).

2 As Noel Malcolm discovered (Malcolm 1981), Hobbes had had his own experience of 'personation', as part of his duties in the Cavendish household. For representative purposes, Hobbes was given a nominal single share in the Virginia Company. He was also used to carrying out other commissions (such as paying bills) on the Cavendishes' behalf.

3 'Persona est is qui suo vel alieno nomine res agit: si suo, persona propria, sive naturalis est; si alieno, persona est ejus, cujus nomine agit, repræsentativa' (Hobbes 1841, vol. IV, 143).

4 Though, even here, actors can create actions through the act of representing them dramatically. So, although an actor can represent an action through mimesis (as in, say, pretending to drink something from a cup), he or she can also represent actions by performing tokens of that very action (such as running across the stage).

5 Of course, if the sovereign is an assembly rather than an individual, the representative will not be a natural person, either. Since Hobbes allows explicitly for this possibility, we have to conclude that he is allowing that political representation may involve neither artificial nor fictional personation, both of which depend on the representative's being a natural person.

6 Hobbes argues, however, in chapter 19 that monarchy is preferable.

7 According to Hampton this argument is to be found in chapters 19, 20, 22 and 29 of *Leviathan*, as well as *De cive*. However, several of the passages she cites (e.g. *L* 144–45, 155–56, 223–24) merely state that the sovereign power is unlimited, and limits the power of subordinate agencies.

8 I explore this theme further in my book *After Politics: The rejection of politics in contemporary liberal philosophy* (Newey 2001).

8

LAW, CRIME, PUNISHMENT

INTRODUCTION

There are two major kinds of law in *Leviathan*: natural law (which *Leviathan* calls the law of nature), and civil law.[1] We encountered natural law in Chapter 4: as its name suggests, it is the law that prevails in the state of nature, that is, when no political authority exists. On the other hand, civil law, which Hobbes discusses in *Leviathan* chapter 26, comprises the laws that obligate those subject to political authority. Without such an authority, there is no civil law.

LAW AS COMMAND

Hobbes' account of civil law in *Leviathan* seems simple enough. He adopts what is sometimes referred to as a *command* theory of law. According to this theory, laws arise as commands: 'it is manifest that law in general is not counsel [i.e. advice], but command' (*L* 183). The identity works both ways, so that anything that counts as law must have been commanded by the sovereign, while whatever the sovereign commands, thereby counts as law. The central contrast here is between law, which commands us to do or to refrain from doing things, and advice or 'counsel'. One of the differences between them, according to Hobbes, is that whereas commands are designed to benefit the commander, advice aims at the benefit not of the adviser, but of the person who is advised (L 176–77). This way of putting it, however, is potentially misleading, since it suggests that the intended beneficiary of civil laws as 'commands' is the commander, that is, the sovereign, whereas Hobbes' whole point is that these laws benefit those who are commanded, the subjects. We can resolve this by bearing in mind that the sovereign acts as the subjects' agent, for their benefit. So in issuing commands, the real commander is the person of the 'state', that is, the subjects.[2]

Commands, unlike advice, must be obeyed. If the person who receives advice ignores it, he or she does so at his or her own risk; for this reason, advice (or 'counsel') cannot be punished (L 177). The mark of a good counsellor is sound judgement (L 52). It is better for the sovereign to hear advice from different counsellors separately, since it is then less likely to be corrupted by the advisers' own interests, and listeners are less prone to be swayed by 'eloquence' instead of sound reasoning (L 181). Though Hobbes does not say so explicitly, the strong implication of his remarks is that counsel is best carried out in a non-public forum, and with a sovereign comprising one person (for which he indicates his preference, L 131–32), or only a few persons, rather than an assembly. The problems that beset mass advice-giving apply equally to the deliberations of a sovereign assembly (L 131, 243).

Of course, not every utterance with the form of a command – that is, in the imperative mood – has the force of law: the person who commands needs to have appropriate authority, and the commands have to be issued as part of a law-making procedure. Hobbes builds on his earlier theory of authorisation to explain what the authority is. The civil law is not merely

a command of any man to any man, but only of him whose command is addressed to one formerly obliged to obey him ... I define civil law in this manner. Civil law is, to every subject, those rules which the commonwealth has commanded him (by word, writing, or other sufficient sign of the will) to make use of, for the distinction of right and wrong, that is to say, of what is contrary, and what is not contrary, to the rule.

(L 183)

The sovereign's commands are rules (Goldsmith 1996, 275). It is not simply a matter of the sovereign's ordering people around. An example of this would be a rule prescribing that drivers keep to the right. This does not command people to drive on the right, because I do not disobey such a command if I choose not to drive at all: the rule tells me what to do if I choose to drive. This is not to say that all rules are conditional in this way – I may simply have to perform certain acts, such as joining the army, if conscripted, or be forbidden to perform others, such as murder. So the rule is what is commanded, but the rule itself may only require that I perform or avoid certain actions if specific conditions are satisfied.

This passage also makes clear that the authority, which by issuing commands compels obedience, is the sovereign. The sovereign, whether it is an individual or an assembly, is thought of as having been set up by the agreement of all the subjects. As we have seen, it follows from this theory that those who are subject to the laws are also the ultimate authors of those laws. Hence a subject who opposes these laws wills a kind of self-contradiction.

THE DILEMMA OF LAW-MAKING

The people are both authors and subjects of the civil law. However, this suggests a dilemma implicit in the theory of authorisation in *Leviathan* chapters 16 to 18, examined in Chapter 7. The theory holds that the ultimate author of the sovereign's acts is the people. As Hobbes himself remarks in *Leviathan* chapter 18, the clearest way to see this is to imagine that the sovereign is the whole people – that is, the people as a body is self-representing. The implication of this is that the person of the sovereign is a natural person, and it then becomes easy to understand how authorisation could occur: the sovereign acts on its own authority, just as I act on my own authority, or you on yours.

This however poses a puzzle for the theory. The problem is well summarised by G.A. Cohen (1996, 167), in discussing authorisation in the philosophy of Hobbes and Kant:

> You might think that, if you make a law, then that law binds you, *because* you made it. For, if you made the law, how can you deny that it binds you, without contradicting your own will? But you might also think the opposite. You might think that, if you are the author of the law, then it *cannot* bind you. For how can it have authority over you when you have authority over it? How can it bind you when *you*, the law*maker*, can change it, at will, whenever you like?

The problem arises from the dual role played by the people. On the one hand, the law binds you because it is law; on the other hand, the law is something that you can make or unmake at will – so how can it bind you?

As we have seen, in Hobbes' theory it is not necessary that the sovereign is not a party to the covenant by means of which the political authority comes into being (*L* 122). This means that the sovereign stands outside the civil law, as Hobbes clearly sees: '[t]he sovereign of a commonwealth, be it an assembly or one man, is not subject to the civil laws' (*L* 184). Here Hobbes restates the dilemma noted above by Cohen, arguing that it is impossible for anyone to bind himself, 'because he that can bind can release; and therefore he that is bound to himself only is not bound' (*L* 184).

But it should be noticed that we have now slipped from talking about the people, to talking about the sovereign. If the sovereign is above the law, while the people are subject to it, then perhaps we should conclude that the sovereign cannot be bound. Nonetheless, the people, by authorising the sovereign that makes law on its behalf, is bound. At this point we recall, mystifyingly, that the people itself is sovereign, or at least the author of what the sovereign does; so how can the people find itself bound, when its agent the sovereign is not?

It is useful to recall the ways in which individuals can undertake to bind themselves by taking on obligations where they previously were not obligated. Civil and commercial contracts, like employment, marriage and insurance policies respectively, are obvious examples. In such cases, the parties voluntarily assume obligations to which they were previously not subject. The answer to Cohen's dilemma suggested by these contractual obligations is that I can indeed bind my will, because it does not follow from the fact that I willed at some time in the past that my will be bound, that I can unbind it at will later on. In becoming an employee of an organisation, for instance, I bind myself – that is, bind my will – to act within the terms of the contract. If I breach one of the terms of the contract, it is not legally open to me to say unilaterally: 'But the terms of the contract were freely agreed by me, so they are subject to my will; and now I will to change them.' For, in contracting, I freely agreed to bind my own will by the terms of the contract.

In understanding private contracts like those just mentioned, we could if we wished divide ourselves in thought into two persons, one of whom exists before the contract, and the other after it. By dividing ourselves in this way into two persons, we can see the will of the one as binding the future actions of the other – even though in this case, of course, they are really one person. Then it becomes clear that the second person, who is bound, has no power to revoke the obligations imposed by the first. The special feature of Hobbes' theory is that those who make the original contract license a third party[3] to act in ways that will obligate their future selves.

But, of course, the employer and employee are distinct persons, whereas, as I have argued, we can see the sovereign and the people as a single natural person. So it seems that Hobbes' theory of sovereignty depends on dividing the lawmaker, who is above the civil laws, from those who are bound to obey them, even though those who make the laws are also those who are subject to them. This way of putting it makes Hobbes' task sound impossible, and Cohen's dilemma looms. But, as I shall argue, the theory of authorisation outlined in the last chapter shows how law can bind the very persons who authorise it.

Cohen's dilemma clearly relies on pressing the implications of the idea that the people and the sovereign are identical. The underlying assumption is this: if A and B are identical, then whatever is true of A is true of B, and whatever is true of B is true of A. This principle, the indiscernibility of identicals, was propounded by the seventeenth-century German philosopher Leibniz. But the relation between sovereign and people is one of identity in a special sense. This is true even if the personnel who fulfil the role of sovereign are the same as the people as a whole – that is, a form of direct democracy prevails in which all the members of the people act together as the sovereign. But it is clearer still when the sovereign is a single individual, or a proper subset of the people. Indeed, there is no need for the sovereign to be drawn from the people who are subject to the sovereign's laws at all.

Identity is being assumed for the purposes of a particular role, that of political representative. As far as this goes, the situation is no different from that of actors playing roles, as Hobbes points out (L 112). For representational purposes we take the actor playing Julius Caesar to be Caesar. But it is clearly false that everything and only that which is true of the actor is true of Caesar: for example, Caesar did not have an actors' union card. Because of this, plenty of descriptions that are true of the sovereign will not be true of the people, and conversely. So the 'indiscernibility of identicals' is only partially applicable here, and we cannot infer that whatever is true of the sovereign must therefore be true of the people.

It is not that we first specify the representative and represented, decide that they are identical, and then infer that whatever is true of the representative must also be true of the represented. Rather we infer their identity from the fact that they are related as representative and represented. When we see them as related in this way, we regard them as identical in some ways, but not others. The sovereign embodies that aspect under which the people can be viewed as acting freely in making laws, even though under another aspect the people must be seen as subject to those same laws.

As often with Hobbes' theory of sovereignty, the implications are easier to see if one imagines that the sovereign is a legislative assembly of all the people. Then it is true that each person, as a member of the assembly, retains absolute freedom in making the law. But this is quite consistent with saying that each person as a private citizen remains subject to the law, as indeed do Members of Parliament or Congress. An MP who breaks the speed limit, for example, cannot plead immunity on the grounds that he or she has the power to make the law, or repeal it, though Parliamentary privilege gives MPs more licence in the chamber of the House of Commons than others (or they themselves) outside it.[4]

The key to Hobbes' solution is that authorisation is a one-off act: the agreement between every man and every other man that creates the 'person' of the state simultaneously also nominates somebody, the sovereign (whether an individual or an assembly), to 'bear the person' of the state, or in other words to act for it. This means, among other things, that the sovereign is nominated to enact legislation on behalf of the community, but that the people as a whole are the 'authors' of the legislation. They are indeed bound to obey the laws passed, and cannot 'unbind' themselves subsequently.[5]

It should be noted that this also explains why the sovereign must be, as Hobbes says, *legibus solutus* – not bound by the laws. This necessarily includes the contract by which the sovereign's role as the people's agent is established. For imagine, contrarily, that the sovereign were so bound. Then he could simply free himself from the terms of the contract by a suitable act of legislation: 'For having the power to make and repeal laws, he [the sovereign] may when he pleases free himself from that subjection, by repealing those laws that trouble him, and making of new; and consequently, he was free before' (*L* 184). For Hobbes, then, since the sovereign has the power to exempt itself from scope of the laws, it cannot be subject to the laws in the first place.

More obviously, the people could have no redress against the sovereign for actions performed in its name. For this to be the case, the sovereign would need to have entered into a contract with the people, whereby the sovereign could be held to account for failing to perform its terms. But, since the sovereign is the people, the latter would be asking for redress against itself.

NATURAL LAW VS CIVIL LAW

As noted earlier, civil law, unlike natural law, can only exist within a political authority. But if they are both genuinely forms of law, an obvious question arises, which continues to exercise legal philosophers today: what is the relation between them? This gives rise to a number of further questions. Does one kind of law contain, or presuppose, the other? Do they cover distinct areas of conduct, and if so, what are these areas? If not, and the different kinds of law overlap, can they come into conflict? Which form of law has priority if they do?

Many of Hobbes' Christian contemporaries assumed that natural law was a law of morality, commanded by God. While Hobbes, in common with his contemporaries and earlier political and legal theorists, such as the thirteenth-century philosopher St Thomas Aquinas, distinguishes between natural and civil law, modern-day legal philosophers usually talk of morality on the one hand, and positive law (that is, the law of polities, or states) on the other. Nonetheless the questions that arise are in many respects identical to those that Hobbes addressed; the answers given to them define different schools of thinking within legal philosophy.

The questions above become sharp when we ask whether any legislation made by the sovereign that is unjust or otherwise immoral nevertheless enjoys the force of law. The orthodox Christian assumption endorsed by the natural law school of thinking was that the answer to this must be 'No' (for a modern defence of this position, see Finnis 1982). Aquinas, for example, took the view that *lex iniusta non est lex* – an unjust law is no law at all – though he did not think that the latter should be resisted in all cases (for further commentary see e.g. Finnis 1998, 184, 272–74). This is quite consistent with thinking that the fact that a duly constituted political authority has enacted a piece of legislation is a reason in itself for obeying it – and many would add that this is a moral reason. On this view, natural law or morality contains civil law. But where they conflict, civil law yields to the claims of morality.

Underlying this pattern of thinking is the assumption that civil law ought to be obeyed, at least if the political authority that enacts the law is itself justified. If this were not true, there would be no basis for saying that they can come into conflict. This is because the status of the civil law is held to depend on prior moral standards of right and wrong. Some writers, however – legal positivists – take the view that there is no intrinsic moral content to the law (for the classic modern statement of this view, see Hart 1961). The main feature of this account is that it assumes that there is a clear procedure for determining whether or not something counts as law.

It has often been assumed or argued that Hobbes was a legal positivist (see Hart 1961, 187–95; Barry 1968, 131–32; Watkins 1973, 114; Hampton 1986, 107–10; Lloyd 1992, 15). Hobbes does anticipate some aspects of this theory, to the extent that *Leviathan*'s basic test to decide whether something counts as law is whether or not it has been commanded by the sovereign. Hobbes' theory is accordingly often identified as a precursor of the 'command' theory of law, whose major statements were *The Province of Jurisprudence Determined* (published in 1832; see Austin 1995) of John Austin (1790–1859) and Hans Kelsen's (1881–1973) 'pure' theory of law. The aim in each case is to remove allegedly extraneous matter from law, particularly the matter of morality, and replace it with something that looks less problematical than morality does. Thereby we avoid various awkward problems that exercise moral philosophers: what morality is, where it comes from, what authority it has, how disputes over it are decided and so on.

Hobbes rejects the conventional assumption that natural law, as the dictate of morality, was created by God. In chapter 46 he argues that the proposition that God created law reduces to absurdity: 'God they [i.e. scholastics such as Aquinas] say is the prime cause of that and all other actions, but no cause at all of the injustice' (L 469). Admittedly Hobbes says, for example, that 'the law of nature ... is the eternal law of God' (L 191), but as we noted earlier, he is quite happy to say that the laws of nature are but 'theorems' (L 111), which people may refer to as God's commands if they wish. This view is reiterated in chapter 26:

> the laws of nature .. are not properly laws, but qualities that dispose men to peace, and to obedience. When a commonwealth is once settled, then are they actually laws, and not before, as being then the

commands of the commonwealth, and therefore *also* civil laws. For it is the sovereign power that obliges men to obey them.

(*L* 185; emphasis added)

This inverts the relation between natural and civil law as it is conceived by natural-law theorists such as Aquinas. The status of natural law as law depends on its being given effect by civil law, rather than vice versa. Because of this, the possibility cannot arise that natural law removes the force of civil law. Mark Murphy argues that 'Hobbes was more a latter-day Thomas Aquinas than an early version of John Austin' (Murphy 1995, 873; for an argument to a similar conclusion, see Fuller 1990). On this interpretation, then, the law of nature overrides civil law.

But the interpretation rests heavily on Hobbes' remark that civil and natural law cannot conflict; that is, the law promulgated by the sovereign cannot be at odds with natural law. Although he does say that civil and natural law must be consistent, Hobbes defines the laws of the political authority so as effectively to rule out the possibility of a clash between them. He states that the sovereign is subject to the law of nature, but Hobbes adds that the sovereign itself is arbiter of what the law of nature requires: 'it is by the sovereign power that it is law; otherwise it were a great error to call the laws of nature unwritten law' (*L* 191). For Hobbes, people in the state of nature can unobjectionably act in all sorts of ways that Aquinas would have held to contravene the law of nature (*L* 90). And they are bound only to desire that the law of nature that commands them to seek peace is generally observed; no individual is required to observe it in his or her actions if this tends to his or her destruction (*L* 110).[6]

In *Leviathan* and in his later work *A Dialogue between a Philosopher and a Student of the Common Laws of England*, Hobbes adopts in extreme form the doctrine that the interpretation, as well as the enactment, of the civil law is dependent on the sovereign (or on judges who are answerable to the sovereign). Part of what this does is to decide what actions or states of affairs the terms 'just' and 'unjust' refer to.[7] The sovereign seemingly has ultimate discretion regarding these questions, which would usually be thought of as issues of moral judgement; so in this sense the sovereign is in effect the arbiter of morality. Matters are very different in the state of nature, where '[t]he notions of right and wrong, justice and injustice have ... no place' (L 90). On this showing, Hobbes is a fairly typical 'positive' law theorist.

Notice however that Hobbes does not deny that natural law exists. He says that the laws of nature come into being when 'a commonwealth is once settled', but 'not before' then. Hobbes must mean by this that though the content of natural law exists and can be known before political authority exists, in the state of nature it lacks the force of law. Though they remain distinct from civil laws, the laws of nature begin and end their career as laws in the commonwealth, the body that creates civil laws. This must be the thought behind his otherwise obscure remark (L 185) that '[t]he law of nature and the civil law contain each other': each contains the content of the other. For this reason, there can be no conflict between them. Hobbes says that natural and civil law are not 'different kinds, but different parts' of the law, of which 'one part being written, is called civil, the other unwritten, natural' (L 185).

Why does Hobbes bother to say this? Why does he not just say that the only true law is civil law, particularly since he insists (L 191) that unless there is a sovereign power to declare what is law, it would be 'a great error to call the laws of nature unwritten law'? The trouble is that Hobbes also says (L 188) that the law of nature is eternal and universal: its content is summed up by the fundamental principle of fairness, which is encapsulated in the negative version of the 'Golden Rule', *Do not that to another, which you think unreasonable to be done by another to yourself* (L 188). If fairness is indeed a universal and unchanging law, then its content cannot depend on that of particular civil laws that vary from one political authority to the next, because civil laws depend on the discretion of the sovereign. This suggests that the sovereign does not enjoy a completely free hand in making the law after all.

Thus another potential contradiction comes to the surface. On the one hand, Hobbes seems to adopt a strongly positivist view of law. The sovereign that makes the laws, effectively makes actions just or unjust (L 386), and this suggests that the sovereign in law-making cannot act unjustly, since the laws themselves determine what is just and unjust. The law cannot be unjust (*L* 239). But now it seems on the other hand that if it commanded a law that violated the principle of fairness in the Golden Rule, the sovereign would indeed act unjustly. Hobbes gives the example (*L* 194) of a law prescribing that anyone removed from his or her home by force may regain it by force, and asks what happens when the home is occupied not because of the use of force, but the owner's negligence. If there is no explicit provision to cover this eventuality, Hobbes says, 'this case is contained in the same law', that is, the person may still regain his or her home by force.

However, if this is what the Golden Rule requires as the fundamental law of nature, then it is surely possible that the sovereign's actions could fail to comply with it. But Hobbes has a subtle if potentially evasive answer to this. Here as elsewhere in *Leviathan* he is concerned by the fact that the meanings of words such as those embodied in law allow of different interpretations ('almost all words are ... ambiguous' – *L* 194; cf. 240). Where disagreements arise, conflict will result. Part of the sovereign's job is to fix the reference of key terms, about which dispute will otherwise rage, with dire consequences for the stability of the political authority. Since its well-being depends on defusing private disagreements, it is vital that legal interpretation has a clear and unambiguous basis. 'The interpretation of the law of nature, is the sentence of the judge constituted by the sovereign authority' (*L* 191).

In actual cases, much judicial work concerns the application to unprecedented cases of existing law, and this also creates the scope for divergent opinions. Hobbes argues that in making judgements in such cases, the presumed intentions of the original legislators should be the guide that is used: this is why in the eviction example just given, it was assumed that the homeowner could regain his or her property by force. But 'the intention of the legislator is always supposed to be equity', that is fair dealing. In other words, the sovereign treats like cases or claims in a like manner. 'It were a great contumely [i.e. offence] for a judge to think otherwise of the sovereign' (*L* 194). So what is now sometimes called the principle of 'interpretative charity' requires us to assume that the sovereign always intends to act fairly.

By way of comparison, we can refer to a crucial passage in the *Dialogue*, which contains Hobbes' mature thinking on law. There the 'Philosopher' (who expresses Hobbes' own views against those of the 'Student') says that the law of equity 'is a certain perfect reason that interprets and amends the law written, itself being unwritten' (Hobbes 1997, 54). But the Philosopher adds immediately that '[w]hen I consider this, and find it to be true … I find my own reason at a stand; for it frustrates all the laws in the world', since this means that 'any man' can invoke reason as 'a pretence for his disobedience' (Hobbes 1997, 54–55).

The law of reason does indeed underlie all law, and every sane adult has the natural power of reason. But it is a cardinal error, in Hobbes' view, to infer from this that anyone endowed with natural reason is an authority on the law. His grounds for saying this are plain: it would lead to the chaos that the political authority is there to prevent. So the reason on that laws rest cannot be 'any private reason; for then there would be as much contradiction in the laws as there is in the schools [i.e. among philosophers]' (*L* 187). Although he accepts that 'justice fulfils the law, and equity interprets the law' (Hobbes 1997, 101), Hobbes is keen to deny the claim that judges 'amend' the law. All they can do is to amend faulty assertations about what the content of the law is. In judging cases, 'the judge does no more but [i.e. than] consider, whether the demand of the party be consonant to natural reason … which interpretation is authentic, not because it is his private sentence [i.e. opinion], but because he gives it by authority of the sovereign' (*L* 191–92).

However, Hobbes adds a twist to this story. The law is contained in the commands of the sovereign, but these commands themselves need interpretation by those subject to them (*L* 190). Since the ultimate basis of civil law is equity, which exists outside any human mind as a law of reason, it is possible that the sovereign gets it wrong (*L* 192). But we as subjects must always treat the sovereign's declarations as final (*L* 195). It would therefore be false to say that the sovereign could not will the violation of the principle of equity. The consequence is rather that subjects, as private interpreters of the law, would never have good reason to think that the sovereign had willed such a violation (*L* 194).

Confronted, for instance, with a case where the sovereign seems to treat like claims differently, we have to assume that despite appearances some relevant difference exists. We could never regard ourselves as justified in interpreting a law in such a way that the legislator could be thought of as having intended to breach equity.

Although the sovereign is the ultimate authority on the meaning of the law, the subjects still have to interpret the law themselves – otherwise they would never be able to know what they are required, permitted or forbidden to do. Accordingly, Hobbes takes care to emphasise that laws must be made known to the subjects. He says for example that '[t]o rule by words, requires that such words be manifestly made known; for else they are no laws': this is to 'take away the excuse of ignorance' (L 246).

This poses problems, given the ambiguity of words. Each person unavoidably uses his or her own judgement in deciding what is commanded, what permitted and what forbidden, having nothing else to go on. The fact that each reader can only be guided by her own use of reason is underlined in chapter 42: 'whosoever persuades by reasoning from principles written, makes him to whom he speaks judge, both of the meaning of those principles, and also of the force of his inferences upon them' (L 354). Nonetheless, Hobbes in chapter 29 identifies such judgements as a prime culprit for the 'weakening' of the political authority (L 223). This problem becomes particularly sharp with the right of self-preservation, which each subject retains from the state of nature. For if I think that an act of the sovereign threatens my life, I am entitled to resist (e.g. L 152, 208, 214). But if anyone may resist the sovereign when they think themselves entitled, chaos again threatens.

While each person can only gather from 'the bare words', what the law means, there is only 'one sense' of the law (L 194) amid individuals' various interpretations of it. This predicament is inescapable, but it does underline the fact that equity, understood as a principle of natural reason, is indispensable to subjects in trying to make sense of the law. For only a presumption of reasonableness will make it possible for each subject to have any basis for judging what the law says. What matters above all, however, is not that everyone's interpretation in fact converges, but that there is known to be a single authoritative interpretation, which is 'the letter' of the law (L 194).

In *Leviathan* more than in his previous works Hobbes stresses that there cannot be legal experts whose opinions are allowed to be at variance with those of the sovereign: 'he is not the interpreter of them [written laws] who writes a commentary on them' (L 193). In effect he argues that since commentaries are even more prone to interpretative disputes than the original texts commented upon, the attempt to clarify the law through commentary – that is, through formal interpretations of the law – is necessarily self-defeating. Even so, in interpreting the law, each person cannot avoid acting as a commentator on the law by the use of natural reason. Hobbes later suggests that individuals' understanding of language converges: 'words have their significance by agreement' (L 253). But, of course, dispute arises precisely when agreement about the meaning of words in their legal contexts is lacking. Then it seems that the only remedy is that the sovereign's word about the meaning of the law is law.

CRIME AND PUNISHMENT

In chapters 27 and 28 of *Leviathan* Hobbes turns his attention to crime and punishment. A criminal intention by itself is insufficient for the commission of a crime. Action is required for crime, though mere intention is sufficient for sin (L 201). While all crimes are sins, not all sins are crimes, since crime only exists where there is a political authority that makes actions criminal (L 201). Crimes can only be perpetrated if the offender was in a position to know that the act in question contravened the civil law – 'the want of means to know the law, totally excuses' (L 208). So, as already noted, there can be prosecutions neither for violations of a law that has not been promulgated, nor of children or demented people (L 208). Since it is impossible to be obligated to do something that is naturally impossible, persons cannot be obligated to obey laws if, by complying with them, they are put under 'terror of present death' (L 208).

Punishment is in its nature a public act (*L* 214), though it need not be carried out in public. It is an 'evil' inflicted 'by public authority, on him that has done ... that which is judged by the same authority to be a transgression of the law', or has omitted to do what is required by law. One of the prime functions that governments perform is to make laws to regulate the conduct of citizens and to inflict punishment on those who break the laws. Accordingly, a central question that theorists of political obligation (philosophers who aim to explain how citizens' duty to obey political authority can be justified) have to tackle is how the authority's imposition of punishment on its citizens can be justified.

Where does this right come from? Hobbes asks, 'by what door the [sovereign's] right or authority of punishing in any case came in' (*L* 214). Other seventeenth-century writers such as John Locke base the right of the sovereign to inflict punishment on a natural right to punish. In Locke's theory, the natural right to punish is granted to each person in the state of nature as an executive power to implement the law of nature, understood by Locke as the law of God. Hobbes' view is rather different. Recall that everybody has a right to everything in the state of nature, in the sense that each person has a right to whatever he or she judges to be needed for self-preservation, and there is nothing in principle that could not in some circumstances be thought necessary for this purpose. The act of agreeing to set up a political authority is the undertaking to 'lay down' (*L* 92) most of these rights, and to authorise the sovereign power. This act of renunciation is one that each prospective subject performs. But as we have seen, Hobbes stresses that the prospective sovereign is not a signatory to the agreement, and is therefore not bound by it.

It is of fundamental importance that the sovereign remains in the state of nature with respect to the subjects (as well as to other sovereigns) after the covenant is made. However, the sovereign, as such, only begins to exist at the point when the state of nature ceases to exist in its full form. The sovereign as such does not exist in the full state of nature. Despite this, the sovereign is thought of as enjoying undiminished the natural rights that everybody enjoys prior to the covenant: 'before the institution of commonwealth, every man had the right to everything, and to do whatsoever he thought necessary to his own preservation ... and this is the foundation of [the] right of punishing ... the subjects did not give the sovereign that right, but only, in laying down theirs, strengthened him to use his own' (L 214). This includes a right to punish offenders.

The key implication of Hobbes' theory, then, is that the sovereign is not granted the right to punish by the citizens, but has it anyway: 'the right which the commonwealth (that is, he or they which represent it) has to punish, is not grounded on any concession or gift of the subject' (L 214). Hobbes argues that the right to punish cannot be transferred from subjects to sovereign, since nobody can be assumed to give the sovereign the right 'to lay violent hands on his person' (L 214). Here again he relies on the idea that I cannot transfer to you a right that I myself do not have. As indicated earlier, my 'right to everything' is not, despite appearances, unrestricted: it is a right to whatever, in the circumstances, I may reasonably think I need for my own preservation. I cannot transfer to the sovereign the right to use violence against me since 'it cannot be intended' (L 214) that I have this right. It cannot be intended because my right to all things necessary to my preservation in the state of nature could not include such a right. So we cannot think of the sovereign's right to punish as having been handed over by the subjects, because it was not theirs to hand over in the first place.

Though the sovereign's right to perform the actions that characterise punishment (e.g. putting offenders to death) already existed in the state of nature, it is only through the political and juridical apparatus that comes into being with political authority that these actions can be described as punishment: 'neither private revenges nor injuries of private men can properly be styled [i.e. called] punishment; because they proceed not from public authority' (L 214–15). An act that merits one form of description in the state of nature acquires a different description when the political authority is set up. The difference lies not in the quality of the act itself, but in the nature of the agent who performs it.

Hobbes concludes, then, that the sovereign simply retains the right from the state of nature: 'the subjects did not give the sovereign that right, but only in laying down theirs, strengthened him to use his own' (L 214). As we have seen, he dismisses the idea that the right to punish could be transferred by the subjects from the rights they hold in the state of nature. He then answers the question where the sovereign's right to punish comes from, if not from the subjects' natural right to all things needed for self-preservation:

> before the institution of commonwealth, every man had a right to do whatsoever he thought necessary to his own preservation; subduing, hurting or killing any man in order thereunto [i.e. in order to preserve himself]. And this is the foundation of that right of punishing which is exercised in every commonwealth.
>
> (L 214)

As with the other powers of the sovereign, then, there is no possibility that the subjects could revoke the right to punish if the sovereign fails to keep its side of the bargain. The sovereign strikes no bargain or agreement with the subjects and has the right to punish irrespective of any agreement. It is unsurprising that the sovereign makes no such deal with the subjects, since the sovereign does not exist until the subjects agree among themselves to lay down their rights. So Hobbes' answer to the question that theorists of political obligation pose regarding the right to punish, is that in a sense the right to punish always exists. In the political authority the right to punish is left over from the sovereign's right to self-preservation.

However, the claim that the sovereign's right to punish must be left over from the state of nature faces certain problems. The argument that I cannot transfer to the sovereign a right to punish me, since I lack that right myself, ignores an obvious possibility. The right to punish could be transferred, if each subject transferred to the sovereign his or her right (including the right to inflict violent death) against everyone else. This would mean that the sovereign would acquire A's right to inflict violence on B, and B's right to do so against A, and so on for all the subjects. So the sovereign's right to punish, derived from transferred rights of self-preservation, would cover everybody.

The idea that the sovereign's right to punish survives from the state of nature also faces the objection that the sovereign may not exist in the state of nature (for a parallel point about Locke, who argued for such a right in the *Second Treatise*, see Nozick 1974, 139). Clearly the sovereign does not exist as sovereign, since before the arrival of political authority, sovereignty itself does not exist. But if the agent that becomes sovereign does not exist in the state of nature, nor do that agent's rights. In this case, there are no rights that survive into political society, so the right to punish cannot be a survival from the state of nature.

So problems arise if we trace the right to punish back to the sovereign's rights in the state of nature. There are other advantages in seeing the right to punish as resulting from mutual transfers of rights among those who subject themselves to the sovereign. It seems to offer a better understanding of the basis for the sovereign's right to punish. The right to all things that each individual possesses in the state of nature exists to promote self-preservation. But if one private citizen murders another, the murderer may pose no threat at all to the sovereign, though Hobbes does argue that crimes are acts against the person of the commonwealth (e.g. *L* 213, 237). The rationale for the sovereign's right to punish rests not on its own right of self-preservation against its subjects, but on the subjects' signalling that they will desist from violence against one another.

The right to punish can then be derived from the fundamental basis of the law of nature, which holds that 'every man ought to endeavour peace ... and when he cannot obtain it, that he may seek and use all helps and advantages of war' (*L* 92). The sovereign gains or retains a natural right to perform certain actions. These actions, under political authority, acquire the description of punishment. In summary, then, although the entitlement to perform those actions, which in the commonwealth count as punishment, already exists in the state of nature, they only merit the term 'punishment' when people have moved out of the state of nature.

By the same token, only those persons can be punished who have accepted political authority, rather than declaring themselves 'enemies' towards it (*L* 216). Enemies can simply be fought and killed without due process (*L* 219). Punishment of the innocent is a transgression of the law of nature (*L* 219), because it violates equity, and no benefit derives from punishing the innocent – another indication, incidentally, that Hobbes did not simply think that the state of nature is one in which anything goes. But those who are not subjects may justifiably have any treatment whatever inflicted upon them, as long as the sovereign believes they pose a danger to the public good (*L* 219). Hence while the rules of punishment regulate and constrain the treatment of wrongdoers, there is in principle no limit to the acts that can justifiably be performed towards 'enemies' – Hobbes' term for those who have not renounced the contract. One consequence of this is that there are no limits on what can be done to non-combatants (or, indeed, combatants) in prosecuting a war with a foreign power.

This treatment, however bad, would not of course count as punishment. This follows from the claim that punishment requires a political authority that commands civil laws. Hobbes says that those who deny an authority to which they previously submitted will be hoist with their own petard.

> [In] denying subjection, he [that is, the person who renounces the covenant by denying the sovereign's authority] denies such punishment as has by the law been ordained; and therefore suffers as an enemy of the commonwealth; that is, according to the will of the representative.
>
> (*L* 216)

Hobbes does not make it very clear exactly which illegal acts are such that their perpetrators count as an 'enemy' of the commonwealth rather than merely as criminals. But such acts must presumably include at least treasonous actions, such as the attempted assassination of the sovereign (if the latter is an individual). Some offences, such as parking violations or petty theft, presumably would not reduce the perpetrator to the status of an enemy of the commonwealth, rather than a criminal within it. But others do. The infliction of capital or other punishment, at least for those crimes that make the perpetrator an 'enemy' to the political authority, is a conceptual impossibility. A further consequence of this view is that no distinction can be drawn between the response by the sovereign to acts of treason and conventional acts of war-making against foreign powers. Hobbes argues that 'rebellion is but war renewed' (L 219), so that the same response is appropriate to each.

This also reinforces the point that the natural law of equity only becomes effective within a political authority, despite the fact that its existence does not depend on that authority. The 'sword' may attack the innocent as well as the 'nocent' in war (L 219), although the law of equity, as Hobbes stresses, forbids punishing the innocent within the commonwealth (e.g. L 192). So the innocent children and grandchildren of enemies are fair game (L 219). The sovereign continues to be subject to equity; as a principle determining just measures of punishment, equity only comes into effect within those relationships that are mediated by the civil law. And, as this is not true of 'enemies', it cannot be a principle regulating their treatment.

In their role as lawmakers, the individual person or persons composing the sovereign have the power to make laws, and hence in Hobbes' theory are themselves outside the law (L 231). But as private citizens, like off-duty MPs or Congressmen or -women, they are as subject to the law as anyone else. As regards punishment, certain actions performed by the sovereign – such as taking goods owned by one of the subjects without the latter's consent – may be construed as acts of punishment in some circumstances, but as theft in others.[8] This is not a 'shadowy' distinction, as one commentator has suggested (Ryan 1996, 339), but an instance of a very familiar role-playing division, without which much of modern life would be impossible.

Hobbes offsets the authoritarianism of *Leviathan* with an element of paternalism. The sovereign is meant to govern for the good – that is, the safety – of the people (L 240). Punishments and rewards are to be applied for the common benefit (L 241). The paternalism extends to a basic provision of social security. Those who are unable to support themselves 'ought not to be left to the charity of private persons, but to be provided for, as far as the necessities of nature require, by the laws of the commonwealth' (L 239). On the other hand those who can work, but do not want to – known in Hobbes' day as 'sturdy beggars' – will 'be forced to work' (L 239).

CONCLUSION

Hobbes thinks, then, that law is whatever the sovereign commands. In deciding whether something is law – be it a document, an utterance or some set of rules or practices – what matters is whether it comes from a suitable source, rather than its content. In this Hobbes agrees with modern legal positivists. But he further argues that the content of the civil law must be consistent with natural law. He is also clear that the sovereign falls under the sway of natural law, just as the subjects do (*L* 237). This certainly qualifies Hobbes' standing as a legal positivist, since positivists deny that natural law or morality should constrain – let alone determine – the content of positive law. For Hobbes, natural law exists as the law of reason. Reason constrains the content of positive law. And positive laws can only be those that the sovereign can intelligibly be regarded as having made.

All sane adults can reason, and therefore tend to think themselves authorities on matters of reason, including the content of the natural law. By common consent, natural law can overrule civil law. So if private reason is allowed free rein, there is a risk that everyone will think himself an authority on the law. This is why the sovereign has to decide what natural law commands. If this seems to be at odds with reason, citizens have to defer to the sovereign's interpretation. This may be sustainable in most circumstances. But the strains of commitment may show when the sovereign's actions stand grossly at odds with the natural dictates of reason as understood by the populace at large. Kleptocratic or murderous regimes would not be justifiable by this standard.

Hobbes traces the sovereign's right to punish offenders to the natural right to use any means that may preserve oneself. As I have suggested, however, in some ways it makes better sense to think of the original right as being held not by the sovereign but by individuals in the state of nature, and then being transferred. If the sovereign did not exist in the state of nature, the sovereign will have no natural right of its own to carry over into political society. Nor is it obvious that a right to pre-emptive action against a possible aggressor in the state of nature can be identified with a right to punish offenders after the fact under civil government. For these reasons, the mutual transfer of right from subjects to sovereign makes better sense of Hobbes' theory. Though it remains in a state of nature with the subjects, the sovereign is bound by natural law to act so as to promote their well-being. Precisely for this reason, however, those who have not submitted to the sovereign are enemies and may be eliminated at will, without due legal process.

FURTHER READING

Leviathan, chapters 25, 26, 27, 28, 29

HOBBES ON LAW

It is useful to compare the main treatment of civil law in *Leviathan* with Hobbes' other political works, particularly *De cive*. The passages in *De cive* dedicated to the theory of civil law and sovereignty are in chapters 13 and 14. Those in the *Elements of Law* occur at chapters 28 and 29. The fullest statement of Hobbes' mature views on the nature of law is contained in his *A Dialogue between a Philosopher and a Student of the Common Laws of England*, edited with an introduction by Joseph Cropsey (Chicago, IL: Chicago University Press, 1997). For an account of the historical background to the *Dialogue*, see Glenn Burgess, *The Politics of the Ancient Constitution: An introduction to English political thought, 1603–42* (University Park, PA: Pennsylvania University Press, 1993). Summaries of Hobbes' views about the different varieties of law can also be found in Martinich, *A Hobbes Dictionary* (Oxford: Blackwell, 1995), 176ff.

COMMENTARY ON HOBBES' LEGAL THEORY

General

The most comprehensive single-volume guide to Hobbes' views on the nature of law is Claire Finkelstein (ed.), *Hobbes on Law* (Burlington, VT: Ashgate, 2005), which contains many of the essays listed below.

For brief surveys of Hobbes' theory of civil law, see Maurice Goldsmith, 'Hobbes on Law', in Tom Sorell (ed.), *The Cambridge Companion to Hobbes* (Cambridge: Cambridge University Press, 1996). Goldsmith defends the traditional view of Hobbes as an early legal positivist. See also Conal Condren, *Thomas Hobbes* (New York: Twayne Publishers, 2000), ch. 5. An interesting argument that Hobbes was in fact a natural law theorist of a kind similar to Thomas Aquinas is contained in Mark Murphy, 'Was Hobbes a Legal Positivist?', *Ethics* 105 (1995), 846–73. See also Timothy Fuller, 'Compatibilities on the Idea of Law in Thomas Aquinas and Thomas Hobbes', *Hobbes Studies* 3 (1990), 112–34.

For a sympathetic treatment of Hobbes' theory, see Robert Ladenson, 'In Defense of a Hobbesian Conception of Law', *Philosophy & Public Affairs* 9 (1981), 134–59. Ladenson argues that Hobbes does not fit in easily with either the positivist or natural law schools as these are conceived in modern legal philosophy. See also Ladenson's contribution to Finkelstein (ed.), *Hobbes on Law*, 'Hobbes on Natural Law and Natural Right'.

The relation between natural and positive law in Hobbes

David Dyzenhaus, 'Hobbes and the Legitimacy of Law', *Law and Philosophy* 20 (2001), 461–98, rejects the traditional 'positivist' interpretation that Hobbes' sovereign is strongly constrained by natural law. See also Dyzenhaus, 'Hobbes and the Legitimacy of Law', in Finkelstein (ed.), *Hobbes on Law*. Sharon Lloyd, 'Hobbes' Self-Effacing Natural Law Theory', *Pacific Philosophical Quarterly* 82 (2001), 285–308, and reprinted in Finkelstein (ed.), *Hobbes on Law*, offers an interpretation close to that given in the text of this chapter: she points out that the claim that natural law overrides or invalidates civil law becomes empty given Hobbes' insistence that the sovereign is the only authoritative interpreter of natural law. David Gauthier, 'Hobbes: The laws of nature', *Pacific Philosophical Quarterly* 82 (2001), 258–84, argues that for Hobbes the law of nature is to be seen as a set of rational guidelines or precepts rather than as commands. On this point, see also Robert Ladenson,

'Hobbes on Natural Law and Natural Right', in Finkelstein (ed.), *Hobbes on Law*.

For Hobbes' views on the law of nature, see the further reading section at the end of Chapter 4. See also Sharon Lloyd, 'Hobbes' Self-Effacing Natural Law Theory'. Lloyd argues that for Hobbes the essence of law consists neither in natural nor in positive law as usually understood, emphasising, as I have in this chapter, the importance of the sovereign in adjudicating disputes over the content of the law of nature; that is, the law of nature (which commands us to seek peace by creating a sovereign) itself dictates a mechanism for resolving disputes about its content (though Lloyd's description of natural law as being on this account 'self-effacing' seems to me potentially misleading). See also David Gauthier, 'Hobbes: The laws of nature'.

Hobbes on punishment

See Mario A. Cattaneo, 'Hobbes' Theory of Punishment', in K.C. Brown (ed.), *Hobbes Studies* (Oxford: Blackwell, 1965). Also David Heyd, 'Hobbes on Capital Punishment', *History of Philosophy Quarterly* 8 (1991), 119–34; and Anita L. Allen and Maria H. Morales, 'Hobbes, Formalism and Corrective Justice', *Iowa Law Review* 7 (1992), 713–39; these essays are reprinted, along with the one by Cattaneo, in Finkelstein (ed.), *Hobbes on Law*. For theoretical background on the right to punish and its origins, see Robert Nozick, *Anarchy, State, and Utopia* (Oxford: Blackwell, 1974), ch. 6, especially 137–42. Useful theoretical background can also be found in A.J. Simmons, 'Locke and the Right to Punish', *Philosophy & Public Affairs* 20 (1991), 311–49.

INTERNATIONAL LAW

For an application of these debates to international law, see Charles Covell, *Hobbes, Realism, and the Tradition of International Law* (Basingstoke: Palgrave, 2004), who tries to redefine Hobbes as an opponent of realism. For a classic statement of Hobbes as a prophet of realism, see Hedley Bull, 'Hobbes and the International Anarchy', *Social Research* 48 (1981), 717–38, reprinted in Finkelstein (ed.), *Hobbes on Law*. See also Robinson Grover, 'Hobbes and the Concept of International Law', in the same volume, which earlier appeared in Timo Airaksinen and M.A. Bertman (eds), *Hobbes: War among nations* (Aldershot: Avebury, 1989). Grover argues that the sovereign is superfluous, since it will only come into being if people are already disposed to keep their covenants; as I have argued above, this ignores Hobbes' claim that covenants need the backing of force.

Further argument on the relevance of natural law to Hobbes' theories of international politics can be found in Noel Malcolm, 'Hobbes' Theory of International Law', in his *Aspects of Hobbes* (Oxford: Clarendon Press, 2002), ch. 13; and Michael Williams, *The Realist Tradition and the Limits of International Relations* (Cambridge: Cambridge University Press, 2005). See also the further reading section at the end of Chapter 10 below.

NOTES

1 In modern usage, civil law is distinguished from criminal law, the distinction being that civil offences are not prosecuted, but only liable to private redress in the courts. In Hobbes' usage, 'civil' refers to any law other than the law of nature (and so would include both the criminal and the civil law in the modern sense).

2 For the details of this argument, see Chapter 7 above.

3 Though this party may be one or more of the contractors themselves, the sovereign is legally a third party distinct from them.

4 For example, they can make personal allegations, which would be actionable if repeated outside the House of Commons.

5 Note that this is different from saying that nothing can make them unbound. Hobbes is quite clear that they can be made unbound, that is, absolved of their obligation to obey the sovereign. He says for example (*L* 153) that '[t]he obligation of subjects to the sovereign is understood to last as long, *and no longer*, than the power lasts, by which he is able to protect them ... the end of obedience is protection' (emphasis added; cf. Hobbes' well-known remark about the 'mutual relation between protection and obedience' at the very end of the book (*L* 491)). The point is, however, that the subjects cannot initiate circumstances (as had Parliament before and during the civil wars) in which the sovereign's power to protect will be undermined.

6 I shall however note a marginal qualification to this view later, when we discuss the law of equity.

7 This cannot however mean for Hobbes that there are no normative truths at all in the state of nature. For the laws of nature, such as the requirement to seek

peace, or to observe contractual agreements, already exist in the state of nature and have normative content.

8 Punitive actions by the state, such as judicial execution, imprisonment or exacting fines, become crimes when performed by one citizen on another (respectively, murder, kidnapping and theft).

9

RELIGIOUS LIBERTY AND TOLERATION

INTRODUCTION

Religion plays a big part in *Leviathan*. In this Hobbes follows his contemporaries, for whom religious questions were of great political importance. Religious questions, both of theology and church organisation, had bulked large in the civil wars. Until a couple of decades ago, most commentators thought that in *Leviathan* Hobbes endorsed a political order in which a single religion – the one prescribed by the sovereign – dominates. Latterly, however, many readers of Hobbes have concluded that he advocated a degree of religious liberty which, although restricted by modern standards, was for his own time rather broad in scope (Ryan 1983, 1988; Tuck 1990; Martinich 1992; Gray 2000).

HOBBES, *LEVIATHAN* AND RELIGION

Religion was sufficiently important to Hobbes to merit a whole section of *Leviathan* to itself. Part 3 of *Leviathan*, entitled 'Of a

Christian Commonwealth', argues, particularly in chapter 42 (the longest in the entire book), that the claims of religious organisations to political power are unfounded. Indeed, Part 4, 'Of the Kingdom of Darkness', continues the same discussion in a more negative and polemical vein.

Although the last two parts of *Leviathan* make up half its total length, modern editors sometimes greatly abridge them or cut them entirely; and they attract much less comment than the first two parts. However, in the last generation or so there has also been a reaction against the comparative neglect of Parts 3 and 4. An early protest against this neglect was entered by John Pocock, who complained that the standard attitude of 'far too many scholars has traditionally been, first, that they aren't really there; second, that Hobbes didn't really mean them' (Pocock 1971, 160). As a result, commentators now tend to take them more seriously than was previously the case.

Nonetheless, much of the argument of Part 3 (and to some extent Part 4) remains rather tedious for modern readers uninterested in biblical interpretation. Hobbes' main aim, especially in Part 3, is to show that the churches' claims to exercise political power lack any scriptural foundation. It is therefore not surprising that his prime strategy is to look in exhaustive detail at the relevant biblical texts. His method is an attritional one. Hobbes grinds his way through the scriptures, arguing that they fail to support those who think the state should be subordinated to religious authorities such as priests, bishops or the Pope. While these parts should not be ignored, and make a significant contribution to the argument of *Leviathan*, the treatment they receive here will in no way be proportionate to their length. The main reason for this is that the main audience envisaged for this book comprised those interested in modern political philosophy and theory rather than biblical interpretation.

In understanding the religious doctrines of *Leviathan*, two questions need to be distinguished. First, 'What are the religious politics of *Leviathan*?'; and second, 'What were Hobbes' own religious views?' It may seem obvious that these are different questions, but some commentators write as if the answer to the second question must be the same as the answer to the first. Some readers of *Leviathan* think that the book relies on orthodox Christian theological assumptions, while others think Hobbes subscribed to some more offbeat version of Christianity. Others argue that the book rejects Christian doctrine across the board, at least in the sense that its arguments do not assume the truth of any form of Christianity; this goes for most of the game-theoretic interpreters of *Leviathan*, discussed in Chapter 5. Of course, the last of these might be true, even if Hobbes was, in his personal religious beliefs, a kind of Christian.

Historians have pointed out (Mintz 1962, 45; Skinner 1964, 332), that the charge most often levelled against Hobbes by his contemporaries, at least after the publication of the English *Leviathan*, was that of 'atheism'. In the seventeenth century, 'atheism' was a blanket term of abuse for anyone whose religious views were regarded as objectionable (Martinich 1995, 31ff., esp. 36), rather than carrying any serious charge of denying God's existence. In much the same way, 'bastard', used today as a generic term of abuse, usually carries no literal charge of illegitimacy.[1] In his essay 'Of Atheism', Francis Bacon wrote that 'all that impugn a received religion, or superstition, are, by the adverse part [i.e. those who disagree with them] branded with the name of atheists' (Martinich 1992, 19ff.). A contemporary, Roger Coke, remarked in the 1660s that Hobbes could not 'walk the streets, but the boys point at him, saying "There goes Hobbes the atheist!"' (Springborg 1996, 347). So the charge of 'atheism' bandied about by Hobbes' contemporaries should be interpreted with caution, at least as a guide to Hobbes' own religious beliefs.

Modern commentators have variously seen Hobbes as a 'Christian atheist' in the phrase used by his contemporary, the Anglican bishop Henry Hammond, to describe Hobbes' views (Tuck 1993a, 329), that is, one who rejected belief or faith in God but held that Jesus was the Messiah; or a theist who believed that the truths of the Christian religion were disclosed by the combined power of reason and supernatural revelation (Martinich 1992, 1–5); or as a sceptical fideist who held that reason is powerless to demonstrate the truth of the Christian religion, which therefore requires a leap of faith (Pocock 1971, 192). Some commentators continue to believe that Hobbes was an atheist in the modern sense – that is, someone who denies the existence of God (Skinner 1988; Wootton 1988, e.g. 711).

As our concern is with *Leviathan*, rather than Hobbes' personal views, I shall only consider the latter much later in this chapter. The book itself gives good reason for not doing so. *Leviathan* argues unequivocally that private beliefs cannot be permitted to shape religious policy. If Hobbes thought (contrary to the interpretation I set out in Chapters 4 to 6) that the reason why we should obey the laws of nature was that God had commanded them, this might affect our understanding of *Leviathan* as political theory. But it is not clear that even this would affect the book's justification for political authority. Hobbes had to provide reasons for accepting his political theory that his contemporaries would be likely to find compelling. As we have already seen, Hobbes said in the 'Review, and Conclusion' that the aim of the book was 'to set before men's eyes the mutual relation between protection and obedience' (*L* 491).

So *Leviathan* had to appeal to those professing a wide range of different religious beliefs, including those who denied that God was the author of the laws of nature (*L* 111). What Hobbes is doing, then, is something much closer to the modern liberal strategy, endorsed by the twentieth-century US political philosopher John Rawls and others, of trying to offer political conclusions that can be justified from a variety of moral and religious perspectives, including those who lack strong religious beliefs (Rawls 1993, 1999, e.g. chs 22 and 26). His aim is to provide conclusions that can be accepted irrespective of deep differences in ideological outlook.

Fortunately, therefore, readers of *Leviathan* do not need to engage with the intricacies of Hobbes' own religious views, at least when it comes to interpreting the book's theory of church and state. Hobbes' religious beliefs would be relevant, if the book simply proposed that these beliefs should be embodied in the political and religious institutions of society. But in fact the book's argument is precisely that the political authority should not institutionalise the religious views of private citizens[2] – of whom Hobbes, obviously, was one. For this conclusion to follow, he needed only to claim that there was no final authority to verify whether religious claims were true, coupled with some other non-religious premises, as we shall see in the following sections.

LEVIATHAN AND RELIGIOUS LIBERTY

In a much-cited passage near the end of *Leviathan*, Hobbes reviews the recent religious upheavals in England, and draws conclusions from them about the best form of religious organisation. The view that he seems to endorse is that the abolition of the Church of England was a good thing, as was the fact that Presbyterianism, which replaced the Church of England, had in turn given way to Independency, a radically decentralised form of church organisation.

> First, the power of the popes was dissolved totally by Queen Elizabeth ... And so was untied the first knot. After this, the Presbyterians lately in England obtained the putting down of Episcopacy: and so was the second knot dissolved. And almost at the same time, the power was also taken from the Presbyterians. And so we are reduced to the Independency of the primitive Christians to follow Paul, Cephas or Apollos, every man as he likes best: which if it be without contention, and without measuring the doctrine of Christ by our affection to the person of his minister ... is perhaps the best. First, because there ought to be no power over the consciences of men, but of the word itself, working faith in everyone, not always according to the purposes of them that plant and water, but of God himself ... and secondly because it is unreasonable in them who teach there is such danger in every little error to follow the reason of any other man endued with reason of his own, to follow the reason of any other man, or of the most voices of many other men.
>
> (*L* 479–80)

Hobbes could make these arguments with relative impunity during the triumph in the late 1640s of Independency, which reconstructed the church along the lines of 'primitive Christian' practice. This was, of course, completely at odds with the Anglican religious order enforced by Charles I and his predecessors, as well as the religious settlement that came into force with the

Restoration after 1660. Hobbes' apparent defence of Independency particularly angered his former friend Edward Hyde. To hedge his bets, however, Hobbes included a sideswipe at the Independents in the handwritten presentation copy of *Leviathan* that Hobbes had had specially made as a gift to the future Charles II in exile in France in 1651 (Hobbes 1991, liv).

Hobbes found himself under parliamentary investigation in the later 1660s during proceedings on the Atheism Bill. By this time the 'Clarendon Code' had reasserted a stringent form of Anglicanism through such measures as the Corporation Acts (1661), the Act of Uniformity (1662), the Conventicle Act (1664) and Five Mile Act (1665), which reinstated the pre-civil-war Church of England and restricted non-Anglican Protestants from preaching their religion outside private households. Against this background, Hobbes prudently excised the passage quoted above, along with many others that would offend against the reinstated Anglican orthodoxy, when preparing the Latin text of *Leviathan* in the mid-1660s (first published in 1668). It is unlikely that his own views about how church and political authority should be related to one another had significantly changed during this period. The English *Leviathan* was effectively banned in England during the 1660s though printed copies circulated, and even publishing his views in Latin would have got him into trouble with the authorities (for further details, see Chapter 11).

RELIGIOUS TOLERATION

In recent decades the view has gained currency that in *Leviathan* Hobbes set out to defend religious toleration (Ryan 1983, 1988; Tuck 1990). Indeed, Richard Flathman goes so far as to say that Hobbes 'go[es] well beyond toleration' (Flathman 1993, 154). In other words, according to this view, Hobbes was trying to justify a political theory that allowed for religious diversity. This interpretation has received its ablest exposition in the writings of Richard Tuck. Hobbes emerges as a defender of toleration not merely because of the generally individualist bias of his thought, but also because of the wide divergences in religious practices that he was prepared to accept. Tuck argues that in its essentials,

Leviathan's case for toleration was '[f]irst, that there was no source of moral or religious judgment in a commonwealth independent of the sovereign; and second, *that the very lack of such a source implied toleration*' (Tuck 1990, 169; emphasis added).

On this reading, the fact that private judgement was an unstable basis for a political order persuaded Hobbes that civil peace can be preserved only by making the sovereign the supreme authority on Scripture. Why, though, should the 'very lack' of a source of moral or religious judgement be thought to imply toleration? The idea, presumably, is that toleration can be justified by an argument along the following lines:

(1) People make an indefinite number of conflicting claims about religion or morality, any one of which may be true.
(2) There is no authoritative source of truths on religion or morality (apart, that is, from the political authority itself).

So,

(3) Nobody knows which, if any, of these claims is true.

But,

(4) Other things being equal, it is surely wrong for a political authority to suppress a true moral or religious claim.

So,

(5) Other things being equal, it is wrong for the authority to suppress any of the claims mentioned in (1), and this amounts to a doctrine of religious or moral toleration.

The first question this raises is whether the argument works. The second question is whether Hobbes himself makes this argument. On the first question, there are two different ways an argument can fail to give us good reasons for believing its conclusions. One is if it draws invalid inferences from the initial premises; the other is if the premises themselves are false.

Premise (4) might be disputed here. Many philosophers have thought that the fact that a claim is true does not mean that there cannot be a good reason for suppressing it. 'Reason of state' is often cited in this connection, and official secrecy provides a clear, if exceptional, illustration of it. John Stuart Mill confronts and dismisses this view in chapter 2 of *On Liberty*, on the grounds that the truth of a doctrine is part of its utility. But it is hard to see why there is necessarily any reason that utility should not be better served by suppressing truths, or promoting falsehoods, than their opposites. Indeed, another nineteenth-century English utilitarian, Henry Sidgwick, thought that a utilitarian society would need to suppress the very fact that it was being run on utilitarian lines. Even most non-utilitarians think that it could be legitimate to suppress truths for reasons of state.

It is not beyond dispute that the truth of a belief provides a compelling reason for not suppressing it. Many modern liberals would argue that the reason why beliefs should not be suppressed is not because they are true, but because they as liberals subscribe to a moral principle such as equal respect for persons, which commits one to respecting their beliefs. Very often, liberals assume or argue that sets of beliefs (such as mutually inconsistent sets of religious doctrines) which cannot all be true should nonetheless all be tolerated. For instance, some religions such as Hinduism are polytheistic, while others, such as Christianity, Islam and Judaism, are monotheistic. The belief that there is at most one god is clearly inconsistent with the belief that there are many gods. If so, the reason why these religions all have a claim to be tolerated cannot be that they are all true. Nor (for most liberals anyway) will the case for toleration be based in general on the claim that each belief has at least a reasonable likelihood of being true: the pedlars of wild conspiracy theories, for instance, benefit as much from a tolerant regime of free speech as do intellectually rigorous scientists.

A second line of response is that the argument will lack bite in the face of religious and moral disagreement over fundamental beliefs. Such disagreement essentially involves dispute over whether the beliefs in question are true, or probably true. Of course, the mere fact of disagreement does not stop one side or the other from being right. But very often no conclusive argument can be given to show who is right. In such cases the repressive political authority may mount an argument for suppression based on the alleged balance of probabilities, perhaps arguing that a clear and present danger lies in permitting the doctrine to flourish. Here an argument from public order may well prove stronger than one based on probable truth.

Did Hobbes really mean to offer an argument of the form (1) to (5), or anything like it? It is not clear that he did. For one thing, although some sources in *Leviathan* seem to endorse versions of (1) to (3), there is not much to support a claim like (4). Indeed, Hobbes argues that even if some doctrine, which the political authority's official religion brands as heretical, happens in fact to be true, subjects are still obligated to obey the laws in general, and those relating to religious conduct in particular. The duty of obedience, for Hobbes, extends to any laws requiring participation in the state religion. Hobbes says that nobody can show someone else that he or she has had a direct communication from God. But if the person who tries to show this is the sovereign, 'he may oblige me to obedience, so as not by act or word to declare I believe him not' (*L* 256).

Nonetheless, there is a passage in chapter 26 that could be taken to support the claim that Hobbes endorsed (4), the view that it would be wrong for a political authority to suppress a true moral or religious claim. He considers the relation between civil and natural law, and concludes that no problem results for the theory 'if the [civil] law declared, be not against the law of nature', and allows only that 'all subjects are bound to obey' the civil law 'in all things not contrary to the moral law' (*L* 198–99). Here he seems to be rejecting the notion that a legitimate civil law could conflict with the moral law, and it might be thought that what motivated this claim, or at any rate exemplified it, was the view that it was necessarily wrong to suppress true religious doctrines. Hobbes seems to be claiming that the natural or moral law trumps the civil law, so that the civil law would be invalid if it contravened morality.

However, as I argued in Chapter 8, Hobbes' views are more sophisticated than this. He is indeed distancing himself from the view that an immoral law, such as one that suppressed the true religion, would be a law in any true sense. So it probably would be wrong to suppress a certain religious doctrine, such as the claim that Christ was divine, if that is true. But a claim of this kind can never be established in such a way as to constitute knowledge.

Indeed, in the very passage that is taken to support (4), Hobbes negates its force. He notes that 'a subject that has no certain and assured revelation particularly to himself concerning the will of God is to obey for such the commands of the commonwealth' (*L* 199). If we spell it out, Hobbes' argument runs as follows: unless a subject has got true and assured revelation from God to do otherwise, that subject has to obey the political authority; the commands of the political authority are themselves to be taken for divine commands; therefore, no subject has got true and assured revelation from God to do otherwise than obey the political authority. This authority could decide, of course, to allow a measure of religious freedom – for example, because in the sovereign's view, this is what God wants. The crucial point for Hobbes, however, is that religious policy follows from the will of the sovereign, rather than because it is based on theological or other considerations that are objectively true.

Hobbes goes further, and argues that anyone who thinks that he or she can disobey the sovereign at will – if for example, the sovereign is an unbeliever – the disobedience is itself anti-Christian. '[W]hen the civil sovereign is an infidel, every one of his own subjects that resists him sins against the laws of God (for such are the laws of nature), and rejects the counsel of the apostles, that admonishes all Christians to obey their princes' (*L* 414). This is tantamount to rejecting (4). It implies that even if a sovereign espouses a false doctrine – which Hobbes, if only to pander to his readers' prejudices, has to assume is a non-Christian doctrine – the subjects are still bound to obey. The conclusion must be that for Hobbes the truth of a doctrine offered no justification for disobeying the religious order promulgated by political authority.

HOBBES' INTOLERANT TOLERATION

Another argument, which also begins with premise (1) above, might go like this:

(1) People make an indefinite number of conflicting claims about religion or morality, any one of which may be true.

But,

(2′) If people are permitted to follow these claims, then political and religious chaos, that is, a breakdown of public order, will result.

So,

(3′) The political authority is justified in enforcing whatever measures, including suppression of beliefs, are necessary for the preservation of public order.

Does Hobbes argue along these lines? A plausible case could be made that he does. As far as (2′) goes, he argues in chapter 29 (*L* 223) that 'among the diseases of a commonwealth' is the prevalence of the belief that 'every private man is the judge of good and evil actions', rather than the civil law, with the result that the political authority is 'distracted and weakened'; this is held to be particularly true when each individual's conscience is held up as an ultimate court of appeal on questions of morality.

As for (3′), in chapter 31 Hobbes argues that

> seeing a commonwealth is but one person, it ought also to exhibit to God but one worship; which then it does, when it commands it to be exhibited by private men publicly. And this is public worship, the property whereof, is to be uniform ... because a commonwealth has no will, nor makes no laws, but those that are made by the will of him or them that have the sovereign power, it follows that those attributes which the sovereign ordains in the worship of God for signs of honour ought to be taken and used for such by private men in their public worship.
>
> (*L* 252–53)

This strongly suggests that the doctrine of *Leviathan* restricts religious liberty. It is not assumed that the public forms of worship are in themselves necessitated by other considerations such as divine revelation. The only relevant question is what the public authority requires in the way of religious observance. Hobbes' idea seems to be that a contradiction would exist if the sovereign willed two different forms of public worship, just as it would if an individual thought there were two mutually exclusive forms of worship, each of which was necessary to salvation. There are also supposed to be pragmatic political grounds for enforcing uniformity: whichever doctrine happens to be true, political chaos is liable to result unless uniformity is imposed. Most people would point out that there may sometimes be pragmatic grounds for toleration rather than coercion, but for Hobbes the point remains that pragmatism will not yield a principled case for toleration. Religious liberty, like other liberties, has to take its chances case by case against concerns such as public order.

Accordingly, in Part 3 of *Leviathan* Hobbes aimed to show that religious claims against secular authority, whether in matter of religion or elsewhere, had no basis in scripture. This strategy in turn demands minimalism about the doctrinal content of religion (i.e. Christianity). Hobbes boils it down to the bare bones in order to pre-empt the threat of sedition fuelled by religious 'inspiration'. It is barely exaggerating to assert that Part 3 is devoted to showing that we can have no good reason, and in particular no biblical warrant, for belief in Christian doctrines beyond those that Hobbes thinks are necessary to make somebody a Christian. These come down to endorsing the claim, which Hobbes seemingly interprets in purely secular terms, that 'Jesus is the Christ', a proposition that he takes as equivalent to 'Jesus is the King [i.e. of the Jews]' (L 407; cf. 273, 299, 346, 408–13).

For Hobbes this is the most that the Bible entitles us to say about the attributes of Jesus. Of God we know nothing at all (L 23; cf. 467) apart from the fact that he exists (L 271). We know nothing of the divine attributes because God is incomprehensible (L 271). It follows, with added force, that we cannot justify engaging in civil disobedience as a result of supposed divine revelation, still less rebellion. As Hobbes knows, these arguments will not suffice to dissuade people from trusting to their own judgements about religion, with the results that he repeatedly bemoans in *Leviathan*. His aim is to establish that claims by religious authorities to political power lack scriptural foundation.

There are many passages in *Leviathan* where Hobbes expresses scepticism about people's claims to have received a text message from the Almighty. For example, in chapter 32 he deflates the view that God reveals himself to man through dreams: 'to say he [i.e. God] has spoken to him in a dream, is no more than to say he has dreamt that God spoke to him' (*L* 257). Miracles are important in this connection, because 'their purpose [is] always to beget or confirm belief' (*L* 302). Hobbes devotes a whole chapter to debunking them (chapter 37). Miracles, at least in post-biblical times, no longer occur (*L* 259, 306), and even if they did there would be no guarantee that they were brought about by God or his agents rather than his enemies (*L* 258), who, as the Bible assures us, also have the power to bring about the miraculous.

Hobbes' account of miracles torpedoes the Roman Catholic doctrine of transubstantiation, the claim that the bread and wine at the service of communion are transformed into the body and blood of Christ. The Catholic doctrine, rejected then as now by the reformed churches of northern Europe, held that this was a literal transformation, which occurs every time the Last Supper is commemorated in the sacrament of the Eucharist. Of course, as Hobbes gleefully points out, a fairground conjuror at least makes it look as though he has transformed a rod into a serpent, or water into blood, whereas after the officiating priest has blessed the sacraments, the bread and wine on the altar still look suspiciously like a wafer and a glass of Cabernet Sauvignon (*L* 305, *L* 422–23). The Catholic doctrine, Hobbes says, is no better than the ancient Egyptian custom of worshipping leeks (*L* 423).

It is presumably with such beliefs (which in context merit the technical term 'superstition'[3]) in mind that Hobbes denounces those

> men [who], vehemently in love with their new opinions, (though never so absurd), and obstinately bent to maintain them, gave those opinions also that reverenced name of *conscience*, as if they would have it

seem unlawful to change or speak against them; and so pretend to know they are true, when they know at most, but that they think so.

(L 48)

This acerbic passage casts extreme doubt on Hobbes' credentials as a precursor of modern liberal theorists of toleration. He does not say that private belief ought to be protected – indeed the above passage expresses contempt for conscience. As Hobbes knew only too well, the elevation of 'conscience' to be the supreme arbiter of moral right and wrong was one of the roots of political disorder (L 223), such as the civil strife in the British Isles during the previous decade. Stability required deference not to these private judgements, but to a supreme political authority.

It is worth noting that Hobbes seems to begin from a similar point to John Locke, a later seventeenth-century defender of toleration. Hobbes considers an argument similar in form to the best-known argument given by Locke for toleration in his *Letter concerning Toleration*. There Locke argues that attempts to impose religious conformity must be doomed to fail, since regimes that try to do this are seeking to achieve uniformity in people's beliefs, and it is simply a fact about beliefs that they cannot be coerced in this way. I believe what I believe, on the basis of evidence or revelation or faith, and the fact that the regime tries to make me believe something different cannot by itself have any impact on this basis.[4]

Hobbes apparently anticipates Locke's views on belief. He does so in rebutting the charge that the state's domination over the church allows rulers to force their subjects to deny Christ. 'To this I answer, that such forbidding is of no effect; because belief and unbelief never follow men's commands' (L 343); in chapter 46 he adds that there is nobody who will 'not hazard his soul upon his own judgment' rather than submit it to the discretion of the civil power (L 472). The clearest statement of this position is perhaps in chapter 26, where Hobbes says of any law that is repugnant to individuals' private conscience that such people are 'bound … to obey it, but not bound to believe it: for men's belief, and interior cogitations, are not subject to the commands, but only the operation of God' (L 198).

But Hobbes does not advance this theory of belief in support of toleration. The fact that beliefs resist these attempts to coerce them can be used to yield a very different conclusion from Locke's: because belief is resistant in this way, it is of little account whether the public authorities are intolerant about religion. The implicit argument, once spelled out, goes as follows: what really matters to each individual is his or her own salvation; salvation depends (if anything) on private beliefs; but these beliefs are impervious to outside repression, for example by the civil authority. This is why it doesn't matter very much to individuals how repressive the civil authority is.

Hobbes suggests that the imperviousness of private beliefs to outside coercion is one side of a coin whose other face is religious uniformity. In chapter 42 he discusses the biblical case of Naaman the Syrian. Naaman (2 Kings 5:17) is said to have converted to the Jewish religion when cured of leprosy by Elisha, but was not described as doing wrong in continuing to go through the motions of worshipping the idol Rimmon, as was required by the secular power (L 343–44). According to Hobbes this shows that what matters is the forum of private conscience, not the publicly prescribed religious forms. He implies that those forms may be enforced in public with as much authoritarianism as one wishes. Hobbes' great coup here is to turn the argument from private conscience on its head, making of it an argument not for religious latitude but for uniformity.

The same applies to Hobbes' discussion of ancient Rome's religious policies in chapter 12, where he remarks that 'the Romans, that had conquered the greatest part of the then known world, made no scruple of [i.e. had no objection to] tolerating any religion whatsoever in the city of Rome itself, unless it had something in it that could not consist with their civil government' (L 83). An example of the latter was the Jewish religion, which denied all political authority under God. The point is that the Romans' willingness to tolerate 'any religion whatsoever' in the city of Rome depended on the submission of the Roman people and their having been placated with bread and circuses.

Hobbes does admittedly leave room for variation in 'things indifferent' to salvation. As we have seen, his conception of the

defining tenets of Christianity is, by the standards of his contemporaries, a minimal one. As a result, the range of actions that
Hobbes deems necessary to salvation is rather limited (*L* 403): it
encompasses only acknowledging the truth of the claim that
'Jesus is the Christ', and obeying the civil laws. This is com-
patible with any political order, even one that denies the truth of
Christianity. While some Christians believe that salvation demands
adherence to a range of other doctrines as well (such as the virgin
birth or the resurrection), it follows for Hobbes that this belief
cannot justify disobedience towards political authority.

Consequently, the minimal content of Hobbes' version of
Christianity should not be confused with toleration. Suppose someone imagined that a much wider range of actions were necessary to
salvation: such a person would not be tolerated if these actions were
at odds with the laws of the land. What does the work, in other
words, is Hobbes' minimalist account of what is required for salvation, and not a principled commitment to toleration as a value.
The minimalism follows from the fact that there is very little, in
Hobbes' view, that the study of scripture can be taken to prove
incontrovertibly about the nature of God. The question is not so
much what is true about God's nature, but what human reason
could be expected to gather about God's nature from the evidence
available to it. It is the fact that in Hobbes' view not much is
required for salvation which leaves a good deal of scope open to
individual subjects to interpret the divine will. Even here, it should
be noted, there are no obvious limits on the degree to which the civil
authority can compel conformity to its prescribed forms of public
worship.

As I noted earlier, one of modern political philosophy's main
concerns is how to impose agreed political principles, such as
principles of justice, on a society in which people hold diverse
beliefs (Raz 1990; Rawls 1993; Gray 2000), and it may be
tempting to think that Hobbes was also engaged in this project.
Many modern philosophers think the best response to this diversity is to draw up principles that are as uncontroversial as possible
between these beliefs. This may have influenced the way in which
Hobbes has been read on religious liberty. The fact that Hobbes
provides the most minimal content to Christian doctrine makes it

tempting to see him as an early liberal. But it would be rash to infer from the fact that these philosophers have often aimed to make room for toleration in the face of diversity that *Leviathan* engages in a similar enterprise.

The 'tolerant' interpretation of *Leviathan* has also recently been advanced by John Gray, albeit on a more pragmatic reading of Hobbes' intentions (Gray 2000, ch. 1). This assumes that the prime and only political good is security: 'For [Hobbes], toleration was a strategy of peace ... In this Hobbesian view, the end of toleration is not consensus. It is coexistence' (Gray 2000, 3). The choice, in short, is between coexistence, and no existence. This is not, however, adequate for those, such as John Rawls, who demand a more ambitious defence of toleration: coexistence in no sense implies that people who are forced, by lack of power, to put up with others, would not happily squash them if they had the power to do so. Such coexistence is not produced by toleration, but impotence: on the stronger reading, toleration requires a readiness to live with others even when it is in one's power to do otherwise. However, confusion may arise over this (even among political philosophers), because of its passing similarity to a principled defence of toleration – namely that a tolerant society is one in which the balance of power between different groups is a good in itself.

Hobbes does remark at the end of *Leviathan* that following the views of other men about what forms of religious doctrine to adopt 'is little better than to venture his salvation at cross and pile [i.e. a game of chance]' (*L* 480; Ryan 1988, 41). This might be thought to suggest that it is too dangerous to entrust one's salvation to the fiat of the worldly sovereign. But Hobbes is explicitly referring here to the beliefs of other private men, not the public religious authority. He is in fact offering a *reductio ad absurdum* argument against those who think that 'there is such danger in every little error', based on human fallibility: those who claim to preach the true religion down to minute details of observance are as fallible as those they presume to guide. Thus this is part of the justification of the handing over to the sovereign of decisions about matters of religious doctrine, not part of an argument for religious liberty.[5]

SOVEREIGNTY AND BIBLICAL INTERPRETATION

Previously, in *Elements of Law* and *De cive*, Hobbes had adopted the conventional position that, since scripture did not interpret itself, the most authoritative account of it was likely to be made by divines, those versed in theology. For example, he maintains quite unambiguously in *De cive* that 'it is the task of a church to settle disputes; and therefore it is for a church, not for individuals, to interpret holy scripture' (Hobbes 1998, 231). In *Leviathan*, however, he changes his position radically. There, in chapter 42, he argues that ministers of the church cannot be the authoritative interpreters of the meaning of scripture.

Not coincidentally, this parallels Hobbes' mature views about the authority of judges in interpreting law. As we saw in Chapter 8, in the *Dialogue on the Common Law* he attacks the claims of judges to authority in interpreting statute as undermining the unitary sovereign: indeed, Hobbes links the two claims explicitly (*L* 378): 'It is the civil sovereign that is to appoint judges, and interpreters of the canonical scriptures; for it is he that makes them laws.' There is a good reason for this: Hobbes thought that the 'person' of the sovereign (whether an individual or assembly) could be the only source of political, ecclesiastical and juridical authority.

This was not because Hobbes believed that the sovereign was likely to be more skilful at biblical interpretation than everyone else. His point was rather, as with the written civil laws, that scripture does not interpret itself, that the divergences in private readings of it are liable (then if not now) to provoke civil strife, and therefore the interests of peace are best served by making the sovereign's interpretation of it authoritative. Religious law in *Leviathan* is the ecclesiastical equivalent of road-safety legislation: it matters little which side of the road people drive on, as long as everybody drives on the same side. What is needed is a salient standard, a point of convergence, which enables each person to conform in public to the behaviour of every other person.

The Naaman passage cited a few pages back does, however, create a further puzzle. Hobbes says that whatsoever a subject, as Naaman was, is compelled to in obedience to his sovereign, and does it not in order to his own mind, but in order to the laws of his country, that action is not his, but his sovereign's; nor is it he that in this case denies Christ before men, but his Governor, and the law of his country.

(L 344)

The problem here should be obvious from the discussion of sovereign representation in Chapter 7. Hobbes' argument depends on the idea that sovereign and people are one person, so that the actions of the agent, that is the sovereign, are owned by those of the author, the people, who are therefore responsible for them. How then can the people be absolved of responsibility if the sovereign denies Christ, or performs some other action tending to damnation? Surely if the people are the author of the sovereign's acts, they must take responsibility for them, and accordingly accept salvation or damnation as the consequence of this.

This problem in some ways parallels the objection lodged by G.A. Cohen against Hobbes' account of law-making, considered in Chapter 8. There the problem was that the people are both master of, and subject to, the civil law, and this seemed to involve a contradiction, or at least to license inferring contradictory conclusions from the same premise. In response I stressed that the sovereign does not become identical with the people, but for certain purposes is taken for the people. The fact that sovereignty is 'absolute', that is, undivided, in Hobbes' theory does not detract from this status.

So, by the same token, the political identity of sovereign and people should not be taken as identity across the board. In particular, identity should not be assumed for the purposes of assessing what might be called religious liability. If the across-the-board identity claim were true, it would be nonsensical to deny that a purely referential expression could be true of the sovereign but not of the people (or vice versa). But, as we have already seen in this chapter, Hobbes makes a great deal of the distinction between judgements by private citizens about religion and morality, on the one hand, and judgements by the public authority on the other.

The point is particularly clear with religion. The 'people' is necessarily disaggregated in matters of faith because each individual has a private conscience. Hobbes says that 'faith is the gift of God; and he works it in each several [i.e. individual] man by such ways, as it seems good to himself' (L 405). There is no such thing as the public conscience, only the several consciences of private men. The Leviathan is a corporate being, whose judgement overrides that of the subjects. But it does not follow that *Leviathan* therefore also has a corporate conscience, which likewise overrides private conscience. Hobbes' argument about the non-coercibility of belief underlines this point.

Hobbes nonetheless insists that disaster ensues when individuals are left to form and act on their private judgements, whether about religion, law or politics; in chapter 29 this is accounted one of the principal causes of 'weakness' in a political authority. It follows that private conscience cannot justify a veto on civil law, as many modern liberals have thought.

> Another doctrine repugnant to civil society is, that whatsoever a man does against his conscience is sin; and it depends on the presumption of making himself judge of good and evil ... the law is the public conscience, by which he has already undertaken to be guided.
>
> (L 223)

As a result – a point as relevant to the religious politics of our day as of Hobbes' – private citizens cannot appeal to conscience as a Get Out of Jail Free card.

LEVIATHAN'S THEOLOGY

Hobbes was a mortalist: he believed that the soul has no existence after the death of the body. In chapter 38, he quotes the Bible itself in support of this view (Job 14:7), to show that 'man dieth and wasteth away, yea man gives up the ghost, and where is he?' (L 310). David Johnston argues (1989, 659) that Hobbes became a mortalist before he started composing *Leviathan* because it removed a threat to his political theory – the fact that the political authority could be trumped by a religious one. If the latter could assert that subjects would suffer eternal damnation if they obeyed a civil law at odds with the law of God, then it would be harder for the political authority to cow its subjects by fear of the worldly consequences of disobedience, since a much worse fate might await those who obeyed such a law.

Hobbes' mortalism thus meant that the soul was not granted eternal life, but was returned to life by God on judgement day. Then the damned would suffer a 'second death'. They would be consigned to hell. In a presumably burlesque passage, Hobbes identifies hell with Gehenna or Tophet, ancient Jerusalem's municipal garbage dump (L 313), where the local authorities seem to have pioneered a waste management scheme using incineration. Hobbes notes that nobody would be so literal-minded as to identify the 'hell' of the Bible with this dump, but argues that otherwise we have to think of hell as a metaphor. According to Hobbes, the damned would be consumed in this fire, but not forever: unlike the saved, they would be able to have sex, and thus perpetuate themselves via their children (L 433). This is the only sense that Hobbes finds he can attach to the idea that the damned would be condemned to eternal torment.

In his interpretation of Jesus' relationship to God, Hobbes also provides a novel adaptation of the theory of personation presented in *Leviathan*, chapters 16 to 18. The orthodox view of that relationship, endorsed by the Church of England before and after the Restoration settlement, was that God was a three-in-one being, comprising God as Father, as Son (i.e. Jesus) and as Holy Spirit – the doctrine of the Trinity. In chapter 41 and in Appendix 1 of the Latin edition of *Leviathan*, Hobbes offers a highly controversial account of the God-Jesus relationship. Jesus, he says,

> represents (as Moses did) the person of God; which God from that time forward, but not before, is called the father; and being still one and the same substance, is one person as represented by Moses, and another person as represented by his son the Christ. For person being relative to a representer, it is consequent to plurality of

representers that there be a plurality of persons, though of one and the same substance.

(L 338)

Here Hobbes draws directly on the theory of personation given in chapters 16–18 of *Leviathan*, which we examined in Chapter 7. The significant feature of the theory for current purposes is Hobbes' claim that 'it is consequent to plurality of representers that there be a plurality of persons'; that is, the same individual is a different person if represented by *A* rather than *B*, even though that individual is, by hypothesis, the same in each case. So God is a different person if represented by Moses rather than Jesus. Nonetheless, God remains in some sense the same individual, whoever represents him.

This was far from being orthodox Anglican (or indeed Christian) doctrine. It was passages like the one above that attracted the charges of 'atheism' from Hobbes' contemporaries, or the charge of denying the orthodox Christian doctrine of the Trinity. Hobbes completely omitted this passage in the 1668 Latin *Leviathan* (Hobbes 1994b, 333). Certainly his view that Jesus stood in the relation of 'representer' to God would have struck most contemporaries as bizarre. For one thing, it placed Jesus on a level footing with Moses, a mere prophet. Second, it seemed to deny that Jesus was, in his own person, divine: the denial of Jesus' divinity was declared to be heretical by the Council of Nicaea in the year 325.

It is odd that Hobbes, who otherwise was only too well aware that his interpretations of Christianity were unorthodox, if not heterodox, should have published the Latin appendices in 1668 and dug himself deeper into the hole that his earlier writings had opened up. Hobbes' minimal characterisation of Christianity sidelines God. If all that Christians are required to believe is that Jesus was King of the Jews, why should they believe in God at all? The 'representative' theory of the Trinity does nothing to dispel this worry. This makes the charge of 'Christian atheism' look plausible. In fact, Hobbes may well have thought that God did exist, since for him the universe is matter in motion, and he thought that there has to be a first mover. But evidently such a being need not be much like the traditional Christian God.[6]

CONCLUSION

Like Hobbes, modern liberals are much concerned with the diversity of beliefs in society. Modern liberals also follow him in trying to produce just principles to govern diverse societies. This may make it look as if Hobbes, like modern liberals, is trying to produce a theory of toleration. But for Hobbes diversity is a problem to be solved by political design, rather than an asset to be accommodated by it. This is one difference from modern liberalism, which seeks to protect the different political claims mounted by 'identity'. Since the facts constitutive of identity may be public (e.g. skin colour), it cannot be banished to the private sphere as readily as beliefs can, though of course the belief that these facts are of overriding political weight can be so banished.

Hobbes' theory is clear that private judgements have to take a back seat in political justification. It is not just that most judgements will lose out, by not being endorsed by the sovereign; they will also prove to lack sufficient rational warrant, and be mere articles of faith. The only consolation, from the perspective of those holding these judgements, is that the beliefs themselves lie beyond the reach of the sovereign. Since Hobbes thinks that few religious beliefs can be justified by reason, there will be very little possibility that the religion prescribed by a sovereign will run counter to such beliefs.

Moreover, since private judgement is inextricably private, subjects can go on having their own convictions regardless of how externally repressive the sovereign is, and it is these convictions that matter to salvation. However, some of the key liberties that modern liberalism stresses are freedom of worship, freedom to proselytise and freedom of association; these freedoms are constitutive of toleration, since they guarantee that citizens will be able to follow their own impulses in these matters, despite the disapproval of others. Nothing in Hobbes' theory requires that these freedoms be present.[7] That is why it is mistaken to construe him as an advocate of toleration.

FURTHER READING

Leviathan, chapters 12, 31; Part 3, especially chapters 32, 36, 37, 42, 43

HOBBES AS AN ADVOCATE OF TOLERATION

A recent work of contemporary political theory that strongly emphasises Hobbes' standing as a theorist of toleration, albeit of a highly pragmatic kind, is John Gray, *Two Faces of Liberalism* (Oxford: Polity Press, 2000). For further defences of the view that Hobbes advocates toleration, see Richard Tuck, 'Hobbes and Locke on Toleration', in Mary Dietz (ed.), *Thomas Hobbes and Political Theory* (Lawrence, KS: University Press of Kansas, 1990). Alan Ryan has defended a 'tolerant' interpretation of Hobbes in his 'Hobbes, Toleration and the Inner Life', in David Miller and Larry Siedentop (eds), *The Nature of Political Theory* (Oxford: Oxford University Press, 1983). See also Ryan, 'A More Tolerant Hobbes?', in Susan Mendus (ed.), *Justifying Toleration: Conceptual and historical perspectives* (Cambridge: Cambridge University Press, 1988).

Johann P. Sommerville, *Thomas Hobbes: Political ideas in historical context* (Basingstoke: Macmillan, 1992), ch. 6, emphasises Hobbes' hostility to conscience as potentially seditious (*L* 223), but argues that nonetheless he was prepared to urge the toleration of heterodox views if these were 'harmless' (Sommerville, *Thomas Hobbes*, 155). The question raised by this argument, particularly for a contextual reading such as Sommerville's, is how far the expression of deviant opinions could count in seventeenth-century conditions as 'in no way undermin[ing] the public peace' (156). In this respect, at least, our world may be radically different from that in which Hobbes was writing. For an argument that the English *Leviathan* is less liberal in its religious prescriptions than the Latin version, see Edwin Curley, 'Hobbes and the Cause of Religious Toleration', in Patricia Springborg (ed.), *The Cambridge Companion to Hobbes' Leviathan* (Cambridge: Cambridge University Press, 2006).

HOBBES' RELIGIOUS VIEWS

A historically well-informed general article on Hobbes' religious beliefs is Patricia Springborg, 'Hobbes on Religion', in Tom Sorell (ed.), *The Cambridge Companion to Hobbes* (Cambridge: Cambridge University Press, 1996). See also Springborg's 'Hobbes, Heresy and the *Historia Ecclesia*', in *Journal of the History of Ideas* 55 (1994), 553–71; Johann P. Sommerville, *Thomas Hobbes: Political ideas in context*; and J.G.A. Pocock, 'Thomas Hobbes: Atheist or enthusiast? His place in a Restoration debate', *History of Political Thought* 11 (1990), 737–49.

Hobbes as an orthodox Christian

See the further reading for Chapter 4 above. For more on Hobbes' own religious views, see also R.J. Halliday, Timothy Kenyon and Andrew Reeve, 'Hobbes' Belief in God', *Political Studies* 31 (1983), 418–33. A more recent restatement of the view that Hobbes was a fairly orthodox Christian can be found in A.P. Martinich, *The Two Gods of Leviathan: Thomas Hobbes on religion and politics* (Cambridge: Cambridge University Press, 1992). Martinich also voices this interpretation in his other works, for example Hobbes (London: Routledge, 2005), ch. 6. The view that Hobbes was an orthodox Anglican is voiced by Samuel Mintz, *The Hunting of Leviathan* (Cambridge: Cambridge University Press, 1962); and Paul J. Johnson, 'Hobbes' Anglican Doctrine of Salvation', in Ralph Ross, Herbert Schneider and Theodore Waldman (eds.), *Thomas Hobbes in His Time* (Minneapolis, MN: Minnesota University Press, 1974).

Criticisms of Martinich's interpretation can be found in Edwin Curley, 'Calvin or Hobbes, or Hobbes as an Orthodox Christian', *Journal of the History of Philosophy* 34 (1996), 257–71. Martinich's reply to the critique is printed after Curley's article.

Hobbes as a heterodox Christian

Richard Tuck defends the 'Christian atheist' interpretation of Hobbes' religious beliefs in 'The "Christian Atheism" of Thomas

Hobbes', in Michael Hunter and David Wootton (eds), *Atheism from the Reformation to the Enlightenment* (Oxford: Oxford University Press, 1992). Tuck also writes on Hobbes' ecclesiology in 'The Civil Religion of Thomas Hobbes', in Nicholas Phillipson and Quentin Skinner (eds), *Political Discourse in Early Modern Britain* (Cambridge: Cambridge University Press, 1993). Further details of Hobbes' views about the relations between church and state can be found in his *Dialogue between a Philosopher and a Student of the Common Laws of England*, edited with an introduction by Joseph Cropsey (Chicago, IL: Chicago University Press, 1997).

Hobbes as an 'atheist'

Traditionally interpreters of Hobbes have taken the view that he was an 'atheist', though (as we saw in earlier in this chapter) this term was often used as a generic term of abuse. Many commentators in the mid-twentieth century were inclined to view Hobbes as either an out-and-out atheist, or as someone for whom religious belief played no significant role either in his personal life or political theory. Leo Strauss, for instance, assumed that Hobbes' own religious protestations were insincere (*Natural Right and History* (Chicago, IL: Chicago University Press, 1953)). Similar remarks apply to Michael Oakeshott's *Hobbes on Civil Association* (Oxford: Oxford University Press, 1975).

The game-theoretic school of interpretation discussed in Chapter 5 proceeds on the assumption that Hobbes was, at least as far as the normative basis of his political theory went, devoid of religious belief. Pasquale Pasquino, 'Hobbes, Religion, and Rational Choice: Hobbes' two Leviathans and the Fool', *Pacific Philosophical Quarterly* 82 (2001), 406–19, presents a 'rational choice' reading of Hobbes' views on religion itself. Richard Peters, *Hobbes* (Harmondsworth: Penguin, 1956), ch. 10, produces an excellently balanced view of Hobbes' own putative religious views and their (ir)relevance to his political theory. For a contrasting view, see Giovanni Fiaschi, 'The Power of Words: Political and theological science in *Leviathan*', *Hobbes Studies* 26, no. 1 (2013), 1–5.

HOBBES AS A HARBINGER OF LIBERALISM

Jonathan Israel defends the view that Hobbes was a precursor of the 'radical Enlightenment', that is, an atheist who denied that political authority could rest on any religious basis, in his *Radical Enlightenment: Philosophy and the making of modernity* (Oxford: Oxford University Press, 2001). See also Richard Flathman, *Thomas Hobbes: Skepticism, individuality and chastened politics* (Newbury Park, CA: Sage, 1993), especially ch. 7. Quentin Skinner, *Liberty before Liberalism* (Cambridge: Cambridge University Press, 1998), argues that Hobbes' conception of liberty prefigured that of modern liberalism. Other portrayals of Hobbes as a proto-liberal can be found in the articles by Ryan and Tuck cited above under 'Hobbes as an advocate of toleration'.

NOTES

1 Hobbes made such accusations himself. In his *Mr Hobbes Considered in His Loyalty, Religion, Reputation and Manners* of 1662, Hobbes responded to the charge of 'atheism' against him by the mathematician John Wallis, that Wallis was by a process of 'projection' seeing in Hobbes the beliefs he feared he harboured himself but dared not confront (Hobbes 1839–45, vol. VII, 353).

2 Except, perhaps, those of the sovereign (assuming that sovereignty is borne by an individual). But even then the sovereign is acting in a public capacity rather than as a private citizen.

3 Hobbes uses 'superstition' to refer to any doctrine that is not promoted or endorsed by the public authority, so it follows that a doctrine could be superstition in one polity but orthodoxy in another.

4 It is not clear that this argument is an argument for toleration at all (Newey 1999, 31–32). Locke's claim that beliefs are immune from coercion seems to be a pragmatic obstacle that prevents regimes that would like to act intolerantly from doing so, rather than a principled defence of religious liberty. It is also possible to dispute the premise that Locke relies on here, which is not to be confused with the claim that it is impossible deliberately to coerce one's own beliefs ('Deciding to Believe', in Williams 1973). While it may well be true that if I believe *p*, I cannot simply decide to believe not-*p*, it does not follow that it is likewise impossible for someone else to try to make me believe not-*p*, as the modern panoply of advertising and other forms of propaganda readily shows.

5 The contrary interpretation places much weight on the 'Review, and Conclusion' to *Leviathan*, with its claim that the independency of the primitive churches was perhaps the most desirable form of church organisation. But Hobbes may well have been trying to ingratiate himself with the Independents, who had defeated

their Presbyterian rivals in the power struggles following the defeat of Charles I. The passage was dropped both in the scribal manuscript presented to the future Charles II and in the Latin *Leviathan*.

6 In Part 3, Hobbes finds himself defending the minimalist interpretation of Christianity, and his arguments depend on showing that no more than this is warranted by the use of reason. So what grounds could there be for Hobbes to believe anything beyond this? Presumably only the grounds that give rise to faith, seen as the irrational counterpart of belief.

7 The freedoms may be granted at the sovereign's discretion, but (unlike modern liberal theories of toleration) nothing in the theory demands that they be granted.

10

LEVIATHAN AND INTERNATIONAL RELATIONS

INTRODUCTION

One of the oddities of Hobbes' legacy is that, though he is widely read by modern political theorists, his strongest influence today is on those who work in an area about which he has comparatively little to say. This is international relations, the study of sovereign states, their behaviour and relationships, and of international bodies and institutions such as the United Nations or European Union. In a way it is not very surprising that Hobbes does not say much about these matters. In the seventeenth century the very subject matter of modern international relations barely existed: familiar features of international politics today, such as the UN, the institutions of global capitalism such as the World Bank, World Trade Organisation and G8·summits, international non-governmental organisations such as Amnesty International and Oxfam, the development of international law, the international criminal court and the doctrine of universal jurisdiction for certain crimes, are of recent – in some cases very recent – origin. All these aspects of the modern world remained well in the future at the time Hobbes was writing *Leviathan*.

It would however be wrong to say that nothing resembling the modern academic study of international relations existed in Hobbes' day. The phenomena that international relations students address – sovereign states and other international bodies and institutions – were well established by Hobbes' time. European politics was marked by rivalry between sovereign states in something like their modern form – indeed, the term 'Westphalian system' is now used to describe the interplay between independent sovereign states inaugurated by the Treaty of Westphalia at the end of the Thirty Years War in 1648, three years before *Leviathan* was first published.

NATURAL LAW AND INTERNATIONAL THEORY

For Hobbes and his contemporaries, the major source of reflection on the relations between states came from the natural law tradition – that is, the tradition of moral theology, strongly influenced by Christianity, which we have already seen at work in *Leviathan*'s description of the state of nature. The chief feature of natural law thinking, for present purposes, lies in the idea that human beings are subject to certain norms of conduct, regardless of whether their behaviour is governed by laws in the everyday sense, namely the enactments of man-made authorities, such as governments (so-called 'positive law'). Usually these norms were thought of as coming from God and as such they existed before, and could override, man-made laws.

Natural law thus provided the backbone of the seventeenth-century study of what we now call international relations. The idea of natural law was clearly well adapted to offer a way of regulating what would otherwise look like a dangerous, unruly branch of political life, namely the relations between states. For man-made positive laws existed only within states, not as a way of governing the relations between states. Again, the idea that posi-tive law could govern the relations between states, for example with regard to conduct in wartime, would have seemed odd to Hobbes, even if the all-too-plain limits now in the enforcement of international law would not. Even now the power of international law to alter the conduct of states remains severely limited. By contrast with often ineffectual bodies entrusted with the enforcement of international law such as the UN, which depend on consensus between powers to mandate military action, sovereign states such as the United States can impose their will through sheer force. All this would have been readily recognisable to Hobbes.

His great contemporary, the Dutch jurist Hugo Grotius (1583–1645), can claim to have pioneered the study of modern international relations. In some ways Grotius foreshadows the modern-day 'liberal' school of thought in international relations. This holds that there are moral standards – embodied for instance in international law – and that these standards may be strong enough in themselves to compel states to live harmoniously together. For Grotius it is human beings' natural sociability, coupled with a natural right to self-defence, which gives them a motive for peaceful coexistence. According to Grotius' major work *The Law of War and Peace*, it is simply a natural fact about human beings as a species that they want to live together in peace, and this means they have a self-interested reason to do what the conventional dictates of Christian morality anyway require of them. In this sense, Christian morality and self-interest happily coincide. One obvious consequence of this for international politics is that states can coexist peacefully without the need for a superstate or other supreme power to keep them in check.

On the face of it, Hobbes rejects Grotius' optimism. As we have seen, Hobbes did not think that humans possessed a natural impulse towards sociability. Rather, their natural impulses, if unchecked, lead to conflict, and Hobbes thought that relations between states exemplified this. Of course, this does not mean that cooperative coexistence is impossible: Hobbes' whole point is that it can be achieved. Indeed, he says explicitly that such cooperation can obtain between sovereign powers, in the form of 'leagues', that is, alliances (*L* 163). But its achievement depends, as we have seen, on the presence of a 'common power' to stabilise expectations about how others will behave. Without this power there is nothing – certainly not a natural impulse towards sociability or benevolence – to stop everything from falling apart. It follows from this that where no common power exists, uncertainty will prevail.

The international sphere, certainly in Hobbes' day and largely still in ours, has lacked a 'common power'. It is however important to distinguish between uncertainty and chaos or 'anarchy' in the popular sense of the word. It does not follow from the absence of a common power that no mutually beneficial action is possible. But it is liable to prove unstable: there is no reasonable expectation that the conditions of cooperation will persist. It is this radical uncertainty that marks, in Hobbes' view, the relation between sovereign states.

I will set out what I take to be the main features of *Leviathan*'s account of international relations. With this in place, we will be in a better position to judge the principal causes of quarrel among international relations interpreters of *Leviathan*, and thus determine the book's significance for our understanding of today's world, as well as Hobbes' own.

INTERNATIONAL POLITICS AS A STATE OF NATURE

Leviathan argues that the international sphere exemplifies the state of nature. In other words, the situation in international politics, where there is no dominant global authority, mirrors that of individual human beings in the state of nature. In a well-known passage in chapter 13 of *Leviathan*, as we saw in Chapter 4, Hobbes uses the example of sovereign states to show that the state of nature is a real and not merely a fictional condition of mankind:

[i]t may peradventure [i.e. perhaps] be thought, there was never such a time, nor condition of war as this, and I believe it was never generally so, over all the world. But there are many places where they live so now. For the savage people in many places of America, except the government of small families, the concord whereof [i.e. whose ability to live together peacefully] depends on natural lust, have no government at all, and live to this day in that brutish manner, as I said before. Howsoever, it may be perceived what manner of life

there would be where there were no common power to fear, by the manner of life which men that have formerly lived under a peaceful government use to degenerate into in a civil war. But though there had never been any time wherein particular men were in a condition of war against one another, yet in all times kings and persons of sovereign authority, because of their independence, are in continual jealousies, and in the state and posture of gladiators, having their weapons pointing and their eyes fixed on one another – that is, their forts, garrisons and guns upon the frontiers of their kingdoms, and continual spies on their neighbours, which is a posture of war.

(L pp89–90)

Hobbes' main point here is clear: national leaders are in a state of war against one another 'because of their independence' – because there is no world government that wields supreme power over them. So Hobbes thought that the state of nature obtained between both individual humans in the state of nature, and persons who exercise sovereign power in international affairs. Remember that the guiding image throughout *Leviathan* shows that when we come together to form a state, it is as if we form a single, giant person with supreme power. International power politics, accordingly, is a battle of the giants, and when giants do battle, the smaller fry are apt to get trampled underfoot – as European conflicts during the first half of the seventeenth century showed all too well.

Nonetheless, a number of problems arise when one tries to understand international affairs as a Hobbesian state of nature.

NON-EQUALITY

First, the international sphere does not obviously bear out Hobbes' claim that the state of nature is one of equality. Hobbes says that individuals in the state of nature are roughly equal in offensive power, since anyone is strong enough to kill, and weak enough to be killed by, anybody else: 'the weakest has strength enough to kill the strongest, either by secret machination, or by confederacy with others' (L 87). But as many commentators such as Charles Beitz and Hedley Bull have pointed out (Bull 1977, 49; Beitz 1979, 40ff.), this does not apply to international relations.

There is no sense in which, for example, the modern-day USA and a developing nation such as Bangladesh are roughly equal in offensive power.

If the actors in the international sphere are manifestly unequal, it seems that the conclusions that Hobbes draws from his description of the state of nature fail to follow. Rough equality in offensive power leads to war (the motive of 'diffidence') because it gives everybody a motive to engage in pre-emptive aggression. Each person can reason as follows: unless I pre-empt, there is no secure expectation that I will not fall prey to such aggression, with the likelihood that I will be killed — because of rough equality, I know that any aggressor will be able to do this. This provides a rational motive for pre-emption. But the USA has no such motive for pre-emptive aggression against Bangladesh, because there is a gross inequality in the two nations' offensive capabilities.

'WAR'

If the equality postulate does not apply to the relations between sovereign states, one of the main conditions for regarding the state of nature as a state of war seems to be lacking. Hobbes characterises the state of nature as a state of war. Then, if sovereign states are in a state of nature, similar to that which obtains between individual human beings where no supreme power exists, then states are necessarily in a 'state of war'. It may sound strange to say this, since we think of 'war' as an exceptional and temporary condition that sometimes prevails between sovereign states that are otherwise at peace, whereas it seems to follow from Hobbes' account that all such states are at war with one another all the time. Two states could be at 'war' in this sense even though there is no history of such hostilities between them, and there may indeed be long-standing treaties of friendship and cooperation (such as between the United Kingdom and Portugal).

UNSOCIABILITY

Hobbes depicts the state of nature for individuals as one of minimal sociability, wholly devoid of the means for 'commodious living', such as industry, agriculture, the arts and sciences, property and so on. Individuals are unable to call on the aid of others to eke out a livelihood. But in our time, as in the mid-seventeenth century, it is clear that sovereign states manage to cooperate for mutual advantage in a wide variety of military, economic, political, scientific and cultural projects, and this was already true to some extent (e.g. in the form of military alliances or trading agreements) in Hobbes' day. International civil society exists – perhaps in a richer way than it did in the seventeenth century – but even, then mercantile and other links, including cultural and dynastic ones, existed between sovereign states. And indeed Hobbes himself, in his famous discussion in chapter 13, points out the *dis*analogy between the individual state of nature and international politics: because in the latter, Hobbes says, sovereigns who have garrisons and other fortifications mounted on their frontiers 'uphold thereby, the industry of their subjects, there does not follow from it, that misery, which accompanies the liberty of particular men' (*L* 90).

NON-STATE ACTORS

This point about sociability leads on to a fourth problem. It seems that individuals are the only entities that exist in *Leviathan*'s depiction of the state of nature. But in the international sphere, there are and always have been non-state actors of various kinds, although they are much more numerous nowadays than they were in Hobbes' time. A prominent example, in the mid-seventeenth century as now, is the Roman Catholic Church. And states themselves combine into supranational bodies for certain purposes, such as defensive alliances or trading. Ethnic, linguistic and religious ties, for instance, often straddle national boundaries.

THE MEANING OF 'DEATH'

Finally, the threat of sudden and violent death is a real prospect for individuals in the state of nature. But it is not really clear what 'death' involves for sovereign states. Even in monarchical states, we can distinguish between the death of the incumbent (a particular person) and the office of sovereign, or the Crown. Of course some states cease to exist, through such causes as fragmentation (as with the former Soviet Union or Yugoslavia), annexation (such as the Baltic states of Latvia, Lithuania and Estonia when they were invaded by the Soviet Union during the Second World War) or merger/absorption (as when the former German Democratic Republic merged with, or was absorbed by, the German Federal Republic). But even here there is partial survival, or indeed full-scale resurrection following apparent 'death', as with the Baltic states' re-emergence after the collapse of the Soviet Union. So, in sum, there seems to be a poor fit between the state of nature, as Hobbes describes it, and international politics.

HOBBESIAN RESPONSES

NON-EQUALITY

It may be that Hobbes envisaged the international sphere as one of equality. But he never explicitly makes this claim in *Leviathan*. The equality in offensive power that Hobbes describes in chapter 13 clearly does not hold good in the international arena. A more plausible suggestion is that the state of nature is an ideal type that is only ever imperfectly realised. Just as the commonwealth is lacunose – that is, the reach of civil power is limited, leaving pockets in which the state of nature persists – so any empirical realisation of the state of nature will contain local deviations from Hobbes' no-holds-barred paradigm, and this applies to international politics as a state of nature.

Even so, Hobbes' central claims about life in the state of nature are hard to sustain. The underlying problem is to provide a grounding for the motive of 'diffidence', as Hobbes describes it in chapter 13. To extract a more empirically plausible view of international politics from *Leviathan*'s state of nature, we have to give up the idea that the rough equality between individuals in the state of nature applies also to states. However, it is important to acknowledge that the difficulty of launching offensive war at a distance tends to narrow the disparity between unequal military powers. In addition, the sheer costs in personnel and *matériel* of belligerence against another power will often deter them from pre-emptive warfare. Each of these considerations raises the relative costs of aggression, so that we can no longer assume that, on cost/benefit grounds, belligerence must be preferable to inaction. So, while international power politics certainly manifests inequality, it does not necessarily precipitate violent conflict.

Rather than equality in killing power, as in the individual state of nature, the international arena displays marked inequalities in force, tempered by logistical and other obstacles. Once equality is modified along these lines, Hobbes' theory delivers more empirically plausible predictions about power play in the global arena. The powerful may be deterred by these obstacles from imposing their will even when confronted with markedly weaker prey. It does not preclude cooperative action where this benefits each party. But the residual inequalities in power suggest that even where cooperation is not zero-sum, the stronger party will be able to extract greater advantage from agreements than the weaker party. The terms of trade between Western nations and the poor south are a case in point.

'WAR'

As we saw in Chapter 4, in a state of 'war' in Hobbes' sense, there is no reasonable expectation that one will not without warning be subjected to attack. 'War' thus includes not just active hostilities but the lack of any stable expectation that such hostilities will break out. But even this, it may be said, exaggerates the instability of international politics. Switzerland, for example, is a small power that does not belong to NATO or any other external defensive alliance. But it is not under constant threat of invasion, nor has it felt constrained to launch pre-emptive attacks on its neighbours. It is hard then to defend the view that the individual state of nature applies to the international sphere, which can display stability despite the lack of even rough equalities of offensive power.

However, this very fact could be turned to Hobbes' advantage – assuming that Hobbes wants to depict international relations as a state of nature. Since rough equality in offensive power does not obtain, there is no universal motive for 'diffidence', that is, for launching pre-emptive aggression against other states. After all, if I know that I am much less powerful than you, and I know that you know this as well, I will also know that you have no reason of pre-emption for attacking me (though of course you may have other reasons). So any given state knows that the cost/benefit sum does not always favour belligerence, and pre-emption will not be the dominant strategy – that is, one that is better whatever others do. And the state will also know that, because other states know that pre-emption is not dominant, they will not have this reason to launch pre-emptive attacks on it (this is far from saying, of course, that nobody will ever have good self-interested reasons to pre-empt).

This modified theory can make better sense of the phenomena of international politics. More powerful states commit acts of aggression freely against less powerful ones, but the reverse seldom happens. Coalitions of small states may act against a larger one. Often states have interests that converge rather than conflict, and they can act jointly on this basis. It should be noted that Hobbes says that even individuals in the state of nature have no hope of survival without the help of 'confederates' (i.e. allies; *L* 102). However, cooperation is likely to persist only as long as their interests match. Even where the interests do coincide, it often proves hard (as nowadays with action on climate change) to concert joint action where each side fears that the others will not keep their side of the bargain. In this respect, self-interest marks both the individual state of nature and the 'international anarchy'; but in the latter case, self-interest will often tell against pre-emptive aggression rather than in favour of it. A case in point is the doctrine of 'mutually assured destruction' familiar from the superpower nuclear rivalry between the USA and Soviet Union during the Cold War.

UNSOCIABILITY

Given that the universal reasons that motivate pre-emptive action in the individual state of nature do not hold generally for sovereign states, the sporadic cooperation evident in international politics also becomes intelligible. For the 'incommodities' of the state of nature arise where nobody can reasonably expect that others will cooperate, and this is clearly so if everyone has good reason to fear pre-emptive aggression from everybody else. But where cooperative expectations are stabilised, first by the absence of any universal reason to fear aggression, and second by the fact that each party stands to gain more from cooperation than conflict, there is no reason why mutually beneficial exchanges, for example commercial ones, should not occur between states.

It is also important to see that, in part, the international system fails to mirror the no-holds-barred state of nature precisely because, in their internal make-up, sovereign states are not anarchic. The civil peace bestowed by government makes room for cooperation both within civil societies and between them. Hobbes allows for at least a rudimentary form of international civil society. He acknowledges, for instance, that the 'amity' between sovereigns may provide the basis of a 'contract' between them, by which subjects may be exempt, while in a foreign country, from laws there (L 154), as with diplomatic immunity.

NON-STATE ACTORS

Hobbes was aware that other international actors existed besides sovereign states. We have already mentioned the Roman Catholic Church, which relies for its continuing mission on a fabric of social and economic institutions. In chapter 22 Hobbes refers to 'corporations of men, that by authority from any foreign person, unite themselves in another's dominions, for the easier propagation of doctrines' (L 163). One of Hobbes' objections (e.g. L 475–76) to the Church of Rome is that it in effect sets up an alternative object of loyalty in states, since its clergy owe allegiance to the Pope rather than to their temporal sovereign.

The price of admitting this is to jettison any full parallel between the individual and international versions of the state of nature. But that has, of course, already been forfeited by abandoning rough equality as an initial postulate. To the extent that these other agents can vie with sovereign states, they add to the complexity of the international arena as a state of nature. But there is no reason in principle why they cannot be treated as self-interested actors in much the same way as sovereign states, to which the state-of-nature motives of competition, diffidence and glory can be ascribed.

THE MEANING OF 'DEATH'

The final point above – that states do not suffer 'death' in the same way as individuals do – can be met more directly. Sovereign states aim, at the minimum, to survive. Whatever else 'survival' may mean, it at least involves not suffering a catastrophic decline in power. This might be thought of as a form of functional arrest equivalent to the death of an individual. As Hobbes says, 'though sovereignty, in the intention of them that make it, be immortal; yet is it in its own nature, not only subject to violent death, by foreign war; but also ... it has in it, from the very institution, many seeds of a natural mortality' (*L* 153).

Some commentators (Beitz 1979; Malcolm 2002) argue that there is no analogue for the death of the individual with respect to sovereign states. It is true that a state may 'die' without its citizens dying. However, this seems to rely on the 'fallacy of division': the inference that if some collective entity has some property, then the parts of the collective must also have it. So, if the parts of the collective lack the property, the collective must also lack it. It is easy to see that this does not apply to collective or corporate entities in general: for example, a club may be poor even though the people who belong to it are well off (they may be too mean to make donations to it); a large crowd of people is not necessarily a crowd of large people (they may be attending a dwarves' convention). Similarly, the fact that, following the 'death' of a state – however this is interpreted – the citizens who used to belong to it can live on as citizens of some other state, does not force us to conclude that states cannot die. Many former citizens of the Soviet Union have survived as citizens of, for example, the Russian Federation.

***

Since equality only underwrites the motive of diffidence, rather than the other 'causes of quarrel' in the state of nature – namely 'competition' and 'glory' – removing the equality postulate leaves these other causes intact in the international sphere. That is, competition and glory make for conflict. It is all too clear how competition for relatively scarce resources can and often does trigger international disputes, including war in the usual sense (as well as a 'war' in Hobbes' sense). Indeed many historians would identify competition for scarce goods as a prime 'cause of quarrel' between nations both in modern times and earlier.

Equally, the motive of 'glory' often prompts wars of aggression by leaders who seek self-aggrandisement through military conquest, or indeed diplomatic brinkmanship. Glory is valued in itself but also instrumentally. It is a means of gaining power. But the reputation that follows from holding others in awe is itself a form of power, as it is likely to deter would-be aggressors. As Hobbes says, the desire for power is 'a general inclination of all mankind, a perpetual and restless desire of power after power'. In the case of 'kings, whose power is greatest', they 'turn their endeavours to the assuring it at home by laws, or abroad by wars' (*L* 70).

So far I have examined Hobbes' state of nature, and asked how well it stands up as a model for international politics. I have suggested that it stands up reasonably well if we abandon the equality postulate. Next we look at Hobbes' prominent role in present-day international relations theory, as a prophet of 'realism'.

HOBBES AS A REALIST

Along with liberalism and Marxism, realism is often identified as one among three traditional schools of thinking about international relations.[1] The realist school explains international relations by the self-interest of the actors involved – usually sovereign states or combinations of them. Hence it claims to take a 'realistic' view of states' actions, rather than (as in the liberal school) devising moral standards by which states' actions are to be assessed, and attempting to work out ways in which these standards can be imposed politically, or arguing (as do traditional Marxist theorists) that the international system is a temporary edifice that will be swept away once capitalism has been superseded.

Hobbes' influence on the realist school derives mainly from his description of the state of nature in *Leviathan* and some of his other works. Commentators have detected in this account four main features, which have led them to classify Hobbes as a realist. These are: self-interest, rationality, amorality and anarchy. We shall look at these in turn.

SELF-INTEREST

Hobbes is commonly thought of as advancing a 'self-interested' theory of human motivation, and this chimes with a key assumption made by the realist school: that states' actions on the international stage are explicable as the product of their self-interested calculation. Moreover, *Leviathan*'s account of the content of these motivations overlaps quite closely with the realist analysis of them. As Hobbes says, 'the passion to be reckoned upon is fear' (*L* 99), and modern-day realists echo this in emphasising the importance of security in states' perceptions of their own interests.

Similarly, as we have seen, two of the three main 'causes of quarrel' that Hobbes identifies in chapter 13 of *Leviathan* – that is, the motives provided by 'competition' and 'glory' (*L* 88) – readily make sense of international conflict in the modern world. The third motive given in chapter 13, namely 'diffidence', has limited applicability to the international sphere. Resources (including security itself) are scarce and lead to competition between states, while terrorist threats and 'weapons of mass destruction' help to even out inequalities of power between big powers and small ones. In some cases, the former may launch pre-emptive action against the latter, as in Iraq in 2003. Finally, the desire for reputation, which underlies the pursuit of glory, is a familiar motivation behind imperialist and expansionist projects down the ages to our own. Glory is an intrinsically scarce good. In fact, each motive proceeds from scarcity. Self-interest shows itself in efforts by each agent to enlarge his or her share.

RATIONALITY

Means–end reasoning

A closely linked feature that many commentators have seen in Hobbes' state of nature is a theory of rationality that holds that rational action is a matter of effective means–end calculation. The paramount end is self-preservation, and the problem facing individuals in the state of nature is to work out how best to achieve this. The laws of nature, which answer this question, are mere 'theorems' (*L* 111). That is, no ends or goals are in themselves more 'rational' than others – the ends that it is rational to promote are those that present themselves with overwhelming motivational force, and to be rational is simply to adopt the most effective means of achieving them.

Rational choice

More particularly, Hobbes is often credited with foreshadowing the rational choice approach to international relations, which tries to understand action by using the devices of game theory such as the prisoner's dilemma (see Chapters 5 and 6). The leading exponent of this view in contemporary international relations theory is Kenneth Waltz (Waltz 1979; Brown 2001, 43ff.). Game theory has played a major part in modern attempts by international relations theorists to explain conflict, for example in their attempts to understand nuclear arms proliferation between the USA and Soviet Union during the Cold War. Similarly it is applied to the problems in securing international cooperation where, in the absence of coercion, states will be tempted to act unilaterally and against the common interest in areas such as pollution control or fisheries policy.

Hobbes' claim that the laws of nature oblige *in foro interno* but not necessarily *in foro externo* (*L* 110), for instance, suggests that I do whatever, in my own rational judgement, best conduces to my preservation. Although it is better for each person if everyone abides by the laws of nature, it does not follow that it is always better for anybody to abide by them – specifically, where others are not doing so. Similarly, Hobbes' remarks about the 'Fool' earlier in chapter 15 (*L* 101–3) seem designed to show that individuals always have a self-interested reason for keeping their agreements, and not just a reason grounded in the fact that impersonal morality tells them that this is right.

AMORALITY

The means–end understanding of rationality contrasts with the view held by some Marxists and most liberals that morality provides statesmen with reasons which may override other, non-moral, considerations. In *Leviathan* it seems that the laws of nature gain their force from the fact that they promote self-preservation, not because they express the dictates of morality, seen as something independent of the natural drive to self-preservation. In Hobbes' own time, of course, the prevalent view was that these reasons gained their force from the Almighty, as the laws of nature, which God had laid down to safeguard human interests. This point remains controversial (see Chapter 4, 'Further Reading').

ANARCHY

Liberals incline to see the international arena as being at least partly regulated by legal instruments and international bodies like the UN. Though there is no world government, international politics is not simply chaos. But there are different ways in which this can be understood. Some liberals optimistically suppose that the principles that underlie norms of international cooperation, including legal norms, may be enough in themselves to make states comply with them. Realists assume, by contrast, that where there is no effective power to regulate behaviour, self-interested actors may nonetheless have good reason to create ordered systems of action. For example, states may use their bargaining power to secure cooperative agreements which, though entered into freely, have something like the force of law. This is self-interested give-and-take, not submission to norms whose moral force is enough in itself to make states abide by their agreements. Nonetheless, the underlying situation on this view is anarchy – cooperation persists only for so long as states have self-interested reason to engage in it.

In the early twenty-first century, the USA's unilateral derogations from the Kyoto Accords, its imposition of steel tariffs, its rejection of an international criminal court and bypassing of international law in making war against Iraq suggest that big powers can dodge frameworks of international cooperation if they are strong enough. Realists say, as Hobbes seems to, that nation states can do this because they can get away with it. If an objector asks why international politics is not mere chaos, the realist can reply that it is not because the actors – sovereign states – recognise that norms have a force independent of military and economic power. Rather it is because stronger states can enforce the norms against weaker non-compliant states if they want to do so.

WAS HOBBES ACTUALLY A REALIST?

It helps in understanding the issues underlying the conflicting interpretations of Hobbes' views to set out schematically the major lines of argument, and points of difference between them. The initial position, on which most commentators agree, is that Hobbes thought that

(IP) International politics is a state of nature (in Hobbes' understanding of the term).

I have set out above the respects in which *Leviathan* endorses (IP). Some interpreters also maintain that

(SN) The state of nature, as Hobbes describes it, is nasty, characterised by selfish individualism, treachery and so on.

And, once (SN) is granted, it readily follows that

(IPSN) International politics is nasty, characterised by selfish individualism, treachery and so on, which is one of the characteristic claims of realism. Interpretations of Hobbes on international relations largely take their bearings from these propositions. Realists such as Hans Morgenthau and Kenneth Waltz, who regard Hobbes as their prophet, are happy both to endorse (IP) and (SN), and to attribute these propositions to Hobbes; they are therefore also happy to take the consequence (IPSN), which informally sets out some of the central tenets of realism, and to attribute that to Hobbes too.

On the other hand liberals such as Charles Beitz who reject realism, concur in ascribing the (IP) + (SN) → (IPSN) inference to Hobbes but, since they reject (IPSN), they reject (IP) as well (they concur with Hobbes' view of the state of nature as set out in (SN)). Still further interpreters, such as Malcolm, contend that, since Hobbes himself did not endorse (SN), he is not committed to (IPSN) – that is, he dissents from one of the central contentions of realism[2] – but endorses instead a version of the more benign liberal view of international relations. Malcolm, whose concern is less with characterising international relations than with the correct interpretation of Hobbes' views about them, affirms something along the following lines:

(SN-Malcolm) The state of nature, as Hobbes described it, is characterised partly by conflicts but also convergences of interest, and actors within it are subject to natural (that is, the moral) law.

Therefore,

(IPSN-Malcolm) International politics, as Hobbes described it, is characterised partly by conflicts but also convergences of interest, and actors within it are subject to natural (that is, the moral) law.

My own view, set out earlier, is that Hobbes subscribes to (IR), subject to the qualification of the equality postulate. He says that 'commonwealths not dependent on one another ... live in the condition of a perpetual war, and upon the confines of battle, with their frontiers armed, and cannons planted against their neighbours' (*L* 149). (SN) also needs to be toned down, as it applies to international politics. Hence we should not accept (IPSN) in its unvarnished form. It is however very important to understand that these caveats to (IPSN) are fully consistent with ascribing self-interested motives to state actors.

Some commentators (Malcolm 2002; M. Williams 2005) have a different reason for rejecting (IPSN), namely that Hobbes did not think that only reasons drawn from self-interest could be normative for human beings. Hobbes says for example in chapter 30 that since 'equity' (in the form of equality before the law) is 'a precept of the law of nature, a sovereign is as much subject [to it] as any of the meanest of his people' (*L* 237; cf. Malcolm 2002, 437–38). He adds that 'the true doctrine of the laws of nature is the true moral philosophy' (*L* 111). So, since the laws of nature apply in the state of nature, and the law of nature is a moral law, the latter applies to international relations if it is a state of nature. Hobbes amplifies this point at the end of chapter 30, 'The Office [i.e. duties] of the Sovereign Representative':

> [c]oncerning the offices of one sovereign to another, which are comprehended in that law which is commonly called 'the law of nations', I need not say anything in this place; because the law of nations and the law of nature is the same thing. And every sovereign has the same right, in procuring the safety of his people, that any particular man can have in procuring his own safety. And the same law that dictates to men that have no civil government what they ought to do, and what to avoid in regard of one another, dictates the same to commonwealths, that is, to the consciences of sovereign princes and sovereign assemblies; there being no court of natural justice but in the conscience only, where not man, but God reigns.
>
> (*L* 244)

Malcolm is particularly concerned to repudiate the idea, which surfaces in discussions of *Leviathan* by both realists and their opponents, that Hobbes thought that justice and morality have no content unless the sovereign wills it, and therefore that international politics is morally null.

It is certainly true, as the quotations above bear out, that Hobbes' views in *Leviathan* cannot be reduced to slogans such as 'might is right'.[3] It is also undeniable that the theory aims to tell people how they ought to behave, and that its prescriptions rest on a substantive claim about the human good – that it consists in, or at least requires, peace. Hobbes carefully distinguishes first between private judgements of good and ill, which express individuals' appetites (*L* 39, 46, p110), and justice, which consists in doing what one has agreed to (*L* 239); and then he distinguishes private judgements from the objective content of the laws of nature, as counsels of peace (*L* 111). While Hobbes does say that no law can be unjust (*L* 239), he thinks this not because he simply believes that might makes right, but because the subjects are thought of as having agreed to whatever laws (within the law of nature) the sovereign sees fit to enact, and what has been agreed to cannot be unjust.

None of this means, however, that the law of nature imposes any stringent check on self-interest as a motive. Natural law is meant only to 'direct and keep [people] in such a motion, as not to hurt themselves by their own impetuous desires, rashness or indiscretion, as hedges are set, not to stop travellers, but to keep them in the way' (*L* 239–40). Hobbes does think that there are objective rules of conduct, enshrined in the laws of nature. '[A]ll men agree on this, that peace is good'; he is prepared to describe these laws as 'moral' in the sense that the study of them is 'the true moral philosophy' (*L* 111). But it does not follow that Hobbes rejected the classic realist view of conduct as self-interested. For example, he famously remarks in chapter 11 that 'I put for a general inclination of all mankind, a perpetual and restless desire of power after power, that ceases only in death'; he adds that the cause of this 'is not always that a man hopes for a more intensive delight ... but because he cannot assure the power and means to live well, which he has [at] present, without the acquisition of more' (*L* 70). Curbs on my behaviour stem not from morality as an external standard, conceived of as distinct from my self-interest – and thus potentially in conflict with it – but from my considering the best means to 'live well'. Hobbes makes this clear in stressing, towards the end of chapter 15, that we are not obliged to follow the laws of nature when they 'procure [one's] own certain ruin'. This is 'contrary to the ground of all laws of nature, which tend to nature's pre-servation' (*L* 110).

Since international politics is a state of nature, as already described, each actor is entitled to do whatever he deems necessary for self-preservation (*L* 91). As I have explained, the best way to achieve this may well be to seek peace rather than acting aggressively. But often, self-preservation requires a state to make war. In such a case, the law of nature will not provide an external reason for peacemaking that will show that the state's action is irrational or unreasonable. Nor will its actions be unjust, since until rights have been transferred by covenant, 'no action can be unjust ... the validity of covenants begins not but with [i.e. only with] the constitution of a civil power sufficient to compel men to keep them' (*L* 100–1).

CONCLUSION

We can conclude, then, that Hobbes' views in *Leviathan* are not so far from classical realism as some recent commentators have claimed. I have endorsed a modified version of the realist position, as follows:

(IP-modified)   International politics is a state of nature (in roughly Hobbes' understanding of the term), except that the equality postulate does not hold generally.

The modified state of nature also transforms (SN).

(SN-modified)   The state of nature, as Hobbes would describe it with the equality postulate qualified, is generally nasty, characterised by selfish individualism, treachery and so on, though self-interest quite often makes peaceful coexistence preferable to war.

This in turn delivers the only slightly modified conclusion,

(IPSN-modified) International politics is generally nasty, charac-terised by selfish individualism, treachery and so on, though self-interest quite often makes peaceful coexistence preferable to war.

The one and only 'ground' of the laws of nature is self-preservation. This offers far too thin a normative basis to make Hobbes a liberal internationalist before his time.

FURTHER READING

Leviathan, chapters 13, 22, 24, 30

HOBBES AS A REALIST

Despite recent attempts at revision, Hobbes remains a central figure in the realist tradition of thinking about international relations. A representative statement is Raino Malnes, *The Hobbesian Theory of International Conflict* (New York: Oxford University Press, 1994). See also Robert Kagan, *Paradise and Power: America and Europe in the new world order* (London: Atlantic Books, 2003). A similar view, but from a standpoint hostile to realism, is expressed by Charles Beitz, *Political Theory and International Relations* (Princeton, NJ: Princeton University Press, 1979), 27–59.

Further influential statements of the 'realist' interpretation of Hobbes can be found in Hedley Bull, 'Hobbes and the International Anarchy', *Social Research* 48 (1981), 717–38; and Bull's *The Anarchical Society: A study of order in world politics* (New York: Columbia University Press, 1977). See also Michael Walzer, *Just and Unjust Wars: A moral argument with historical illustrations* (Harmondsworth: Penguin, 1980).

HOBBES AS AN OPPONENT OF REALISM

An interpretation that tries to underline the ethical dimension of Hobbes' thinking on international affairs, is Michael Williams, *The Realist Tradition and the Limits of International Relations* (Cambridge: Cambridge University Press, 2005), and the same author's 'Hobbes and International Relations: A reconsideration', *International Organisation* 50 (1996), 213–36. See also Charles

Covell, *Hobbes, Realism, and the Tradition of International Law* (Basingstoke: Palgrave, 2004) for a further attempt to revise the accepted realist interpretation of *Leviathan*. Another statement of the same view can be found in A. Nuri Yurdusev, 'Thomas Hobbes and International Relations: From realism to rationalism', *Australian Journal of International Affairs* 60 (2006), 305–21. For earlier attempts to distance Hobbes from the realist tradition, see John Vincent, 'The Hobbesian Tradition in Twentieth-Century International Thought', *Millennium: Journal of International Studies* 10 (1981), 91–101, and Cornelia Navari, 'Hobbes and the "Hobbesian Tradition" in International Thought', *Millennium* 11 (1982), 202–22.

A further departure from the realist interpretation of Hobbes is offered by Noel Malcolm, 'Hobbes' Theory of International Relations', in his *Aspects of Hobbes* (Oxford: Clarendon Press, 2002), ch. 13. Malcolm argues that Hobbes should be understood not as a realist but as a 'rationalist', who regarded improvement in human behaviour, whether in domestic or international politics, as genuinely possible. A briefer statement of Malcolm's views can be found in Malcolm, 'What Hobbes Really Said', *National Interest* 81 (Fall 2005), 22–28, which stresses the alleged disanalogy between the prevalence of death and equality in the state of nature compared with the international sphere.

INTERNATIONAL RELATIONS AS A STATE OF NATURE

Richard Tuck, *The Rights of War and Peace: Political thought and the international order from Grotius to Kant* (Oxford: Oxford University Press, 1999), ch. 4, argues that sovereign states are not merely analogous to, but in fact Hobbes' model for, free individuals in the state of nature and that the right to aggressive war-making follows, for Hobbes, from this. Here Tuck is advancing his view that the main problem that Hobbes' political theory sets out to solve is epistemic scepticism – the general doubt that we can know anything (see Chapter 3 above). However, as with the individual state of nature, conflict would result from scarcity even if knowledge were attainable.

For a rejection of the view that any significant relation holds between the international sphere and the state of nature, see David Boucher, 'Inter-community and International Relations in the Political Philosophy of Hobbes', *Polity* 23 (1990), 207–32. Further scepticism that any significant analogy holds between the relations of individuals in the state of nature and those between sovereign states, is expressed in Beitz, *Political Theory and International Relations*, 40–52; Bull, *The Anarchical Society*, 49–50.

HOBBESIAN WORK IN INTERNATIONAL RELATIONS THEORY

A work that has been influential in international relations theory and which assumes the 'realist' interpretation of Hobbes is Martin Wight, 'The Three Traditions of International Theory' in his *International Theory: Three traditions* (Leicester: Leicester University Press, 1991). The classic modern statement of the realist position is Kenneth Waltz, *Theory of International Politics* (Reading, MA: Addison-Wesley, 1979). Good introductory textbooks on international relations theory in general are Chris Brown, *Understanding International Relations*, 2nd edn (Basingstoke: Palgrave, 2001); and David Boucher, *Political Theories of International Relations: From Thucydides to the present* (Oxford: Oxford University Press, 1998).

OTHER

Other attempts by Hobbes scholars to understand the role of international relations in his theory include Malcolm Forsyth, 'Thomas Hobbes and the External Relations of States', *British Journal of International Relations* 5 (1979), 196–209; and Robinson Grover, 'Hobbes and the Concept of International Law', in Timo Airaksinen and Martin Bertman (eds), *Hobbes: War among nations* (Aldershot: Avebury, 1989), 79–90. For an entertaining attempt to transplant Hobbes' theory into modern conditions, see Arthur Ripstein, 'Hobbes on World Government and the World Cup', also in Airaksinen and Bertman (eds), which foregrounds Hobbes' notion of 'glory' and its role in international politics. See also

Kinji Akashi, 'Hobbes' Relevance to the Modern Law of Nations', *Journal of the History of International Law* 2 (2000), 199–216.

Among modern interpreters of Hobbes, David Gauthier's *The Logic of Leviathan: The moral and political theory of Thomas Hobbes* (Oxford: Clarendon Press, 1969) includes an appendix in which he speculates about how Hobbes' theory might be applied to international relations. A briefer attempt along similar lines is contained in Howard Warrender's *The Political Philosophy of Hobbes* (Oxford: Clarendon Press, 1957), 118–20. Jean Hampton looks at Hobbesian explanations for international power politics in her 'Hobbesian Reflections on Glory as a Cause of Conflict', in Peter Caws (ed.), *The Causes of Quarrel: Essays on peace, war, and Thomas Hobbes* (Boston, MA: Beacon Press, 1989).

NOTES

1 These schools of thought have of course been augmented more recently by approaches such as constructivism.
2 Not the only such contention, since it is important to realists to affirm the view of international politics as represented by (IPSN), that is, to contend that there is no overarching law that shows that actors who behave as (IPSN) describes are acting contrary to reason or to morality. However, realists such as Raino Malnes (Malnes 1994, e.g. 32–33) are also inclined to attribute this view to Hobbes.
3 See the discussion of this topic above in Chapter 6.

11

LEVIATHAN
EARLY RESPONSES

INTRODUCTION

For better or worse, most works of political philosophy published today have little impact beyond a small audience of specialist scholars and academics. Even books such as John Rawls' *A Theory of Justice*, first published in 1971, which has become a classic and has been intensively discussed by political philosophers, are little read even by educated readers who do not specialise in the field. Rawls is far from being a household name, although the questions that *Theory of Justice* addresses – the basis of political authority, on what basis to distribute the benefits of social cooperation, the scope of individual liberty, and so on – overlap significantly with those that figure in political debate.

One index of comparison between the 'impact' of *Leviathan* is the likely print run of *Leviathan*: between 1,200 and 1,500 for the first edition of 1651 (Malcolm ed., Hobbes 2012, vol. I, 225), at a time when the population of England was around 5 million. Today, with a UK population 12 times that, and very large

English-speaking populations overseas, most works of political theory have an initial print run of 1,000 copies or less (a figure that has not been much affected by the advent of e-publishing). Sales of *Leviathan* seem to have been sluggish at first, though the book's publisher Andrew Crooke had allowed for a largish print run of between 1,200 and 1,500 copies (Malcolm ed., Hobbes 2012, vol. I, 225). The first edition, which appeared in 1651, sold at the high price of 8 shillings and 6 pence; by the 1680s, when a second edition of *Leviathan* (the 'Bear' edition) had been published, the work was fetching between 12 and 16 shillings a copy second-hand (Malcolm ed., Hobbes 2012, vol. I, 231ff.). Moreover, readers had already had access to Hobbes' political theory via the *Elements of Law*, published in 1640, and *De cive*, published in Latin in 1642; the English translation of this work, entitled *Philosophicall Rudiments concerning Government and Society*, appeared in the same year as *Leviathan* itself.

Hence those curious to find out Hobbes' thoughts on politics and government had a number of options, and as some contemporaries pointed out, *De cive* and its translation presented those thoughts in more concise form than the bulky and prolix *Leviathan*. There is some evidence that the latter's first edition, with a print run of perhaps a thousand copies, failed to sell out: I noted earlier that Samuel Pepys had tried to obtain a copy of *Leviathan* in 1668, by which time new copies were selling at the very high price of 30 shillings each: this may have been because the great fire of 1666 in London had destroyed many copies; a number of booksellers' premises were consumed in the fire; the book had also acquired scandal value, as the House of Commons was at this time investigating *Leviathan* as part of the proceedings on the Atheism and Profaneness Bill (Malcolm ed., Hobbes 2012, vol. I, 231–33). The copy Pepys mentions may have been one of the de luxe 'large-paper' versions of the first edition. If the book Pepys mentions was a copy of that edition, it suggests that the first print run had not sold out even seventeen years after publication (Parkin 2007, 96).

However, as with most aspects of *Leviathan*'s publishing history, matters are less straightforward than this. First, the copy Pepys mentions may not have been a new one, but one unsold from the print run of the 1651 'Head' edition. Second, relatedly, in early modern England there was a brisk underground trade in pirated editions of books; for instance, in the 1580s Roger Ward was found to have illegally published around 10,000 pirated copies of the 'alphabet books' commonly used to teach the rudiments of writing. Anyone with a printing press could pirate copies of a book – for instance, Hobbes' own *Elements of Law* was pirated from manuscript copies in circulation in editions published between 1650 and 1652 (Malcolm 2002, 464).

Moreover, because of the opportunity cost of keeping type set, books – including *Leviathan* – were printed in a piecemeal fashion, and incomplete versions could enter circulation or be cannibalised to create new editions. Third, particularly under systems of press regulation such as that in place in 1650s and 1660s England, where the Stationers' Company acted as a cartel licensing book publication, a samizdat-style readership was liable to emerge even with publications that, like *Leviathan*, had got a licence but were expensive – which is not to say that the Stationers' Company was a monopoly, as there was a clear split between the company insiders and those traders who operated outside and opposed the cartel (Astbury 1978, 301; Treadwell 2002, 771). The importance of the Stationer's Company was, however, underlined during the Restoration period: the Printing Act of 1662 'preventing abuses in printing seditious, treasonable and unlicensed books and pamphlets' aimed at control of the press by ensuring prepublication vetting by the Stationers' Company (Treadwell 2002, 756ff.; Astbury 1978); books could only be imported to the country via the Port of London, where suspect consignments could be seized by the Company's inspectorate. Moreover, since books were generally sold unbound, parts of them could be detached and circulated separately.

The result is that it is hard to get any clear picture of the number of copies of *Leviathan* in circulation in the 1650s and 1660s, after its first publication; high prices certainly offer some evidence that demand exceeded supply. As Malcolm notes, 'the most obvious reason for printing a second edition of *Leviathan* [during the late 1660s, in what became the "Bear" or second English printing of the book] was to cash in on the notoriety of the book, which had pushed its price to unusually high levels' (Malcolm 2002, 343). During the 1650s as many as three people seem to have proposed translating *Leviathan* into French, though no version appeared in that language for over a hundred years (Malcolm 2002, 467ff.); in part this was because of the circulation of the Latin *De cive* on the continent and because *Leviathan* itself appeared in Latin by 1668.

The length of *Leviathan*, its often polemical tone, and Hobbes' delight in intellectual iconoclasm and epigrammatic aperçus made the book an unusually productive source for those in search of mud to sling at political and religious opponents. Often Hobbes expressed, or could be made out to have expressed, extreme thoughts that in some milder form might be held by one's adversaries, so that the super-strength Hobbesian version of the idea might be held up polemically as a logical or causal consequence of the milder view. The other side of that coin, of course, was that opponents could return the favour, and make one's own views seem dangerous or eccentric by dressing them in Hobbesian garb.

LEVIATHAN AND THE ENGAGEMENT

It is beyond argument that Hobbes became notorious for views that became associated with his name under the label 'Hobbism'. The term, always used pejoratively, referred to a variable set of doctrines that Hobbes was thought to have espoused, including atheism, the absolute subordination of the church to the state, psychological and ethical egoism, monarchical absolutism, anti-clericalism, the 'rebel's catechism' that endorsed insurrection against authority, libertinism, a 'Socinian', 'Arian' or Unitarian denier of the Trinity, a 'caesaro-papist' proponent of merging the church into the state, the 'Pelagian' denial of the doctrine of original sin, and so on. Not all of these charges were without foundation; for instance, Hobbes was hard put to deny the charge of caesaro-papism, given that *Leviathan* proposed the wholesale subordination of the church to secular authority. On some of the other accusations, Hobbes' text left more room for interpretation.

As we have already seen, *Leviathan* has been read as an intervention in the debate over 'Engagement' – that is, whether people (particularly those who had supported the king during the civil war) should take an oath of loyalty or 'Engagement' to the new republican regime following Charles I's execution; this was a particularly thorny question for landowners, who faced the sequestration of their estates if they failed to 'compound' (i.e. to pay a fine and pledge not to take up arms again) with Parliament's Committee for Compounding with Delinquents. Meanwhile, the Presbyterians, who had supported Parliament in the first civil war, switched sides in the second, and at the end of 1648 (when the king had again been defeated), found themselves pushed out of political power in what amounted to a military coup (Pride's purge). But the new dominant party, the Independents, knew that their power rested on thin ground. Hence their need to elicit people's allegiance to the new regime.

In February 1649 members of the executive Council of State were directed to take the oath of Engagement. In October 1649 the oath was extended to all MPs, as well as clergymen, government officials, teachers and members of the armed forces. Then, at the start of 1650, Parliament passed the Act for Subscribing the Engagement, which required all males over eighteen to swear the following oath: 'I do declare and promise, That I will be true and faithful to the Commonwealth of England, as it is now Established, without a King or House of Lords' (Firth and Rait 1911, 325ff.). In October 1650 Parliament ordered the removal of clergy (mainly Presbyterians) who had refused to take the oath.

At this time, of course, Hobbes was still exiled in France. However, certain problems beset the thesis, prominently argued by Quentin Skinner (2002, vol. III, ch. 10), that *Leviathan* was intended as a 'contribution to the lay theory of engagement' (Skinner 2002, vol. III, 306), which along with other contributions such as those of Anthony Ascham, Marchamont Nedham, John Drew and Francis Osborne, who on broadly pragmatic grounds counselled submission to the new regime. One problem with this thesis is chronological. Little hard evidence about the precise date at which Hobbes started work on *Leviathan* is available, but the best estimate (Malcolm ed., Hobbes 2012, vol. I, 8–9), is that Hobbes had begun writing it by spring or early summer 1649, at which point only the members of the Council of State had been required to take the oath. Indeed, Hobbes may have started compiling notes that eventually formed the basis for *Leviathan* considerably earlier, in the mid-1640s (Malcolm ed., Hobbes 2012, vol. I, 10–11); in which case it follows with added force that the original impulse to write the book was not supplied by the Engagement debate.

Second, if this was its aim, *Leviathan* does not suit the purpose very well. The book was both expensive and very long. It begins by tackling a range of non-political topics such as logic, geometry, human psychology and semantics, and takes many pages to get to the political theory set out in Part 2 of the book. *Leviathan* then embarks on a lengthy disquisition on theology in Part 3. This inevitably blunts its polemical effectiveness. By contrast, political pamphlets of the day were often composed quickly for a specific occasion and might run to 8,000 words; *Leviathan* is over 200,000 words long. Nor does Hobbes seem to have rushed to get it out, although if he did indeed begin work on it in earnest in spring or early summer 1649, he wrote it very fast. The trouble taken with the book, notably the production of a de luxe large-paper limited edition and the scribal manuscript prepared for presentation to Prince Charles (see Chapter 2), also does not suggest that Hobbes was in a hurry to join battle over the Engagement, which had in any case been enacted into law well before *Leviathan* was completed.

More specifically, third, the arguments that Hobbes gives are in some respects not very well adapted to the job of justifying the Engagement. If there is one interpretation on which virtually every reader of *Leviathan* agrees, it is that Hobbes advocates the subordination of religious to political authority. This could with some shuffling be reconciled with the dominant Independent party, which held that there should be no established church and that local congregations should be free to organise themselves on broadly self-governing lines – though nothing in *Leviathan* obviously rules out an Anglican-style established church under the secular sovereign, and indeed precisely this arrangement, with the restored king as Supreme Head of the Church of England, was reinstated in England after 1660 to Hobbes' apparent contentment. Hobbes' uncompromising support for secular domination of the church was unlikely to go down well with neither of the two main constituencies of opinion that the new regime needed to get onside, namely civil war royalists and the Presbyterians.

This is backed up by Hobbes' remarks in *Leviathan* about oaths. This may strike modern readers as an odd concern for a political theorist to address. But for Hobbes' seventeenth-century readers the force of an oath would be conventionally taken as a summons to God to witness the oath-taker, and hold him to account should he fail to do what he had undertaken. Hobbes' discussion of oaths is the passage in the book that seems most obviously relevant to the Engagement which was, after all, administered by means of an oath. It occurs in chapter 14, just after Hobbes has stated that 'the passion to be reckoned upon, is fear' (*L* 99). There he remarks that 'the oath adds nothing to the obligation. For a covenant, if lawful, binds in the sight of God, without the oath, as much as with it: if unlawful, bindeth not at all' (*L* 100). The 'obligation' stems from transfer of right, carried out either by word or, more usually, by deed, when a subject acts as if the sovereign authority rules and accepts protection from it (cf. *L* 485) – the oath adds nothing. Since this was conventionally understood as an avowal before God, Hobbes' position on oaths added fuel to accusations of atheism. Likewise the Engagement added nothing that was not provided by the fact that Parliament, presided over by the Council of State, wielded power and, through the army, could furnish protection.

Finally, there is the testimony of Hobbes himself. In *Considerations, upon the Reputation, Loyalty, Manners and Religion of Thomas Hobbes of Malmesbury*, written in 1662, Hobbes refers to the Solemn League and Covenant of 1643, a pact between the English Parliament and the Scottish Presbyterians, which also involved a form of political undertaking or engagement, as 'a very great Crime', as was 'the imposing of the Engagement', i.e. the one imposed on all men in England by the 1650 Act (Hobbes 1839–45 [1680], 13–14).

Of course, it is fair to point out that Hobbes' position about making one's peace with the post-monarchical regime at the end of the 1640s had been noticeably less hostile. It is usual to regard these protestations as retrospective self-justification produced over ten years after the Engagement debate, when the monarchy had been restored and Hobbes had a vested interest in making his younger self look less accommodating to the republican regime than he was at the time. But it is also possible that Hobbes was being less disingenuous than he may seem. He had, after all, been closely associated with the royalist cause, and indeed the Stuart royal family, during his exile in Paris, acting as a tutor to Prince Charles. While there were certainly aspects of *Leviathan* that provoked disquiet among Hobbes' more conservatively minded royalist confrères like Edward Hyde, as we shall see, the book was some way from being the 'Rebel's catechism' that Hobbes' antagonist John Bramhall alleged. Although – the main point that bothered Bramhall – the scope of the subject's right to resist the sovereign remained unclear in the theory, if Bramhall had been correct, Hobbes could hardly have also supported the republican regime's right to exact obedience in the form of an Engagement that the theory itself said subjects could break at will. Indeed, this scope for rebellion might be thought to leave the door open for future acts of rebellion, such as those aimed at restoring the monarchy.

The *Considerations* is noteworthy both for what Hobbes reaffirms about the obligation to obey the republican regime, and what he denies. He first points out that *Leviathan* could not have been written in defence of 'Oliver's title' since Cromwell did not become Lord Protector until two years after its publication. Hobbes says that royalists 'were forced to compound' in order to save 'their Lives and Fortunes, which in [*Leviathan*] he hath affirmed they might lawfully do, and consequently not lawfully bear Arms against the Victors' (Hobbes 1839–45 [1680], 20). His point is that royalists had done everything within their power to assist the king, 'and were consequently at liberty to seek the safety of the Lives and Livelihood wheresoever, and without Treachery'.

The case, Hobbes says, is different with parliament's supporters like Wallis, since they sought to undermine the king's power while he still wielded it. Hobbes then reiterates the remark in *Leviathan*'s 'Review, and Conclusion' that 'every man is bound as much as in him lies, to protect in war the authority by which he is himself protected in time of peace' (*L* 484; Hobbes 1839–45

[1680], 21–22). He also repeats the point that submission is tokened by words or 'other sufficient signs' when 'the means of his life are within the guards and garrisons of the enemy' (*L* 484). At this point Hobbes makes a crucial clarificatory point: '[i]t was not necessary', he says, to add the rider 'Unless they came into those Guards and Garrisons by their own Treason' (Hobbes 1839–45 [1680], 23). In other words, the 'mutual relation between protection and obedience' (*L* 491) did not extend to those who, by rebelling against their protection, found protection instead in a usurping power. That excluded Presbyterian opponents of Charles I like Wallis, and precluded agreements like the Solemn League and Covenant. For them, an engagement made without right would not be made right by the addition of an oath. On the other hand, 'submission implieth them all' – that is, what conquest is, when it occurs, and in what the conqueror's right consists, lies in the act of submission. Hobbes adds, that '[c]onquest is not the victory itself, but the acquisition by victory, of a right over the persons of men' (*L* 485). So the royalists who compounded had in effect already submitted to the new regime, and done so with right; and again, an oath of engagement was extraneous.

On these grounds, then, the suggestion that *Leviathan* should be seen primarily as a contribution to the debate about the Engagement oath seems unpersuasive, and even the 'Review, and Conclusion', the part of the book most obviously suited to serve such a purpose, fails to provide conclusive reasons to engage. It could still, however, be seen as giving reasons for ex-royalists to compound, and therewith to submit to the new regime.

FURTHER POLITICAL CONTROVERSY

At the start of this chapter we saw that evidence about the circulation of *Leviathan* after it was first published is quite sketchy. What is clearer, however, is that a number of authors in England felt constrained to enter the lists against *Leviathan* in the years after 1651. One of the problems Hobbes faced was that *Leviathan* offered a series of trenchant arguments on a wide variety of controversial questions. This eclecticism tended to wrong-foot readers, who might find themselves by turns repelled and attracted by the views the book expressed. It also made the book a particularly fertile source of argumentative straw men. This was clearest with the reactions to *Leviathan*'s treatment of the basis of political authority, and the theological arguments that Hobbes made in Part 3 of the book, which exerted a formative influence on the reception of the book first in England and later on the continent.

Samuel Mintz's *Hunting of Leviathan* (Mintz 1962, 157–60) includes a list of anti-Hobbes pamphlets and other works published from 1650 onwards. As that cut-off date indicates, not all of the works respond to *Leviathan* – Hobbes was involved in several other polemics during the 1650s, including those with John Wallis and with Bishop Bramhall, though these controversies sometimes spilled over into one another; for instance, Wallis' *Elenchus geometriae Hobbianae* of 1655, aimed mainly at refuting Hobbes' efforts at 'squaring the circle', also aims to undermine the theology and ecclesiology of *Leviathan*. But a number of authors did specifically target *Leviathan*.

Many of these writers were considerable figures in their own right. They include the political theorist Sir Robert Filmer (1588–1653), in *Observations on Mr Hobbes' Leviathan* in 1652; *Leviathan Drawn Out with a Hook*, published in 1653, by Alexander Ross (1590–1654), who produced the first English version of the Qur'an; and the Cambridge Platonist Henry More's (1614–87) *Antidote to Atheism* of the same year. The *Humble Advice* of 1655, written by Richard Baxter (1615–91), a prominent Nonconformist cleric, called for *Leviathan* to be burned (Parkin 2007, 114); as we shall see, this call was taken up considerably later. Seth Ward (1617–89), Savilian Professor of Astronomy at Oxford and future Bishop of Salisbury, published *In Thomae Hobbii philosophiam* in 1656, and John Bramhall (1594–1663), the one-time Bishop of Derry and future Archbishop of Armagh, wrote *Castigations of Mr. Hobbes* and *The Catching of the Leviathan* in 1658. An early signal of opposition to the book was the *Beacon* petition of 1652, named after a pamphlet entitled *A Beacon Set on Fire* (Collins 2007, 483–90).

A Beacon Set on Fire (1652), compiled by Luke Fawne and other Presbyterian booksellers, includes a catalogue of blasphemies deemed to be 'not Popish' (Parkin 2007, 114; Lemetti 2011, 159). This latter list includes various claims ascribed to Hobbes in *Leviathan*. The petitioners were a consortium of booksellers led by Luke Fawn, and though their prime target was the suppression of 'Popish' publications, they also called for *Leviathan* to be suppressed on grounds of blasphemy (Parkin 2007, 114). The *Beacon* tract set off an extended pamphlet war, which had a strong ideological backdrop. The Beacon petitioners were Presbyterians, who had sold, and in some cases also authored, publications for the Westminster Assembly of Divines, a Presbyterian-dominated body that had been commissioned in the 1640s by the Long Parliament to examine Church of England reform. Early in 1652, seven or eight months after *Leviathan* was published, Thomas Hill, a Presbyterian former member of the Assembly, wrote to Richard Baxter to tell him that Baxter's 'deep detestation of Hobbes his Leviathan hath awakened some of us to consider what is fitt to be done therein' (Collins 2007, 484–86).

The *Beacon*, which appeared a few months later, lists some of Hobbes' most egregious blasphemies, drawn from Part 3 of *Leviathan*. Among the doctrines objected to by the petitioners was Hobbes' claim that the sovereign alone was final arbiter of scriptural interpretation (e.g. *L* 355); his 'mortalism', i.e. his belief that the soul did not endure for eternity (*L* 430ff.); and his claim that there was no obligation to practise the true faith if the sovereign commanded otherwise (e.g. *L* 343). The pamphlet war continued, with an intervention by Baxter himself, but the petitioners failed in their efforts to get *Leviathan* banned. As the 1650s progressed, however, a number of other writers engaged with Hobbes' text.

George Lawson's *An Examination of the Political Part of Mr. Hobbs His Leviathan* was published in 1657; Lawson, a village clergyman, was a political theorist in his own right. Lawson disputes many of Hobbes' theological premises and the political conclusions drawn from them, for example declaring that 'Civil Government derives its Being from Heaven; for it is a part of Gods Government over mankind' (Rogers 1995, 16). Not surprisingly, Lawson finds some of Hobbes' theological views unpalatable, such as his claim that the 'right of Gods soveraignty is derived not from Creation, but his irresistible Power' (Rogers 1995, 110) – a claim that, as we have seen, makes God's sovereignty seem to depend on sheer force, as indeed the *Leviathan* passages in Job appear to say. Mainly, however, Lawson focuses on the political claims made in *Leviathan*, relying on a familiar argumentative fork: those of Hobbes' claims that were true were not new, while those that were new were not true: '[m]any of his Rules I confess are good, but most of them are such as are very ordinary and commonly known ... in those points wherein he is singular, he can hardly be excused from error' (Rogers 1995, 107).

One cause of *Leviathan*'s hostile initial reception was that many of Hobbes' erstwhile royalist allies felt that he had turned his coat. Insofar as the latter held a theory of legitimate political authority, it was usually based on the notion of divine right (Sommerville 1986, 5ff.; Skinner 2002, vol. III, 288), defended by the future James I in *The Trew Law of Free Monarchies* of 1598 (James I 2002, 61):

> their obedience, I say, ought to be to him, as to Gods Lieutenant in earth, obeying his commands in all thing, except directly against God, as the commands of Gods Minister, acknowledging him a Iudge set by GOD ouer them, hauing power to iudge them, but to be iudged onely by GOD, whom to onely hee must giue count of his iudgement.

In other words, monarchs were accountable for their actions – but only to God, to whom they owed their position in the first place. The biblical *locus classicus* for defences of this position was St Paul's letter to the Romans, where Paul says that 'there is no power but of God: the powers that be are ordained of God' (Romans 13:1). The implication, stated directly in the next verse, is that to resist the sovereign is, by extension, to resist God himself.

Not much in *Leviathan* echoes such a view. Hobbes does in fact cite in paraphrase the opening of Romans 13 (*L* 342–43), but in this passage he uses the biblical text against the claim that churchmen can wield power granted by God against the secular sovereign. It can be thought of as an opportunistic argument pitched on ground that Hobbes' opponents were committed to occupying. Hobbes' own view is that legitimate authority derives from a transfer or waiving of right in respect of the sovereign (e.g. *L* 485). This means that the sovereign is a human creation, whose legitimacy, contrary to the position held by conservative monarchists such as Filmer, depends on the several decisions by each individual to give up natural rights: unless a person does this she cannot be regarded as a subject, but only as an enemy of the commonwealth (*L* 216, 485).

At the same time, royalists felt that Hobbes allowed far too much scope for rebellion by his denial in *Leviathan* that the right to resist could be wholly alienated to the sovereign (*L* 93, 96). In the early 1650s, hard on the heels of the overthrow, trial and execution of Charles I, his defeated supporters were alert to the possibility that political theory might be used or indeed designed to justify the rebellion. In the pamphlet wars that raged at the time, a number of writers were prepared to defend either the regicide itself, or to commend pragmatic accommodation with the post-royal regime. Recent events had, after all, made rebellion far from an abstract or academic contingency. And what was justified in retrospect, might also be justified in prospect, or even become a self-fulfilling prophecy. Above all, the notion of an original agreement to set up government was anathema to royalist traditionalists, given the divine right doctrine. This was not simply because God was removed from the picture as the source of right. It was also because the rights of nature which are ultimately transferred to the sovereign are conferred by the subjects, who hold these rights before the inception of government. Thus the source of right lay in the people and (it might be thought, although Hobbes rejects this possibility (e.g. *L* 122)) what can be conferred can also be revoked.

Hobbes was accordingly censured for basing the obligation to obey the sovereign not upon the will of God, but that of human beings, and this consenter contract-based reasoning was anathema to many royalists: they disliked the corollary that a king might be held to account for failing to keep his side of the agreement with his subjects, as this was thought tantamount to licensing 'sedition'. While Hobbes emphasises that the sovereign retains all his rights intact from the state of nature, and to this extent has 'absolute' authority, the inalienable right to resist might be thought to limit this absolutism. But in fact for critics like Hyde, this was doubly wrong. First, Hyde objected to this particular limitation of sovereign power, which Hobbes had extended even to condemned criminals; second, and in contrast, Hyde thought that Hobbes had made the monarch's other powers too broad, and more generally that it was the *failure* to put the relationship of sovereign and subjects on a contractual footing that made the agreement ripe for abuse.

The idea that *Leviathan* amounted to a primer for rebellion was widely held. 'Was there ever such a trumpeter of rebellion heard before?' Bramhall asked rhetorically in his *The Catching of Leviathan* (Martinich and Battiste 2011, 347), just after the passage where he describes the book as a rebel's catechism. For Christian royalists like Bramhall, furthermore, Hobbes' theory lacked any firm moral foundation. His depiction of moral anarchy in the state of nature was shocking to those who thought of the pre-political condition of human beings as subject at least to the governance of moral laws (the laws of nature) whose author was God. For Hobbes, by contrast, those in the state of nature were subject to no moral restraint in their pursuit of self-preservation; the laws instituted in the commonwealth were not unjust, so long as they had been consented to, as the sovereign power has.

Its lack of obvious orthodoxy, or obvious lack of orthodoxy, on so many fronts made *Leviathan* a rhetorical pawn in successive political controversies. Imputations of 'Hobbism' were routinely made to castigate or ridicule opponents. Accusations of Hobbism bulked large, for example, in the debate over church organisation that followed the re-establishment of the Church of England after 1660. The 'latitudinarians' in the Church of England after the Restoration advocated religious unity among Protestants in the face of threats from both 'Papists' within the country, particularly after Charles II's Declaration of Indulgence of 1672 that suspended penal laws against Roman Catholics, and the popular ferment from 1678 of the 'Popish Plot', a fictitious Catholic conspiracy to assassinate the King; and from outside the country, from the Catholic powers on the continent, notably France and Spain. However, the Latitudinarians faced opposition on the dissenting wing of Protestantism, who resented both the relaxation of the anti-Catholic laws and the 'Clarendon Code' enacted between 1661 and 1665, which enforced Anglicanism's dominance and penalised dissenting minorities.

From the perspective of these non-Anglican dissenting sects, Anglicans' defence of latitudinarianism looked – or could be made to look – uncomfortably close to *Leviathan*'s 'Erastian' subordination of the church to the sovereign (Parkin 2007, 361). One obvious source of worry for Protestants as the 1670s progressed was the fact that as Charles had no surviving legitimate children, the heir presumptive was his younger brother James, Duke of York, who was correctly suspected to be a Roman Catholic. Hence the hard-to-deny consequence of the Hobbes' claim that subjects should conform themselves to the sovereign's religion, whatever it might be, was that the country would sooner or later be required to turn Catholic. Latitudinarians like John Tillotson (1630–94), who eventually became Archbishop of Canterbury, tried to distinguish their position from Hobbes' but with little success (Parkin 2007, 359).

Tillotson ran into difficulties over a sermon entitled *The Protestant Religion Vindicated*, preached in 1680 before the King, when Tillotson was Dean of Canterbury. He stated, 'I cannot think ... that any pretence of conscience warrants any man' other than those inspired as were the Apostles, 'to affront the established religion of a nation, though it be false, and openly to draw men from the profession of it'. The *Biographia Britannica* account of this episode recounts that 'a witty Lord, standing at the King's elbow when this was delivered, said *Sir, Sir, do you hear Mr Hobbes in the pulpit?*' The account goes on to report Dr Hickes (George Hickes, an Anglican priest and scholar of linguistics) as saying that the Bishop of Ely Peter Gunning 'complained of this sermon in the House of Lords, as containing a doctrine that would serve the cause of Popery'.[1] Hence Hobbes, notwithstanding his vitriolic anti-Catholic rhetoric in *Leviathan* Part 4, which likens the papacy to 'the Kingdom of Fairies' (*L* 482), could be cited even in accusations of crypto-Catholicism.

OFFICIAL PERSECUTION AND PROHIBITION

Not only did *Leviathan* attract controversy in the war of words that followed its publication; the book also gained unwelcome attention from the authorities, both under the Protectorate of Oliver Cromwell in the 1650s, and during the Restoration period after 1660. While Hobbes' detractors drew on his other writings when making their case against him, there is no doubt that *Leviathan*, with its wide-ranging and controversial views – not only on political theory, but on human psychology, the basis for social order, the structure of the family, the mortality of the soul, the materiality of nature, the punishment of the damned, the Trinity, legal and ecclesiastical authority, and much else – provided a large target for critics to aim at. Hobbes' rhetoric also invited controversy: at times it was wilfully iconoclastic.

When *Leviathan* was published, printed matter was subject to censorship. In 1557, Queen Mary had granted the Stationers' Company its charter, which awarded the company a monopoly of book production in exchange for the Company's acting as state censor. The new republican regime passed a Printing Act in 1649 (renewed in 1653), to 'restrain from too arbitrary and general an exercise' the 'irregularity and licentiousness of printing', with a tariff of penalties applicable to the bookseller, printer, and above all the author in case of breach. That *Leviathan* should be threatened with censorship was an irony probably not lost on him: in chapter 18 of the book he had argued that 'it is annexed to the sovereignty to be judge of what opinions and doctrines are averse, and what conducing to peace; and consequently, on what occasions, how far, and what, men are to be trusted withal, in speaking to multitudes of people; and who shall examine the doctrines of all books before they be published'. The sovereign could in principle intervene personally (as James I had done) to decide what publications were to be suppressed. The reason, given most clearly in chapter 29, was simple: unrestricted publication allowed for the fomenting of sedition against the sovereign, by for example 'the reading of the books of policy' (*L* 225). Nonetheless, *Leviathan* circulated freely in England during the remainder of the republican period, and after the Restoration.

At the same time, some of the accusations made by Hobbes' critics were echoed by public officials. In 1657, according to the diary of Sir Thomas Burton, MP for Westmorland, a man named Robinson (probably Humphrey Robinson, a Stationer's Company official charged with censoring the presses during the Protectorate) had presented *Leviathan* to the Committee for Bibles as 'a most poisonous piece of atheism',[2] but in this case no further action seems to have been taken.

However, as has already been mentioned, *Leviathan* was also subject to investigation during the later 1660s as part of the House of Commons proceedings on a bill against 'atheism' then going through Parliament. After the restoration of the Stuart monarchy, Parliament passed the Licensing Act (1662), which subjected books to vetting by the bishops of the reinstated Church of England before publication. The government press surveyor and licenser, Sir Roger L'Estrange, had determined to enforce the press licensing system more rigorously, while Charles II's fear of the bishops' response had led him to stop the publication of *Behemoth*, Hobbes' narrative of the civil wars (Malcolm 2002, 348): this added a further layer of irony, since *Leviathan* itself argues that the church should be subordinated in all secular matters to the sovereign, i.e. the temporal authority (e.g. *L* 391–92). Anglican as well as Nonconformist clerics were quick to identify the great fire of London in 1666 as a mark of God's wrath towards a sinful people (Field 2008, 362ff.). John Milward MP noted in his diary on 3 September 1666 that two sermons had been preached before the House of Commons calling for a reformation of the nation's morals (Milward 1938, 37; cf. Kuchta 2009, 47). In this fervid atmosphere, in October 1666, just over a month after the fire, a 'Bill against Atheism, Profaneness and Swearing' was introduced to the House of Commons.

Milward noted in his diary that *Leviathan* was among the books called for investigation (Milward 1938, 25). On 17 October the house ordered the committee created by the bill to investigate 'such Books as tend to Atheism, Blasphemy, or Profaneness, or against the Essence or Attributes of God', one of which was named as *Leviathan*. The committee overseeing the bill was charged with investigating 'in particular … the Book of Mr. Hobbs called

The Leviathan; and to report the Matter, with their Opinions, to the House'.[3] This rattled the now seventy-eight-year-old Hobbes, who, as White Kennett related some decades later, 'was then at Chatsworth, and appear'd extreamly disturb'd at the News of it; fearing that messengers would come for him, and the Earl would deliver him up, and the Two Houses commit him to the Bishops, and they decree him a Heretick, and return him to the Civil Magistrate for a Writ *de Haeretico comburendo* [i.e. to have him burned as a heretic]' (Kennett 1708, 109–10).

The bill was given a final reading in the Commons in January 1667 and passed up to the Lords, where it received a second reading in October. However, the measure met with strong opposition, mainly because its content, dealing as it did with beliefs rather than observable practices, was seen as not being legally enforceable. The bill stalled after 1668, but was revived in the House of Lords in February 1674 and again in November 1675 (Milton 1993, 520). No doubt Hobbes' fears of being burned as a heretic were indeed baseless – the last person to be committed to the flames for heresy was the Anabaptist Edward Wightman, executed at Lichfield in 1612 – although the Writ *de Haeretico comburendo*, introduced in the reign of Henry IV, remained a valid legal instrument until 1677.

In fact, as *Leviathan* had been published in 1651, it was covered by the Indemnity and Oblivion Act of 1660, which limited score-settling from the pre-Restoration period to those who had authorised the execution of Charles I (Milton 1993, 519; Malcolm 2002, 350). Hobbes acknowledged as much in his 1662 *Apology* for *Leviathan* (Hobbes 1839–45, vol. VII, 4), which attempted to dispel the impression that *Leviathan* had been written expressly to legitimate the regicide of Charles I and the Commonwealth regime that followed it. There had been no legal authority to judge heresy in 1651, as the Court of High Commission had been abolished (Kennett 1708, 110–11), although the common law offence of heresy remained until 1677, but even in this case the order had to be made by the Lord Chancellor acting on a directive from the sovereign (Milton 1993, 523ff.). After Hobbes' death, a provincial vicar, John Dowel, in his *The Leviathan heretical ... justified by the refutation of a book of his entituled The Historical*

Narrative of heresie of 1683 sought to expose Hobbes' defiance of religious orthodoxy. As the title indicates, Dowel aimed to refute Hobbes' self-justification, in his tract *The Historical Narrative* of 1668, for having written *Leviathan* during the English republic.

Nonetheless, *Leviathan* afforded ample scope for imputations of heterodoxy, if not heresy, not least in the appendices to the Latin translation of *Leviathan*, on which Hobbes had been working since the mid-1660s. There Hobbes defends an interpretation of the Trinity, adapted from the account of political representation given in the English *Leviathan* and in *De homine*, which was to say the least unorthodox; and in fact this interpretation had already been foreshadowed in the 1651 edition of *Leviathan* (*L* 338): 'For *person* being relative to a representer, it is consequent to plurality of representers that there be a plurality of persons, though of one and the same substance'. The implication was that the single person of God was severally represented by the Father, the Son and the Holy Spirit, though Hobbes in this same passage allows that Moses was also a representer of God. None of this was likely much to endear Hobbes to the authorities, despite the fact that after the fall of Clarendon (Hobbes' former friend Edward Hyde) in 1667, Hobbes had a significant ally at court in Lord Arlington, a member of the so-called 'Cabal' by whom Clarendon had been ousted. In the late 1660s Hobbes set to work on *An Historical Narration concerning Heresy*, which seems to have been complete by 1668 (Champion 2012). But it, like other late works, such as his *Dialogue* between a philosopher and a student of the common law, would not be published in Hobbes' lifetime.

LEVIATHAN AND THE UNIVERSITIES

In the decades following its publication, *Leviathan* sparked controversy in the universities of both Oxford and Cambridge. 'Hobbism' became something of a 'boo' word in the intellectual atmosphere of 1650s and 1660s England, and remained so for a long time after. Like 'Socinian' (a term used in its stricter sense to describe the doctrines of the Italian theologian Faustus Sozzini or Socinus (1539–1604), and more specifically his rejection of the Trinity), 'Hobbism' was used as a generic term of abuse against thinkers or writings that the speaker wanted to put beyond the pale of civilised discourse. This fate befell Daniel Scargill (1647–1721), who was elected fellow of Corpus Christi College, Cambridge, in 1667. The basis for imputing 'Hobbism' to Scargill seems to have been fairly thin, and may have blurred Hobbes' positions with the views, which were in some respects akin to Hobbes', of the ancient Greek atomist philosopher Epicurus. Scargill's transgression lay in part at least in his defence of the view that the origins of the world allowed of mechanistic explanation and that the nature of the universe does not suffice to prove God's existence (Parkin 1999, 88–89). As a result of these and other expressed views, Scargill was summoned to appear before a Cambridge University court in 1668 and was suspended pending a public recantation of his controversial views; despite having recanted, he was excluded from the college in 1669 after what seems to have been an orchestrated smear campaign (Parkin 1999, 91–92).

But this was not the end of the matter: Scargill was able to draw on support at court, and soon letters arrived from the King demanding that Scargill be reinstated to his fellowship at Corpus Christi (Parkin 2007, 247), notwithstanding his 'asserting and publishing certaine haereticall opinions tending to Atheisme' (quoted in Milton 1993, 539). A little later the Archbishop of Canterbury Gilbert Sheldon (an old associate of Hobbes' from the 'Tew circle' of the 1630s (Tuck 1979, 11)) added his own voice. Ralph Cudworth, notable as one of the pre-eminent Cambridge Platonists, also lobbied for Scargill's removal (Mintz 1962, 50). The public recantation that Scargill then produced contained a full confession of his misdemeanours.

In the preamble to the printed version of the recantation Scargill acknowledges that he has gloried in 'being a disciple of Hobbes and an atheist' (Schuhmann 1998, 204). Hobbes' friend and biographer John Aubrey noted that 'Mr. Hobbes wrote a letter to ... (a colonell, as I remember) concerning Dr. Scargill's recantation sermon, preached at Cambridge, about 1670 [in fact 25 July 1669]'. Aubrey adds that Hobbes put this letter 'into Sir John Birkenhead's hands to be licensed [i.e. for publication]' (Schuhmann 1998, 204–5; Birkenhead had been a civil war royalist and occupied a court position in the 1660s as Master of Requests). Birkenhead turned down the request, Aubrey says, 'to collogue [i.e. keep in with] and flatter the bishops' – whose opposition to *Leviathan* had already put paid to its being reprinted, as Samuel Pepys had noted the previous year.

In his address Scargill does not hold back on self-denigration. He confesses to having held 'a foolish proud conceit of my own wit' and to have used his university position to voice 'diverse wicked, blasphemous, and atheistical positions', as well as succumbing to the moral lapses with which the college and university authorities, such as the Master of Corpus Christi, John Spencer, had sought to tar his character. Among the 'Hobbist' opinions that Scargill charges his earlier self with holding are the beliefs that

> [a]ll right of dominion is founded only in power; that if the devil be omnipotent he ought to be obeyed; that all moral righteousness is founded on the positive law of the civil magistrate only; that the scriptures of God are not law, farther than they are enjoined by the civil magistrate; that the civil magistrate is to be obeyed though he should forbid the worship of God, or command theft, murder and adultery.
>
> (Scott 1812, vol. VII, 370)

Scargill reaffirms his rejection of these doctrines later in the recantation, adding to these 'execrable positions' the notion 'that there is a desirable glory in being, and being reputed, an atheist; which I implied when I expressly affirm that I gloried to be an Hobbist and an atheist' (Scott 1812, vol. VII, 371).

Few of these positions, at least according to the interpretation of *Leviathan* given earlier in this book, could in fact be ascribed to Hobbes (at least as the author of that work), as distinct from representations of them given by others, such as John Bramhall, who had polemical motives for distorting Hobbes' views (Parkin 2007, 250). As we have seen, Hobbes' argument insisted that political legitimacy is created by transfer of right, not by sheer force, 'there being no obligation on any man, which arises not from some act of his own' (*L* 150); the idea that the kingdom of heaven might be founded on 'unjust violence' is repudiated by the critique of the 'Fool' in *Leviathan*, chapter 15 (*L* 101–2); that though the content of right and wrong depends on the covenant of civil government (*L* 90, 239, 245), the claim that injustice itself is the violation of contract cannot itself be grounded contractually, and is thus a law of nature (*L* 103; cf. 232); and that the sovereign is subject to the natural law of equity, which forbids, for instance, the use of sovereign wealth for personal gain (*L* 237; cf. 240). The one point at which Scargill's list of 'Hobbist' doctrines is accurate is that divine law requires the positive sanction of the sovereign's command to give it legal force (*L* 357; cf. 197–98), but even here Hobbes leaves room to construe him as saying that the sovereign is the authoritative expositor of a pre-existing divine law (*L* 244, 248; cf. 324), whose normativity can be seen, accordingly, as originating with God (*L* 224; cf. 192).

But the crucial point for Scargill was now to be seen to be anti-Hobbist. In fact, Scargill himself acknowledges that this may make his new protestations of orthodoxy incredible, since (as we saw in Chapter 8 when discussing Hobbes' use of the Old Testament story of Naaman the Syrian in 2 Kings 5 (*L* 343–44)) the true Hobbist would curb the public expression of any private beliefs, including one's own, that contradicted official political or religious doctrine (cf. Parkin 1999, 95; 2007, 249–50); to this extent the 'recantation' was fully consistent with Hobbes' views as expressed in *Leviathan* (*L* 344, 414). Scargill seems here to license an 'esoteric' reading of his text along the lines favoured by followers of Leo Strauss (though here, as ever, it is a nice question how far an author may travel towards obliquity in masking his true intentions from all but initiates).

Among the charges levelled at Scargill, in the campaign of character assassination to which the Cambridge University authorities subjected him, was 'libertinism' or lax morals. Scargill admitted the truth of the charge in his recantation: 'I have lived in great licentiousness; swearing rashly, drinking intemperately, boasting myself insolently, corrupting others by my pernicious principles and example'. Few tried to tar Hobbes himself, whose personal life was modest – his old friend Edward Hyde called him 'a Man of Probity', who had 'lived a life free from scandal'

(Rogers 1995, 181) – with the brush of libertinism. But some of the moral doctrines defended in *Leviathan*, such as its claim that in the state of nature 'there be no propriety, no *mine* and *thine* distinct' (*L* 90) and its apparent relativism ('one man calls *wisdom* what another calls *fear*; and one *cruelty*, what another *justice*' (*L* 31)) readily lent themselves to being presented as a libertine's charter, and Hobbes' opponents were not slow to exploit this.

In Oxford University Hobbes had some intellectual allies, such as Henry Stubbe of Christ Church (1632–76), a classical scholar and physician. On 9 December 1656 Stubbe wrote to Hobbes urging him to 'speake fauourably of this vniuersity, wherein yo^u haue many fauourers, and wch hath uindicate yo^u so much by slighting both the lectures & bookes of yor Antagonists' (Malcolm ed., Hobbes 1994a, vol. I, 379) – a good indication both of Hobbes' support in Oxford, and of his need for it given the number of detractors he faced, including some, like John Wallis, in Oxford itself. As was mentioned earlier, Stubbe had corresponded with Hobbes about a projected Latin translation of *Leviathan* (Malcolm ed., Hobbes 1994a, vol. I, 271), though this plan came to nothing and eventually Hobbes translated the book into Latin himself.

However, Hobbes also had numerous enemies, including some in high places in Oxford. One of the most implacable of them was John Wallis (1616–1703), the Savillian Professor of Geometry. Hobbes first tangled with Wallis over the 'squaring of the circle', a problem that Hobbes claimed to have solved in his *De corpore* of 1655. The dispute between the two men was exacerbated by several factors, notably the outspokenness of each, Hobbes' bristling at what he saw as his exclusion from the scientific establishment of the Royal Society (of which Wallis was a member) and Wallis' Presbyterianism – one of Hobbes' diatribes against Wallis evoked his 'Absurd Geometry, Rural Language, Scottish Church Politics, and Barbarisms'. The dispute, however, spilled over from mathematics to politics. As their pamphlet-war continued into the 1660s, Wallis published *Hobbius heautontimorumenos* (1662) which, as well as continuing the mathematical dispute, accused Hobbes in effect of being a time-server, and having written *Leviathan* 'in Defense of Olivers Title', i.e. of Cromwell's supremacy (though Cromwell did not become Lord Protector until 1653, well after the book was written) (Skinner 2002, vol. III, 328 n. 20).

Hobbes in response published the anonymous *Considerations, upon the Reputation*, which has already been cited. When *Leviathan* was published, Hobbes contends,

> He staid about Paris, and had neither encouragement nor desire to return into *England*, he wrote and published his *Leviathan*, far from the intention either of disadvantage to His Majesty [royalists regarded Charles II's reign as having begun at the execution of Charles I, i.e. on 30 January 1649] or to flatter *Oliver* (who was not made Protector till three or four years after) or purpose to make way for his return.
>
> (Hobbes 1839–45 [1680], 7–8)

Hobbes goes on to say that there is 'scarce in it a page that does not upbraid both him and you' (i.e. both Cromwell and Wallis). Hobbes puts his return from France to England to the fact that 'he would not trust his safety with the *French* Clergy' (Hobbes 1839–45 [1680], 8).

Another powerful antagonist of Hobbes' at Oxford was John Fell, the Dean (that is, principal) of Christ Church after the Restoration. When Anthony Wood wrote his *Athenae Oxonienses*, a biographical compendium on Oxford alumni, including Hobbes, Fell deputed two translators to turn the text into Latin, but then did the editing of the Latin version himself. Fell took the opportunity of excising the favourable remarks that Wood had made about Hobbes in his original version of the *Athenae*, substituting remarks 'to the great dishonor and disparagement of the said Mr. Hobbes' (Wood 1817, vol. III, 1213), notably concerning his lack of competence in mathematics as evidenced by the Wallis polemics. Hobbes wrote a letter of complaint (dated 20 April 1674) to Wood, who passed it on to Fell; the Dean 'read it over carelessly, and not without scorn; and when he had done, bid Mr. Wood tell Mr. Hobbes "that he was an old man, had one foot in the grave; that he should mind his latter end [presumably his impending showdown with the Almighty]"' (Bliss ed., Wood 1817 [1813], vol. I, cxxxvi).

As White Kennett wrote in his memoir of the Cavendish family, published early in the eighteenth century, 'It is no trampling on the ashes of Mr. Hobbs to say that he was a great coward' (Kennett 1708, 113). Hobbes' fears about incineration, though perhaps exaggerated (Milton 1993, 514), gained some credence posthumously. Notwithstanding this support in Oxford, Hobbes' ideas came under attack from the university authorities in the years after his death. There was an attempt to implicate his ideas in the death by suicide of an Oxford fellow, William Cardonnel, in 1681 (Parkin 2007, 369–70; cf. Malcolm 2002, 309); Humphrey Prideaux, the orientalist and scholar of Christ Church, said that Cardonnel had associated with the Earl of Devonshire and that his mind had 'been poisoned by Hobs' during his stay at the Cavendish family seat at Chatsworth (Malcolm 2002, 310).

Two years later, *Leviathan* was publicly burnt in Oxford, together with *De cive* and other 'seditious' books. The exposure of the Rye House plot to assassinate Charles II and his brother James, Duke of York, impelled defenders of the Church of England to reaffirm Anglican orthodoxy against the perceived doctrinal threats to it; their ulterior purpose was to discredit the Whig opposition which had sympathised with the plot. In the wake of the plot's exposure the authorities sought to stamp down on the opposition. *Leviathan* provided a soft target for the Oxford authorities when the Rye House plot was discovered on 12 June 1683. They moved quickly, commissioning an investigation into anti-government literature in mid-July. The Regius Professor of Divinity at Oxford, William Jane, was commissioned to survey opposition literature, notably the English republican writings from the civil war period, but also works by Hobbes (Parkin 2007, 371ff.). Anthony Wood related that

[s]ome of the principal heads of this University had found therein [i.e. in *Leviathan*] as in that *De Cive*, several positions destructive to the sacred persons of Princes, their state and government, and all humane society [and so] the venerable Convocation did, by their judgment and decree past among them on the 21. of *July* 1683,

condemn them as pernitious and damnable and thereupon caused the said two books to be publickly burnt.

(Wood 18 7, vol. II, 480)

The action was carried out by the university marshal at the instigation of Convocation, the university's governing body, immediately after the *Judgment and decree* against the books had been pronounced. Book-burning may seem a strange act for a university to carry out, and for modern readers recalls similar acts by totalitarian regimes such as the Nazi one. But for the Oxford authorities the Rye House plot offered the chance to reaffirm the university's pro-court credentials at a time when Hobbes' political theory had become associated with the Whigs; in this John Fell was again a prime mover (Parkin 2007, 371). The servile preamble to the *Judgment and decree* excoriates the 'execrable villainy' of 'the barbarous assassination' plot, and declares that Oxford has found it 'to be a necessary duty' to expose 'those impious doctrines' that 'gave rise and growth to these nefarious attempts' (Scott 1812, vol. VIII, 424).

The *Judgment and decree* listed various errors committed by the targeted authors, of whom Hobbes was cited more often than anyone else. It roundly condemned twenty-seven 'propositions' declared to be 'false, seditious, and impious, and most of them heretical and blasphemous, infamous to the Christian religion, and destructive to all government', in each case naming the authors who had affirmed them (Scott 1812, vol. VIII, 420). Among the propositions attributed to Hobbes were the following:

The Seventh.
Self-preservation is the fundamental law of nature, and supersedes the obligation of all others ...
The Tenth.
Possession and strength give a right to govern, and success in a cause, or enterprize, proclaims it to be lawful and just ...
The Eleventh.
In the state of nature, there is no difference between good and evil, right and wrong; the state of nature is a state of war, in which every man hath a right to all things.

The Twelfth.

The foundation of civil society is this natural right ...

The Thirteenth.

Every man, after his entering into society, retains a right of defending himself against force, and cannot transfer that right to the commonwealth ...

The Fourteenth.

An oath superadds no obligation ... and notwithstanding their pacts and oaths, [subjects] may lawfully rebel against, and destroy their sovereign.

(Scott 1812, vol. VIII, 424–25)

The Hobbesian credentials of this list are fairly strong. The seventh proposition can be substantiated from *Leviathan*'s basis for the laws of nature (*L* 91); at least the first part of the tenth, from the 'Review, and Conclusion' (*L* 486), as long as the requisite transfer of right has occurred; the eleventh, from chapter 13 (*L* 90); the twelfth, from chapter 17 (*L* 120); the thirteenth, concerning the inalienability of the right to defend oneself, from chapter14 (*L* 93); the futility of adding an oath to a covenant, the fourteenth proposition, at the end of that chapter (*L* 100). The propositions, taken together, were held to lead to depravity, corruption, sedition, rebellion, regicide and atheism.

'LIBERTINISM' AND *LEVIATHAN*

Hobbes' writings, and *Leviathan* in particular, had become in England (matters were different on the European continent, as I explain below) a shape-shifting albatross to be hung about the neck of political opponents. The extraordinary pliability of Hobbes' text provides at least part of the explanation for this. For instance, most religious orientations – Erastians, Episcopalians, Anglicans, Independents, atheists, Unitarians – apart from those committed to theocracy, could take some comfort from the book, as well as finding much to object to. So *Leviathan* could be used by either side to make opponents look as though their positions were uncomfortably close to, or indeed identical with, Hobbes'.

Similar remarks apply to the main political affiliations in Restoration England, particularly the major cleavage between the 'court' and 'country' factions (the future Tories and Whigs, respectively). This double-sidedness meant that while one's opponents could usually be tarred with the brush of 'Hobbism', the same went for oneself, and this imparted a certain nerviness to political debates that traded in Hobbes' name. *Leviathan* said enough about enough things and in a way that, by design or otherwise, was ambiguous, for disputants to find in it a veritable arsenal of polemical munitions. The universities were important in conditioning Hobbes' reception because what is now thought of as political theory had a proportionately much larger readership, as already noted, among the public than it now has. The authorities worried, among other things, that the doctrines of *Leviathan* were not merely false, but actively corrupted those who read the book.

Part of the basis for this worry lay in Hobbes' English prose style. Hobbes' idiom in *Leviathan* is characteristically direct, conversational and dialectical. Hobbes buttonholes the reader, forcing engagement with his line of questioning. For example, in chapter 30, in discussing public education: 'But are not (may some man say) the universities of England learned enough already to do that? Or is it you will undertake to teach the universities? Hard questions. Yet to the first, I doubt not to answer ...' (*L* 237). Or in chapter 21, when asking whether men condemned to death are free to resist the sovereign: 'have not they the liberty then to join together, and assist and defend one another? Certainly they have: for they but defend their lives, which the guilty may as well do, as the innocent' (*L* 152).

The cumulative effect of such passages, where a line is argued, Hobbes poses a rhetorical question, then comes back with a disarmingly straightforward response, is to help to make the positions Hobbes defends, and their justification, seem self-evident. At the same time, as Quentin Skinner has shown, *Leviathan* 'is arguably the most rhetorical of all Hobbes' works' (Skinner 1996, 427).[4] A venerable rhetorical technique, encapsulated in the Latin tag *Ars est celare artem*, is to use the arts of rhetoric itself in order to conceal the use of rhetoric, and one way this can be done is by disavowing the use of 'eloquence' in favour of plain speaking. In fact Hobbes was long lauded as a champion of an unembellished style of writing (see Lund 2012, 40); Sir James Mackintosh's *On the Progress of Ethical Philosophy* described it as 'the very perfection of didactic language. Short, clear, precise, pithy, his language never has more than one meaning' (Mackintosh 1834, 58).

Space does not permit an adequate treatment of rhetoric in *Leviathan*, to which Skinner devoted a major book; it argues that Hobbes performed a volte-face about rhetoric in *Leviathan*. Having earlier repudiated it, Hobbes came to see that unaided reasoning would be insufficient to make readers accept his conclusions, and so he resorted to the eloquence he had previously avoided (Skinner 1996, 426ff.). Here I mention only Hobbes' use of rhetorical technique to affect a plain-spoken tone. He says that '[t]he light of humane minds is perspicuous words, but by exact definitions first snuffed, and purged from ambiguity' (*L* 36). A misuse of words, deliberate or otherwise, can mislead. Indeed their misuse seems for Hobbes to involve a form of semantic commodity fetishism: 'words are wise men's counters, they do but reckon by them; but they are the money of fools' (*L* 29). Hobbes makes clear the perils of failure to use words clearly in chapter 5. 'Metaphors, and senseless and ambiguous words, are like *ignes fatui* [literally 'stupid fires'; but used here as a metaphor for false enlightenment or illusion]; and reasoning upon them, is wandering amongst innumerable absurdities' (*L* 36).

These programmatic statements, made early in the book, lead one to expect that *Leviathan* itself will use an unadorned style. But, whether or not the disavowals are intended to lead readers to drop their guard – as with the figure just cited of *ignes fatui*, a metaphor wrapped in a simile – Hobbes does not, as we have already seen, confine himself to 'perspicuous words'. One widely held reading, then and since, was that Hobbes could not avow his true beliefs, particularly on religion, without dissimulation, the result being that many passages in *Leviathan* display carefully crafted ambiguity, for example on the status of the laws of nature (*L* 111), on miracles (chapter 37), or Hobbes' repeated avowals that the content of Christianity can be boiled down to the proposition that 'Jesus is the Christ' (e.g. *L* 273, 299, 407, 409–10).

Alongside the widespread exploitation of Hobbesian texts to blacken political adversaries, there was a select, but not negligible, group of persons drawn to *Leviathan* by its very notoriety. During the Restoration period, though not much before, Hobbes' name came to be associated with what was often called 'libertinism' or 'licence', namely decadent laxity in one's moral outlook and conduct, expressed in such disorders as drinking, gambling, swearing and sexual promiscuity. With the rise of the Whig party as a faction organised in opposition to the court of Charles II and the Anglican ascendancy after the Restoration, the lubricious mores of the King and his court could be used to stain Hobbes by association: as we saw earlier, Hobbes had acted as a tutor to Charles when both were in exile in France.

Indeed, it became a commonplace that Hobbes had degraded the morals of the gentry by making turpitude fashionable, in such dens of vice as the new coffee houses in London. Commentators voiced alarm that Hobbesian doctrine was cankering the minds and manners of the young. Moralists noted that Hobbes, partly because of his ambiguity but also because of his plausible literary style, seduced the gullible, empty-headed and novelty-seeking into swallowing his doctrines by intellectual stealth. In the preface to his riposte to *Leviathan*, Clarendon noted that 'frequent reciting of loose and disjointed sentences, and bold Inferences' by Hobbes' admirers 'have too much prevail'd with many of great Wit and Faculties'; this had duped them into thinking Hobbes' views 'more innocent, or less mischievous, then [they] upon a more deliberate perusal will find them to be' (Lund 2012, 36ff.).

In the early nineteenth century the historian Macaulay wrote that 'Hobbism soon became an almost essential part of the character of the fine gentleman' (quoted in Mintz 1962, 137). The Oxford antiquary Anthony Wood said of John Wilmot (1647–80), the notoriously rakish second Earl of Rochester, that his exposure in youth to the court of Charles II 'not only debauched his manners, but made him a perfect *Hobbist* in principle' (Wood, 1817, vol. III, 1229): the implication presumably being that Rochester had been debauched by Charles, whom Hobbes had previously corrupted while acting as the prince's tutor while in exile in Paris. On his deathbed Rochester was reported as saying that

'Mr Hobbes and the philosophers have been my ruin', and renounced them for the Bible.[5] Earlier in life Wilmot had conveyed some strikingly Hobbesian thoughts in his 'Satire against Reason and Mankind', published in 1679, the year of Hobbes' death, but written some five years earlier (Parkin 2007, 306):

> For hunger or for love they [i.e. non-human animals] fight or tear,
> Whilst wretched man is still in arms for fear.
> For fear he arms, and is of arms afraid,
> By fear to fear successively betrayed;
> Base fear, the source whence his best passions came:
> His boasted honor, and his dear-bought fame;
> That lust of power, to which he's a slave,
> And for the which alone he dares be brave ...

Rochester here encapsulates in poetic form a number of Hobbesian thoughts. The first few lines summarise Hobbes' view that 'the passion to be reckoned upon, is fear' (*L* 99), and that the natural condition of mankind is war (*L* 88). Rochester's 'For fear he arms and is of arms afraid' voices Hobbes' view that from the 'diffidence of one another, there is no way for any man to secure himself so reasonable as anticipation' (*L* 88). As far as honour is concerned, Hobbes says that the worship of God follows 'those rules of honour, that reason dictates to be done by the weak to the more potent men, in hope of benefit, [or] for fear of damage' (*L* 249–50). Hobbes anticipates Rochester in describing as 'a general inclination of all mankind, a restless desire of power after power, that ceases only in death' (*L* 70); in particular, when discussing duels, Hobbes says that 'the ground of courage is always strength or skill, which are power' (*L* 67), including the power that arises from reputation (*L* 62): compare Rochester's 'That lust of power, to which he's [i.e. man is] a slave,/ And for the which alone he dares be brave'. Other passages from the 'Satire' also show Hobbesian influence (Parkin 2007, 306ff.).

Thus Hobbes' ideas could penetrate or by thought to penetrate, beyond the confines of the academy, into the wider social world. The idea that 'Hobbism' could indeed infiltrate the whole intellectual and cultural life of the nation was, indeed, something of a trope among Hobbes' adversaries, who of course promoted his notoriety by the very fact of criticising him. In a late Restoration comedy, George Farquhar's *The Constant Couple*, first performed at Drury Lane in 1700, the amoral Vizard is seen reading a book; his uncle, Smuggler, presumes that he is 'at his meditation', reading 'some book of pious ejaculations', a fond thought immediately dispelled by Vizard, who exclaims, 'This Hobbes is an excellent fellow!' (see Skinner 2002, vol. III, 268). The implication, clearly, is that Hobbes' writings were reputed to be primers of vice, and would be recognised by audiences as such. By this time the lapse of the Licensing Act in 1695 meant that *Leviathan* could circulate legally again, and indeed it seems that the third printing of the book, the 'Ornaments' edition, dates from this period, though it should not be inferred from this fact that *Leviathan* now was entirely freed of harassment by the authorities (Malcolm 2008 and Malcolm ed., Hobbes 2012, vol. I, 258ff.); indeed, a new Blasphemy Act was passed in 1698 (Malcolm ed., Hobbes 2012, vol. I, 262).

One marker of Hobbes' notoriety was the critique of him by John Eachard (?1636–97), a fellow and later Master of St Catherine's College, Cambridge. Eachard's *The Grounds and Occasions of the Contempt of the Clergy* (1670) probed the causes of anticlericalism in England generally. *The Grounds and Occasions* provoked outrage among the clergy, and in response, Eachard published a further pamphlet in which he took a sideswipe at Hobbes, possibly to acquit himself of charges of 'Hobbist' sympathies – Hobbes was taken as a prime exponent of anticlericalism (though *The Grounds and Occasions* had appeared anonymously (Parkin 2007, 289)). This proved to be the prelude to a full-frontal attack on Hobbes by Eachard, dedicated to Archbishop Sheldon, entitled *Mr. Hobbs' State of Nature Considered* (1672), written as a dialogue between 'Timothy' ('God-honouring') and 'Philautus' ('self-loving'), who voices the Hobbist position. Eachard mentions 'another sort of more shrewd and judicious despisers' of the clergy, 'who have a very strange opinion of religion, scripture, and the clergy'; he adds 'I need not, I suppose, Sir, tell you, that these are the disciples of Mr. Hobbs', bemoaning the fact that fashionable gentry have been easily converted 'to his doctrine and opinions' (Eachard

1705, 147). Some gentlemen, Eachard adds, believe 'that if there were any God at all, it must be a kind of wooden god, such as Mr. Hobbs' god' (Eachard 1705, 148) – presumably intended as a glance at Hobbes' materialist view of God, which many contemporaries thought tantamount to atheism.

Eachard makes some effective criticisms of Hobbes, though a lot of the pamphlet's humour is rather laboured and argues past Hobbes rather than against him. In picking up *Leviathan*'s claim that the state of war consists not only in armed conflict but 'in the known disposition thereto' (*L* 88–89), Eachard points out that Hobbes had argued in *De cive*, chapter 1, §12, that 'war ... is fully declar'd either by Words, or Deeds', rather than consisting in the mere absence of a sovereign. Eachard also mocks Hobbes' claim in chapter 13 of *Leviathan* that the fact that people lock their doors and chests, and ride out armed, shows that they take the possibility of attack or theft seriously. To this Eachard retorts that there is no reason to think that the typical human being is 'a *Whore*, a *Bitch*, a *Drab*, a *Cut-Purse*' and so on, but 'because there be *Dogs*, *Foxes*, *Hogs*, *Children*, *Fools*, *Madmen*, *Drunkards*, *Thieves*, *Pyrats* and *Philautians*' (Eachard 1705, 71). However, Hobbes anticipates this criticism, arguing that he does not thereby 'accuse man's nature in it' (*L* 89), any more than do those who ride armed against the risk of bandits or who lock the doors and chests in their homes. But it often suited polemicists' purposes to portray Hobbes as being more misanthropic than the text of *Leviathan* warranted.

LEVIATHAN OUTSIDE BRITAIN

In essence, '*Leviathan* outside Britain' during the period we have been examining – basically the first fifty years following the English *Leviathan*'s publication – refers to the book's reception in continental Europe. The conditions for its reception were different there from in England.

While the text of *Leviathan* clearly spoke to the political upheavals in Britain during the 1640s and 50s, it might be thought to speak, less directly, to immediate political conditions in France or the Netherlands (though large parts of Germany had been consumed in the long-running conflict that concluded with the Treaty of Westphalia in 1648). Nonetheless, the period of the Fronde upheavals in France between 1648 and 1653 – in the first half of which period Hobbes himself was exiled in Paris – directly raised some of the concerns central to *Leviathan*, notably the balance between sovereign authority and the protection of local or sectional particularisms. The Fronde began when the Parlement of Paris revolted against a royal attempt to impose taxes on it. Like Charles I's summoning of Parliament in 1640, the French Crown (Louis XIV's mother Anne of Austria ruled as regent during his minority) had been forced to seek tax revenues to recoup the cost of foreign war (though the Parlement was a judicial rather than legislative body). In due course the Fronde rebellion developed into a civil war waged by Louis de Bourbon, Prince de Condé, against the regency regime led by the Queen and Cardinal Mazarin, both of whom were foreigners; the wars concluded with Condé's defeat by royalist forces, though not before parts of the country, such as Provence, had degenerated into internecine conflict. Insofar as the Fronde had any unifying motive, it was opposition to the Court, and it was in this area that Hobbes' political theory had particular resonance in France.

However, since English at the time was a peripheral European language (Malcolm 2002, 462), *Leviathan* had little intellectual impact on the continent before Johannes Blaue published the Latin translation in Amsterdam in 1668. Nonetheless, there is evidence of some demand for the text specifically of *Leviathan* from French intellectuals. On the testimony of Hobbes' friend Charles du Bosc, who wrote to him from southern France in 1659:

> Mr Andrew Croocke [Andrew Crook, the publisher of *Leviathan*] sent me halfe a dozen *de Homine* and one *Leuiathan* for frends ... Mr Lantin of Dijon while we were there had the reading de Homine. Three of these I sent for, are for him, and the Leuiatan. All ye learned men I know desire that Leuiathan were in french or Latine.
>
> (Malcolm ed., Hobbes 1994a, vol. I, 504; cf. Malcolm 2002, 466)

Another French friend, François du Verdus, wrote to Hobbes in 1656 to tell him that he had begun translating *Leviathan* into French (Malcolm 2002, 398), but Du Verdus' English was not up to the task and this attempt came to naught (Malcolm 2002, 467). Nor would there be a French translation of *Leviathan* until the eighteenth century, and then only of an abridged version of the text (Malcolm 2002, 468).

One reason for the slow progress in translating *Leviathan* into French was probably that continental readers had already gained access to Hobbes' political theory via *De cive* rather than *Leviathan*. *De cive* became generally available in Latin from 1647 (a private limited edition had circulated since 1642), as well as in a French translation by Hobbes' friend Samuel Sorbière from 1649. The demand for the Latin text seems to have been brisk: in a letter from Sorbière to Hobbes of August 1647 he tells him that 'there are no more copies left of [*De cive*]', although the publisher Elsevier 'is getting requests from everywhere for hundreds of them', to the point where Elsevier was already contemplating a second edition (Malcolm ed., Hobbes 1994a, vol. I, 161).

The relatively low level of demand for *Leviathan* can be gauged, in part, from the paucity of translations into other European languages during the seventeenth century; though of course that itself might be thought to reflect lack of demand. Nonetheless, there clearly was demand for Hobbes' writings on the continent, and specifically for *Leviathan*. The Latin text of 1668, reissued in 1670, met the requirements of scholarly readers, for whom Latin functioned as a lingua franca, but the text also gained a vernacular readership among Dutch speakers. *Leviathan* was translated into Dutch in 1667 by Abraham van Berkel (Malcolm ed., Hobbes 2012, vol. I, 164), a scholar of Leiden University and member of Spinoza's circle (Israel 2001, 185–86); this may reflect a demand for the work for readers not only in the Dutch Republic but also the Spanish Netherlands, north Germany and the Baltic littoral, where Dutch was also read (Malcolm 2002, 465–66); the continued use of Low German in northern Germany made Dutch accessible to native germanophones. One library of 42,000 titles auctioned in 1718 in Hamburg contained Latin, German and Dutch books to the virtual exclusion of other languages

(Israel 2001, 139). But, apart from the Latin version of *Leviathan*, no complete translations into languages other than Dutch appeared during the seventeenth century. A partial Russian translation was made in the later eighteenth century (Malcolm 2002, 463 n. 23), but no full French translation of the text was published until the twentieth century. Hence for most European scholars, who had no English – an exception was Samuel Pufendorf (Malcolm ed., Hobbes 2012, vol. I, 164–65) – the main conduit carrying *Leviathan*'s argument into Europe was the Latin edition; even vernacular translations were sometimes from the Latin rather than English version of the text, as with the first German translation of *Leviathan*, which appeared in the 1790s (Malcolm 2002, 469).

As in England, *Leviathan* faced problems of censorship. One obstacle that a contemporaneous French version of Hobbes' text would have faced, if openly published in France or imported from abroad, was the increasingly stringent censorship regime (Sawyer 1990, 137); a royal edict or *règlement* of 1618 imposed severe penalties for publishing or distributing prohibited books and pamphlets, or those deemed to be seditious (Sawyer 1990, 25). A letter of 1637 from Hobbes' friend Marin Mersenne to the French philosopher Descartes (to whose *Meditations on First Philosophy* Hobbes later wrote a critical response) lamented the fact that 'never has the censorship of books been so stringent as at present' (Martin 1999, 25). While the Fronde period saw an explosion in pamphleteering in France, the end of the Fronde in 1652 was marked by the reissue by the Paris Parlement of edicts against seditious publications, and in this atmosphere a French-language *Leviathan* would have had trouble in passing the censors.

As Malcolm shows, the fact that Hobbes' ideas about politics and religion entered the European forum first via *De cive*, and only much later via vernacular European languages (by contrast, the English version of *De cive* had only appeared in November 1650, some six months before the English *Leviathan* was published) meant that their reception on the continent fell into two stages (Malcolm 2002, ch. 14), defined by the publication dates of *De cive* (effectively 1647), and the Latin *Leviathan* (1668). While plenty of European commentators were ready to criticise Hobbes' political construction in *De cive*, the lack in this work of a distinct theologico-political section within the book, corresponding to the third part of *Leviathan*, meant that they generally restricted themselves to attacking Hobbes' political conclusions, or the claims about human nature and natural law on which they were taken to rest.

As among Hobbes' English readers, for instance, the *De cive* account of the state of nature as a state of war came in for criticism, being deemed to be both 'wicked' and 'absurd' (Malcolm 2002, 474). Commentators found disturbing Hobbes' denial of an original state of human benevolence, or at least of peaceful coexistence, and his assertion that acts such as murder did not violate the law of nature. These aspects of the theory had already been in circulation in Europe for a couple of decades by the time the Latin *Leviathan* was published, and it was accordingly the theological matter in the second half of the book, as well as the appendices of the Latin translation (of which there was no counterpart in the English version), that excited the largest volume of critical comment after 1668. One measure of the continental penetration of *Leviathan* was its addition to the Roman Catholic Church's index of prohibited books in 1703 (*De cive* had been put on the index as early as 1654). The banned volume was the Latin rather than the English *Leviathan* (though in fact Hobbes' *oeuvre* was to be added to the index in its entirety in 1709).

Much of the initial reaction to *Leviathan*, in part because of the reputation of *De cive*, resembled that in England. Accusations such as 'Spinozism', 'Socinianism' and 'atheism' were bandied about with much the same profligacy as was, say, the charge of 'Communism' during the McCarthyite era in the Cold War United States. One of Hobbes' important early commentators on the continent was the German philosopher and jurist Samuel Pufendorf (1632–94), whose *De iure naturae ac gentium* accepts some of Hobbes' premises while reaching markedly different political conclusions. Pufendorf notes that to compel someone forcibly and to obligate them (that is, to subject them to a moral or legal requirement) are distinct notions. He then objects that Hobbes, in granting subjects the right to resist, also gives the sovereign the right to compel subjects: this indeed may seem at odds with the famous passage at the start of chapter 14, where

Hobbes says that though writers are prone to confuse *ius* and *lex* – that is, right and law – they should be distinguished because 'law and right differ as much as obligation and liberty; which in one and the same matter are inconsistent' (*L* 91).

Modern commentators differ over how to interpret Hobbes' reception on the European continent. For some, such as Jonathan Israel, Hobbes defies inclusion in the 'radical Enlightenment', because of his commitment to political absolutism. '[G]iven Hobbes' politics, and his attitude to ecclesiastical power and censorship ... he simply was not, and could not have been, the source and inspiration for a systematic redefinition of man, cosmology, social hierarchy, sexuality and ethics' of the kind that Israel credits Spinoza with having been (Israel 2001, 159; cf. 602). But matters are less straightforward than this. For one thing, not all of Hobbes' readers took him to be defending absolutism, as we saw with Bramhall. And as we have also seen, Hobbes' English-speaking commentators, though broadly in agreement about his absolutism, found nevertheless plenty to object to in other matters that *Leviathan* addresses, and this gave him a radical cachet that commentators were already bemoaning by the 1670s. Nor is it clear why Hobbes' 'attitude to ecclesiastical power' – namely, its unqualified subordination to temporal authority – should disqualify him as a radical, though it should be added that the term 'radical' may be too contextually variable or observer-relative to be of much help in the historiography of ideas.

Certainly, the underground on the continent, for whom the main form of ecclesiastical power was that wielded by the Roman Catholic Church, found in Hobbes a theoretical counterweight to ultramontanism, the view that temporal authority should be subordinated to that of Rome. Ultramontanism was a doctrine particularly associated with the Jesuits, and their Jansenist opponents in France turned to Hobbes for support. In the early nineteenth century the French conservative thinker Joseph de Maistre (1753–1821) remarked on the affinity between Hobbes and what he called the 'principal doctrine' of Jansenism:

It is well known that this philosopher argued that everything is necessitated, and that in consequence *liberty*, properly so called, does

not exist, nor freedom of choice. 'We call those agents free,' he
says, 'who act with deliberation; but deliberation in no way excludes
necessity, because the choice was necessary, just like the
deliberation'.[6]

De Maistre goes on to remark that Hobbes' compatibilism is
echoed by the Jansenist view that freedom of the will is consistent
with the necessitation of actions, as long as external coercion is
absent. Hobbes' thinking can be detected in the *Essais de morale et
de politique*, an influential Jansenist text published in 1687 that
draws extensively on his political theory (Malcolm 2002, 507). It
should also be noted that in some cases, like this, Hobbes'
political ideas were endorsed despite his religious views rather
than because of them. As the anonymous author of the *Essais*
remarks in the preface,

> It would be hard to deny that the principles of the English author
> Hobbes in his book *De cive* are followed in these essays. But far
> from denigrating them, they will increase the admiration in which
> these principles are held, since all intelligent people concur that it
> would be hard to write with more soundness than has this wise man.
>
> (Anon. 1687, 6)[7]

The author immediately adds, however, that 'one would not want
to say the same about what he has written about religion, and he
has not been followed in these matters'. Nonetheless, the author
goes on to endorse an account of man in the state of nature
('l'homme vivant hors de toute societé'). It is typical of the continental response to Hobbes, at least outside the Dutch-speaking
area, that it is *De cive* rather than *Leviathan* that is cited. There
follows a notably Epicurean disquisition, in which are high-
lighted not Epicurus' atomism, which might be thought of as
echoed by Hobbes' own writing as well as associates of his such as
Gassendi, or materialism (the latter was of course particularly
problematic for religious orthodoxy), but the quest for *ataraxia* or
tranquillity – including, particularly, freedom from fear. It is
taken for granted that Hobbes' political theory could be detached
from his religious views, as was often not the case with his

interlocutors in England. In part the latter response stemmed from the polemical urge to blacken Hobbes in any way that his writings seemed to permit, but it also reflected a difference in the way that his texts were read, that English readers took the political theory as part of larger theologico-political system. The most obvious, and rather prosaic, reason for this was that after 1651 *Leviathan* became the flagship version of Hobbes' political theory in England, and its structure explicitly invited readers to interpret it in this way. With *De cive*, on the other hand, though it too was written as part of a larger philosophical system, it was issued separately, and could be read as a free-standing political treatise.

By the same token, those on the continent who were attracted by Hobbes' lack of religious orthodoxy could either look past the absolutism of his political theory or qualify it, and not only on the grounds of the retained right to resist the sovereign. Important in this regard is Hobbes' theory of punishment, which allowed for a deterrent-based rather than purely retributive account of legal penalties: 'it is of the nature of punishment to have for end, the disposing of men to obey the law' (*L* 215); Hobbes affirms that punishment of the innocent violates the law of nature (*L* 219); subjects ought not to have contradictory demands made of them by the sovereign (*L* 211); acts elicited under 'terror of present death' are 'totally excused', as are criminal acts performed through lack of the means to know the law (*L* 208). Hobbes was indeed to exert an important influence on the Italian penologist Cesare Beccaria (1738–94), who argues in his *An Essay on Crimes and Punishments* that social utility is the basis of legal punishment in which the level of the penalty is decided by the minimum needed to deter others, where the background state of nature is one of war and individuals forgo rights to buy security (Beccaria 1983, e.g. 64, 66, 91).

CONCLUSION: HOBBES IN OUR TIME

Though this chapter has focused on early responses to *Leviathan*, I will briefly sketch major more recent (that is, in the last hundred years or so) readings of the book. At the outset it should be stressed that this is a very large subject, which could easily fill a book by itself. I will mention only what strike me as the major currents of interpretation, several of which have come up at various points in this book and have been mentioned in the further reading sections. Of course, my views as to what count as major currents of interpretation is itself an interpretation, from which other commentators may dissent.

Early in the twentieth century, A.E. Taylor (1869–1945) voiced what came to be called the 'deontic' reading of *Leviathan* and Hobbes' other political works, which was developed further by Howard Warrender in the 1950s (Warrender 1957). It was also endorsed by F.C. Hood (1964). In Taylor's words,

> Hobbes' ethical doctrine proper, disengaged from an egoistic psychology with which it has no logically necessary connection, is a very strict deontology, curiously suggestive ... of some of the characteristic theses of Kant.
>
> (Taylor 1938, 408)

This thesis was put forward as a counter to the then dominant 'egoistic' reading of *Leviathan*, according to which the nub of Hobbes' political theory is to explain how mutually disinterested and self-seeking agents can combine to create a political structure conducive to common well-being. Some more recent writers, such as Martinich 1992, are also sympathetic to this reading. Some of these accounts, such as Hood's, explicitly see God as the foundation for morality, in that the obligatoriness of moral norms is held to lie in their status as divine commands; others, by contrast, see morality as having intrinsic normativity. An interesting variant on these readings is Darwall 1996, chapter 3. Either way, these writers assimilate the normative force of Hobbes' laws of nature to that of moral requirements, rather than simply seeing the former as 'prudential' rules designed to promote self-preservation and the goods of 'commodious living'.

The deontic reading has also gained some currency in international theory, where again the background to it is furnished by a received interpretation. In this case the received reading has it that Hobbes is a prophet par excellence of 'realism', the view that international politics is to be understood primarily as the upshot of interaction between sovereign states who aim to promote their own well-being, including self-preservation above all; they thus, on this view, parallel the 'egoistic' reading of individuals in the state of nature (see above, Chapter 10). By contrast, some readers of *Leviathan* in international theory see the laws of nature as having deontic force distinct from that of prudential norms (e.g. Malcolm 2002, ch. 13). Similar lines of interpretation, in this case applied to Hobbes' notion of law, can also be found in Fuller 1990 and Murphy 1995.

Another very significant trend, which arose partly in reaction to the deontic theory, is that pursued by the contextualist or Cambridge school of interpretation. This methodology, whose intellectual antecedents lie in R.G. Collingwood's (1889–1943) philosophy of history and the linguistic philosophy of J.L. Austin (1911–60), that the meaning of texts from the history of political thought, such as *Leviathan*, should be recovered by attending to the historical context within which they were produced. Sometimes this is taken to be very local political debates, such as that over Engagement, but often interpreters work simply on the basis that the texts have a history – they were produced in a determinate time and place by authors with an intellectual background (in Hobbes' case, both in scholastic philosophy and humanism), and this shapes how they should be read. The historical context used in interpretation extends to the texts' reception, and this forms the basis for Skinner's view that when one examines the contemporary reception of Hobbes' theory, the divine command account of natural law becomes 'incredible' (Skinner 2002, vol. III, 282–85; cf. vol. I, ch. 4). It is incredible because it is claimed to be at odds with the way in which virtually all of Hobbes' contemporary readers, friends as well as foes, read him.

The success enjoyed by contextualists in converting historians of ideas to their approach has opened a bifurcation between their approach and that of analytical political theorists. Skinner himself has tried to close this gap by interpreting Hobbes as a party to debates over republican freedom that remain current in political theory (Skinner 2008; cf. Pettit 1997); on Skinner's reading, Hobbes' 'negative' conception of liberty won out historically over the 'neo-Roman' idea of liberty as non-domination. Some historians of ideas have in turn criticised Skinner for reading both Hobbes and his contemporaries through the lens of modern debates (Worden 1998). More generally, critics of contextualism emphasise the difficulty of defining historical contexts, and the threat of hermeneutic circularity (Boucher 1985); these problems arise in particularly acute form with Hobbes, whose intellectual career spanned seven decades, and with *Leviathan* specifically, given the polymorphous nature of the text, and the nearly twenty-year gap between the writing of the English and Latin versions of it.

Leo Strauss' (1899–1973) interpretation of Hobbes, first set out in 1932 in an article in French, but published a few years later as a book in English translation (Strauss 1952), was formative for some generations of political scientists and theorists. On Strauss' reading, Hobbes' political philosophy marked a decisive break with 'traditional' thinking about politics, derived from Aristotle, scholasticism and a religiously based theory of natural law. Despite this, however, Hobbes' innovativeness in Strauss' view rests not on his espousal of a scientific or naturalistic philosophy, but a new liberal moral attitude based on the 'passions' of human beings. Despite his advocacy of the geometric method and his active interest in what is now called natural science, Hobbes' political theory was formulated without reference to the latter – a view that George Croom Robertson had already expressed in the late nineteenth century – and in fact stood in some tension with it. Hobbes did not think that all passions had equal status, but rather elevated the passion for self-preservation over others. Not surprisingly the view that Hobbes' thinking heralded a sharp rupture with his predecessors has led to charges that this is to read him unhistorically (e.g. Skinner 2002, vol. I, 64, 71–72).

Strauss had also criticised the use made of Hobbes by Carl Schmitt (1888–1985) in the latter's *The Concept of the Political* of 1932. For Schmitt, Hobbes, far from being a proto-liberal, was to be seen as a kind of prophet manqué of the techno-bureaucratic state. It needs to be added that Schmitt, a German and a Nazi party member from 1933, adopts a narrative in his *Leviathan in the State Theory of Thomas Hobbes* (Schmitt 2008) which is anti-Semitic in intent and specifically holds Jewish liberals responsible for what Schmitt saw as the frustrated apotheosis of the mechanical state. For Schmitt, unlike Strauss, the contractual elements in Hobbes' theory were an aberration, and at best to be seen as a symbolic device for representing political relationships, rather than a mechanism that itself creates them. Schmitt argues that the image of the Leviathan is symbolically inappropriate: he objects to Hobbes' political means, but not to his aim, which is (as Schmitt sees it) to present representation itself in a compelling political form. What Schmitt describes is a 'crack' in the artifice that would later be exploited to engineer a liberal state. Schmitt's interpretation could hardly be further from Strauss.

The notion of the state as artifice is also prominent in the reading of *Leviathan* by the British conservative thinker Michael Oakeshott (1901–90). Oakeshott's interpretation of Hobbes went through a number of changes, but in its final form, presented in Oakeshott's *On Human Conduct*, it saw Hobbes' commonwealth as a *societas* or 'civil association', which Oakeshott distinguished from a *universitas* or 'enterprise association': while civil associations have no particular ends, but bind members by means of rules, enterprise associations exist to promote shared objectives. An obvious objection is that Hobbes' commonwealth does exist to promote a particular end, namely that of preserving the lives of its members. Civil association is the solution to the problem of war. But Oakeshott thought that war was apt to make civil degenerate into enterprise association – a community for mutual defence – so that the best footing on which politics could be placed was precisely the Hobbesian one of preventing war. Oakeshott seems to have thought that political symbolism and myth could work to make this Hobbesian predicament cause for celebration rather than regret. In a discussion written much earlier than *On Human Conduct* Oakeshott remarks that Hobbes' vision

> will appear an unduly disenchanted interpretation of the mystery of human life. But there can be no mistaking its character. It is myth, not science. It is a perception of mystery, not a pretended solution ... Hobbes recalls us to our morality with a deliberate conviction, with a subtle and sustained argument.[8]

Oakeshott's view of *Leviathan* is thus double-edged: while the image it presents is 'disenchanted', in the sense due to Max Weber – it is a world in which magical thinking has been superseded by scientific rationality – it also reports a 'mystery'. There is something in this. Just as Schmitt saw in Hobbes a thinker who engages in what Schmitt called 'political theology', by secularising concepts (in particular, that of sovereignty) with theological origins; so for Oakshott Hobbes, even while putting forward a rationalistic view of politics as stemming from individual self-interest, finds himself drawn back to a vision of politics that goes beyond what can be framed in these terms alone.

One effect of contextualism has been that some writers, in reaction, largely or wholly dispense with historical considerations when interpreting *Leviathan*. In some cases (e.g. Kateb 1989; Sorell 1986) the interpreters simply bring their critical acumen to bear on the text by reading it and making the best sense they can of it, perhaps supported by their readings of other texts by Hobbes, such as *De cive*, *The Elements of Law*, and so on. Where these other texts are brought into play, the attempt is still to reconstruct Hobbes' own thinking, since what he says in *De cive* about, say, rights in the state of nature is held to give clues as to what he says about the same subject in *Leviathan*. Of course, since the ancillary texts themselves need interpreting, the problem of 'grounding' a particular reading threatens to open up a hermeneutic circle or regress. Other writers make no bones about dispensing with historical information in general, and with the 'mythology of coherence' in particular, when comparing different texts by the same author (Skinner 2002, vol. I, 70).

The influential group of Hobbes' interpreters who take his theory as an account of rational choice in the state of nature have already been dealt with in Chapter 5. They include Gauthier (1969), Kavka (1986), Hampton (1986) and Kraus (1993). As I suggested earlier, the charge that this reading is ahistorical, because game theory was not invented until the twentieth century, is question-begging. If it is said that Hobbes does not use the relevant terminology of pay-offs, dominance and so on, that is clearly true. But all interpretation that goes beyond direct quotation involves paraphrase, often in a language different from that in which the interpreted work was written. Often the interpreter is addressing the author's intentions, and in particular what the author would recognise as an adequate account of what he or she was doing. But in this case it might simply be true that Hobbes would have recognised game theory as a helpful formalisation of certain features of the state of nature. But, in any case, any insistence that there is only one way, or a best way, of interpreting a text like *Leviathan* fails to do justice to the variety of ways in which readers can respond to it and find interest in it.

In Chapter 10 I also indicated Hobbes' influence on the 'realist' school in what is now called international theory, the view that international relations are best understood as a form of realpolitik. Hobbes' thinking exerted a strong influence on those such as Hans Morgenthau credited with founding the school, as well as more recent 'structural realist' thinkers like Kenneth Waltz. International theorists who write on realism tend to situate Hobbes in a line of thinking founded by Thucydides that goes by way of Machiavelli, and reaches its apotheosis in the Augsburg and Westphalia treaties of 1555 and 1648 respectively. Various interpretative objections may be made against the simplifications involved in this reification of realist thought, notably that the intellectual bond between Machiavelli, a theorist of republican freedom, and Hobbes is rather tenuous. At the same time, the idea that international politics is approximated by Hobbes' state of nature also influenced those, such as Hedley Bull, who were not themselves realists, but thought that the 'international anarchy' bore strong Hobbesian features.

There are many other *Leviathans*. University expansion over the past few generations has led to many more scholars working on Hobbes, and as academic life places a premium on originality, his readers have found many new angles from which to interpret him. Richard Tuck sees Hobbes as owing a primary debt to scepticism, notably of the ancient Greek Carneades (Tuck 1988b), but also as being a kind of 'utopian' (Tuck 2004). Others see Hobbes in *Leviathan* as an exponent of rhetoric (Condren 1990; Johnston 1986; Skinner 1996); there are sympathetic and not-so-sympathetic feminist readings of Hobbes (Hirschmann and Wright 2012), interpretations of him as a Christian thinker (Martinich 1992), as proponent of modern scientific methodology in the analysis of politics (Goldsmith 1966), as a sceptic (Tuck 1988b), an Epicurean (Springborg 2010) and so on. There is no obvious sign that interest in *Leviathan* is abating, so no doubt the years to come will throw up yet further interpretations of the book. As with Jorge Luis Borges' fictional persona Pierre Menard, someone who set out to write a final or definitive interpretation of *Leviathan* would in effect be committed to rewriting the book – in other words, writing it again.

FURTHER READING

GENERAL

Nowadays the fullest account of *Leviathan*'s early reception is to be found in Jon Parkin, *Taming the Leviathan: The reception of the political and religious ideas of Thomas Hobbes in England 1640–1700* (Cambridge: Cambridge University Press, 2007). Parkin shifts the emphasis in his book, arguing that the studied ambiguity of Hobbes' writings, including *Leviathan*, lent his book to creative misinterpretations that fluctuated according to the prevalent political debates of the day and their protagonists' polemical aims. *Leviathan* was, accordingly, read quite differently during the Protectorate of the 1650s than under the resurgent Anglican regime during the Restoration period a decade later. As the title of his book indicates, however, Parkin's attention is confined the reception of *Leviathan* in England. See also Parkin's 'The Reception of Hobbes' *Leviathan*', in P. Springbord (ed.), *The Cambridge Companion to Hobbes' Leviathan* (Cambridge: Cambridge University Press, 2006), 441–59. Juhana Lemetti, *Historical Dictionary of Hobbes' Philosophy* (Lanham, MD: Scarecrow Press, 2011), has a short article on 'Hobbes and Hobbism' that lists some of the main contemporary responses to *Leviathan*. Noel Malcolm's edition of *Leviathan* devotes a part of chapter 3 to responses to it (Malcolm ed., Hobbes 2012 vol. I, 146–62).

LEVIATHAN AND THE 'ENGAGEMENT' DEBATE

The classic statement of the view that *Leviathan* is to be seen as an intervention in the political debate over the oath of loyalty or 'Engagement' to the new republican regime in England is Quentin Skinner, 'Conquest and Consent: Thomas Hobbes and the Engagement controversy', in G.E. Aylmer (ed.), *The Interregnum: The quest for settlement* (London: Macmillan, 1972); reprinted in *Visions of Politics*, vol. III: *Hobbes and civil science* (Cambridge: Cambridge University Press, 2002). Jon Parkin gives a brief overview of the Engagement controversy in *Taming the Leviathan*, 85–90. An important appraisal of the 'de facto' case for engagement is provided by Kinch Hoekstra, 'Hobbes De Facto? "A Review, and Conclusion"', in Tom Sorell and Luc Foisneau (eds), *Leviathan after 350 Years* (Oxford: Oxford University Press, 2004), 33–74. Noel Malcolm expresses reservations about Skinner's thesis in his introductory volume to the Clarendon edition of *Leviathan* (Oxford: Clarendon Press, 2012), vol. I, 67ff. Malcolm's main point is that the claim often cited in support of the thesis from *Leviathan*'s 'Review, and Conclusion' about the 'mutual relation between protection and obedience' (*L* 491) was not original with Hobbes; he adds, though, rather confusingly, that other writers' construal of this relation was different from Hobbes', since it relies on a moral reciprocity between rulers and ruled, whereas in Hobbes' view it lies at the basis of rule itself (Malcolm ed, Hobbes 2012, 68).

FURTHER POLITICAL CONTROVERSIES

The first full study of contemporary responses to *Leviathan* was Samuel Mintz's *The Hunting of Leviathan* (Cambridge: Cambridge University Press, 1962). Mintz argues that Hobbes exerted a powerful and insidious influence on his readers: while most of them rejected either outright or in large part the political and religious positions Hobbes defends in *Leviathan*, Mintz contends that they were forced willy-nilly to adopt Hobbes' own methods of argument in making their case. The list of pamphlet responses to *Leviathan* that Mintz gives (Mintz 1962, 157ff.)

includes a number of significant contemporary interventions but is not comprehensive (cf. Rogers 2007, 437 n. 1).

The Cambridge Companion to Hobbes' Leviathan, edited by Patricia Springborg (Cambridge: Cambridge University Press, 2007), devotes a section to the reception of *Leviathan*. There John Rogers gives a good survey of the varying constituencies of opinion that *Leviathan* antagonised in 'Hobbes and His Contemporaries'. Perez Zagorin discusses Hyde's reaction to *Leviathan* in 'Clarendon against *Leviathan*', arguing that Hobbes' absolutist account of sovereignty in *Leviathan* alienated Hyde, who favoured a monarchy with powers limited by retained rights on the part of the subjects. Also in the *Cambridge Companion*, Jeffrey Collins' 'The Presbyterians and *Leviathan*' examines attempts by Presbyterians and their allies during the 1650s to get the book banned. For a valuable account of Hobbes' own response to the reception of *Leviathan*, see also Philip Milton, 'Hobbes, Heresy and Lord Arlington', *History of Political Thought* 14, no. 4 (1993), 501–46.

Some thirty years after Mintz, Mark Goldie gave a critical overview of Hobbes' critics in 'The Reception of Hobbes', in J.H. Burns and Mark Goldie (eds), *The Cambridge History of Political Thought, 1400–1700* (Cambridge: Cambridge University Press, 1991). For an anthology of responses by Hobbes' contemporary critics to *Leviathan*, see G.A.J. Rogers (ed.), *Leviathan: Contemporary responses to the political theory of Thomas Hobbes* (Bristol: Thoemmes Press, 1995), which includes *A Brief View and Survey of ... Leviathan* by Edward Hyde (the Earl of Clarendon), and John Bramhall's *The Catching of Leviathan*.

LEVIATHAN AND THE UNIVERSITIES

Jon Parkin discusses the Daniel Scargill case in 'Hobbism in the Later 1660s', *Historical Journal* 42, no. 1 (1999), 85–108, as well as in *Taming the Leviathan*, 244–52. For the Scargill case, see also Mintz, *Hunting of Leviathan*, 50ff. The Oxford University *Judgement and Decree* of 21 July 1683 against Hobbes is reprinted in Walter Scott (ed.), *A Collection of Scarce and Valuable Tracts*, 2nd edn, vol. VIII (London, 1812).

For discussion of Hobbes' putative heresy, see Justin Champion, '"The Kingdom of Darkness": Hobbes and heterodoxy', in Sarah Mortimer and John Robertson (eds), *Consequences of Religious Heterodoxy 1600–1750* (Leiden: Brill 2012). Also J.A.I. Champion, 'An Historical Narration concerning Heresie: Thomas Hobbes, Thomas Barlow, and the Restoration debate over "heresy"', in David Loewenstein and John Marshall (eds), *Literature and Heresy in Early Modern English Culture* (Cambridge: Cambridge University Press, 2006), 221–53.

LEVIATHAN OUTSIDE BRITAIN

For the reception of *Leviathan* in continental Europe for the first century or so after its publication, see Noel Malcolm, 'Hobbes and the European Republic of Letters', in *Aspects of Hobbes* (Oxford: Oxford University Press, 2002), which deals with European reaction to Hobbes' thought generally, and not only with specific regard to *Leviathan*. See Malcolm also for the Cardonnel family's links with Hobbes (Malcolm 2002, 259–316); also see Malcolm's edition of *Leviathan* (Oxford: Clarendon Press, 2012), vol. I, ch. 3, and pp. 87–91, for remarks about early attempts to translate *Leviathan* into French.

NOTES

1 *Biographia Britannica* 1773, vol. VI, 3948.
2 *Journal of the House of Commons*, vol. VIII 1660–67 (1802), 636.
3 It should be noted for accuracy that Skinner is referring to Hobbes' Latin translation of *Leviathan*; but Skinner sees the Latin translation as marking a further elaboration of an already highly rhetorical text.
4 Oxford *DNB* entry for Rochester, quoting Seward 1799 *Biographiana*, 2 vols, vol. II, 509, cited in Mintz 1962, 141.
5 Sir Thomas Burton, *Diary* (14 January 1657), 349, cited in Milton 1993, 515.
6 My translation. See de Maistre 1852, vol. IV, 101ff.
7 My translation here, and below.
8 Michael Oakeshott, '*Leviathan*: A myth', Online Library of Liberty, <http://oll.libertyfund.org/?option=com_staticxt&staticfile=show.php%3Ftitle=668&chapter=165297&layout=html&Itemid=27> (accessed 29 August 2013).

CONCLUSION

Why bother to read *Leviathan* today? The short answer, for many
readers, will be, 'Because I've got to do an essay/exam on it.'
I hope to have provided some help for readers in this unenviable
position, and indeed this book has largely been written with
them in mind. Even for these readers, however, it is worth
standing back to consider both the main outlines of Hobbes'
theory, and what reasons one might have for reading the book
even if doing so were not a matter of bleak necessity.

The main thing Hobbes has to say concerns the nature of
political authority. What distinguishes his theory from others is
not so much that Hobbes tries to justify this authority – many
theorists have done that – but how he does so. First, as we have
seen, he depicts the alternative to politics, the state of nature, as
desolate. Hobbes' characterisation of chaos is instantly recognisable, and lodges in the minds even of those who are ignorant of,
or reject, his remedy for it. The state of nature resonates precisely
because we are familiar with the collapse of order at home, in the
classroom, on the sports field, in public demonstrations or in
society at large. As far as it goes, the right answer to the question
'Why is political authority justified, for Hobbes?' is indeed,
'Because the alternative is so grim.'

Second, Hobbes' solution – at least as I have interpreted it in this book – makes the justification of political power depend on consent. He is at pains to stress that it is the 'transfer of right' that creates authority. Justification is not conferred merely because the state of nature is grim, or because the person or body to whom right is transferred wields overwhelming power over those who transfer it. So Hobbes' justification calls on another familiar idea, that in order to achieve legitimate authority, as distinct from brute force, we need consent. The twist in the tail, for modern liberals, is that Hobbes makes the conditions for consent very undemanding: on his view, the traveller who surrenders his valuables to a highwayman, the coward who caves in to the bully, the baby who takes its mother's milk, have all given sufficient signs of consent. In particular, I consent to someone's power over me even if I submit purely from the fear of 'present death'.

Third, because the conditions of consent are so weak, and because we have good reason to avoid present death if we can, Hobbes thinks both that we have good reason to consent to political authority, and that we very often do consent. His claim that authority is justified contrasts with both anarchists and liberal defenders of authority, both of whom tend to impose stringent conditions if authority is to be justified. In fact, Hobbes' theory exposes a common feature of these positions – their rejection of worldly political realities in favour of an ideal. Liberals tend to think that the obligations that political authority claims are justified only in an ideal world, and anarchists do not think them justified even there. What Hobbes gives us, by contrast, is the reality of politics, and above all, of power.

It does not matter, for Hobbes, how we come to consent. The sovereign has the same rights and duties regardless of whether political power comes about by mutual agreement or by conquest. As I have argued, this can be seen as a rejection of the idea that, in order to justify political authority, political theorists need to tell a story about how people in the state of nature would rationally decide to leave it. This approach faces the problem of showing that the story is true, or can be taken as though it were true. In *Leviathan* Hobbes cuts through these worries by arguing that protection and obedience are mutually reinforcing. As long as protection is there, we have sufficient ground for obedience, and in not rebelling, we consent.

Fourth, *Leviathan* is based on a self-interested theory of motivation and reasons for action. The motive for obligation is the overriding impulse for self-preservation. The obligation itself arises from the consent of the subjects – but, as we have seen, the bar for consent is very low. While this self-interested view may not be very morally edifying, it does at least answer to entrenched features of the world we inhabit. This is not simply because human altruism is in short supply much of the time. It is also because even wholly philanthropic action does not occur in a political vacuum. Consider the practicalities of aiding those rendered needy by natural or man-made disaster abroad. Effective delivery requires a political, and often military, presence on the ground. Even a boundlessly wealthy philanthropic organisation, in negotiating with local leaders over when, how and what to provide in aid, and to whom, would be taking political decisions.[1] This becomes clear, for instance, when we ask to whom the organisation would be accountable, and on what basis.

Fifth, *Leviathan* comes up with a wholly new theory of political representation. In fact, the very idea of representation was much less familiar to Hobbes' contemporaries than it is to us. The sovereign does not – and for Hobbes, cannot – represent the subjects directly, but represents instead an imaginary person, the person of the state. The upshot of this is a paradox. In order to preserve our belief in the reality of representation, we have to believe in a fiction, which is not only thought of as acting, but as doing so in our name. The fiction of the state of nature supports this by providing a story whose anticlimactic end – our failure rationally to escape from the state of nature – gives reasons for not making that fiction reality. The alternative is to realise a further fiction, that of the sovereign as representative of the people, taken as one being.

In part because of this paradox, the idea of representation remains politically contentious, as well as familiar. Protests against the 2003 Iraq War mobilised in the United Kingdom under the slogan 'Not in my name'. But of course the action of going to war was carried out in the name of the British people. This summarises one of the constitutive tensions in modern democratic politics, which can be put down directly to the paradox of representation: that in democracies, political authority acts in the name of the people, even though no such being exists. This fictional being is then called upon to sanction the speaker's preferred outcomes, and to disown the others.

Leviathan also sidelines God. Hobbes numbered among his opponents not only old enemies who had fought with Parliament against Charles I in the civil wars, but erstwhile friends such as Edward Hyde, later Lord Clarendon. Hyde found the doctrines of Leviathan – especially its stress on consent, with the implicit notion of popular sovereignty – repellent. What Hyde and other royalists really disliked about the book was its denial that, in the words of the famous passage from scripture, often cited to justify political authority, 'The powers that be are ordained by God' (Romans 13:1). Rather, for Hobbes, power is handed up to the sovereign from the people.

Not only does this mean that monarchs are not ultimately sovereign: it also means elbowing God aside as the source of political authority. The subjects create the sovereign and, as Hobbes says in the first few sentences of *Leviathan*, thereby emulate God as creator. Human beings have no need of divine authorisation. What matters is not whether Hobbes' theory can, at a stretch, be accommodated to conventional religious (that is, Christian) morality and theology. It is that the theory makes no demand that God play more than a walk-on part.

***

At the start of this book I said that *Leviathan* is haunted by the spectre of violent political disorder. Hobbes offers his theory of absolute sovereignty as a way of laying the ghost. But, as I hope to have made clear, the ghost is never finally exterminated. The seeds of disorder are perpetual, and omnipresent, particularly in humans' tendency to back their own private judgements over the claims of the public authority.

Leviathan is a kind of parody of the biblical Book of Job. In Job, an all-powerful God allows the serial infliction of misery on an innocent man, Job himself. When Job asks God about the justification for this, God says, in effect: I do this, because I can. 'Whatsover is under the whole heaven is mine' (Job 41:11). Job's response is one of abject surrender, like that of the subjects to the sovereign. When he answers God, 'I abhor myself, and repent in dust and ashes' (Job 42:6), his tribulations come to an end. We are told that he is given twice as much as he had before.

God's response to Job may seem primitive, even crude. It questions the very basis for talking about justification in situations like Job's. God offers not so much a form of justification, as a dismissal of the question. His overpowering might, it seems, makes right. And that means, it may be thought, that we can no longer talk about 'right' here. Morality serves only as an instrument of power – or insofar as it offers any check on power it is feeble, a straw to swat the wind.

In the end there is no good answer to Hobbes' query, posed in the 'Fool' passage, of what we should say if the Kingdom of Heaven is taken over by 'unjust violence' (L 101), and the powers that be are ordained by injustice. The meek will not inherit the earth. On its publication *Leviathan* offered scant comfort for those who wished to see an old corrupt order overthrown by the rule of saints, a kingdom of the righteous. Nor for us now, borne along on the back of Hobbes' uncatchable monster.

NOTE

1 As Bernard Williams made clear; see his 'Humanitarianism', in Williams 2005, e.g. 152.

BIBLIOGRAPHY

PRIMARY SOURCES

Anon. 1687. *Essais de morale de de politique, où il est traité de l'origine des sociétés civiles, de l'autorité des Princes & du devoir des sujets.* Lyon: Thomas Amaulry.

Beccaria, C. (1983) *Essay on Crimes and Punishments.* 4th edn. Boston, MA: International Pocket Library.

Burton, T. 1828. *Diary of Thomas Burton, Esq., Member in the Parliaments of Oliver and Richard Cromwell.* Edited by John Towill Rutt. London: Henry Colburn.

de Maistre, J. (1852) *Du Pape: Suivi de l'Eglise gallicane dans son rapport avec le souverain pontife.* Paris: H. Goemaere.

Hobbes, T. 1679. *Thomae Hobbesii malmesburiensis vita.* London.

———1839–45. *The English Works of Thomas Hobbes of Malmesbury.* Edited by W. Molesworth. London.

———1841. *Thomas Hobbes Malmesburiensis opera philosophica quae latine scripsit omnia.* Edited by W. Molesworth. London.

———1946. *Leviathan.* Edited by M. Oakeshott. Oxford: Oxford University Press.

———1968. *Leviathan.* Edited by C. B. Macpherson. Harmondsworth: Penguin.

———1969. *The Elements of Law, natural and politic.* Edited with a preface by F. Tönnies, edn revised by M. M. Goldsmith. London: Cass.

———1971. *Léviathan.* Edited by F. Tricaud. Paris: Sirey.

———1976. *Thomas White's De Mundo Examined.* Translated and edited by H. Whitmore Jones. London: Bradford University Press.

———1983. *De Cive: The Latin version.* Edited by H. Warrender. Oxford: Clarendon Press.

——1986. *The Rhetorics of Thomas Hobbes and Bernard Lamy*. Edited by J.J. Harwood. Carbondale, IL: Southern Illinois University Press.

——1990. *Behemoth*. Edited by F. Tönnies, with an introduciton by S. Holmes. Chicago, IL: Chicago University Press.

——1991. *Leviathan*. Edited by R.F. Tuck. Cambridge: Cambridge University Press.

——1994a. *The Correspondence of Thomas Hobbes*. 2 vols. Edited by N. Malcolm. Oxford: Oxford University Press.

——1994b. *Leviathan. With selected variants from the Latin edition of 1668*. Edited by E. Curley. Indianapolis, IN: Hackett.

——1995. *Three Discourses*. Edited by N.B. Reynolds and A.W. Saxonhouse. Chicago, IL: Chicago University Press.

——1996. *Leviathan*. Edited with an introduction by J.G.A. Gaskin. Oxford: Oxford University Press.

——1997. *A Dialogue between a Philosopher and a Student of the Common Laws of England*. Edited with an introduction by J. Cropsey. Chicago, IL: Chicago University Press.

——1998. *On the Citizen* [English translation of *De cive*]. Edited by R.F. Tuck and translated by M. Silverthorne. Cambridge: Cambridge University Press.

——1999. *Hobbes and Bramhall on Liberty and Necessity*. Edited by V. Chappell. Cambridge: Cambridge University Press.

——2002. *Leviathan*. Edited by A.P. Martinich. Peterborough, ON: Broadview.

——2003. *Thomas Hobbes Leviathan*. 2 vols. Edited by G.A.J. Rogers and K. Schuhmann. London: Continuum.

——2008. 'The Making of the Ornaments: Further thoughts on the printing of the third edition of *Leviathan*'. *Hobbes Studies* 21, no. 1: 3–37.

——(ed.) 2012. *Thomas Hobbes: Leviathan*. 3 vols. Oxford: Clarendon Press.

Kennett, W. 1708. *Memoirs of the Family of Cavendish*. London: H. Hills.

Milward, J. 1938. *The Diary of John Milward, Esq., Member of Parliament for Derbyshire, September, 1666 to May, 1668*. Edited by Caroline Robbins. Cambridge: Cambridge University Press.

Rogers, G.A.J. (ed.) 1995. *Leviathan: Contemporary responses to the political theory of Thomas Hobbes*. Bristol: Thoemmes Press.

——2007. 'Hobbes and His Contemporaries'. In P. Springborg (ed.), *The Cambridge Companion to Hobbes' Leviathan*. Cambridge: Cambridge University Press

Selden, J. 1892. *The table talk of John Selden*. Edited with an introduction and notes by S. Harvey Reynolds. Oxford: Clarendon Press.

SECONDARY SOURCES AND OTHER WORKS

Airaksinen, T. and Bertman, M.A. (eds) 1989. *Hobbes: War among nations*. Aldershot: Avebury.

Akashi, K. 2000. 'Hobbes' Relevance to the Modern Law of Nations'. *Journal of the History of International Law* 2: 199–216.

Alexandra, A. 1992. 'Should Hobbes' State of Nature Be Represented as a Prisoner's Dilemma?'. *Southern Journal of Philosophy* 30: 1–16.

Allen, A. and Morales, M. H. 1992. 'Hobbes, Formalism and Corrective Justice'. *Iowa Law Review* 7: 713–39.

Allingham, M. 2002. *Choice Theory*. Oxford: Oxford University Press.

Ashcraft, R. 1978. 'Ideology and Class in Hobbes' Political Theory'. *Political Theory* 6: 27–54.

——1988. 'Political Theory and Practical Action: A reconsideration of Hobbes' state of nature'. *Hobbes Studies* 1: 63–88.

Astbury, R. 1978. 'The Renewal of the Licensing Act in 1693 and Its Lapse in 1695'. *Library*, 5th series, 33, no. 4: 296–322.

Aubrey, J. 1898. *Brief Lives, chiefly of contemporaries, set down by John Aubrey, between the Years 1669 and 1696*. 2 vols. Edited by A. Clark. Oxford: Clarendon Press.

Austin, J. 1995. *The Province of Jurisprudence Determined*. Edited by W.E. Rumble. Cambridge: Cambridge University Press.

Axelrod, R. 2006. *The Evolution of Cooperation*. Rev. edn. New York: Perseus.

Ball, T. 1985. 'Hobbes' Linguistic Turn'. *Polity* 17: 739–60.

——1996. *Reappraising Political Theory: Revisionist studies in the history of political thought*. Oxford: Clarendon Press.

Barnard, J. and D.F. McKenzie (eds) 2002. *The Book in Britain, Volume IV: 1557–1695*. Cambridge: Cambridge University Press.

Barry, B. 1968. 'Warrender and His Critics'. *Philosophy* 43: 117–37.

——1995. *Justice as Impartiality*. Oxford: Clarendon Press.

Baumgold, D. 1988. *Hobbes' Political Theory*. Cambridge: Cambridge University Press.

——1990. 'Hobbes' Political Sensibility: The menace of political ambition'. In Dietz 1990.

Beitz, C. 1979. *Political Theory and International Relations*. Princeton, NJ: Princeton University Press.

Berlin, I. 1969. *Four Essays on Liberty*. Oxford: Oxford University Press.

Blackburn, S. 1998. *Ruling Passions: A theory of practical reasoning*. Oxford: Oxford University Press.

Boonin-Vail, D. 1994. *Thomas Hobbes and the Science of Moral Virtue*. Cambridge: Cambridge University Press.

Bostrenghi, D. (ed.) 1992. *Hobbes e Spinoza, scienza e politica: Atti del Convegno internazionale, Urbino, 14–17 ottobre, 1988*. Naples: Bibliopolis.

Boucher, D. 1985. *Texts in Context: Revisionist methods for studying the history of ideas*. Dordrecht: Martinus Nijhoff.

——1990. 'Inter-Community and International Relations in the Political Philosophy of Hobbes'. *Polity* 23: 207–32.

——1998. *Political Theories of International Relations: From Thucydides to the present*. Oxford: Oxford University Press.

Brett, A. 1997. *Liberty, Right and Nature: Individual rights in later scholastic thought*. Cambridge: Cambridge University Press.

Brown, C. 2001. *Understanding International Relations*. 2nd edn. Basingstoke: Palgrave.

Brown, K.C. (ed.) 1965. *Hobbes Studies*. Oxford: Blackwell.

——1978. 'The Artist of the *Leviathan* Title-Page'. *British Library Journal* 4: 24–36.

Brown, S.M. 1965. 'The Taylor Thesis: Introductory note', and 'The Taylor Thesis: Some objections'. In K. Brown 1965.

Bull, H. 1977. *The Anarchical Society: A study of order in world politics*. New York: Columbia University Press.

——1981. 'Hobbes and the International Anarchy'. *Social Research* 48: 717–38.

Burgess, G. 1990. 'Contexts for the Writing and Publication of Hobbes' *Leviathan*'. *History of Political Thought* 11: 675–702.

——1993. *The Politics of the Ancient Constitution: An introduction to English political thought, 1603–1642*. University Park, PA: Pennsylvania University Press.

Burns, J.H. and Goldie, M. (eds.) 1991. *The Cambridge History of Political Thought, 1400–1700*. Cambridge: Cambridge University Press.

Carmichael, D.J.C. 1990. 'Hobbes on Natural Right in Society: The *Leviathan* account'. *Canadian Journal of Political Science* 23: 3–21.

Cattaneo, M. 1965. 'Hobbes' Theory of Punishment'. In K. Brown 1965.

Caws, P. (ed.) 1989. *The Causes of Quarrel: Essays on peace, war, and Thomas Hobbes*. Boston, MA: Beacon Press.

Champion, J. 2006. 'An Historical Narration Concerning Heresie: Thomas Hobbes, Thomas Barlow, and the restoration debate on over "heresy"'. In Loewenstein and Marshall 2006.

——2012. "'The Kingdom of Darkness': Hobbes and heterodoxy". In Mortimer and Robertson 2012.

Cohen, G. A. 1996. 'Reason, Humanity and the Moral Law'. In *The Sources of Normativity*, by C. M. Korsgaard *et al*. Cambridge: Cambridge University Press.

Collins, J. 2005. *The Allegiance of Thomas Hobbes*. Oxford: Oxford University Press.

——2007. 'Silencing Thomas Hobbes: The Presbyterians and *Leviathan*'. In P. Springborg (ed.), *The Cambridge Companion to Hobbes' Leviathan*. Cambridge: Cambridge University Press.

——2013. 'Thomas Hobbes, Heresy, and the Theological Project of *Leviathan*'. *Hobbes Studies* 26, no. 1: 6–33.

Condren, C. 1990. 'On the Rhetorical Foundations of *Leviathan*'. *History of Political Thought* 11: 703–20.

——1994. *The Language of Politics in Seventeenth-Century England*. New York: St Martin's Press.

——2000. *Thomas Hobbes*. New York: Twayne Publishers.

Copp, D. 1979. 'Collective Actions and Secondary Actions'. *American Philosophical Quarterly* 16: 177–86.

——1980. 'Hobbes on Artificial Persons and Collective Actions'. *Philosophical Review* 89: 579–606.

Corbett, M. and Lightbown, R. 1979. *The Comely Frontespiece*. London: Routledge & Kegan Paul.

Covell, C. 2004. *Hobbes, Realism, and the Tradition of International Law*. Basingstoke: Palgrave.

Curley, E. 1990. 'Reflections on Hobbes: Recent work on his moral and political philosophy'. *Journal of Philosophical Research* 15: 169–250.

———1992. '"I Durst Not Write So Boldly" or, How to read Hobbes' theological-political treatise'. In Bostrenghi 1992.

———1996. 'Calvin or Hobbes, or Hobbes as an orthodox Christian'. *Journal of the History of Philosophy* 34: 257–71.

———2006. 'Hobbes and the Cause of Religious Toleration'. In P. Springborg (ed.), *The Cambridge Companion to Hobbes' Leviathan*. Cambridge: Cambridge University Press.

Curthoys, J. 1998. 'Thomas Hobbes, the Taylor Thesis and Alasdair Macintyre'. *British Journal for the History of Philosophy* 6: 1–24.

Chwaszcza, C. 2012. 'The Seat of Sovereignty: Hobbes on the artificial personality of the commonwealth or state'. *Hobbes Studies* 25, no. 1: 123–42.

Dalgarno, M. T. 1976. 'Analysing Hobbes' Contract'. *Proceedings of the Aristotelian Society* 76: 209–26.

Darwall, S. 1996. *British Moralists and the Internal 'Ought', 1640–1740*. Cambridge: Cambridge University Press.

Dietz, M. (ed.) 1990. *Thomas Hobbes and Political Theory*. Lawrence, KS: University Press of Kansas.

Dunn, J. and Harris, I. (eds) 1997. *Hobbes*. 3 vols. Cheltenham: Edward Elgar.

Dworkin, R. M. 1975. 'The Original Position'. In N. Daniels (ed.), *Reading Rawls*. Oxford: Blackwell.

———1986. *Law's Empire*. Cambridge, MA: Belknap Press.

Dyzenhaus, D. 2001. 'Hobbes and the Legitimacy of Law'. *Law and Philosophy* 20: 461–98.

Eachard, J. 1705. *Dr Eachard's Works. To which are added five letters*. London: J. Phillips.

Edmundson, W.A. 1998. *Three Anarchical Fallacies: An essay on political authority*. Cambridge: Cambridge University Press.

Ewin, R.E. 1991. *Virtues and Rights: The moral philosophy of Thomas Hobbes*. Oxford: Westview.

Field, J.F. 2008. *Reactions and Responses to the Great Fire: London and England in the later seventeenth century*. PhD thesis. Newcastle University. <https://theses. ncl.ac.uk/dspace/handle/10443/676>.

Finkelstein, C. (ed.) 2005. Hobbes on Law. Burlington, VT: Ashgate.

Fiaschi, G. 2013. 'The Power of Words: Political and theological science in *Leviathan*'. *Hobbes Studies* 26, no. 1: 1–5.

Finnis, J. M. 1982. *Natural Law and Natural Rights*. Oxford: Clarendon Press.

———1998. *Aquinas*. Oxford: Oxford University Press.

Firth, C. H. and Rait, R.S. (eds) 1911. *Acts and Ordinances of the Interregnum, 1642–1660*. London.

Flathman, R.E. 1993. *Thomas Hobbes: Skepticism, individuality and chastened politics*. Newbury Park, CA: Sage.

Forsyth, M. 1979. 'Thomas Hobbes and the External Relations of States'. *British Journal of International Relations* 5: 196–209.

Fuller, T. 1990. 'Compatibilities on the Idea of Law in Thomas Aquinas and Thomas Hobbes'. *Hobbes Studies* 3: 112–34.

Gauthier, D. 1969. *The Logic of Leviathan: The moral and political theory of Thomas Hobbes*. Oxford: Clarendon Press.

——1986. *Morals by Agreement*. Oxford: Clarendon Press.

——1987. 'Taming *Leviathan*'. *Philosophy & Public Affairs* 17: 280–98.

——1988. 'Hobbes' Social Contract'. In Rogers and Ryan 1988.

——2001. 'Hobbes: The laws of nature'. *Pacific Philosophical Quarterly* 82: 258–84.

Gert, B. 1969. 'Hobbes and Psychological Egoism'. In B. Baumrin (ed.), *Hobbes' Leviathan: Interpretation and criticism*. Belmont, CA: Wadsworth.

——1996. 'Hobbes' Psychology'. In Sorell 1996a.

Goldie, M. 1991. 'The Reception of Hobbes'. In J. H. Burns and M. Goldie (eds), *The Cambridge History of Political Thought 1450–1700*. Cambridge: Cambridge University Press.

Goldsmith, M.M. 1966. *Hobbes' Science of Politics*. New York: Columbia University Press.

——1980. 'Hobbes' "Mortall God": Is there a fallacy in Hobbes' theory of sovereignty?' *History of Political Thought* 1: 33–50.

——1981. 'Picturing Hobbes' Politics'. *Journal of the Warburg and Courtauld Institutes* 44: 232–37.

——1989. 'Hobbes on Liberty'. *Hobbes Studies* 2: 23–29.

——1996. 'Hobbes on Law'. In Sorell 1996a.

Grant, H. 1996. 'Hobbes and Mathematics'. In Sorell 1996a.

Gray, J. 2000. *Two Faces of Liberalism*. Oxford: Polity Press.

——2002. *Straw Dogs: Thoughts on humans and other animals*. London: Granta Books.

Grover, R. 1989. 'Hobbes and the Concept of International Law'. In T. Airaksinen and M.A. Bertman (eds), *Hobbes: War Among Nations*. Aldershot: Avebury.

——1980. 'The Legal Origins of Thomas Hobbes' Doctrine of Contract'. *Journal of the History of Philosophy* 18: 177–94.

Haji, I. 1991. 'Hampton on State-of-Nature Cooperation'. *Philosophy and Phenomenological Research* 51: 589–601.

Halliday, R.J., Kenyon, T. and Reeve, A. 1983. 'Hobbes' Belief in God'. *Political Studies* 31: 418–33.

Hampton, J. 1986. *Hobbes and the Social Contract Tradition*. Cambridge: Cambridge University Press.

——1989. 'Hobbesian Reflections on Glory as a Cause of Conflict'. In Caws 1989.

——1991. 'Reply to Haji'. *Philosophy and Phenomenological Research* 51: 603–9.

——1997. *Political Philosophy*. Boulder, CO: Westview.

Hanson, D.W. 1984. 'Thomas Hobbes' "Highway to Peace"'. *International Organization* 38: 329–54.

——1990. 'The Meaning of "Demonstration" in Hobbes' Science'. *History of Political Thought* 11, no. 4: 587–626.

Hardin, R. 1991. 'Hobbesian Political Order'. *Political Theory* 9: 156–80.

Harman, J. D. 1997. 'Liberty, Rights, and Will in Hobbes: A response to David van Mill'. *Journal of Politics* 59: 893–902.

Harrison, R. 2003. *Hobbes, Locke, and Confusion's Masterpiece: An examination of seventeenth-century political philosophy*. Cambridge: Cambridge University Press.

Hart, H. L. A. 1961. *The Concept of Law*. Oxford: Clarendon Press.

Hartman, M. 1986. 'Hobbes' Concept of Political Revolution'. *Journal of the History of Ideas* 47: 487–95.

Heyd, D. 1991. 'Hobbes on Capital Punishment'. *History of Philosophy Quarterly* 8: 119–34.

Hirschmann, N. and Wright, J. 2012. *Feminist Interpretations of Thomas Hobbes*. University Park, PA: Pennsylvania State University Press.

Hoekstra, K. 2003. 'Hobbes on Law, Nature and Reason'. *Journal of the History of Philosophy* 41, no. 1: 111–20.

——2004. 'The De Facto Turn in Hobbes' Political Philosophy'. In Sorell and Foisneau 2004.

Hohfeld, W. 1923. *Fundamental Legal Conceptions as Applied in Judicial Reasoning, and other legal essays*. Edited by W. Wheeler Cook. New Haven, CT: Yale University Press.

Honig, B. and Mapel, D.R. (eds) 2002. *Skepticism, Individuality and Freedom: The reluctant liberalism of Richard Flathman*. Minneapolis, MN: University of Minnesota Press.

Hood, F.C. 1964. *The Divine Politics of Thomas Hobbes: An interpretation of Leviathan*. Oxford: Clarendon Press.

——1967. 'The Change in Thomas Hobbes' Definition of Liberty'. *Philosophical Quarterly* 17: 150–63.

Horton, J. 1992. *Political Obligation*. Basingstoke: Macmillan.

Hunter, M. and Wootton, D. (eds) 1992. *Atheism from the Reformation to the Enlightenment*. Oxford: Oxford University Press.

Israel, J. 2001. *Radical Enlightenment: Philosophy and the making of modernity*. Oxford: Oxford University Press.

Jacquot, J. 1952. 'Sir Charles Cavendish and His Learned Friends'. *Annals of Science* 8: 13–27.

James I. 2002. C.H. McIlwain (ed.). *The Political Works of James I*. Union, NJ: Lawbook Exchange.

Jesseph, D. 1996. 'Hobbes and the Method of Natural Science'. In Sorell 1996a.

——1999. *Squaring the Circle: The war between Hobbes and Wallis*. Chicago, IL: University of Chicago Press.

Johnson, P.J. 1974. 'Hobbes' Anglican Doctrine of Salvation'. In R. Ross, H. Schneider and T. Waldman (eds), *Thomas Hobbes in His Time*. Minneapolis, MN: Minnesota University Press.

Johnston, D. 1986. *The Rhetoric of Leviathan: Thomas Hobbes and the politics of cultural transformation*. Princeton, NJ: Princeton University Press.

——1989. 'Hobbes' Mortalism'. *History of Political Thought* 10: 647–63.

Kagan, R. 2003. *Paradise and Power: America and Europe in the new world order*. London: Atlantic Books.

Kateb, G. 1989. 'Hobbes and the Irrationality of Politics'. *Political Theory* 17: 355–91.

Kavka, G.S. 1983a. 'Hobbes' War of All against All'. *Ethics* 93: 291–310.

——1983b. 'Right, Reason and Natural Law in Hobbes' Ethics'. *Monist* 66: 120–33.

——1986. *Hobbesian Moral and Political Theory*. Princeton, NJ: Princeton University Press.

King, P. (ed.) 1983. *The History of Ideas: An introduction to method*. London: Croom Helm.

——1993. *Thomas Hobbes: Critical assessments.* 4 vols. London: Routledge.

Kramer, M. 1997. *Hobbes and the Paradoxes of Political Origins.* London: Macmillan.

Kraus, J.S. 1993. *The Limits of Hobbesian Contractarianism.* Cambridge: Cambridge University Press.

Kuchta, D. 2009. 'The Three-Piece Suit'. In P. McNeil and V. Karaminas (eds), *The Men's Fashion Reader.* Oxford: Berg, 44–53.

Ladenson, R. 1981. 'In Defense of a Hobbesian Conception of Law'. *Philosophy & Public Affairs* 9: 134–59.

Leijenhorst, C. 1996. 'Hobbes' Theory of Causality'. *Monist* 79: 426–47.

Leites, E. (ed.) 1988. *Conscience and Casuistry in Early Modern Europe.* Cambridge: Cambridge University Press.

Lemetti, J. 2011. *Historical Dictionary of Hobbes' Philosophy.* Lanham, MD: Scarecrow Press.

Levy Peck, L. 1996. 'Hobbes on the Grand Tour: Paris, Venice, or London?' *Journal of the History of Ideas* 57: 177–82.

Lewis, D. 1969. *Convention: A philosophical study.* Oxford: Basil Blackwell.

Lips, J. 1927. *Die Stellung des Thomas Hobbes zu den politischen Parteien der großen englischen Revolution.* Leipzig.

Lister, A. 1998. 'Scepticism and Pluralism in Thomas Hobbes' Political Thought'. *History of Political Thought* 19: 35–60.

Lloyd, S. 1992. *Ideals as Interests in Hobbes' 'Leviathan': The power of mind over matter.* Cambridge: Cambridge University Press.

——2001. 'Hobbes' Self-effacing Natural Law Theory'. *Pacific Philosophical Quarterly* 82: 285–308.

——2010. *Morality in the Philosophy of Thomas Hobbes: Cases in the law of nature.* Cambridge: Cambridge University Press.

Loewenstein, D. and J. Marshall (eds) 2006. *Literature and Heresy in Early Modern English Culture.* Cambridge: Cambridge University Press.

Lubiénski, Z. 1932. *Die Grundlagen des ethisch-politischen Systems von Hobbes.* Munich: Ernst Reinhardt.

Lund, R. 2012. *Ridicule, Religion and the Politics of Wit in Augustan England.* Devon: Ashgate.

Lund, W.R. 1988. 'The Historical and 'Political' Origins of Civil Society: Hobbes on presumption and certainty'. *History of Political Thought* 9: 223–35.

Macdonald, H. and Hargreaves, M. 1952. *Thomas Hobbes: A bibliography.* London: Bibliographical Society.

Mackintosh, J. 1834. *A General View of the Progress of Ethical Philosophy, Chiefly during the Seventeenth and Eighteenth Centuries.* 2nd edn. Philadelphia: Carey, Lea and Blanchard.

McLean, I. 1981. 'The Social Contract in *Leviathan* and the Prisoner's Dilemma Supergame'. *Political Studies* 29: 339–51.

McNeilly, F.S. 1966. 'Egoism in Hobbes'. *Philosophical Quarterly* 16: 193–206.

——1968. *The Anatomy of Leviathan.* London: Macmillan.

Macpherson, C. B. 1962. *The Political Theory of Possessive Individualism: Hobbes to Locke.* Oxford: Clarendon Press.

——1965. 'Hobbes' Bourgeois Man'. In K. Brown 1965.

Malcolm, N. 1981. 'Hobbes, Sandys, and the Virginia Company'. *Historical Journal* 24: 297–321.

——1996. 'A Summary Biography of Hobbes'. In Sorell 1996a.

——2002. *Aspects of Hobbes*. Oxford: Clarendon Press.

——2005. 'What Hobbes Really Said'. *National Interest* 81 (Fall): 22–28.

——2007. 'The Making of the Bear: Second thoughts on the printing of the second edition of *Leviathan*'. *Hobbes Studies* 20, no. 1: 2–39.

——2008. 'The Making of the Ornaments: Further thoughts on the printing of the third edition of *Leviathan*'. *Hobbes Studies* 21, no. 1: 3–37.

Malnes, R. 1994. *The Hobbesian Theory of International Conflict*. New York: Oxford University Press.

Martin, H.-J. 1999. *Livres, pouvoirs et société à Paris au XVIIe siècle*. Geneva: Droz.

Martinich, A. P. 1992. *The Two Gods of Leviathan: Thomas Hobbes on religion and politics*. Cambridge: Cambridge University Press.

——1995. *A Hobbes Dictionary*. Oxford: Blackwell.

——1997. *Thomas Hobbes*. London: Macmillan.

——1999. *Thomas Hobbes: A Biography*. Cambridge: Cambridge University Press.

——2005. *Hobbes*. London: Routledge.

Martinich, A. P. and Battiste, B. (eds) 2011. *Leviathan Parts I and II*. Peterborough, ON: Broadview.

Mathie, W. 1986. 'Reason and Rhetoric in Hobbes' *Leviathan*'. *Interpretation* 14: 281–98.

May, L. 1980. 'Hobbes' Contract Theory'. *Journal of the History of Philosophy* 18: 195–207.

McLean, I. (1981) 'The Social Contract in *Leviathan* and the Prisoner's Dilemma Supergame', *Political Studies* 29: 339–51.

McNeil, P. and Karaminas, V. (eds) 2009. *The Men's Fashion Reader*. Oxford: Berg.

Mendus, S. (ed.) 1988. *Justifying Toleration: Conceptual and historical perspectives*. Cambridge: Cambridge University Press.

Miller, D. (ed.) 1991. *Liberty*. Oxford: Oxford University Press.

Miller, D. and Siedentop, L. (eds) 1983. *The Nature of Political Theory*. Oxford: Oxford University Press.

Milton, P. 1993. 'Hobbes, Heresy and Lord Arlington'. *History of Political Thought* 14, no. 4: 501–46.

Mintz, S. 1962. *The Hunting of Leviathan: Seventeenth-century reactions to the materialism and moral philosophy of Thomas Hobbes*. Cambridge: Cambridge University Press.

Missner, M. 1983. 'Skepticism and Hobbes' Political Philosophy'. *Journal of the History of Ideas* 44: 407–27.

Morrow, J. 1993. *Game Theory for Political Scientists*. Princeton, NJ: Princeton University Press.

Mortimer, S. and Robertson, J. (eds) 2012. *Consequences of Religious Heterodoxy 1600–1750*. Leiden: Brill.

Murphy, M. 1995. 'Was Hobbes a Legal Positivist?'. *Ethics* 105: 846–73.

Nagel, T. 1959. 'Hobbes' Concept of Obligation'. *Philosophical Review* 68: 68–83.

Navari, C. 1982. 'Hobbes and the 'Hobbesian Tradition' in International Thought'. *Millennium* 11: 202–22.

Neal, P. 1988. 'Hobbes and Rational Choice Theory'. *Western Political Quarterly* 41: 635–52.

Newey, G. 1996. 'Reason Beyond Reason: "Political obligation" reconsidered'. *Philosophical Papers* 25: 21–46.

——1999. *Virtue, Reason and Toleration: The place of toleration in ethical and political philosophy.* Edinburgh: Edinburgh University Press.

——2001. *After Politics: The rejection of politics in contemporary liberal philosophy.* London: Palgrave.

Nozick, R. 1974. *Anarchy, State, and Utopia.* Oxford: Blackwell.

Nuri Yurdusev, A. 2006. 'Thomas Hobbes and International Relations: From realism to rationalism'. *Australian Journal of International Affairs* 60: 305–21.

Oakeshott, M. 1975. *Hobbes on Civil Association.* Oxford: Oxford University Press.

——1991. *Rationalism in Politics and other essays.* Indianapolis, IN: Liberty Fund.

Okin, S. M. 1982. '"The Soveraign and His Counsellours": Hobbes' reevaluation of parliament'. *Political Theory* 10: 49–75.

Parkin, J. 1999. 'Hobbism in the Later 1660s: Daniel Scargill and Samuel Parker'. *Historical Journal* 42, no. 1: 85–108.

——2006. 'The Reception of Hobbes' *Leviathan*'. In P. Springborg (ed.), *The Cambridge Companion to Hobbes' Leviathan.* Cambridge: Cambridge University Press.

——2007. *Taming the Leviathan: The reception of the political and religious ideas of Thomas Hobbes in England 1640–1700.* Cambridge: Cambridge University Press.

Pasquino, P. 2001. 'Hobbes, Religion, and Rational Choice: Hobbes' two *Leviathan*s and the Fool'. *Pacific Philosophical Quarterly* 82: 406–19.

Peters, R.S. 1956. *Hobbes.* Harmondsworth: Penguin.

Pettit, P. 1997. *Republicanism: A theory of freedom and government.* Oxford: Oxford University Press.

——2008. *Made with Words: Hobbes on language, mind, and politics.* Princeton, NJ: Princeton University Press.

Phillipson, N. and Skinner, Q.R.D. (eds) 1993. *Political Discourse in Early Modern Britain.* Cambridge: Cambridge University Press.

Pitkin, H.F. 1964a. 'Hobbes' Concept of Representation – Part I'. *American Political Science Review* 58: 328–40.

——1964b. 'Hobbes' Concept of Representation – Part II'. *American Political Science Review* 58: 902–18.

——1967. *The Concept of Representation.* Berkeley, CA: University of California Press.

Plamenatz, J. 1965. 'Mr Warrender's Hobbes'. In K. Brown 1965.

Pocock, J.G.A. 1971. *Politics, Language and Time: Essays on political thought and history.* London: Methuen.

——1990. 'Thomas Hobbes: Atheist or enthusiast? His place in a restoration debate'. *History of Political Thought* 11: 737–49.

Popkin, R.H. 1982. 'Hobbes and Scepticism'. In L. Thro (ed.), *History of Philosophy in the Making.* Washington, DC: University Press of America.

Pritchard, A. 1980. 'The Last Days of Hobbes: Evidence of the wood manuscripts'. *Bodleian Library Record* 10: 178–87.

Prokhovnik, R. 1991. *Rhetoric and Philosophy in Hobbes' Leviathan*. New York: Garland.

Rawls, J. 1971. *A Theory of Justice*. Oxford: Oxford University Press.

——1993. *Political Liberalism*. New York: Columbia University Press.

——1999. *Collected Papers*. Edited by S. Freeman. Cambridge, MA: Harvard University Press.

Raz, J. 1990. 'Facing Diversity: The case of epistemicabstinence'. *Philosophy & Public Affairs* 19: 3–46.

Reik, M.M. 1977. *The Golden Lands of Thomas Hobbes*. Detroit, MI: Wayne State University Press.

Rhodes, R. 1992. 'Hobbes' Unreasonable Fool'. *Southern Journal of Philosophy* 30: 177–89.

Ripstein, A. 1989. 'Hobbes on World Government and the World Cup'. In T. Airaksinen and M.A. Bertman (eds), *Hobbes: War among nations*. Aldershot: Avebury.

Robertson, G.C. 1886. *Hobbes*. London: William Blackwood and Sons.

Rogers, G.A.J. and Ryan, A. (eds) 1988. *Perspectives on Thomas Hobbes*. Oxford: Oxford University Press.

Rogow, A.A. 1986. *Thomas Hobbes: Radical in the service of reaction*. New York: Norton.

Ross, R., Schneider, H. and Waldman, T. (eds) 1974. *Thomas Hobbes in his Time*. Minneapolis, MN: Minnesota University Press.

Runciman, D. 1997. *Pluralism and the Personality of the State*. Cambridge: Cambridge University Press.

——2000. 'What Kind of Person is Hobbes' State? A reply to Skinner'. *Journal of Political Philosophy* 8: 268–78.

——2003. 'The Concept of the State: The sovereignty of a fiction'. In Q.R.D. Skinner and B. Stråth (eds), *States and Citizens: History, theory, prospects*. Cambridge: Cambridge University Press.

Ryan, A. 1983. 'Hobbes, Toleration and the Inner Life'. In Miller and Siedentop 1983.

——1988. 'A More Tolerant Hobbes?'. In Mendus 1988.

——1996. 'Hobbes' Political Philosophy'. In Sorell 1996a.

Sacksteder, W. 1984. 'Hobbes' Philosophical and Rhetorical Artifice'. *Philosophy and Rhetoric* 17: 30–46.

Sawyer, J.K. 1990. *Printer Poison: Pamphlet propaganda, faction politics, and the public sphere in early seveneteenth- century France*. Berkeley: University of California Press.

Scanlon, T.M. 1999. *What We Owe to Each Other*. Cambridge, MA: Belknap Press.

Schedler, G. 1977. 'Hobbes on the Basis of Political Obligation'. *Journal of the History of Philosophy* 15: 165–70.

Schmitt, C. 2008. *The Leviathan in the State Theory of Thomas Hobbes: Meaning and failure of a political symbol*. Translated by Erna Hilfstein and George Schwab. Chicago, IL: Chicago University Press.

Schochet, G. 1990. 'Hobbes and the Voluntary Basis of Society'. In Dietz 1990.

Schuhmann, K. 1998. *Hobbes, une chronique*. Paris: J. Vrin

——2004. 'Leviathan and De cive'. In Sorell and Foisneau 2004.

Scott, W. 1812. A Collection of Scarce and Valuable Tracts. 2nd edn. London. Vol. VIII.

Shapin, S. and Schaffer, S. 1985. Leviathan and the Air-pump: Hobbes, Boyle, and the experimental life, including a translation of Thomas Hobbes, Dialogus physicus de natura aeris. Princeton, NJ: Princeton University Press.

Sheridan, P. 2011. 'Resisting the Scaffold: Self-preservation and the limits of obligation in Hobbes' Leviathan'. Hobbes Studies 24, no. 2: 137–57.

Simmons, A.J. 1991. 'Locke and the Right to Punish'. Philosophy & Public Affairs 20: 311–49.

Skinner, Q.R.D. 1964. 'Hobbes' Leviathan'. Review of The Divine Politics of Thomas Hobbes, by F. C. Hood. Historical Journal 7: 321–33.

——1966a. 'Thomas Hobbes and His Disciples in France and England'. Comparative Studies in Society and History 8: 153–67.

——1966b. 'The Ideological Context of Hobbes' Political Thought'. The Historical Journal 9: 286–317.

——1969a. 'Meaning and Understanding in the History of Ideas'. History and Theory 8: 3–53.

——1969b. 'Thomas Hobbes and the Nature of the Early Royal Society'. Historical Journal 12: 217–39.

——1972a. 'Conquest and Consent: Thomas Hobbes and the Engagement controversy'. In G.E. Aylmer (ed.), The Interregnum: The quest for settlement 1646–1660. London: Macmillan.

——1972b. 'The Context of Hobbes' Theory of Political Obligation'. In M. Cranston and R.S. Peters (eds), Hobbes and Rousseau. New York: Doubleday.

——1986. 'The Paradoxes of Political Liberty'. In S. McMurrin (ed.), The Tanner Lectures on Human Values, vol. VII. Cambridge: Cambridge University Press, 227–50.

——1988. 'Warrender and Skinner on Hobbes: A reply'. Political Studies 36: 692–95.

——1989. 'The State'. In T. Ball, J. Farr and R. Hanson (eds), Political Innovation and Conceptual Change. Cambridge: Cambridge University Press.

——1990. 'Hobbes on the Proper Signification of Liberty'. Transactions of the Royal Historical Society, 5th series, 40: 121–51.

——1991. 'Thomas Hobbes: Rhetoric and the construction of morality'. Proceedings of the British Academy 76: 1–61.

——1993. '"Scientia Civilis" in Classical Rhetoric and in the Early Hobbes'. In Phillipson and Skinner 1993.

——1996. Reason and Rhetoric in the Philosophy of Hobbes. Cambridge: Cambridge University Press.

——1998. Liberty before Liberalism. Cambridge: Cambridge University Press.

——1999. 'Hobbes and the Purely Artificial Personality of the State'. Journal of Political Philosophy 7: 1–29.

——2002. Visions of Politics, vol. I: Regarding method. Cambridge: Cambridge University Press.

——2002. Visions of Politics, vol. III: Hobbes and civil science. Cambridge: Cambridge University Press.

———2008. *Hobbes and Republican Liberty*. Cambridge: Cambridge University Press.

Skyrms, B. 1996. *The Evolution of the Social Contract*. Cambridge: Cambridge University Press.

Slomp, G. 2000. *Thomas Hobbes and the Political Philosophy of Glory*. London: Palgrave.

Smith, M.A. 1994. *The Moral Problem*. Oxford: Blackwell.

Sommerville, J.P. 1986. *Politics and ideology in England 1603–1640*. London: Longman.

———1992. *Thomas Hobbes: Political ideas in historical context*. London: Macmillan.

Sorell, T. 1986. *Hobbes*. London: Routledge.

———1988. 'The Science in Hobbes' Politics'. In Rogers and Ryan 1988.

———1990a. 'Hobbes' Persuasive Civil Science'. *Philosophical Quarterly* 40, no. 3: 342–51.

———1990b. 'Hobbes' Un-Aristotelian Political Rhetoric'. *Philosophy and Rhetoric* 23, no. 2: 96–108.

———1993. 'Hobbes without Doubt'. *History of Philosophy Quarterly* 10: 121–35.

———(ed.) 1996a. *The Cambridge Companion to Hobbes*. Cambridge: Cambridge University Press.

———1996b. Editor's 'Introduction'. In Sorell 1996a.

———1996c. 'Hobbes' Scheme of the Sciences'. In Sorell 1996a.

Sorell, T. and Foisneau, L. (eds) 2004. *Leviathan after 350 Years*. Oxford: Clarendon Press.

Spragens, T.A. 1973. *The Politics of Motion: The world of Thomas Hobbes*. London: Croom Helm.

Springborg, P. 1975. 'Hobbes and the Problem of Ecclesiastical Authority'. *Political Theory* 3: 289–303.

———1994. 'Hobbes, Heresy and the Historia Ecclesia'. *Journal of the History of Ideas* 55: 553–71.

———1996. 'Hobbes on Religion'. In Sorell 1996a.

———(ed.) 2006. *A Critical Companion to Hobbes' Leviathan*. Cambridge: Cambridge University Press.

———2010. 'Hobbes' Fool, the *Stultus*, Grotius, and the Epicurean Tradition'. *Hobbes Studies* 23: 29–53.

Sreedhar, S. 2010. *Hobbes on Resistance*. Cambridge: Cambridge University Press.

State, S. 1985. 'Text and Context: Skinner, Hobbes and theistic natural law'. *Historical Journal* 28: 27–50.

Strauss, L. 1952. *The Political Philosophy of Hobbes*. Chicago, IL: University of Chicago Press.

———1953. *Natural Right and History*. Chicago, IL: Chicago University Press.

Taylor, A.E. 1965. 'The Ethical Doctrine of Hobbes'. In K. Brown 1965. Orig. publ., *Philosophy* 13 (1938): 406–24.

———1997. *Thomas Hobbes*. Bristol: Thoemmes Press.

Thomas, K. 1965. 'The Social Origins of Hobbes' Political Thought'. In K. Brown 1965.

Tierney, B. 1997. *The Idea of Natural Rights: Studies on natural rights, natural law and Church law*. Atlanta, GA: Scholars Press.

Trainor, B.T. 1985. 'The Politics of Peace: The role of the political covenant in Hobbes' *Leviathan*'. *Review of Politics* 47: 347–69.

——1988. 'Warrender and Skinner on Hobbes'. *Political Studies* 36: 680–91.

Treadwell, M. 2002. 'The Stationers and the Printing Acts at the End of the Seventeenth Century'. In Barnard and McKenzie 2002, vol. IV.

Tricaud, F. 1971. Editor's introduction. In *Léviathan*. Edited and translated by F. Tricaud. Paris: Sirey.

——1979. 'Quelques éléments sur la question de l'accès aux textes dans les études hobbesiennes'. *Revue Internationale de Philosophie* 129: 393–414.

Tuck, R.F. 1979. *Natural Rights Theories: Their origins and development*. Cambridge: Cambridge University Press.

——1988a. 'Hobbes and Descartes'. In Rogers and Ryan 1988.

——1988b. 'Optics and Sceptics: The philosophical foundations of Hobbes' political thought'. In Leites 1988.

——1989. *Hobbes*. Oxford: Oxford University Press.

——1990. 'Hobbes and Locke on Toleration'. In Dietz 1990.

——1991. Editor's introduction and a note on the text. In *Leviathan*. Edited by R.F. Tuck. Cambridge: Cambridge University Press.

——1992. 'The "Christian Atheism" of Thomas Hobbes'. In Hunter and Wootton 1992.

——1993a. *Philosophy and Government 1572–1651*. Cambridge: Cambridge University Press.

——1993b. 'The Civil Religion of Thomas Hobbes'. In Phillipson and Skinner 1993.

——1996. 'Hobbes' Moral Philosophy'. In Sorell 1996a.

——1998. Editor's introduction. In *De cive*. Edited by R.F. Tuck and translated M. Silverthorne. Cambridge: Cambridge University Press.

——1999. *The Rights of War and Peace: Political thought and the international order from Grotius to Kant*. Oxford: Oxford University Press.

——2002. 'Flathman's Hobbes'. In B. Honig and D.R. Mapel (eds), *Skepticism, Individuality and Freedom: The reluctant liberalism of Richard Flathman*. Minneapolis, MN: University of Minnesota Press.

——2004. 'The Utopianism of *Leviathan*'. In Sorell and Foisneau 2004.

Tully, J. (ed.) 1988. *Meaning and Context: Quentin Skinner and his critics*. Cambridge: Polity Press.

van Mill, D. 1995. 'Hobbes' Theories of Freedom'. *Journal of Politics* 57, no. 2: 443–59.

——2001. *Liberty, Rationality and Agency in Hobbes' Leviathan*. New York: SUNY Press.

Vincent, J. 1981. 'The Hobbesian Tradition in Twentieth-Century International Thought'. *Millennium: Journal of International Studies* 10: 91–101.

Waldron, J. 2001. 'Hobbes and the Principle of Publicity'. *Pacific Philosophical Quarterly* 82: 447–74.

Waltz, K. 1979. *Theory of International Politics*. Reading, MA: Addison-Wesley.

Walzer, M. 1980. *Just and Unjust Wars: A moral argument with historical illustrations*. Harmondsworth: Penguin.

Warrender, H. 1957. *The Political Philosophy of Hobbes: His theory of obligation*. Oxford: Clarendon Press.

——1960. 'The Place of God in Hobbes' Philosophy'. *Political Studies* 8: 48–57.

——1962a. 'Obligation and Right in Hobbes'. *Philosophy* 37: 352–57.

——1962b. 'Hobbes' Conception of Morality'. *Rivista Critica di Storia della Filosofia* 17: 433–49.

——1965. 'A Reply to Mr Plamenatz'. In K. Brown 1965.

Watkins, J.N.W. 1973. *Hobbes' System of Ideas*. 2nd edn. London: Hutchinson.

Wernham, A.G. 1965. 'Liberty and Obligation in Hobbes'. In K. Brown 1965.

Whelan, F.G. 1981. 'Language and Its Abuses in Hobbes' Political Philosophy'. *American Political Science Review* 75: 59–75.

Wight, M. 1991. *International Theory: Three traditions*. Leicester: Leicester University Press.

Williams, B. A.O. 1973. *Problems of the Self*. Cambridge: Cambridge University Press.

——2005. *In the Beginning Was the Deed: Realism and moralism in political argument*. Princeton, NJ: Princeton University Press.

Williams, M. 1996. 'Hobbes and International Relations: A reconsideration'. *International Organisation* 50: 213–36.

——2005. *The Realist Tradition and the Limits of International Relations*. Cambridge: Cambridge University Press.

Wood, A. 1817. *Athenae Oxonienses: An exact history of all the writers and bishops who have had their education in the University of Oxford, to which are added the Fasti, or Annals of the said University* [vol. I, ed. Philip Bliss, 1813]. London: F.C. & J. Rivington.

Wood, S.W. 1971. 'Confusions in Hobbes' Analysis of the Civil Sovereign'. *Southwestern Journal of Philosophy* 2: 195–203.

Woolhouse, R. 1988. *The Empiricists*. Oxford: Oxford University Press.

Wootton, D. 1988. 'Lucien Febvre and the Problem of Unbelief in Early Modern England'. *Journal of Modern History* 60: 695–730.

Worden, B. 1998. 'Factory of the Revolution'. Review of *Liberty before Liberalism*, by Q.R.D. Skinner. *London Review of Books* 20, no. 3: 13–15.

Wright, G. 1991. 'Thomas Hobbes: 1668 Appendix to *Leviathan*'. *Interpretation* 18: 323–413.

Zagorin, P. 1993. 'Hobbes' Early Philosophical Development'. *Journal of the History of Ideas* 54: 505–18.

——2000. 'Hobbes without Grotius'. *History of Political Thought* 21: 16–40.

——2006. 'Clarendon against *Leviathan*'. In P. Springborg (ed.), *The Cambridge Companion to Hobbes' Leviathan*. Cambridge: Cambridge University Press.

Zaitchik, A. 1982. 'Hobbes' Reply to the Fool: The problem of consent and obligation'. *Political Theory* 10: 245–66.

Zappen, J.P. 1983. 'Aristotelian and Ramist Rhetoric in Thomas Hobbes' *Leviathan*: Pathos versus ethos and logos'. *Rhetorica* 1: 65–91.

Zarka, Y.C. 1996. 'First Philosophy and the Foundations of Knowledge'. In Sorell 1996a.

INDEX

Please note that page numbers relating to Notes will have the letter 'n' following the page number.

Anglicanism, 16, 235, 236, 252, 289, 300
anti-clericalism, 315
anti-Semitism, 326–27
apologists, 'de facto' (for new English republican regime), 17, 31, 149
Aquinas, St Thomas, 211, 212, 213, 227
aristocracy, 14
Aristotle, 65, 326; Hobbes' antipathy towards, 13, 64, 65; Hobbes' translation of *Rhetoric*, 16, 23
Armstrong, Neil, 75
art/artifice, and nature, 63
artificial man, in *Leviathan*/ commonwealth, 44, 48, 49, 62–63
artificial persons/artificial personation, 174, 175, 177, 179, 180, 184, 200, 203n; direct form, 178, 183; non-fictional versus fictional, 176
Ascham, Anthony, 17, 31, 288
assurance game (AG) (game theory), 121, 122, 125, 126, 127, 131, 136, 171n
astronomy, 15, 22, 23, 24
atheism: Atheism Bill, investigation of Hobbes (1666–68), 18, 43, 236, 285, 300–301; Hobbes as atheist in modern sense, 233–34, 256, 290; Hobbes as 'Christian atheist', 233–34, 252, 255–56; as term of abuse, 233
Aubrey, John: biographer of Hobbes, 20–21, 24–25, 53, 303, 304; *Brief Lives, chiefly of contemporaries*, 35; on Hobbes (senior), 13
Austin, John, 213, 325; *Province of Jurisprudence Determined*, 212
authorisation theory, 98, 154, 187, 337; authorisation as one-off act, 210; law as command, 205–6; law-making dilemma, 207, 208, 210; political representation, 175, 179, 183
authoritarianism, 7, 224
authority: absence of established, 68, 91; and commands, 205, 206; for deciding and enforcing orthodoxy, 67; laws of nature, 101–2; legitimacy of, 295; on miracles, 6; of others, taking on trust, 66, 67; and personhood, 188; political *see* political authority; of sovereign, 4–5, 206; of writers, 11
authorship: author as purely imputed person, 188; authorisation by Hobbes, 48; Bible, 5; in Hobbes' theory of representation, 173–76, 179, 181; intentions of author, 32, 33, 34, 41, 58, 77–78
automata (engines), 62
Axelrod, Robert, *Evolution of Cooperation*, 139
axioms, 25, 67
Aylmer, G.E., 331

Bacon, Francis (1561–1626), 23; on atheism, 233; *Essays*, 14
Ball, Terence, *Reappraising Political Theory: Revisionist studies in the history of political thought*, 202–3
ballistics, 24
Bangladesh, 264
barrister/lawyer (example of form of representation), 175, 176, 177
Barry, Brian, 110, 168
Baumgold, Deborah, *Hobbes' Political Theory*, 201
Baumrin, Bernard, *Hobbes' Leviathan: Interpretation and criticism*, 111–12
Baxter, Richard, 294; *Humble Advice*, 293
Beacon Set on Fire, A (pamphlet), 293–94
Beccaria, Cesare, 323
Beitz, Charles, 263, 276; *Political Theory and International Relations*, 280
beliefs: coercion, resistance to, 244, 245, 250, 257n; conflicts of, 68; death, Hobbes' views on, 20; denouncing by Hobbes, 243–44; mistaken or malformed, 51, 74; and motivation, 72; private, 245;

Printed in Great Britain
by Amazon